THE PROBLEM OF UNIVERSALS IN INDIAN PHILOSOPHY

The Problem of Universals in Indian Philosophy

RAJA RAM DRAVID

Edited by

DR. KANSHI RAM

MOTILAL BANARSIDASS PUBLISHERS
PRIVATE LIMITED • DELHI

First Edition: Delhi, 1972
Second Revised Edition: Delhi, 2001

ISBN: 81-208-0832-0

Also available at:
MOTILAL BANARSIDASS
236, 9th Main III Block, Jayanagar, Bangalore 560 011
41 U.A. Bungalow Road, Jawahar Nagar, Delhi 110 007
8 Mahalaxmi Chamber, Warden Road, Mumbai 400 026
120 Royapettah High Road, Mylapore, Chennai 600 004
Sanas Plaza, 1302 Baji Rao Road, Pune 411 002
8 Camac Street, Calcutta 700 017
Ashok Rajpath, Patna 800 004
Chowk, Varanasi 221 001

Printed in India
BY JAINENDRA PRAKASH JAIN AT SHRI JAINENDRA PRESS,
A-45 NARAINA, PHASE-I, NEW DELHI 110 028
AND PUBLISHED BY NARENDRA PRAKASH JAIN FOR
MOTILAL BANARSIDASS PUBLISHERS PRIVATE LIMITED,
BUNGALOW ROAD, DELHI 110 007

TO THE DEAR MEMORY
OF
MY BELOVED MOTHER

FOREWORD

Philosophers, both in the East and the West, have been considerably exercised over the problem of Universals. Are they real entities, or are they mere fictions and fabrications of the human mind, or do they have some objective status, although not as factual entities? The Platonic and the Aristotelian standpoints are well-known, as are the solutions offered by the Nyāya-Vaiśeṣika and Buddhism. Dr. Raja Ram Dravid gives in the following pages a full, clear, scholarly and eminently readable acccount of this problem as viewed by Indian Philosophers. In three rather long chapters, he also attempts a good exposition and analysis of the problem in Western thought. The main emphasis is, however, on the Universal in Indian thought, and Dr. Dravid is only secondarily concerned with Western philosophy.

Starting with the Nyāya-Vaiśeṣika and Mīmāṁsā Realisms, he goes to the Buddhist, Jaina, Vedānta (Advaita and Viśistādvaita) and the Grammarian School of Bhartrhari. The various issues connected with this problem, the nature of the universals, their mode of existence and cognition and connection with words and things, are discussed at length with great analytical skill and insight. The merits and demerits of each point of view are brought out very clearly. I may draw particular attention to the excellent analysis of Buddhist Nominalism (Apohavāda) and the views of the Grammar School as instances in this regard.

In writing this book Dr. Dravid has used the texts written by the masters of the different systems, instead of relying, as is generally done, on introductory texts. Again, he has not been content with the stating and examining of views system-wise. He has also treated separately the principal thinkers of each system taking care to show how the doctrines formulated by the different systems evolved, and how, and this is very important, the different masters of each system differed in many important respects. He has amply shown that the different schools are the different attempts to clarify the ontological and metaphysical insight at the root of the different systems.

The author has also attempted in the final chapter (Chap. XV) to give his own solution of the problem. It is on the pattern of Resemblances which are recurrences and are to that extent universal. To quote his own words:

"Thus we have maintained that there are identical qualities and relations which recur over and over again in our experience. In the same way there are also resemblances—resembling qualities, resembling objects and resembling situations—which repeat themselves in innumerable instances. All these recurrences involve universals. The term universal, in our view, is applicable not only to identical qualities and relations, but also to similarities, because the essential meaning of the term, as we understand it, is recurrence. These recurrent identities and similarities are the principles of grouping; they form the foundations of our thought and speech. There is nothing subjective about them, as the Buddhist maintains." (p. 383) Whether this re-statement of the age-old problem is a better view of the Universals is for the readers to judge.

Dr. Dravid has written an outstanding and scholarly work, and I have great pleasure in recommending it to all serious students of philosophy.

April, 1972

T. R. V. Murti
Professor Emeritus and Ex-Director
Centre of Advanced Study in Philosophy
Banaras Hindu University

PREFACE

The concept of universal and the problems arising out of it form one of the most fundamental and most debated topics of Indian Philosophy. All systems of thought make important contributions on this subject. The whole discussion centres round the contention of the Nyāya-Vaiśeṣika that the existence of universals is required not only epistemologically to explain our knowledge of things but also ontologically to explain the nature of the world. In the West also there have been periods when the problem of universals was the dominating theme of philosophical speculation. One such period was that of Plato and Aristotle, another was the Medieval. Even in the modern period philosophers, both of the rationalist and the empiricist schools, have paid serious attention to the porblem. In my view, the problem is equally important and fundamental for our present day thinking also, for understanding of universals is necessary in order to understand knowledge.

I have endeavoured in this book to give a critical and comprehensive account of the discussion on universals in Indian Philosophy. I have examined and evaluated the various theories of universals advocated by different systems and suggested in the end a line of approach to the solution of the age-old problem. This in no way is the first attempt to give an account of the problem of universals in Indian Philosophy. Such renowned scholars as Stcherbatsky in *Buddhist Logic* and Dr. Satkari Mukherjee in *The Buddhist Philosophy of Universal Flux* and *The Jaina Philosophy of Non-absolutism* have discussed the problem in some detail. In recent times Dr. D. N. Shastri in *Critique of Indian Realism* and Dr. G. N. Shastri in *Philosophy of Word and Meaning* have added a useful discussion on this subject. But the accounts of these authors are limited in scope naturally because the topic of universals forms only a small part of their work. Hence, a comprehensive and critical discussion of this fundamental problem covering all the important theories of universals in Indian philosophy and their mutual conflicts and criticisms, and a comparative study of them with their Western counterparts was very much needed. I have ventured to undertake this task. However, I do not make any claim for completeness, for, I feel, a more exhaustive and more scholarly discussion of this subject is possible. This work is only a humble attempt in that direction.

In the forth-coming chapters I have discussed the theories of universals advocated by the Nyāya-Vaiśeṣika, the Mīmāṁsā, the Advaita Vedānta, the Viśiṣṭādvaita, the Grammarian, the Jaina and the Buddhist schools of thought. I have not discussed the Sāṅkhya view separately because it is not essentially different from the Advaita view. The controversy between the Nyāya-Vaiśesika and the Mīmāṁsā realist on the one hand and the Buddhist nominalist on the other, which forms the heart of the discussion on universals in Indian Philosophy, spreads over several chapters and forms a fairly large part of the whole work. I have discussed not only the epistemological and metaphysical approach to the problem of universals but also the semantic aproach made by the various systems of Indian Philosophy. In this context the view of the Grammarians with special reference to Bhartṛhari has been discussed in some detail. Towards the end I have devoted three chapters for a brief discussion of some of the main trends of thought on universals in Western Philosophy—beginning from Plato to the contemporary Philosophers — and for comparing and contrasting them with their Indian counterparts.

The stand-point from which I have approached the problem may, in a sense, be called realistic. However it is not identical with anyone of the traditionally propounded realisms. It is a stand-point which is represented in contemporary Western Philosophy by such writers as H. H. Price, B. Blanshard, R. I. Aaron and others with some minor variations. This stand-point recognises the objectivity of thought and language and stresses upon the role of experience in the formation of basic concepts. It avoids the extremes of both realism and nominalism and approaches the problem of universals in a less dogmatic manner.

In the preparation of this book I have gone to the original sources for my information. I have studied standard texts of each system of Indian Philosophy and drawn my material from them. I have also consulted available translations and expositions of some of the Sanskrit works, but my conclusions are based on my own study and interpretation of the original texts. With regard to Western theories, however, I have drawn my material either from the original writings of the philosophers or from the standard translations and expositions of their works. For the purpose of my discussion I have made use of terms and concepts and the various classifications current in Western Philosophy. This is unavoidable for one who is discussing a problem in Indian Philosophy through the medium of a foreign language. The implicit danger in such a procedure is of blurring the distinctions between the concepts of two different traditions and of the imposition of the ideas of one tradition on the genuine thoughts of the other. I have taken utmost care to guard against such a danger. I have tried my best to see that the differences between Indian and Western ideas are not ignored and passed over, but duly emphasised.

It is with great pleasure and sense of gratitude that I record my obligations to the various scholars from whom I have derived invaluable help in the preparation of this work. My first obligation is to my revered teacher Prof. T. R. V. Murti (ex-Directer, Centre of Advanced Study in Philosophy, Banaras Hindu University) who gave me insight into the subject through his innumerable discussions. He very kindly consented also to write a foreword to this book. My indebtedness to him is too deep to be expressible in words. I am deeply indebted also to my brother and teacher Padma Bhushan Pandit Raj Rajeshwar Shastri Dravid, late Pt. Harirama Shastri Shukla, Pt. Jagannatha Upadhyaya, Pt. Darbarilal Kothia and Pt. Ramchandra Sastri for helping me in understanding and interpreting some of the difficult Sanskrit texts. I am also thankful to the renowned publishers M/s Motilal Banarsidass for selecting my book for publication.

Varanasi *R. R. Dravid*
April, 1972

ABBREVIATIONS

Ad. Sid.	*Advaitasiddhi* of Madhusūdana Sarasvatī with Gauḍabrahmānandī, 2nd Ed., Bombay, 1937.
Ap. Sid.	*Apohasiddhi* of Ratnakīrti, in *Six Buddhist Nyāya Tracts,* Ed. by Har Prasad Shastri, B. I., Calcutta, 1910
AS	*Aṣṭasāhasrī* by Vidyānanda, Nirnaya Sagar Press, 1915.
ĀM	*Āptamīmāṁsā* of Samantabhadra, Nirnaya Sagar Press, 1915.
ĀTV	*Ātmatattvaviveka* of Udayanācārya, Ch. S. S., 1940
BL	*Buddhist Logic* by Stcherbatsky, F. Th., two vols., Dover Publications, New York, 1962.
CPB	*Central Philosophy of Buddhism* by Dr. T. R. V. Murti, George Allen and Unwin, London, 1955.
Dink.	*Dinakarī,* a commentary by Dinakara Bhaṭṭa on Nyāya Siddhānta Muktāvalī. See NSM.
HR	Helārāja's commentary on *Vākyapadīya,* Kāṇḍa III, Part I. See VP.
JN	*Jñānaśrī Mitra Nibandhāvali,* Kashi Prasad Jayswal Research Institute, Patna, 1959.
JPN	*The Jaina Philosophy of Non-Absolutism* by Dr. Satkari Mukherjee, Calcutta, 1944.
Kir.	*Kiraṇāvalī* of Udayana with *Bhāṣya* of Padmanābha, Banaras, 1919.
Kir. Bhā.	*Kiraṇāvalībhāṣya.* See Kir.
KKK	*Khaṇḍanakhaṇḍakhādya* of Śrīharṣa, Achyuta Grantha Mālā, Banaras, 1961.
Kus.	*Nyāyakusumāñjali* of Udayana with *Prakāśa* and *Bodhinī,* Ch. S. S.
MB	*Mahābhāṣya* of Patañjali with *Pradīpikā,* Nirnaya Sagar Press, 1971.
MBP	*Mahābhāṣyapradīpikā,* a commentary on *Mahābhāṣya.* See MB.
MM	*Mānameyodaya* of Nārāyaṇas, Theosophical Publication House, Adyar, Madras, 1933.

NB	*Nyāyabindu* of Dharmakīrti with Dharmottara's Ṭīkā, B. I. Series, Calcutta, 1929.
NK	*Nyāyakandalī* of Śrīdhara. See PPB.
NM	*Nyāyamañjarī* of Jayanta Bhaṭṭa, Banaras, Medical Hall Press.
NS	*Nyāyasūtras* of Gautama with *Vātsyāyanabhāṣya,* Ed. and Tr. by Ganganatha Jha, Pub. Indian Thought, Allahabad, 1915.
NSM	*Nyāyasiddhāntamuktāvalī* of Viśvanātha Pañcānana, with *Dinakarī* and *Rāmarudrī,* Ch. S. S., 1951.
NV	*Nyāyavārttika* of Uddyotakara, Ch. S. S., 1915.
PKM	*Prameyakamalamārtaṇḍa* of Prabhācandra, a commentary on PMS. See PMS.
PMS	*Parīkṣāmukhasūtra* of Māṇikyanandī, Ed. by Mahendra Kumar Shastri, Nirnaya Sagar Press, Bombay, 1941.
PNT	*Pramāṇanayatattvālokālaṅkāra* of Vādideva Sūri with *Syādvādaratnākara,* a commentary by the author himself, Kashi Jaina Yashovijaya Grantha Mala No. 5, 1905, (Vīra Samvat 2439).
PP	*Prakaraṇapañcikā* of Śālikanātha with *Nyāyasiddhi,* a commentary, Ed. by Subrahmanya Sastri, Pub., B.H.U., 1961.
PPB	*Praśastapāda's Bhāṣya with Śrīdhara's Nyāyakandalī,* Ed. by Vindhyeshwari Prasad Dwivedi, V. S. S. Banaras, 1995.
PR	Puṇyarāja's commentary on *Vākyapadīya* Kāṇda II. See VP.
PTN	*Padārthatattvanirūpaṇam* of Raghunātha Siromaṇi Banaras Mahamaṇdal Press, 1915.
PV	*Pramānavārtikam* of Dharmakīrti with *Vṛtti* by Ācārya Manorathanandī, Ed. by Rahula Sankrityayana.
PVV	*Vrtti* on *Pramāṇavārtika.* See PV.
SBT	*Saptabhaṅgītaraṅgiṇī* of Vimaladāsa, Nirnaya Sagar Press.
SDD	*Sāmānyadūṣaṇadikprasāritā* by Paṇḍita Aśoka, *Six Buddhist Nyāya Tracts,* B. I., Calcutta, 1910.
SM	*Syādvādamañjarī* of Mallişeṇa, Ed. by A.B.Dhruva, Bhandarkar Research Institute, Poona, 1933.
SR	*Syādvādaratnākara* of Vādideva Sūri. See PNT.
SS	*Sarvārthasiddhi.* See TMK
ST	*Sanmatitarka* of Siddhasena Divākara with *Tattvabodhavidhāyinī,* a commentary by Abhayadeva Sūri, Pub. by Gujarat Vidyāpīṭha, Ahmedabad, 1930.
ŚD	*Śāstradīpikā* by Pārthasārathi Miśra, Pub. by Vidya Vilasa Press, Kashi, 1907.

ŚV	*Ślokavārtika* of Kumārila, Ed. by Dr. Kunhan Raja, Madras University Press, 1946.
TBV	*Tattvabodhavidhāyinī* of Abhayadeva Sūri. See ST.
TMK	*Tattvamuktākalāpa* of Vedāntadeśika with *Sarvārthasiddhi*, a commentary by the author himself, Ed. Annaṅgarācārya, Madras, 1941.
TP	*Tattvapradīpikā* of Citsukhācārya, Pub. Udasina Saṁskrita Vidyalaya, Kashi, 1956.
TS	*Tattvasaṅgraha* of Śāntarakṣita with *Pañjikā* by Kamalaśīla, G. O. S. Baroda, 1926.
TSP	*Tattvasaṅgrahapañjikā* by Kamalaśīla. See TS.
TT	*Nyāyavārtika-tātparya-ṭīkā* by Vācaspati Miśra, Ed. by Rajeshwara Shastri Dravida, Ch. S. S., 1925.
Ved. Par.	*Vedāntaparibhāṣā* by Dharmarāja Adhvarīndra, Ed. by S. S. Suryanarayana Sastri, Adyar Library, 1942.
VP	*Vākyapadīya* of Bhartṛhari, Kāṇḍa I with *Vṛtti* by the author himself, Sarasvatī Bhavana Grantha Mālā, 1963; Kāṇḍa II with Puṇyarāja's Commentary, Banaras Saṁskrit Series; Kāṇḍa III (Part I) with commentary by Helārāja, Poona, 1963.
VPV	*Vṛtti* on *Vākyapadīya*. See VP.
VS	*Vaiśeṣikasūtras* of Kaṇāda with *Upaskāra* by Śaṅkara Miśra and *Vivṛti* by Jayanārāyaṇa Tarkapañcanana, Ed. and Tr. by A. E. Gough, E. J. Lazarus and Co., Banaras, 1873.

CONTENTS

CHAPTER I

INTRODUCTION

The problem of universals is one of the most fundamental problems of philosophy. It is a very common, subtle and difficult topic of philosophical controversy It arises directly from our reflections upon experience, thought and language. We have, broadly speaking, two kinds of knowledge of things: sensuous and conceptual. Sensuous knowledge presents a thing in its concrete and particular aspect, whereas conceptual knowledge presents the same thing without any note of particularity. Although what we see and touch are particulars, when we think these particulars we cannot help using general concepts. Our judgement about a particular object affirms that it is of a certain kind, that it is of a certain genus and certain species. In other words, the objects outside the mind, as presented by sensuous knowledge, are particulars, whereas our concepts of them are general or universal. The same is true of our language also. It is a significant fact that almost all words in our language, except proper names, are general, whereas what exist in the outside world are particulars. It is by virtue of this generality that concepts and words become applicable to quite indefinite number of existing and possible objects.

Now the question naturally arises: are these concepts and words true? Do they give us any knowledge of the outside world? Does the universal concept in the mind, or the general word in our language, stand for something that is objectively real? In other words, are there universals just as there are particulars? How are the universals, if any, related to particulars? These and other allied questions have formed the topic of fundamental importance both in Indian and Western Philosophy. It is, indeed, of central importance to inquire as to what is the relation between mental concepts and objective reality. If universal concepts are said to have no foundation in extramental reality, i.e., if they are regarded as purely subjective constructions, then a rift between thought and reality is created. All our knowledge expressed through universal concepts would, in that case, become false. The problem extends to human knowledge in general, and if universal concepts are denied objective foundation, the result would be scepticism.

The problem of universals is raised in various ways: (i) What, if anything, in the objective reality does correspond to the universal concepts in the mind? Or, in other words, what do general words, such as man, red, colour, etc., stand for in the extramental reality? This is the ontological problem. (ii) How are Universal concepts formed? This is the psychological problem. Both these above problems are intimately related. (iii) If universal concepts are simply thought-constructions, how does scientific knowledge of the world become possible? This question is of fundamental importance. Ultimately, however, the problem of universals is the epistemological problem of the relation of thought to reality.

The most natural answer to the ontological question is that concepts and words stand for what a number of things have in common, that is to say, they stand for universals. This view, which is known as realism, has two forms: one asserting that universals are entities different from particulars having a being of their own and in some way related to the particulars, and the other asserting that universals are only common features of particulars having no being apart from them. The one is known as *extreme realism* and the other as *moderate realism.* Both these forms of realism are controverted by two rival theories, namely, *conceptualism* and *nominalism.* According to conceptualists, there are no universals in the outside world; they are merely concepts in the human mind. The nominalists, on the other hand, maintain that the only universals are words and they are made universal by being used of a number of different particulars. They reject not only the universals of the realist, but also the universal concepts of the conceptualists. The conceptualists agree with the nominalists in refusing to give universals a place in the objective reality, but they insist that they cannot be merely a matter of nomenclature which might be quite arbitrary. The universals, they argue, must at any rate be concepts in the minds that use the words. It is for these universal concepts and not for any universals external to the mind using them that the words stand.

Both conceptualism and nominalism would have to face the question what basis in reality there is for the generalisation inherent in experience, thought and language? So far as the realist is concerned he can answer the question in a simple and straightforward manner by saying that the basis in question lies in the discovery of universals inherent in the objective reality, although he would have to face other formidable questions. But the answer is not so simple for the conceptualist and the nominalist. The conceptualist would have to explain how mental concepts are formed, how they can be general if the data of experience from which they are formed are particular, and how words are general in their significance. Similarly, the nominalist would have to explain how words become general and how they can be successfully used in the absence of universal determinants for such usage in outside reality. Some conceptualists and nominalists explain the problem on the basis of similarities and differences discovered amongst particulars. Others deny that there is any basis for concepts and words in outside reality; the generality of words and concepts, they hold, is purely subjective, or *a priori*, having no basis whatever in the outside reality.[1]

All the four kinds of views mentioned above are represented in Indian Philosophy. Extreme realism is advocated by the Nyāya-Vaiśeṣika and the Mīmāṁsā schools of thought. The Nyāya-Vaiśeṣika, as a matter of fact, provides the starting-point of the whole controversy over universals in Indian Philosophy by his theory of *Sāmānya* or *Jāti*. The theory asserts that universals are an independent category of reality. They are real class-essences inhering in particulars by virtue of which the latter fall into natural classes. These class-essences provide the foundation for general conceptions and designations of things. The Nyāya-Vaiśesika however admits that all classifications or generalisations are not necessarily based on real class-natures; they may in many cases be based on certain accidental or adventitious features, as, for example, in the case of the class of 'blind men', or 'cooks' or 'teachers' But so far as natural classes are concerned, the classes such as 'cow', 'tree', 'substance', 'colour', 'quality', etc., we must recognise, he insists,

1. The kind of nominalism, which recognises objective resemblance as the basis of the usage of general words, would be of a moderate type as distinguished from the extreme type which recognises no such basis. It would not be fundamentally different from the kind of conceptualism which also recognises resemblance among objects as the basis of universal concepts in the mind. Similarly, the kind of conceptualism which does not recognise any objective basis for universal concepts in the mind would not be fundamentally different from extreme nominalism, for ontologically there would be no difference between the two.

real class-essences, or universals, providing the bases for such classifications. The Nyāya-Vaisesika further asserts that these universals are eternal entities different from particulars in which they inhere. They are eternal because they are unaffected by the generation, change and the destruction of particulars. They are different from particulars because their cognitions are distinct from the cognitions of the latter. If the difference of cognitions is not admitted to prove the difference of objects, the whole universe would become one. However, the difference between the universal and the particular, according to the Nyāya-Vaiśesika, is not a bar to their intimate relationship. Two things might be different and yet be intimately or inseparably related. The fact that the universal and the particular are never found separately proves that they, notwithstanding their mutual difference implied by their distinct cognitions, are intimately related. This relation which is called *samavāya* (inherence) is of a unique kind. It is an independent category of reality serving to unite two different things into an inseparable union.

The realism of the Nyāya-Vaiśeṣika is strongly supported by the Mīmāṁsā. The school of Prabhākara accepts the Nyāya-Vaiśesika theory of universals almost without modification. But the school of Kumārila introduces an important modification by denying absolute difference between the universal and the particular. It replaces the relation of inherence by *identity-in-difference* (*bhedābheda*). It is argued that absolute difference between the universal and the particular is contrary to experience. They are always felt as both identical and different. The judgement 'this is cow', for example, expresses both identity and difference between 'this', (the particular) and 'cow', (the universal). If experience is our sole guide for determining the nature of reality, then the universal, the Mīmāṁsaka argues, must be admitted to be both identical with and different from the particular. Besides, the relation of inherence (*samavāya*), as conceived by the Nyāya-Vaiśesika, being a category by itself, is external to the relata and, therefore, it cannot in any intelligible sense be said to relate them. Thus the school of Kumārila, though accepting the realism of the Nyāya-Vaiśeṣika, rejects latter's notion of absolute difference between the universal and the particular.

The extreme realism advocated by the Nyāya-Vaiśeṣika and the Mīmāṁsā is vehemently criticised by all the other systems of Indian Philosophy. All of them agree in rejecting the Nyāya-Mīmāṁsā theory of universals, and the arguments advanced by them against this theory are almost the same. The main arguments are, firstly, that no universal entity apart from the particular is ever discovered in experience, and secondly, that if the universal is a real entity, on par with the particular, then it could not be a universal, i.e., be in innumerable particulars at the same time. Although all the critics of the Nyāya-Mīmāṁsā realism agree in rejecting it, they differ in their views on universals. They advance different theories of universals according to their respective stand-points.

The Jaina approaches the problem of universals from his non-absolutistic stand-point. He agrees that concepts and words have basis in outside reality, but this basis, he holds, does not consist in absolute universals. In reality there are neither absolute universals nor absolute particulars. The universal and the particular are not two realities but related aspects of one and the same complex reality. As aspects of a complex reality, the two are relatively identical and relatively different. This is obviously a moderate kind of realism. This was the position held by ancient Jaina thinkers, but some later Jaina writers deviate from it. The objective basis of universal concepts, according to these Jaina writers, is not an *identity* but *similarity of development* (*sadṛśapariṇāma*). This evidently is a kind of conceptualism. The universal (*sāmānya*), according to this view, is not an identical feature common to different particulars, but *similarity* which is different in different particulars. Apart from the two trends mentioned above there is also a third trend present in the Jaina thought. One Jaina writer Abhayadevasūri refuses to recognise the universal in any form, either as identity or as similarity. The universal, in his view, is a subjective construction having no reality whatsoever. Concepts and words have no objective basis; they stand for a number of particulars which alone have real being. This obviously is nominalism. Thus there are three distinct trends, namely, moderate realism, conceptualism and nominalism, present in the Jaina thought. It would therefore be necessary to consider which of these three trends consistently represents the fundamental non-absolutistic stand-point of the Jaina.

The extreme realism of the Nyāya and the Mīmāṁsā is rejected also by the Advaitist. He approaches the problem of universals from the stand-point of absolute identity. He recognises the necessity of accounting for the objective basis of universal concepts, but he denies that it is necessary for this purpose to postulate an ultimate plurality of eternal and ubiquitous universals as is done by the Nyāya. He holds that the purpose can be served by admitting one ultimate universal *Being* (*sattā*) appearing in various *names and forms* (*nāma-rūpa*) by the force of *primordial nescience* (*avidyā*). For the Advaitist *Being* alone is the true universal; all other universals are only appearances of it. He rejects the Nyāya conception of universals as eternal class-essences (*jāti*) and advocates in its place the conception of universals as *categories* (*nāma-rūpa*) *of Being*. These categories, as also the particulars falling under them, are empirically real, but ultimately they are non-different from the *universal Being*. The Advaitist thus distinguishes between two levels of reality: the ultimate and the empirical. The ultimately real is the universal Being (*Brahman*), the substratum of all beings, and the empirically real are universals (*nāma-rūpa*) and particulars. Even within the empirical level the universal possesses a higher grade of reality than the particular, as it functions as a principle of unity. The universal, in the Advaitic view, is the limited empirical substratum of its particular appearances, just as Being is the unlimited ultimate substratum of all appearances. From the Advaitic point of view therefore particulars are related to universals as appearances to reality. That is to say, universals are not *predicates* of particulars, as the realist thinks, but *subjects* of which particulars are *predicates*. It is for this reason that the universal is said to be more real than the particular. But this gradation is true only within the empirical order; ultimately speaking all universals, as also all particulars, are merely appearances of the *universal Being*.

The Sāṁkhya also rejects the Nyāya conception of universals and advocates a view similar to that of the Advaita. The only difference is that the universal Being, for the Sāṁkhya, is not *Brahman* but *Prakṛti*, and universals and particulars are not appearances but modifications of the primordial Being. The universal is the identical substance underlying particular manifestations. The Viśiṣṭādvaitin, on the other hand, does not accept the Advaitic conception of universals, though he too rejects the Nyāya conception of them. His view of universals is similar to that of the Jaina conceptualist. The universal, according to him, is *close resemblance* (*sausādṛśya*) amongst particulars. There is no evidence, he argues, for the universals of the Nyāya conception, nor is there any logical necessity of postulating their existence. Class notions and generalisations are explainable on the basis of resemblances which alone are discovered in experience. He rejects also the Advaitic conception of Being as the universal substratum of all appearances. Being, in his view, is always a *predicate* (*dharma*) and not a *subject* (*dharmī*). It is universal only as the *predicate* of all that exists.

The severest attack on all forms of realism comes from the side of the Buddhist. He rejects not only realism but also conceptualism which accepts resemblance among particulars as the objective basis of universal concepts in the mind. He approaches the problem of universals from the stand-point of absolute difference. Reality, according to him, is constituted of momentary particulars which are absolutely discrete and disparate. There is no identity or similarity in reality. All notions of identity and similarity therefore are fancies of imagination. All class-concepts are *constructions of thought* (*apohas*), they are mere *names*, having no objective foundation whatsoever. This is pure and simple nominalism. It asserts the subjectivity of all conceptual knowledge. The Buddhist tries to establish his nominalism on a secure foundation by distinguishing between two orders of reality: the *ultimate* (*paramārtha*) and the *empirical* (*saṁvṛti*). The ultimate is the world of unique point-instants (*svalakṣanas*) which are given in pure sensation, and the empirical is the world of universals (*sāmānyalakṣaṇas*) which are given by the understanding. Thought and language are concerned with the latter and not with the former. The world of universals is created by the understanding in order to comprehend the flowing reality. Such creation is natural to human mind; it is due to the innate constructive tendency (*anādi-avidyā-vāsanā*) common to all human beings. But since the real by nature is non-relative, or non-conceptual, thought and language fail to touch it. Nevertheless, conceptual knowledge is not absolutely valueless; it has practical value, though ultimately it is illusory. Our classifications and generalisations, though lacking in objective foundation, are pragmatically useful, for they form the basis of successful conduct in life The Buddhist advances a penetrating criticism of the realist's position and defends his nominalism by acute logic.

The problem of universals is approached in Indian Philosophy from the side of *meaning* also. Almost all words in our language, except proper names, are general. They cannot, like proper names, be said to stand for individuals. The question therefore arises: What is the meaning of general words? Various systems of Indian

Philosophy answer the question from their respective stand-points. The issue is two-fold : (i) whether the meaning of general words is universal, or particular, or both, and (ii) whether the meaning of general words is anything real. For the Mīmāṁsā and the Advaita the direct meaning of words is only universal; the particular is meant only by implication. For the Nyāya-Vaiśesika, on the other hand, the word denotes a particular qualified by the universal. The Grammarian who makes a significant contribution to this question is divided into two schools: one holding the particular and the other holding the universal as the sole meaning of words. Bhartrhari is a great champion of the latter view. He is an absolutist like the Advaitist, and holds universals to be empirically real as the meaning of words, though they are ultimately non-different from the *Word-Absolute* (*Śabda-Brahma*). It is noteworthy that all the views mentioned above attach some kind of reality to the meaning of words. But the Buddhist denies that the meaning of words is anything real. Words, according to him, do not express the real at all. The real being the unique point-instant, it is indeterminate, or unspeakable. He accepts that the meaning of words is universal, but the universal in his view is a construction of thought and not an element in reality. The controversy between the realist and the Buddhist nominalist over the question of the reality of the meaning of words forms the most important part of the whole discussion on the problem of universals in Indian Philosophy.

The concept of universals and the problems arising out of it have been perennial topics of discussion in Western Philosophy also. The starting-point for the discussion was provided by Plato's theory of *Ideas.* Plato in his Dialogues advocated an extreme form of realism. He argued that the existence of universals was required not only ontologically to explain the nature of the world which we experience, but also epistemologically to explain the nature of our experience of it. He held that universals were primary realities transcending the world of sense-experience, and that sensible objects were merely imperfect copies of them and were real only to the degree in which they represented the perfect form, or the universal. This extreme realism of Plato was rejected by Aristotle who advocated, in its place, a moderate form of realism. He agreed that universals were real, but denied that they had any being apart from the individual. Individuals alone were primarily real and universals were real only as their immanent features. These two forms of realism, the Platonic and the Aristotelian, provided the foundation for prolonged discussions on universals in Western Philosophy.

In the Medieval period there arose a great controversy over the question of the existence of universals. In the beginning the Platonic realism was favoured, but it soon gave way to the moderate realism of Aristotle under the pressure of criticism by the adversaries of realism. Finally, however, both the forms of realism were rejected in favour of conceptualism.

In the modern period conceptualism was the predominant trend of thought. Although the nominalistic trend was also present, for instance, in the thought of Thomas Hobbes, it did not find much favour among the leading philosophers of this period. Both the empiricists and the rationalists accepted universals in some sense as concepts in the mind. But there was an important difference between the two. The empiricists held that all universals were empirically derived from observed resemblances amongst particulars. The rationalists, on the other hand, held that some universals, which were fundamental to human knowledge, were not empirically derived, that is to say, they were *a priori*. The fundamental concepts of human knowledge, such as being, substance, cause, etc. were inherent in the nature of the mind itself; they could not be derived from experience, like the concepts of dog, chair, etc., since they were presupposed by all knowledge. The rationalists thus accepted the conceptualism of the empiricists, but protested against their empiricism. It is important to note that Kant who was the critic of both the rationalists and the empiricists, shared in the rationalist's protest against the latter.

All the traditional views on universals in Western Philosophy finally boil down to two ontological theories, namely the *Philosophy of Universals* and the *Philosophy of Resemblances*. In the contemporary period, the realists, on the one hand, and the Logical Positivists and the Linguistic Analysts on the other, dispute over the problem of universals at great length. The one upholds universals and the other resemblances as the ontological basis of thought and language. The realists try to reduce all resemblances to universals and the opponents of realism try to reduce all universals to resemblances. It is, therefore, important to ask: Is such a reduction by either side justified? That is to say, can we legitimately reduce either all universals to resemblances, or all resemblances to universals? The solution of the problem of universals would depend to a great extent on a satisfactory answer to this question.

It is, however, true that contemporary attitude towards universals is frequently one of apathy. There are philosophers of our day who dismiss the problem of universals as unreal. Some philosophers hold that the question about universals is unreal because it is non-sensical; the term 'universal' has no significance, for there are no universals in the world over and above the particulars. Others hold the question to be unreal on the ground that it is concerned not with real objects, but only with words; it is simply a question about how words are used, or should be used, about whether abstract nouns, for example, are to be classed with proper names. It will be shown in the course of this work that both these contentions are unjustified. Firstly, it is untrue to say that there are no universals in any sense of the term, although it may be true that the kind of universals postulated by the realist have no existence. Secondly, it is untrue to say that the question about universals is purely verbal, since the use of universals both antedates the use of words and is presupposed by it. The recognition of something as the same or similar does not depend upon the acquaintance with words. Such recognition arises not only in adult human beings, but also in infants before the use of language begins, and in animals who have no acquaintance with words at all. Besides, the use of words itself would not be possible without the apprehension of the universal; one could not use the word 'cow', for example, in one's recognition of cows unless one recognised the mark or sound 'cow' as an instance of the word (universal). And thirdly, even if it be conceded that the problem of universals is purely linguistic, i.e., concerned solely with the classification of words, it cannot be said to be unreal, for the critics themselves hold the problem, interpreted in this way, to be a very urgent one which they are most anxious to solve. It will be our endeavour to show in this work that although it is an error to suppose that the problem of universals is one about entities having the same sort of existence as particular things, it is equally erroneous to suppose that it is concerned purely with language, or proper use of words. There are epistemological and ontological problems involved even in our use of words, which are real enough to demand a solution. The problem cannot simply be brushed aside by saying that there is no problem to solve, or that the problem is unreal.

In the following chapters we shall examine the various views of universals referred to above. Although our main task is a critical discussion of the problem of universals in Indian Philosophy, we shall devote three chapters in the end to a brief discussion of the problem in Western Philosophy also. We will compare and contrast the various views belonging to these two traditions wherever it can relevantly be done. Our approach will be critical. We shall try to see, in the first place, whether a view is self-consistent, and secondly, whether it is reasonably justifiable. The conclusion which we arrive at is that the solution of the problem of universals can be found only in a comprehensive view based on the truths of experience and not in a dogmatic adherence to anyone of the traditional theories, viz., realism, conceptualism and nominalism.

CHAPTER II

THE EXTREME REALISM OF THE NYĀYA-VAIŚEṢIKA

The starting-point of the controversy over universals in Indian Philosophy was provided by the Nyāya-Vaiśeṣika doctrine of *sāmānya* or *jāti*, which set forth the fundamental realistic position in the most extreme form. The basic stand-point of the Nyāya-Vaiśeṣika is realistic and pluralistic. The world, according to it, is constituted of real objects existing independently of the cognising mind. The proof for the existence of such a world is the experience itself.[1] There could be no knowledge if there was no universe external to us. If the idealistic position concerning the external world is admitted, the claim for knowledge has to be entirely given up. The evidence of uncontradicted experience, the Nyāya argues, cannot be denied, as it would mean the cessation of all intellectual activity. Our mind contains no ideas which are independent of, or prior to, experience.[2] We cognise things directly without any intervention of ideas. The very possibility of ideas, according to the Nyāya, rests on the existence of external objects. Hence, if the external reference of our knowledge is questioned, the result would be annihilation of all knowledge.

Now, what does the external world reveal to us? According to the Nyāya-Vaiśeṣika, it reveals both diversity and unity. The variety of our cognitions necessarily implies the plurality of the reals. The manifold knowledge that we have of the external world cannot adequately be explained except on the ground of the plurality of things.[3] But, at the same time, the world reveals to us also the fact of unity inherent in the objects. Just as the variety of our cognitions implies diversity, so does

---

1. *Saṃvideva hi bhagavatī vastūpagame naḥ śaraṇam. Upaskāra* of Śaṅkara Miśra on VS, III, ii, 26.
2. NK, p. 267.
   The Nyāya-Vaiśeṣika accepts the fundamental empiricistic position that there are no *innate* ideas, or *a priori* concepts. All knowledge begins in experience and its total content is derived from experience.
3. NK, p. 267. *na hi viṣayātiśayam antareṇa pratibhāsātiśayo'vakalpate.* NM, Pt. I, p. 124.

the very possibility of cognitions imply the fact of unity. If things were absolutely disparate without having any bond of unity, their comprehension would have been beyond the capacity of human intellect. Hence, things must be admitted to possess common features which enable us to classify them and give them a common designation. These common features are what the Nyāya-Vaiśeṣika calls '*sāmānya*' or '*jāti*'. These are the universals existing in the external world uniting the particulars into various classes. These universals are as real as the particulars in whom they subsist. A denial of the reality of universals, as the conceptualists and nominalists do, would be, according to the Nyāya-Vaiśesika, a denial of the possibility of all knowledge.

1. *The definition of the universal (jāti)*

Praśastapāda defines the universal as the unity which is the cause of identical conception of particular things, and which subsists identically and wholly in each of its subjects.[4] Precisely, the universal, according to Praśastapāda, is the basis on which a community of nature is apprehended in numerically different things. Uddyotakara points out in this connection that when the universal is defined as the cause of identical conceptions, what is meant is not that all identical conceptions are based on universals, but that the universal is invariably the basis of identical conceptions, for an identical conception, in the Nyāya view, may arise even in the absence of the universal (*jāti*).[5] Concepts such as 'man', 'cow', 'pot', etc. are based on real universals (*jāti*), because they correspond to natural classes, i.e., classes to which things belong by birth. But concepts such as 'cook', 'teacher', 'blind-man', etc., though based on objective features, do not imply universals, since they do not correspond to natural classes. They correspond to certain adventitious features of things, not to their permanent class-essences. Now, the possibility of general conceptions even in the absence of the universal shows that Praśastapāda's definition of the universal as 'the cause of general conceptions' is not

4. svaviṣayasarvagatam abhinnātmakam anekavṛtti ekadvibahuṣu ātmasvarūpānugamapratyayakāri svarūpābhedena ādhāreṣu prabandhena vartamānam anuvṛttipratyayakāranam. PPB, p. 311. Cf. samānaprasavātmikā jātiḥ. NS, II, ii, 70.

5. tat samānapratyayotpattikāraṇam jātiriti jātau niyamo na samānapratyayotpattau, jātimantareṇāpi drstatvāt. NV, p 333.

quite precise. Vācaspati Miśra, therefore, rightly regards this definition as unsatisfactory. He remarks that 'this is to be accepted as a definition of the universal in so far as it serves to distinguish it from the individual and the configuration.[6]

The Neo-Naiyāyikas redefine the universal (*jāti*) in order to make its conception precise. They define it as 'that which is eternal and inherent in many individuals.'[7] Thus the universal is said to have three essential characteristics: (1) eternality, (2) commonness, and (3) inherence. In the absence of any of these qualifications the definition of the universal will be too broad. The first qualification is necessary to prevent conjunction (*saṁyoga*) from being included in the definition. Conjunction, in the Nyāya view, possesses the other two characteristics, but it is not eternal. The second qualification is necessary to exclude the dimension (*parimāṇa*) of *ākāśa* which is both eternal and inherent, but not common. And the third qualification is indispensable to avoid the inclusion of absolute non-existence (*atyantābhāva*) under the definition of the universal. The absolute non-existence is eternal and common, but not inherent in anything. Thus all the three qualifications, according to the Naiyāyika, are essential for a precise definition of the universal. This definition also succeeds in excluding adventitious characteristics which sometimes form the basis of our class conceptions. It is noteworthy that the older definition emphasised the essential function of the universal, viz., the generation of class-concepts, though it was found to be logically unsatisfactory. The new definition, on the other hand, though logically precise, says nothing explicitly about the relation of the universal to our knowledge. Nevertheless, it brings out the essential characteristics of the universal, from the Nyāya-Vaiśesika point of view, which serve to distinguish it from the other categories.

2. *The universal as distinct from the particular*

It is clear from the above definitions of the universal that, for the Nyāya-Vaiśeṣika, it has an existence distinct from the particular. The universal and particular, though intimately related, are regarded as existentially, or ontologically, different. Now, what is the ground for admitting the existence of such universals? Uddyotakara summarises

---

6. Vyaktyākṛtibhyām bhedakatvamatrena caitallaksanam na tu sarvathā veditavyam. TT, p. 485.
7. Nityatve sati anekasamavetatvam. NSM p. 55; cf. *Tarkasaṁgraha.*, p. 60.

the arguments for the existence of universals as distinct from the particulars in the following manner.[8]

(a) The general conceptions, e.g., of 'cows', 'horses', etc., must have causes other than the particular cows and horses, because, they have a distinctive character of their own, just like the conception of 'blue'.

(b) The universal 'cow', or 'cowness', must be something distinct from the particular cow because it forms the object of another cognition, like the cognitions of colour and touch.

(c) The universal 'cow' must be distinct from the particular cow because it is designated by a distinct name 'cowness', like *caitra* and horse.

(d) The conceptions of the particular 'cow' and the universal 'cow' must be due to different causes, because they have distinctive features of their own, like the conceptions of colour, etc.

All the four arguments stated above are essentially one and the same. They emphasise in different ways one and the same point, viz., that the universal must be regarded as different from the particular because its cognition is distinct from that of the latter. The distinct cognition of the universal, according to the Nyāya, must be due to its distinct character which must also be the basis of the distinct name given to it. If the difference of cognitions is not accepted as necessarily implying the difference of their objects, the result will be a great confusion. There will neither be real distinctions amongst things, nor any practical activity based on them. Hence, the existence of the universal as distinct from the particular has to be recognised.[9]

Thus the universal for the Nyāya-Vaiśeṣika is an independent category of reality; it is absolutely different from everything else including the particular in which it resides. It is also opposed to the

---

8. NV, pp. 333-34. Cf. Kumārila's proofs for the existence of universal in ŚV, *Vanavāda*, 44-48.

9. The rule that 'the difference of cognitions implies the difference of their objects' is accepted by the Naiyāyika with a qualification. It is said to be true only in those cases where the difference of cognitions is not due to its own character, but to its contents, e.g., perceptual cognitions of 'cow' and 'horse'. But in those cases in which the difference of cognitions is due, not to their contents but to their class-character (*jāti*), e.g., the perceptual and inferential cognitions of one and the same thing, the difference of cognitions does not imply the difference of their objects. See ĀTV, p.144

particular in essential characteristics. It is by definition eternal and common, while the particular is non-eternal and non-common. Thus, there is no common bond uniting the universal and the particular.[10] In fact, the difference between the universal and the particular, in this view, is more radical than the difference between two particular things. Two particulars may have an identical class-essence, but there is no such identity common to the universal and the particular.

Now, if the difference between the universal and the particular is so radical, how can the two be related? The Nyāya-Vaiśeṣika does not consider absolute difference between things as a bar to their being intimately related. The relation of the whole to its parts, and that of the material cause to its effect, according to him, exemplify that two things can be inseparably related inspite of their mutual difference. The Vaiśeṣika postulates an independent category of relation, viz., *samavāya* (*inherence*), to explain this kind of relationship. It is defined as the relation between inseparable things standing to one another as the support and the supported, and as the cause of the idea 'this is in that'.[11] This *samavāya* is said to account for the intimate relation between the universal and the particular. The *cowness* is in the cow and it is cognised as such due to the relation of *samavāya* between them. The *samavāya* itself has no affinity with either the particular or the universal. It is conceived as an eternal and independent category of reality itself. Its sole function is to relate two different things, the universal and the particular, the whole and the parts, etc. into inseparable union, and, at the same time, preserve their mutual difference.

The main contention of the Nyāya-Vaiśeṣika is that the felt difference between the universal and the particular cannot be denied. The opposed characters of coordinating and differentiating cognitions necessarily imply objective difference. The universal must be differentiated from the particular also because it is unaffected by the production, change and destruction of the particular. Along with their mutual difference, the intimate relation between the universal and the particular is also a felt fact. The one is never apprehended without the other. Hence, while determining the relation between

10. PPB, p. 314; cf. NK, p. 315.

11. ayutasiddhānām ādhāryādhārabhūtānāṁ yaḥ sambandhaḥ ihapratyayahetuḥ sa samavāyaḥ. See *Padārthadharmasaṁgraha* of Praśastapāda, p. 14; cf. VS, VII ii, 26.

the universal and the particular, both their mutual difference and intimate relationship have to be taken into account. The only relation which satisfies both these conditions, according to the Nyāya-Vaiśeṣika, is *samavāya* as defined above.

Now, if the universal and the particular, as also their cognitions, are absolutely different from one another, then why is the universal not apprehended independently of the particular? The reason, according to the Naiyāyika, is that the cognition of the universal depends upon the cognition of the particular. It is not possible to apprehend the universal without the particular, because, the causal factors producing the cognition of the former are included in those producing the cognition of the latter.[12] The perception of the universal, Śrīdhara points out, depends upon two factors : the particular that manifests it (*abhivyañjaka*) and configuration (*avayavasaṁsthānaviśeṣa*).[13] That is, the universal is perceivable only in sensible objects. It does not have independent perceptibility, otherwise it should be perceivable even in non-sensible things like atoms. This however should not be taken to mean that the universal has no perceptibility at all, for, in that case, it should remain unperceived even in sensible objects. Udayana therefore remarks that the universal must be admitted to have a natural perceptibility (*svarūpayogyatā*), but its perception depends upon the perception of the particular in which it inheres. In the case of the non-perception of the latter, the former naturally remains unperceived.[14]

It is noteworthy that, for the Nyāya-Vaiśesika, perceivability of the particular is a condition for the perception of the universal, not for its inherence. The universal, according to this school, inheres even in non-perceivable things such as atoms, minds and souls.[15] This

12. na ca vyaktyā vinā sāmānyasphuraṇam kāraṇābhāvāt. vyaktisphuraṇa-sāmagrīniviṣṭā hi jātisphuraṇasāmagrī. Kus. Pt. I, p. 262.
13. NK, p. 317.
14. tasmād vyaktigrahaṇayogyatāntargataiva jātigrahaṇayogyateti tadanupalambhe jāteranupalambha eva. Op. cit., p. 262.
15. The Naiyāyika and the Vaiśeṣika differ on the question of the perceptibility of soul. For the former the soul is perceived through the mind (*manas*) as the object of the notion of 'I'. (See NV, III, i, 1, and Dink., p. 162). But, for the latter, the perception of the soul, where it is both the perceiver and the perceived, is not admissible. He, however, admits that the soul may be perceived in immediate yogic intuition. (See VS, III, ii, 6, and IX, i, ii; and also NK, p. 196). But even if the perception of self be admitted, one can perceive one's own self and not that of others. So, the universal 'soulness' (*ātmatvajāti*) can never be perceived, since the perception of a universal by hypothesis, depends on the perception of more than one instance.

obviously means that the universals soulness (*ātmatva*), mindness (*manastva*), atomness (*paramāṇutva*) and the like are never perceived. The existence of these universals, and also of others whose existence is doubted, can be proved, according to the Naiyāyika, by logical inference. The existence of universal soulness (*ātmatva*), for example, is inferred on the ground that it is required as 'the determinant of the inherent causality of pleasure, pain, etc.'[16] Similarly, inferential proofs based on causality may be advanced for the existence of the universals 'mindness' and 'atomness' also. As a mater of fact, the modern exponents of the Nyāya-Vaiśeṣika school lay greater emphasis on the logical necessity of accepting the existence of universals rather than their givenness in perception. They make use of the principle that the causality of a thing cannot be undetermined and the determinant of causality must be a universal. For example, the existence of universal 'substancehood' (*dravyatva*), whose perception may be doubted, is sought to be proved on the ground that it is required as 'the determinant of the inherent causality of an effect, or of conjunction and disjunction.' Similarly, 'earthhood' (*pṛthivītva*) is proved as 'the determinant of the inherent causality of smell.'[17] This shows that, for the Naiyāyika, the notion of causality as a uniform and necessary relation between things necessarily implies the existence of universals. Udayana has argued this point very strongly. Before we proceed any further it would be worthwhile considering his arguments on this subject.

3. *Universal as the determinant of causality*

Udayana argues for the existence of the universal (*jāti*) on the basis of the principle of causality. His main argument is that causal relation being necessary and uniform, it can be said to exist, not between particulars as such, but between particulars having a determinate class-nature (*jāti*). If causal relation is supposed to hold between bare particulars, then we cannot explain our notion of the *potential* (*savarūpayogya*) cause. We search for the specific material which has potentiality for the desired effect. This potentiality, or causal efficiency

16. ātmatva-jātistu sukhaduḥkhādisamavāyikāraṇatāvacchedakatayā siddhyati. NSM, p. 153.
17. See NSM, pp. 48-49, 105-6.

(*kāraṇatva*), is possessed by a thing by virtue of its class-nature (*jāti*). The determinate class-nature of a thing is an experienced fact, and it forms the basis of our practical life. A denial of this, says Udayana, will be contrary to the nature of things as discovered by us.[18] Further, if the universal is not admitted as the determinant of the causal potency of a thing, absurd consequences will follow. A parti-cular effect, in that case, should be produced by anything and, in turn, be capable of producing anything. Consequently practical life based on class-distinctions should become absolutely impossible. But such a view, Udayana argues, is supported neither by experience nor by logic.[19]

The above argument asserts that the cause-effect relation is completely determined by the class-natures (*jāti*) of cause and effect. Neither can different kinds of things produce the same kind of effect, nor can different kinds of effects follow from the same kind of cause. Udayana anticipates an objection against this theory. It might be contended that different kinds of causes are seen to produce the same kind of effect. Fire, for example, is produced by various kinds of causes, viz., *tṛṇa, araṇi* and *maṇi.* Does it not disprove the theory set out above? Udayana answers that the *sameness* of fire produced by different kinds of causes is only apparent. One and the same effect seems to follow from different kinds of causes, because we do not sufficiently analyse the effect. If we take pains to do so, we would discover that there are sub-classes (*avāntarajāti*) of fires corresponding to the different kinds of causes which produce them. These subtle class-differences of fires may not be easily observable, but they can be discovered by minute observation. If different kinds of causes are believed to produce the same kind of effect, then anything might produce anything. Consequently, both causation as a necessary relation and inference based on it would be annihilated. For ordinary purposes it may not be necessary to find out minute differences of fires; we may generally infer from fire the possible causes which might have produced it. But logically, Udayana argues, it cannot be

18. niyatajātīyasvabhāvatāvyāghātāt. Op. cit., p. 67.
Jayanta maintains that bare particulars devoid of class-nature (*jāti*) are never experienced at all. (yathārūpādyasambaddhā na vyaktirupalabhyate tathaiva jātyayukteti kā te vyasanasantatiḥ.) NM, Pt. I, p. 286.

19. Op. cit., pp. 69-70.

maintained that a determinate kind of effect can be produced by different kinds of causes.[20]

Udayana anticipates another objection against his theory. It might be argued that just as there are different sub-classes of fire corresponding to different kinds of causes, so also there may be different sub-classes of smoke produced by different kinds of causes. Fire may be accepted as the cause of one kind of smoke, but the possibility of other kinds of smoke produced by things other than fire cannot logically be denied. Therefore, neither the presence of smoke would imply the presence of fire, nor the absence of fire would imply the absence of smoke. Consequently inference from smoke to fire will be impossible.

Udayana answers that this objection is not at all effective against his theory. It may be effective against the Buddhist who does not admit real universals (*jāti*) determining the production of an effect. What his theory asserts is only that sub-classes of effects are to be admitted where different kinds of causes are observed to produce superficially the same kind of effect, just as in the case of fire. But where such is not the case, as in the instance of smoke, where the effect (smoke) is invariably seen to be produced by a determinate kind of cause (fire) and nothing else, the assumption of sub-classes of the effect is quite gratuitous. In all such cases, Udayana maintains, the causal relation must be admitted to be determined by the class-natures (*jāti*) of the cause and the effect which are observed to be invariably related.[21] It may be urged again that corresponding to the sub-classes of fire distinguished above, there must also be sub-classes of smokes produced by them. Udayana answers that if it is urged as an objection to his theory, then it is quite acceptable to him (*iṣṭāpatti*). This objection concedes his basic contention that causality cannot be explained without admitting determination by the universals (*jāti*). Also the admission of sub-classes of smoke would not hinder the inference of fire from it; one can always infer the presence of some kind of fire on perceiving a determinate kind of smoke.[22]

20. Ibid., pp. 83-84. Udayana's theory, it may be noted, is in conformity with the modern scientific view about causation in so far as the latter has discarded the older theory of the plurality of causes.

21. pratyakṣānupalambhagocaro jātibhedo na kāryaprayojaka iti vadato bauddhasya śirasyeṣa prahāraḥ. asmākantu yatsāmānyākrāntayor yayor anvayavyatirekavattā tayos tathaiva hetuhetumadbhāvaniścayaḥ. Ibid., p. 89.

22. Ibid.

The substance of Udayana's contention is that specific class-natures of things must be admitted to account for the determinate causal relations between them. The thread, for example, is the material cause of cloth, not merely as an existent, but as a thing having a specific class-character, viz., *threadness.* Similarly, the cloth, too, is the efffect of thread not as an existent, but as a thing having a specific class-character, viz., *clothness.* In other words, the cause-effect relation, according to Udayana, connects the cause of the nature of *thread* with the effect of the nature of *cloth.* The connection holds between *the thread as such,* and *the cloth as such.* and cannot therefore hold between any other pairs of things. This theory does not merely assert that every effect must have a cause, but also that a definite *kind* of effect must have a definite *kind* of cause, and *vice versa.* It is not within our scope to discuss the nature of causal relation in detail. Yet the principle underlying Udayana's argument seems to be undeniable. It must be granted that causal relation holds between particulars having determinate characteristics, and that these characteristics are general in nature. It is not that any two particulars are related as cause and effect, but only those having certain general features. If this principle is accepted, then the reality of the universal (in some sense) would be undeniable.

4. *Jāti and Upādhi*

An important feature of the Nyāya-Vaiśeṣika theory of universals is that it does not recognise all general characteristics as universals (*jāti*). The universal, according to this theory, is the natural and eternal class-essence, such as 'redness', 'cowness', 'potness', etc., which is the permanent feature of particular things. Other general characteristics such as 'cookness', 'tallness', 'blindness', etc., which are adventitious features, are recognised not as universals (*jāti*) but as *upādhis.* The distinction of *jāti* and *upādhi* becomes necessary for the Nyāya also because of its conception of the categories of reality (*padārthas*). Given its conception of the universal, things belonging to the categories of *substance, quality* and *action* can alone be legitimately regarded as possessing genuine class nature (*jāti*). The other categories, viz., *universal, particularity, inherence* and *non-existence,* although we might have general conceptions of them, cannot be said to have real class-natures (*jāti*) inhering in them. Now the question naturally arises, what is the logical basis for the distinction of *jāti* and *upādhi?* Udayana enumerates six *impediments* called *jāti-bādhakas,* the presence of anyone of which is said to be sufficient to disqualify a characteristic from being recognised as a universal.[23] As this topic forms an important part of the Nyāya-Vaiśeṣika theory of universals, we propose to discuss it in some detail. The six impediments are stated as follows :

1. *Vyakterabheda*: The character belonging to a single thing, e.g., '*ākāśatva*', is not a universal.[24]

2. *Tulyatva*: Two general names having the same meaning do not stand for different universals, e. g., '*ghaṭatva*' and '*kalaśatva.*'

3. *Sāṅkarya*: Cross-dividing characters which co-exist in some instances and also exclude one another in others, e.g., '*bhūtatva*' (being an element) and '*mūrtatva*' (having limited dimension), are not to be recognised as universals.[25]

4. *Anavasthā*: The character, the recognition of which as a universal leads to infinite regress, e.g., '*universality*' (*jātitva*), is not to be regarded as a *jāti*, but as an *upādhi*. If 'universality' was regarded as a universal inhering in all the universals, then another 'universality' will be required to synthesise the former with the latter. Similarly, a third 'universality' would be needed to synthesise the second with the other universals in which it inheres, and so on *ad infinitum*. Therefore, the concept of 'universal' is not to be regarded as corresponding to one more universal, namely, 'universality'.

5. *Rūpahāni*: Ultimate differences (*viśeṣas*) of the Vaiśeṣikas cannot have any principle of unity, as it would contradict their essential nature. If '*viśeṣatva*' was regarded as an identity (universal) inhering in the '*viśeṣas*', then their mutual difference would be annihilated. '*Viśeṣas*' being principles of ultimate differences, they cannot be differentiated from one another on the basis of any other characteristic. Hence, if they were regarded as identical in being '*viśeṣas*', it would contradict their self-differentiating nature, and they will be no more '*viśeṣas*'.[26]

---

23. vyakterabhedastulyatvaṁ saṅkaro'thānavasthitiḥ.
rūpahānirasambandhọ jātibādhakasaṅgrahaḥ.
Kir., p. 33; also cited in NSM, pp. 58-59.
24. This is implied by the Nyāya definition of the universal itself.
25. Both '*bhūtatva*' and '*mūrtatva*' are present in the four elements, viz., earth, water, fire and air, but the former is present without the latter in *ākāśa*, and the latter without the former in *manas* (mind). Such general characters, according to the Naiyāyika, are *upādhis*, not *jāti*.
26. Sec. PPB, pp. 13 and 32f. Also see Dink., pp. 58-59.

6. *Asambandha* : The universal in the Nyāya-Vaiśeṣika view is, by definition, 'inherent' in its subjects. This implies that the thing in which nothing can *inhere* cannot be the substrate of a universal. The categories of inherence (*samavāya*) and non-existence (*abhāva*), according to the Nyāya-Vaiśeṣika view, cannot have anything inhering in them. If '*samavāyatva*' is regarded as a universal *inhering* in inherence (*samavāya*), then it would have to inhere in both its substrate and its relation with it, which is absurd. Such a position would also lead to infinite regress. Hence, nothing can be conceived as inhering in inherence. Similarly, no universal can be conceived to inhere in negation because it is not a positive entity. Therefore, '*samavāyatva*' and '*abhāvatva*' are not to be regarded as universals.[27]

It is evident from the above account that the theory of '*jātibādhakas*' is formulated in conformity with the ontological scheme of the Nyāya-Vaiśeṣika. Any character in the case of which one or more of these impediments are present, is to be regarded as an *upādhi*. It is to be noted that these impediments operate in distinguishable ways. The first and the third impediments debar a character from being regarded as a universal. The second impediment nullifies the apparent distinction between two characters each claiming to be a separate universal. And the last three impediments prevent a thing from being the substrate of the universal. The special function of the last three impediments is to keep the inherence of the universal (*jāti*) restricted to the categories of substance, quality and action. Of the six impediments (*jātibādhakas*) described above, the legitimacy of all except one is quite obvious. Given the Nyāya-Vaiśeṣika conception of the universal and its conception of the various categories, all impediments except the third logically follow. But it is not quite clear why the Naiyāyika refuses to recognise cross-dividing characters as universals. It would be worthwhile considering his arguments in this connection.

It is to be noted that a section of the neo-Naiyāyikas do not regard cross-division as an impediment (*jātibādhaka*). The opponents of cross-division hold that two universals cannot be partially coincident and partially exclusive. The neo-Naiyāyikas refuse to accept this rule.[28] They maintain that when general conceptions corresponding to cross dividing characters are present without giving rise to any

27. See Dink., p. 59.
28. tādṛśaniyame mānābhāvān na sāṅkaryaṁ jātibādhakam iti navyāḥ. Dink., p. 58.

logical absurdities patent in other cases considered above, there is no reason why the characters in question should not be recognised as universals. According to this view, three classes of universals may be distinguished on the basis of their mutual relationships. (i) Universals which never coincide, e.g., 'cowness' and 'horseness', (ii) those between any two of which the extension of one completely includes the extension of the other, e.g., 'substancehood' and 'earthhood', and (iii) those which are partially coincident and partially exclusive, e.g., '*bhūtatva*' and '*mūrtatva*'. The older Naiyāyikas accept the first two types alone as genuine universals (*jāti*) and the third as '*upādhi*'.[29]

Udayanācārya is a great champion of the older school. He maintains that two universals cannot coincide if there is opposition between them, i.e., if their extensions are mutually exclusive. And if they coincide, the extension of one must completely include the extension of the other.[30] Vardhamāna raises an important point in this connection. If cross-dividing attributes are not to be recognised as universals, then many of the accepted universals, such as 'potness', 'goldness' etc., would become *upādhis,* since these universals are partially coincident and partially exclusive.[31] The opponents of cross-division might reply that 'potness' as such is not a universal at all. Further sub-classes of pots, such as 'gold pot' 'clay pot', etc., must be made and the universals determining them in those characters, viz., 'gold potness', 'clay potness', etc., will be the genuine universals.

Udayana advances an argument which he thinks to be fatal to the supporters of cross-division. He argues that if two mutually exclusive universals can be coincident, then the possibility of the co-inherence of 'cowness' and 'horseness' also would have to be admitted. It may be urged that the two cannot be coincident because causes producing cows and horses are different. Udayana rejects this argument as unsound because the said causes being imperceptible we are not in a position to make any definite assertions about them. Besides, once it is admitted in principle that two mutually exclusive universals can be coincident, it can be conceived that causes producing cows and horses might be identical. The fact that 'cowness' and 'horseness' have not been perceived together so far is in itself no guarantee for

---

29. See Introduction to *Bhāṣāpariccheda* by Dr. Satkari Mukherjee, p. xxii.
30. evam, vidhirūpayorvyāvṛttirūpayorvā jātyorvirodhe sati na samāveśaḥ. samāviṣṭayośca parāparabhāvaniyamaḥ. Op. cit., p. 187.
31. See *Prakāśa* on Kus. Pt. I, p. 188.

such non-perception in future also. There is nothing to prevent us from thinking, Udayana argues, that both 'cowness' and 'horseness' may inhere together in some creature somewhere at some time.[32]

Udayana obviously assumes that in nature there is no cross-division. Classes (genera and species) are systematically divided from the highest to the lowest. The lower classes, though included in the higher ones, mutually exclude each other. In reality there can be nothing which belongs to two mutually exclusive natural classes at any time. If nature permitted overlapping of mutually exclusive natural classes, then all class-divisions would become completely meaningless. It is for this reason that Udayana refuses to recognise cross-dividing attributes as universals. If Udayana's assumption concerning the constitution of nature is granted, then his conclusion which logically follows from it is inescapable. If nature is what Udayana thinks it to be, then cross-dividing attributes cannot be regarded as real class-essences (*jāti*). They may, however, be regarded as general attributes (*upādhis*) of things.

The neo-Naiyāyikas refuse to accept Udayana's view concerning the constitution of nature. In their view, there is no convincing reason to support Udayaṇa's contention that two co-inhering universals must be related as higher and lower. If partial exclusion of one by the other is not considered a bar in the case of universals related as higher and lower, then what cogent reason is there for denying universality to the attributes which are partially coincident and partially exclusive? Udayana's argument that if mutually exclusive universals are admitted to coexist in the same substrate, then 'cowness' and 'horseness' may also be admitted to coexist in some creature, is not sound at all. Those universals which are found to be totally exclusive of one another need not be conceived as existing together. But there can be no logical bar against two mutually exclusive universals from being coexistent in the same substrate if it is attested by experience. Udayana's argument that if this restriction is not accepted, there can be no guarantee against the future coexistence of two universals now found to be totally exclusive, is unsound. The same argument can be directed against his own position also. What is the guarantee that two universals now found to be related as higher and lower will not be found to be partially coincident and partially

32. Op. cit., p. 192.

exclusive, or totally exclusive, at some point in future? Nothing prevents us from thinking that 'potness' may exist in future without 'substancehood'. But such thinking does not nullify the facts as they are discovered in the present. Characters such as '*bhūtatva*' and '*mūrtatva*', which are partially coincident and partially exclusive, are, according to neo-Naiyāyikas, facts of experience like other universals. Hence, they must be recognised as genuine universals.[33]

Although there is disagreement between the old and the new schools of the Nyāya concerning cross-division, there is perfect agreement over the remaining five impediments. Any attribute which is subject to one or more of these impediments is not to be recognised as '*jāti*' but as '*upādhi*'. This distinction of '*jāti*' and '*upādhi*' brings out clearly the Nyāya-Vaiśeṣika conception of universals as real natural class-essences existing in the objective world. General attributes other than universals, which are called '*upādhis*', are also real characters of things discovered by us in the external world. These attributes form the bases of many of our generalisations and classifications. '*Upādhis*' are again distinguished by the Naiyāyika into '*sakhaṇḍa*' and '*akhaṇḍa*'. The former is an analysable character while the latter is an unanalysable one. One and the same character may be understood as '*sakhaṇḍa*' or '*akhaṇḍa*' according to different contexts. '*Ākāśatva*', for example, is a '*sakhaṇḍopādhi*, when it is defined as 'being the substrate of sound' (*śabdāśrayatva*), but when it is understood as 'the determinant of the inherent causality of sound' (*śabdasamavāyikāraṇatāvacchedaka*), it is an '*akhaṇḍopādhi*', for a determinant is not further determined and hence is unanalysable.[34]

The last point needs some elucidation. The real, in the Nyāya-Vaiśeṣika view, is a complex of substance and attributes. Therefore, the content of all knowledge is a complex of adjective (*prakāra*) and substantive (*viśeṣya*). No genuine cognition can fail to take note of

33. Cf. Introduction to *Bhāṣāpariccheda* by Satkari Mukherjee, p. xxii.

According to Viśiṣṭādvaitin also there is no valid reason to deny universality to cross-dividing attributes. The universal must be recognised wherever there is identical cognition (*anuvṛttadhīreva hi sarvatra jātisadbhāve pramāṇam*). To the objection that in that case mutually exclusive universals, such as 'cowness' and 'horseness', may also be said to subsist together, the Viśiṣṭādvaitin replies that on this question experience alone is the determinant (*upalambhasyaiva niyāmakatvāt*). That is, if two universals are never experienced together, there is no ground for supposing their coexistence in the same substratum.

See TMK, V, 111, and SS on it, pp. 310-11.

34. Ibid., p. xxiii.

these two elements in the real and the relation existing between them. The adjective functions as the determinant of the thing cognised. It is the adjectival part, according to the Naiyāyika, which makes the thing what it is; it constitutes its very nature which serves to distinguish it from other things.[35] It is significant to note that, for the Nyāya, the cognition which is really felt is always determinate. The existence of indeterminate cognition preceding the determinate one is accepted by him only due to logical reasons.[36] It is the determinate cognition which is really known, and the object is always felt in it as qualified by its adjectival essence (*prakāra*).

Now, this *prakāra*, whether it is a universal (*jāti*) or an *upādhi*, when cognised as an element in the real, must be felt as undetermined. For instance, in the perceptual judgement 'this is cow', the substantive (cow) is determined by its adjectival essence (cowness), because the thing is cognised as 'cow.' But 'cowness', which functions here as the determinant, is itself undetermined by another adjective qualifying it. If a determinant is supposed to be determined by a further determinant, the result would be a deadlock. But when an attribute is independently understood as the meaning of a term, i.e., when it is not understood as the determinant, it must be felt as determined by a qualifying adjective. For instance, when the *universal* 'cowness' is understood as the meaning of the *word* 'cowness' independently of its relation to the particular cows, it is felt as determined by 'cowness-ness' the character of being 'cowness'. Now this 'cowness-ness' which is felt as the determinant must be an *akhaṇḍopādhi* which is undetermined and is also unanalysable.[37]

Thus, according to the Nyāya, the real is always cognised as determined by some attribute, except the universal (*jāti*) and the unanalysable characteristic (*akhaṇḍopādhi*) which are felt as the determinants. It may be asked, why does the Nyāya recognise *akhaṇḍopāhi* as a determinant when it is not a real class-essence (*jāti*) of a thing? The Nyāya would answer that it is because of two reasons. Firstly, the universal (*jāti*) alone cannot function as the determinant in all cases because, as we have already seen, all general characters

35. NSM, pp. 186-7; cf. Keith: *Indian Logic and Atomism*, p. 45.
36. For a detailed discussion on this point see Ch. V.
37. NSM, pp. 186-7; cf. Satkari Mukherjee: *Introduction to Bhāṣāparicched*a, pp. xvii and xviii.

cannot be admitted to be universals. And secondly, *upādhi* functions as well as the universal as a principle of synthesis. Therefore, there is nothing wrong in recognising *akhandopādhi* as a determinant of the real.

5. *Existence as the Highest Universal*

Having discussed the Nyāya distinction of universals and other general characteristics, we should now proceed to give a more detailed account of the Nyāya conception of universals. Universals are distinguished by the Nyāya-Vaiśeṣika into two types: '*para*' and '*apara*'. The universal having the widest extension is called '*para*', and all the rest having lesser extension are called '*apara*' Existence (*sattā*), according to the Nyāya-Vaiśeṣika, is the highest universal (*parasāmānya*). It extends over the greatest number of objects, and is the cause of their conception as 'existents'. The supreme function of a universal is *synthesis*, and 'existence' being the ground of synthesis alone is the universal *par excellence*.[38] The other universals, viz., those of substance , quality, action, etc., are less extensive. They are not the bases of synthesis alone, but also of differentiation. They synthesise the members of their own class and also serve to differentiate them from the members of other classes. They are, therefore, both universal (*sāmānya*) and particular (*viśeṣa*). The essential function of these universals being synthesis they are primarily *sāmānya*; they are called *viśeṣas* only in a derivative sense, for they serve to distinguish things belonging to different classes.[39] The universals of lesser extension (*apara*) are again divided into two types: those having intermediate extension (*parāpara*) and those having the least extension (*apara*). 'Substancehood', for example, is less extensive than 'existence' and more extensive than 'earthhood'. Hence it belongs to the intermediate type. The universals, such as 'cowness', 'potness', etc., are least extensive (*apara*), for there are no universals of lesser extension under them.[40]

It is necessary to clear a misunderstanding which is likely to arise from Kaṇāda's statement that 'the distinction of universal and particular is relative to thought'.[41] This should not be taken to mean that generality and particularity, according to Kanāda, are thought-

38. bhāvo 'nuvṛttereva hetutvāt sāmānyameva. VS, I, ii, 4; cf. PPB, p. 11.
39. Ibid., I, ii, 5-6. Also see *upaskāra* on these *sūtras*.
40. NSM, p. 60; cf. NK, p. 13.
41. sāmānyaṁ viśeṣa iti budhyapekṣam. VS, I, ii, 3.

constructions, as it is very likely to be interpreted. It only means that the conception of the universal as a coordinative or differentiative feature is relative to thought. Also the distinction of generality and particularity implicit in the distinction of universals as higher and lower is relative to thought.[42] In other words, the universal, according to Kanāda, may be viewed as a *general* or as a *particular* feature. When it is viewed as the principle of synthesis, it is a general feature, and when as the principle of differentiation, it is a particular feature. 'Cowness', for instance, is both a general as well as a particular feature; it may be viewed as the basis of synthesis of all cows, or as the basis of differentiation of cows from other things. The *sūtra* of Kaṇāda, referred to above, does by no means suggest that the universal is a fabrication of mind. Kaṇāda was not a conceptualist, for he admits universals as elements in the real. They are, for him, as real as particulars; only our view of them, as coordinative or differentiative features, is relative to thought.

It is also necessary to note that the Nyāya distinction of universals as higher and lower does not mean that the former includes the latter. The universal (*jāti* or *sāmānya*) of the Nyāya is not equivalent to 'genus' or 'species'. The universal is the attribute common to many things, while genus or species is the class of things having such an attribute. The class of 'existents' is a genus including the classes of substance, quality and action, which may be called its species. But the universal 'existence' does not include within itself the universals 'substancehood', 'qualityhood', etc., Similarly, the universal 'substancehood' does not include within itself the universals 'earthhood', 'cowness', 'potness', etc, though earth, cows and pots are included within the class of substance. Thus all the universals, according to the Nyāya-Vaiśeṣika, exclude one another. The evidence for their exclusiveness is said to be found within experience itself. Two reasons are advanced in support of this view. Firstly, each universal subsists in a specific group of things (*vṛttiniyama*) which is well defined and demarcated from the other groups of things. And secondly, the cognition of each universal is distinct from the cognition of the other (*pratyayabheda*).[43] These reasons, according to the

42. tatra sāmānyasya tadviśeṣasya ca lakṣaṇam buddhireva. *Upaskāra* on VS, I, ii, 3. Also see *Vṛtti* on the same : paratvarūpaṁ sāmānyatvam aparatvarūpaṁ viśeṣatvañca na niyataṁ kintu budhyapekṣam iti.

43. dravyādiṣu vṛttiniyamāt pratyayabhedācca parasparataścānyatvam. PPB, p. 314.

Nyāya-Vaiśeṣika, conclusively prove that universals are mutually exclusive.

We have noted above that the highest universal 'existence' is distinguished from other universals on the ground that it is the basis of synthesis alone, while others are the bases of both synthesis and differentiation. Again, 'existence' being a universal (*jāti*) it can subsist only in the first three categories of substance, quality and action for reasons discussed in the last section. Now a couple of important questions arise here. If the universal 'existence' is confined to the first three categories of the Vaiśeṣikas, does it not serve as the ground of differentiation between them and the remaining four categories? And does it not also mean that objects belonging to the first three categories alone have existence, not others? Śrīdhara anticipates these questions and answers that the categories of substance, quality and action cannot be distinguished from others on the basis of 'existence' because other categories also (with the exception of non-existence (*abhāva*) are felt as having a 'self-being' (*svarūpasattā*).[44] In other words, according to Śrīdhara, though the universal 'existence' does not inhere in the categories of generality, particularity and inherence, yet these latter are not non-existents, for they are positively felt as having a kind of being It may again be urged that the universal 'existence' at least serves to differentiate the first three categories from that of non-existence and hence it is the basis of differentiation also. To this Śrīdhara replies that 'existence' is denied as the basis of differentiation amongst positive categories only. So, even if the first three categories are distinguished from that of non-existence on the basis of the universal 'existence', it does not affect the Nyāya-Vaiśeṣika position.[45]

Śrīdhara's answers to the questions raised above are obviously unsatisfactory. However it can be seen that he could not have given a more satisfactory answer. 'Existence' being a universal by hypothesis, it could inhere only in the first three categories. Also the categories of generality, particularity and inherence could not be regarded as 'non-existents', since, in that case, they would cease to be positive (*bhāvarūpa*). So, Śrīdhara postulates a kind of 'self-existence' for these categories, which, though not the same as the universal

44. yadyapyeṣa sāmānyādibhyo vyāvartate tathāpi na tebhyaḥ svāśrayaṁ vyāvartayituṁ śaknoti, teṣāmapi svarūpasattāsambuddhisaṁvedyatvāt. NK, p. 12.

45. Loc. cit.

'existence', is yet not a negation of it. Evidently, the notion of 'self-existence', as different from the universal 'existence' and yet non-different from it, defies comprehension. If this 'self-being' is different from 'existence', then the first three categories can be differentiated from the other three positive categories on the basis of 'existence'. And if the 'self-being' and 'existence' are not different, then there is no sense in denying the subsistence of 'existence' in the other three positive categories. In the former case, the universal 'existence' would not remain the basis of synthesis alone, but would also be the basis of differentiation. In the latter case, 'existence' would be the common character of all the positive categories and, therefore, cease to be a universal (*jāti*) of the Nyāya-Vaiśeṣika conception. Moreover, when the categories of substance, quality and action can be distinguished from the category of non-existence on the basis of the universal 'existence', there is no sense in denying 'existence' as the basis of differentiation. Hence, the contention of the Nyāya-Vaiśeṣika that 'existence' is the basis of synthesis alone does not stand to reason.

It is however not difficult to understand why the Nyāya holds fast to the view that the universal 'existence' is the basis of synthesis alone. The reason is that if 'existence' is admitted to be the basis of differentiation also, then the categories of generality, particularity and inherence in which 'existence' does not inhere would turn out to be mere concepts having no actual existence. This position could not be acceptable to the Naiyāyika, as it is directly opposed to his fundamental metaphysical assumptions. Another way in which he could solve the difficulty was by regarding 'existence' as the common character of all the positive categories. But this, too, is not acceptable to him because 'existence', in that case, would cease to be a universal of his conception. The Naiyāyika is not prepared to surrender his conception of 'existence' as the highest universal (*jāti*) synthesising the categories of substance, quality and action.

The proof for the distinct reality of the universal 'existence' according to the Nyāya, is furnished by the experience itself. Kaṇāda maintains that it is on the basis of 'existence' (*sattā*) that we cognise substance, quality and action as 'existing' (*sat*).[46] In other words, our cognitions, such as 'substance exists', 'quality exists', etc., prove the

46. sad iti yato dravyaguṇakarmasu sā sattā. VS, I, ii, 7.

reality of 'existence' as a universal (*jāti*).[47] Kanāda declares also that 'existence' is something different from the existents, viz., substance, quality and action.[48] The reason for this is obvious. If the universal 'existence' is regarded as identical with the existents, then the plurality of substances, qualities and actions, as also the distinctions between these three categories, would be completely obliterated.[49] Another reason why 'existence' is asserted to be different from the existents is that no single existent or a category is as extensive as the universal 'existence'. These two reasons, according to the Naiyāyika, are sufficient to establish the distinct reality of the highest universal 'existence'.

The above discussion of the Nyāya-Vaiśeṣika conception of 'existence' reveals that for this school there are three types of reals. The first consists of the categories of substance, quality and action in which the universal 'existence' inheres. The second type consists of the categories of generality, particularity and inherence in which the universal 'existence' does not inhere, yet which have a kind of positive 'self-existence'. The third type of real is non-existence (*abhāva*) which has neither 'existence' nor a positive 'self-being', and yet is a real entity. These different types of reals are explained by the Naiyāyika by making distinctions between 'existence' (*sattā*), 'being' (*bhāvatva*) and 'reality' (*astitva*). For a fuller comprehension of the Nyāya-Vaiśeṣika theory of universals we propose to discuss these distinctions in some detail.[50]

6. *Existence versus Being and Reality*

According to the Nyāya-Vaiśeṣika, all the seven categories of objects possess the characteristics of 'reality' (*astitva*), knowability (*jñeyatva*) and namability (*abhidheyatva*).[51] The 'reality' of a thing is nothing but its peculiar individuality which prevents it from being identified with anything else.[52] It also means that the real is independent of the

---

47. sattā jātiśca dravyaṁ sat, guṇaḥ sannityādyanugatapratītyaiva siddhyati. Dink., p. 60.
48. dravyaguṇakarmabhyo'rthāntaraṁ sattā. VS, I, ii, 8.
49. The Naiyāyika is anxious to avoid the Advaitic position of the identity of all existence, as it is fundamentally opposed to his pluralistic stand-point.
50. The terms 'existence', 'being' and 'reality' are being used here in specially defined senses. They correspond to '*sattā*', '*bhāvatva*' and '*astitva*' respectively as defined by the Nyāya-Vaiśeṣika.
51. PPB, p. 16.
52. yasya vastuno yat svarūpaṁ tadeva tasya astitvam. NK, p. 16.

knowing mind. The other two characteristics of knowability and namability emphasise that there is no reality beyond experience and language. The Nyāya-Vaiśeṣika is opposed to all forms of subjectivism as it is to agnosticism and mysticism.[53]

The characteristic of 'reality', according to the Nyāya-Vaiśeṣika, is not a common attribute but the very individuality of a thing. It is numerically and functionally different from the universal 'existence'. The 'reality' of a real is identical with it. If it were different, it would have to be admitted as a distinct category. Moreover, if 'reality' of a thing is regarded as something different from it, the thing in itself will be an unreal fiction. The universal 'existence', on the other hand, is a distinct entity subsisting in its subjects by inherence (*samavāya*). Further, 'reality' for the Naiyāyika, is logically prior to 'existence'; a thing must be real before it is an existent.[54] A thing can be real without having 'existence', but it cannot have 'existence' without being real. Even non-existence, according to the Nyāya, is real, since it has its distinctive self-individuality. This insistence on the distinct reality of the objects of experience is a distinctive feature of the Nyāya-Vaiśeṣika pluralism. Śrīdhara clearly states that the reality of a thing necessarily implies its 'otherness' which is invariably experienced as *peculiar* in each case.[55] In other words, the self-identity of a thing is nothing but its distinction from others. The two constitute a unity; they are distinguishable only in thought.

With regard to the categories of generality, particularity and inherence the Nyāya maintains that, though they are devoid of the universal 'existence', they are felt and judged as existing facts (*sadbuddhiviṣaya*). That is, so far as our experience is concerned, all the six positive categories present themselves to our consciousness identically. But the question is, how are the categories devoid of 'existence' felt and judged as 'existents'? Śrīdhara explains that the felt 'existential' character of the categories in question is not intrinsic to them.[56] Each of these categories has a self-being (*svarūpasattva*) which is absolutely different from the universal 'existence'. This 'self-being' is their very individuality which is quite different from the latter. But our understanding mistakes the character of 'self-being'

53. Cf. Sadananda Bhaduri : *Studies in the Nyāya-Vaiśeṣika Metaphysics*, pp. 9-10.
54. nāpi astitvam anarthakaṁ niḥsvarūpe sattāyāḥ samavāyābhāvāt. NK, p. 16.
55. yadeva vastunaḥ pratyātmikaṁ svarūpaṁ sa eva bhedaḥ........tacca pratyekaṁ vilakṣaṇameva saṁvedyate. Ibid., p. 29.
56. Ibid., p. 19.

possessed by the categories of generality, etc., 'existence' and wrongly imputes to them a character which they in fact do not possess.[57] That is to say, the felt 'existential' character of these categories is not real, but an imposition of thought. This however should not be taken to mean that they are unreal. Each of these categories being felt as having a 'self-being', they have an undisputable claim to reality.

The later Naiyāyikas try to synthesise all the six positive categories under one concept of 'being' (*bhāvatva*). 'Existence' is said to subsist directly by inherence in the first three categories, and indirectly in the other three positive categories. The indirect relation in the case of generality and particularity is said to be *co-inherence* in a common substratum (*ekārthasamavetatva*), and in the case of inherence, which is incapable of inhering, *co-residence* in the same substratum (*ekārthavṛttitva*).[58] Being (*bhāvatva*) is nothing but some kind of positive relation to 'existence' (*sattā*), whether direct or indirect. It is due to the possession of 'being' that all the six positive categories are felt and judged as 'existents'.

There are obviously certain basic differences between the two groups of positive categories as conceived by the Vaiśesika. The categories of the first group, viz., substance, quality and action, include eternal as well as non-eternal entities, while those of the second group, viz., generality, particularity and inherence, are all eternal entities. Again, the categories of the first group operate as the causes of both subjective as well as objective facts; they produce their own cognitions in the self and also effects in the objective world. But the categories of the second group have causal efficiency only in relation to certain subjective facts. The universal is the cause of general conceptions (*anuvṛttibuddhi*), particularity is the basis of the cognition of difference (*vyāvṛttibuddhi*) and inherence is the cause of the notion of constitutive locus (*ihabuddhi*). These functions of the categories of the second group not only serve to differentiate them from those of the first group, but constitute the only proof of their reality.[59]

Some neo-Naiyāyikas however refuse to acknowledge any difference between 'existence' (*sattā*) and 'being' (*bhāvatva*).[60] It is argued that no such universal as 'existence' is discovered in perception.

57. sāmānyādiṣu satsaditi anugamaḥ svarūpasattvasādharmyeṇa sattādhyāropāt. Ibid.
58. See *Kiraṇāvalī-bhāṣya* of Padmanābha, p. 44.
59. *Kiraṇāvalī*, p. 30.
60. See PTN, of Raghunātha, pp. 48-49; also Dink., p. 60.

What is perceived is an existent thing and no 'existence' subsisting in it. Existence is not a common attribute like 'cowness', 'potness', etc., which are perceived as inhering in their substrates. Besides, when the categories of the second group are also judged as existents, there is no sense in regarding 'existence' as a universal confined to the first group only. 'Existence', according to these Naiyāyikas, is the same as 'being'. To assert that 'the pot exists' is to assert that 'the pot has being'. This identification of 'existence' (*sattā*) and 'being' (*bhāvatva*) reduces the former to an *upādhi*. 'Being', or 'existence', is conceived here as a character synthesising all the six positive categories of the Vaiśeṣika. This conception, it is claimed, has the merit of avoiding all the difficulties arising out of the assumption of 'existence' as the highest universal confined to the first three categories. Besides, the assumption of 'existence' as a universal, it is held, is unnecessary, as it serves no particular purpose.

An attempt to save the 'universality' of 'existence' is made by a section of the modern Naiyāyikas. It is argued that out of the six positive categories of the Vaiśeṣika, only the first three include destructible entities. Now, the destructibility of a thing presupposes its existence. This means that the thing itself is the primary cause of its own destruction. This causality of the thing must be intrinsically determined, since, as shown in a previous section, there can be no undetermined causality. We cannot destroy anything and everything, but only that which has potency for destruction. The determinant of this potency for destruction can be nothing but the universal 'existence'.[61] That which exists can alone be destroyed. This does not mean that all that exists is destructible, but that all that is destructible is an existent fact.

The above argument has one serious defect. It proves the previous non-existence (*prāgabhāva*) of a thing also as having 'existence'. The previous non-existence of a thing, according to the Naiyāyika, is destroyed when the thing is produced. If 'existence' is the determinant of the causality of destruction, then the previous non-existence of a thing also must be regarded as having 'existence'. This would amount to the absurdity of attributing existence to something which is the negation of it.

61. dhvaṁsakāraṇatāvacchedakatayā sattājātisiddheḥ. Dink., p. 60.

In order to avoid this defect another proof is advanced.[62] The argument runs like this : The 'inherent causality' of all the effects in which 'existence' inheres is determined by 'substancehood'. Corresponding to this inherent causality there is 'producedness' in the effects which belong to one or the other of the three categories of substance, quality and action. This 'producedness' must have a determinant which is the common attribute of all the three categories. Such an attribute can be nothing but the universal, 'existence', since there is no other attribute which is common to these three categories only. Put in plain words, this argument asserts (i) that the effects belonging to the categories of substance, quality and action alone have substance as their inherent cause, (ii) that this fact must be determined by an attribute which inheres in these three categories alone, and (iii) that this attribute can be nothing but the universal 'existence'. This argument obviously avoids the defect of the previous one, since non-existence does not have any inherent cause. Now, even if this argument is admitted to prove that 'existence' is the attribute common to the categories of substance, quality and action determining the effects belonging to them in relation to the inherent causality of substance, the old problem of explaining the felt existence of the other categories remains. The Naiyāyika has to face the dilemma : if 'existence' is recognised as a universal (*jāti*) confined to the first three categories, then the felt existence of the other positive categories goes unexplained; and if it is accepted as an attribute synthesising all the six positive categories, then it cannot be regarded as a universal. The problem is fundamental : it originates from the Nyāya-Vaiśeṣika conception of the categories itself. It seems to be insoluble unless the Nyāya-Vaiśeṣika surrenders its conception of 'existence' as a universal.

7. *Criticism of the Nyāya view of 'existence' by other schools*

The Nyāya-Vaiśeṣika theory of 'existence' as a universal (*jāti*) is criticised by other schools of thought. We would mention here briefly the criticisms of only two of them, viz., the Prābhākara school of Mīmāṁsā and the Advaita Vedānta. The Prābhākara, who agrees with the Nyāya theory of universals almost wholly, disagrees with it on the question of admitting 'existence' as the highest universal.

62. vastutastu samavāyena sattāvacchinnaṁ prati tādātmyena dravyatvena kāraṇatayā janyatāvacchedakatayā sattājātisiddheḥ. Dink., p. 61.

Śālikanātha agrees that the universal must be admitted wherever there is cognition of 'the same'.[63] But no identity, he argues, is apprehended in our experience of things belonging to different classes. We do not apprehend any identity, for instance, between a mountain and an ant-hill, or between a smell and a taste. Hence there is no ground for admitting 'existence' as a universal. So far as our use of the word 'existence' is concerned, it does not necessarily imply a corresponding universal, just as the use of the word 'cook' does not imply the universal 'cookness'. Nevertheless, the usage of the word 'existence' is not without objective foundation. The objective character, '*upādhi*', determining the use of the word 'existence' is, according to Śālikanātha, 'cognisability by a valid means of knowledge' (*pramāṇasambandhayogyatā*).[64] This cognisability is nothing but the 'self-being' (*svarūpasattā*) of things. Even the Nyāya has to recognise 'self-being' of things, otherwise the relation of 'existence' to fictitious entities like 'hare's horn' could be logically conceivable. We call only those things as 'existent' which have 'self-being', or are objects of valid cognition.[65] Moreover, Śālikanātha points out, our assertions of things as past or future would be true only with reference to the 'self-being' of things and not with reference to the universal 'existence' which is by hypothesis eternal. Similarly, our doubts also pertain to the 'self-being' of things. Once it is ascertained, there is no fresh doubt about their 'existence'. Even in the Nyāya view, the term 'existence' as applied to the categories of universal, particularity and inherence means the characteristic of 'self-being' (*svarūpa-sattā*) and not the universal 'existence'. Hence, there is no reason why the same characteristic may not be regarded as the meaning of the word 'existence' in the case of the categories of substance, quality and action also.[66]

Some of the above objections to the Nyāya-Vaiśeṣika theory of 'existence' as the highest universal have been anticipated and answered by Śrīdhara. He maintains that, though there is considerable difference between a mountain and an ant-hill, yet they are not absolutely dissimilar. There is something common to them by virtue of which they are called 'existents', and this common element can be

63. pūrvarūpānukārinī yadi dhīrudīyate, tato'bhyupeyetaiva jātiḥ. PP, p. 97.
64. Ibid.
65. Ibid., p. 99. Cf. *Pūrva Mīmāṁsā* of Ganga Nath Jha, p. 72.
66. Ibid.

nothing but the universal 'existence'.[67] Śrīdhara rejects the view that the concept of 'existence' corresponds to the character of 'self-being' possessed by things. The said character being as particular as the thing to which it belongs, it cannot be the basis of the general concept of 'existence'. If the universal 'existence' is not admitted, Śrīdhara argues, the common designation of things as 'existents' would go unexplained.[68]

Śrīdhara is opposed also to the identification of the universal 'existence' with 'cognisability by a valid means of knowledge'. He argues that if 'existence' means 'cognisability', then a thing must be regarded as non-existent before it is cognised. And if a non-existent thing can be cognised subsequently, then there is no reason why 'hare's horn' should remain uncognised. Hence the existence of things must be admitted to be prior to their being cognised through a valid source of knowledge. Further, Śrīdhara asks, do the valid sources of knowledge exist or not? If they do not, they cannot prove anything. And if they do, then according to the above view, they must be cognisable by another valid means of knowledge. Such a process obviously leads to infinite regress. Hence, 'existence', Śrīdhara concludes, can be equated neither to the 'self-being' of things, nor to their 'cognisability by a valid source of knowledge'. It must be accepted as a universal in its own right.[69]

The Advaita Vedānta also rejects the Nyāya-Vaiśeṣika conception of 'existence' as a universal (*jāti*). According to the Advaitist, what is apprehended in our cognitions of things as 'existents' is the foundational existence *Brahman* itself. Just as in the erroneous cognition of shell as 'this is silver' the element of 'this' is felt as the substratum of the illusory silver, so also in the true cognition of pot as an 'existent' the ground of 'existence', *Brahman* itself, is invariably felt.[70] Madhusūdana Sarasvatī considers three alternative answers to the question as to what determines our cognition of things as existents (*sat*). It may be said to be determined either by the apprehension of the universal 'existence' (*sattājāti*), or by the 'self-being' (*svarūpasattā*) of things, or by the non-cancellation of things through past, present and future (*kālatrayābādhyatva*). He rejects all the three alternatives as untenable.

---

67. NK, p. 12.
68. Ibid.
69. Ibid.
70. kiñcedaṁ rūpyamityatra idamitivat san ghaṭaḥ ityatrāpi sadityadhiṣṭhānabhūtaṁ brahmaiva bhāsate. Ad. Siddhi, p. 353.

The first alternative is rejected by the Advaitist on the ground that the Nyāya itself admits the felt existence of the categories in which the universal 'existence' does not inhere. If the cognition of existence can arise in the absence of the universal 'existence', then how can the latter be regarded as the basis of the former? The Nyāya has explained that the universal 'existence' is related directly to the categories of substance, quality and action and indirectly to the other categories. The cognition of existence in the case of the latter is due to this indirect relation with the universal 'existence'. The Advaitist rejects this explanation as unsatisfactory. It is not intelligible, he says, how different relations give rise to an identical cognition. If this view is accepted, it would eliminate all distinctions of relations.[71]

The second alternative also is found by the Advaitist to be untenable. The 'self-being' of things being as particular as the things themselves, it cannot account for the general cognition of things as existents.[72] And if an identical cognition is said to arise even in the absence of a common character, then the realist theory of universals (*jāti*) will be uprooted. Besides, the Advaitist argues, if one immanent Being can explain our apprehensions of existence in every case, there is absolutely no sense in assuming a plurality of 'self-beings'. Similarly, the third alternative also is rejected by the Advaitist on the ground that the said 'non-cancellation through past, present and future' is not perceivable. Moreover, even in the case of illusory perception the object is felt as 'existent', though it is subsequently cancelled when the right cognition arises. Thus all the three alternative solutions are found by the Advaitist to be unsatisfactory. He therefore concludes that the only right solution to the problem of explaining the felt existence of things is to accept one universal substratum the Existence Itself, which is felt as 'existent' (*sat*) in every case.[73]

The Advaitic criticism of the Nyāya theory of universal 'existence' is quite logical. The Nyāya must either deny that the categories other than those of substance, quality and action are felt as 'existents', or deny that 'existence' is a universal (*jāti*). The Nyāya wants to maintain both and thus falls into a contradiction. The Advaitist approaches the

71. vijātīyasambandhena samānākārapratītyanupapatteḥ, anyathā sambandhabheda eva na siddhyet. Ibid.
72. This criticism would apply to the Prābhākara view also.
73. tasmādekaṁ sarvādhiṣṭhānameva saditi sarvatrānubhūyata iti yuktam. Ibid., p. 354.

problem of the felt existence of things from his own metaphysical stand-point. There is one universal Existence, according to him, appearing under various names and forms. There is no real plurality of 'beings'. 'Being' is one and uniform, and it is this 'Being' which is felt in our apprehensions of things as existents (*sat*). The Advaitist rejects the Nyāya conception of existence as a '*jāti*' different from the existents. It is, according to him, the very 'essence' of things, the real universal. Existence is universal not as a predicate, but as the subject of all predicates. The particular existents, according to the Advaitist, are the empirical determinations of the Universal Existence which constitutes their reality. As we shall see later, the Advaitist admits only one universal as real, viz., the Universal Existence, *Brahman*, and regards the plurality of universal (*jāti*) of the Nyāya as illusory determinations of it.[74]

8. *Concluding remarks*

We may now recapitulate the Nyāya theory of universals as expounded in the foregoing sections. The main contention of the Nyāya is that knowledge and causal relations between things cannot be explained if the reality of universals is not recognised. Our general cognitions of things as 'cow', 'red', 'jar', etc., necessarily imply the existence of general entities, or universals. These universals are the common attributes of things making their coordinative cognition possible. It is further contended by the Nyāya that coordinative cognition being different from the differentiative cognition, the universal must be regarded as different from the particular in which it inheres. If the difference of cognitions is not admitted to imply the difference of objects the whole universe will be a unity. The difference of universal

---

74. According to the Viśiṣṭādvaitin, however, the universal 'existence' must be recognised wherever it is apprehended. When in the case of universals too there is apprehension of existence, there is no reason to deny its inherence in them. As a matter of fact, existence, according to the Viśiṣṭādvaitin is nothing different from 'authenticity' (*tattvato nirūpaṇe prāmāṇikatvādvyatirekeṇa sattvamanyannāsti*). This 'authenticity' is self-authentic; it is not derived from the authenticity of anything else, as it would involve infinite regress. The Viśiṣṭādvaitin repudiates the Advaitic conception of existence as identical with *Brahman*. Existence, in his view, is a predicate and not a subject (*sattvaṁ hi dharma eva na punardharmī*). Hence, if *Brahman* is held to be identical with existence, it will be a predicate, and thus require the postulation of a substratum for it. Consequently, by virtue of being a predicate superimposed on something other, *Brahman* would also become illusory (*mithyā*). See TMK, V, 122; SS, pp. 315-16.

and particular is said to be proved also by the fact that the universal is unaffected by the generation, change and destruction of the particular. It is an eternal entity as contrasted with the particular which is perishable. This mutual difference between the universal and the particular, according to the Nyāya, is not a bar to their intimate relationship. The fact that the universal is never apprehended without the particular proves that the two are inseparably related. This inseparable relation is defined as 'inherence' (*samavāya*) which is an independent category of reality, and which serves to unite two different things into an intimate union.

Thus the universal, as conceived by the Nyāya-Vaiśeṣika, is an eternal entity identically inhering in numerically different particulars as their common attribute. It is due to such universals that coordinative cognitions of things as 'man', 'cow', 'blue', etc., become possible. We have also noted that the Nyāya recognises the existence and possibility of general conceptions which are not based on universals. To explain this it introduces the distinction of *jāti* and *upādhi*. The former is said to be the essential class-nature of a thing inseparable from it, such as the 'cowness' of the cows or the 'jarness' of the jars. It is the real universal (*sāmānya*) recognised as an independent category of reality. The latter is any other general characteristic which is adventitious, or which is not recognisable as a universal for one or the other reasons already discusssed. Our general conceptions, according to the Nyāya, may be based either on *jāti* or on *upādhi*.

By his theory of universals, the Nyāya-Vaiśeṣika seeks to explain the systematic and intelligible character of the world of experience from his own pluralistic and realistic point of view. The world of particulars is said to be united in the highest or the most comprehensive universal 'existence'. This unity is not intrinsic to things, since, in that case, all plurality will be obliterated. This is conceived as an external unity possessed by the individual things as their common attribute. The same holds true in the case of all universals. The class of 'existents' is divided into the categories of substance, quality and action. These categories are again divided into sub classes systematically related as higher and lower down to the lowest or the most determinate classes. All these classes are determined by the respective universals which are exclusive of one another. All the sub classes, too, under a higher class are mutually exclusive. The idea of a thing belonging to two different classes not related as higher and lower is repugnant to the Naiyāyika (except for a small section of them). It is for this reason that he rules out cross-division as illegitimate classification.

The Nyāya-Vaiśeṣika theory of universals as delineated above evidently gives rise to a host of questions. Some of the important questions are : Does the existence of general conceptions necessarily imply the existence of general entities, or universals, different from the particular things? Does the universal exist just as the particulars do? If the universal is an entity like the particular, how does it inhere simultaneously in different particulars? If the universal is absolutely different from the particular, how can it be its predicate? If *samavāya* (inherence) is itself an entity different from both the universal and the particular, how can it relate them at all? And if *upādhis* can equally well explain our general conceptions and function as the principles of synthesis, what is the necessity of assuming a separate category of universals? These and other related questions are actually raised by the opponents of the Nyāya-Vaiśeṣika realism, and the Naiyāyika also has gallantly tried to defend his position. We shall be concerned with these discussions in the forthcoming chapters.

It must, however, be admitted in favour of the Nyāya-Vaiśeṣika that he has drawn our attention to a very important point, namely, that if objects of experience were absolute particulars, i.e., if they were absolutely discrete and disparate, we could not come to have any idea of unity or similarity. We could not come to possess any concepts, and even if we had them in some manner, they could not be applied to anything. We could not have conceptual knowledge of the world at all. Our valid experience, in that case, would be confined to certain immediate intuitions which, by their very nature, would be inexpressible and incommunicable. Also, if things were absolutely dissimilar, we could not explain why we use one and the same word, say, 'man' for different individuals. These considerations would compel us to recognise the reality of universals in some sense. But the extreme realism of the Nyāya-Vaiśeṣika seems hardly defensible. At any rate, universals cannot be regarded as a separate class of entities. The Naiyāyika had the right intuition of the problem, but he did not give, in our opinion, a right answer to it. The weakness of the Nyāya doctrine would become more and more apparent as we proceed through our discussion.

CHAPTER III

THE REALISM OF THE MĪMĀṀSĀ

The closest ally of the Nyāya-Vaiśeṣika in realism is the Mīmāṁsaka who staunchly defends the reality of universals. Both the schools of Mīmāṁsā—The Bhāṭṭa and the Prābhākara—advocate the reality, eternality and the pervasiveness of universals (*jāti*). The Prābhākara theory of universals is almost the same as that of the Nyāya-Vaiśeṣika except for certain differences concerning the nature of inherence relating the universal and the particular. But the difference between the Bhāṭṭa and the Nyāya-Vāiśeṣika on the question of the relation of the universal to the particular is fundamental. The former rejects inherence (*samavāya*) altogether and substitutes in its place the relation of *identity-in-difference* (*bhedābheda*). We shall mostly confine our discussion to these differences and avoid unnecessary repetition as far as possible.

1. *Kumārila's Theory of universals*

According to Kumārila, the universal (*jāti*) is *ākṛti*, that is, it is that by which the individual is specified or characterised. It is the common nature (*sāmānya*) determining the identical cognitions of different individuals.[1] Every individual object has the dual characters of individuality and universality which are the bases respectively of its particular and general cognitions. The universal and the individual are mutually dependent; there can be neither a universal without the individual, nor an individual without the universal.[2] If individuals

1. jātimevākṛtiṁ prāhur vyaktirākriyate 'yayā',
sāmānyaṁ tacca piṇḍānām ekabuddhinibandhanam. ŚV, *ākṛti*, 3.
Ākṛti also means configuration. But Kumārila does not use the word in that sense for the following reasons. Firstly, there are classes of things like air, fire, sound, etc. which have no configuration. Secondly configuration, being different in different individuals, is not a common character. And thirdly, configuration being subject to destruction, cannot be a universal (*jāti*) which is eternal. ŚV, *Vanavāda*, 16-17. Cf. *Pūrva Mīmāṁsā*, pp. 72-73.
2. ŚV, *ākṛti*, 9-10.

were devoid of common character, no general conceptions could arise. Kumārila accepts the Nyāya distinction of *jāti* and *upādhi*. All concepts do not correspond to universals (*jāti*); some of them correspond to *upādhis* also. The concept of 'universal' itself, for example, does not correspond to any 'universalness' (*jātitva*) recognisable as a universal. It can be said to correspond only to an *upādhi*. But it will be wrong to conclude from this that all class-concepts are of the same type.[3] If the existence of universals is denied, there can be neither inference nor verbal knowledge because, individuals being innumerable, no universal relation can be established on their basis.[4]

The universal, according to Kumārila, cannot also be equated to similarity (*sārūpya*). If similarity means identity in some respect and difference in others, then it presupposes the universal. And if similarity involves no identity, then it cannot be the basis of identical concepts. If there were no universals but only similarities, then, on perceiving two cows, we could only say that they are *similar* and not that they are 'cows' in the sense that both belong to the *same* class of 'cows'. Our cognition of them is of the form 'this is the same as that' and not 'this is similar to that'.[5] This proves that the above cognition is based on identity and not on similarity. And even where our cognition is based on similarity, it is explainable, according to Kumārila, only on the basis of identity. When we assert that 'all cows have similar bodies', what is meant is that all cows have bodies belonging to one and the same class. There is no other way of explaining similarity not involving reference to identity. Hence, if identical class-essences are not admitted to be real, there can neither be similarity nor any identical concept.[6]

The class-concept, Kumārila points out, must be distinguished from the group-concept like that of 'forest'. The term 'forest' is only a collective name signifying nothing other than the collection of the

3. Ibid., 20-24.
4. aniṣyamāṇe sāmānye vṛttiḥ śabdānumānayoḥ,
naiva syānna hi sambandho bhedairānantyato bhavet. Ibid., 39; cf. ŚD, p. 387. For Kumārila's arguments for the existence of universals which are similar to those advanced by Uddyotakara in the previous chapter. See ŚV, *Vanavāda*, 44-48.
5. ŚV, *ākṛti*, 66-69; cf. ŚD, p. 409.
6. Ibid., 74-75.

individual trees.[7] But the term 'cow', for instance, does not signify the collection of cows. This contrast is clearly established by our use of the term 'cow' for each individual cow, while the term 'forest' is not used for each individual tree. There is also another difference. From the epistemological point of view, the cognition of the universal 'cow' is different from the cognition of the individual cows. But the cognition of 'forest' is not different from the cognition of 'trees'.[8]

Kumārila considers also the question as to how the cognition of the universal arises. Every individual thing, according to him, has some peculiar properties which assimilate it with one class and differentiate it from others. In the case of cow, for instance, it is the possession of dew-lap, etc., which distinguishes it from all other classes of animals. These characteristic marks are not to be regarded either as the manifesters of the universal 'cow' or as its attributes. They serve only to specify the class. If dew-lap, etc., are regarded as the manifesters or as the attributes of the universal 'cow', then there could be no cognition of the latter until the former are cognised. This would mean that the cognition of the universal 'cow' depends on the cognition of other universals (dew-lap, etc.). Such a position would evidently lead to infinite regress. This would make the cognition of any universal impossible.[9] Therefore, it must be admitted that just as the constituent parts of an individual thing bring about the idea of its extension by the mere fact of their existence, so also they bring about the cognition of the universal (*jāti*) and other properties belonging to it.[10]

Obviously, for Kumārila, the cognition of the universal has a kind of directness like the cognition of the individual or of its properties. It is independent of the specifying marks in the sense that it does not depend on their cognition. But it is also dependent on them in the sense that it does not appear in a place where the individual having those specific properties is absent. Kumārila maintains that the cognition of the specifying marks invariably follows the cognition of the universal, for the two are inseparable. In one sense, he says, the specifying properties may be regarded as attributes of the universal

7. ŚV, *Vanavāda*, 54-55.
8. Ibid., 71-73.
9. Ibid., 2-5.
10. tasmāt sadbhāvamātreṇa mahattvādivad eva dhīḥ,
kriyate' vayavaiḥ piṇḍe tathā jātiguṇādiṣu. Ibid., 7.

also, since there is no absolute difference between the properties and the individuals possessing them, and between the individual and the universal.[11]

A question is frequently raised as to whether the universal subsists in each individual instance wholly or partially. Such a question, according to Kumārila, is illegitimate, because it cannot be raised in respect of universals which are impartite. We cognise the universal as subsisting in numerous individuals; this fact leaves no room for any further questioning.[12] Moreover, there is no rule restricting subsistence to two kinds only, viz., total and partial. There is a third kind of subsistence, as exemplified in the case of the universal, where the questions of total and partial subsistence are quite irrelevant. This third kind of subsistence, Kumārila argues, must be admitted, as it is a perceptual fact. If it is urged that its validity is doubtful, for it is not perceived in any other instance except in the case of universals, then a similar doubt may be raised with regard to total and partial subsistence also. They too, it may be urged, stand in need of proof as they are not perceived anywhere except in their own instances. A perceptual fact, therefore, must be admitted to be self-valid. It does not stand in need of validation by another perceptual fact, as such a process would lead to infinite regress.[13]

2. *The relation between universal and particular*

So far Kumārila's view is found to be in full agreement with that of the Nyāya-Vaiśeṣika. But a major difference between them arises on the question of relation between universal and particular. The relation of universal to particular, according to Kumārila, is purely a natural or internal one and is not based on anything external to them.[14] This relation is said to be identity (*tādātmya*). 'Cowness', for example, subsists only in creatures having dew-lap, etc., simply because it is identical with them. This identity is due to the very nature of the universal and the particulars manifesting it.[15] It is according to Kumārila, a perceptual fact. Similarly, the difference between univer-

11. Ibid., 9-10.
12. Ibid., 33-35; cf. ŚD, p. 402.
13. Ibid., 36-38.
14. svābhāvikaśca sambandho jātivyaktyor na hetumān. ŚV, *ākṛti*, 31.
15. Ibid., 47.

sals, and that between particulars is also a natural one discovered by us in valid perceptual experience.[16]

This theory of Kumārila, gives rise to some important questions. How can the universal, one might ask, be identical with different individuals? Would not such an identity make either the unity of the universal or the mutual difference of individuals false? In other words, how can the universal be one and many at the same time? How can it be both the class-essence (*jāti*) and the individuals characterised by it? Kumārila maintains that the contradictions alleged by these questions are not true at all. What is based on valid perceptual experience cannot be set aside as contradictory. We do perceive individuals as identical with their class-essence, and *vice versa.* When we cognise individuals in their class-nature, they are apprehended as identical; and when we cognise the universal in its individual instances, they are apprehended as different. The dilemma of one and many can also be answered in a similar way. The universal is a unity in itself, but it is also diverse in the form of its individual instances.[17] Kumārila explains further that when our cognition pertains to the individual, the consciousness of the class-character is latent, and when our cognition refers to the class-character of the individual, the consciousness of its individuality is latent. As a matter of fact, both the class-character and the individuality invariably form the contents of our cognitions of things. The abstraction of universal from the individual may be regarded as wrong, but no one can deny the existence of universal element in our cognition of individuals.[18]

3. *Criticism of the Nyāya view*

Pārthasārathi Miśra, an eminent follower of Kumārila, criticises the Nyāya theory of relation between universal and particular.[19] The

16. Ibid., 48-50. Cf. *Pūrva Mīmāṁsā* by Ganganath Jha, p. 73.
17. Ibid., 55-57.
According to Kaumārila, the unity of universal cannot be questioned on the ground of its relation with different individuals, because one and the same universal is perceived to be related with different individuals in the same way. Just as an individual is recognised as 'the same' at different times and places, so is the universal recognised to be 'the same', though subsisting in different substrates.
yathā ca vyaktir ekaiva dṛśyamānā punaḥ punah,
kālabhede 'pyabhinnaiva jātir bhinnāśrayā satī. ŚV, *Vanavāda,* 32; also see 30-31.
18. ŚV, *ākṛti,* 59-62.
19. This criticism would apply also to the Prābhākara view.

universal, according to the Nyāya, though absolutely different from the particular, is not found separately because it is inseparably related with the latter by inherence (*samavāya*). Inherence is defined by the Nyāya, as a relation generating the idea of constitutive locus with regard to inseparable things (*ayutasiddhānām ihapratyayahetuh*). Pārthasārathi denies that we have any idea of constitutive locus at all. Our cognition of 'cow', for example, is of the form 'this is cow', and not of the form 'this has cowness'.[20] Again, he asks, what is inseparable existence (*ayutasiddhi*)? It might be answered that it is the absence of separate existence. But how are we to understand separate existence? Pārthasārathi maintains that it can be understood in two ways: either as having separate motions (*pṛthaggatimattva*) or as having separate substrates (*pṛthagāśrayāśrayitva*), the absence of which would constitute inseparable existence. If separate existence is understood in either of the above senses, then the relation between part and whole cannot be called *samavāya*, since parts move even when the whole does not move. Also the whole and parts have different substrates. The whole subsists in its parts, and the parts in their parts. Similarly, the substrates of the universal and of the individuals in which it subsists are also different. So they, too, cannot be said to be related by *samavāya*.[21] These difficulties, according to Pārthasārathi, can be avoided if *samavāya* is redefined as 'the relation by which an attribute (*ādheya*) generates the cognition of its own form in its substrates (*ādhāra*).[22] For example, the relation by which 'cowness' generates the cognition of its substrates as 'cows' is *samavāya*.

This conception of *samavāya*, according to Pārthasārathi, should be acceptable to those who advocate absolute difference between universal and particular. Besides avoiding the difficulties inherent in their conception of *samavāya*, it also safeguards the difference between universal and individual. They can very well maintain that our cognition of an individual as 'cow' does not eliminate individual

20. ŚD, p. 390.
21. Nārāyaṇa, the author of *Mānameyodaya*, points out the difficulties arising out of the conception of *samavāya* as a relation external to its relata. If *samavāya* is non-different from its relata, there is no relation, and if it is different, there is infinite regress. Thus the Nyāya conception of *samavāya* leads to the impossibility of relation between universal and particular. *Mānameyodaya*, p. 291.
22. yena sambandhenādheyam ādhāre svānurūpāṁ buddhiṁ janayati, svākāreṇa bodhayatītyarthaḥ sa sambandhaḥ samavāya iti. ŚD, p. 391.

differences. The judgment 'this is cow', which expresses this cognition, besides signifying an intimate relation between the individual and the universal, also expresses difference between the two. Thus, the redefinition of *samavāya* as 'the relation by which the individual is cognised in the form of the universal' would make the 'difference view', according to Pārthasārathi, more acceptable.[23]

Pārthasārathi's own view in this regard is the same as that of Kumārila. He maintains that the universal is both identical with and different from the individual. This is said to be proved by our cognition of an individual in the form of the universal. The judgment 'this is cow' expresses both identity and difference between 'this' and 'cow', the individual and the universal. The usual objection to this view based on the abstract opposition between identity and difference, according to Pārthasārathi, has absolutely no force, since the two are found together.[24] If the cognition of identity were sublated by the cognition of difference, just as the cognition 'this is silver' is sublated by the cognition 'this is not silver', then the two would be contradictory. But the cognitions of identity and difference in respect of the universal and the individual are perfectly compatible with one another. In the cognition 'this is cow', for instance, both unity and difference are together apprehended. A self-identical thing is cognised as having dual nature—the particular and the universal. The applicability of both the terms 'this' and 'cow' to one and the same object (*sāmānādhikaraṇya*) proves the non-difference of the particular and the universal. Also the two terms 'this' and 'cow' being non-synonymous (*aparyāya*), they signify difference between the two. This evidence of experience, according to Pārthasārathi is too strong to be set aside by the alleged contradiction.[25]

23. Ibid., pp. 392-93.
24. na virodhaḥ sahadarśanāt. Ibid., p. 393.
25. iyaṁ gauriti buddhidvayam aparyāyeṇa pratibhāsamānam ekaṁ vastu dvayātmakaṁ vyavasthāpayati—sāmānādhikaraṇyaṁ hy abhedam āpādayati, aparyāyatvañ ca bhedam, ataḥ pratītibalād avirodhaḥ. Ibid., pp. 393-94.
The author of *Mānameyodaya* argues that if the idividual and the universal are regarded as absolutely identical, then one of them would be unreal. And if they are regarded as absolutely different, then we cannot explain why 'cowness' subsists only in cows and not in horses. Again, if the individual and the universal were absolutely identical, the *subject* and the *predicate* terms of the judgment 'this is cow', would become synonymous. And if they were absolutely different, then our perceptual judgment could not be 'this is cow', but 'this and cowness'. Both these consequences being evidently undesirable, the individual and the universal must be regarded as both identical and different. *Mānameyodaya*, pp. 233-34.

Pārthasārathi admits that there would be contradiction if the individual and the universal are asserted to be both identical and different in one and the same character. But if the assertions of identity and difference are made in the context of different cognitions, there would be no contradiction. For example, when the universal is referred to in its own character, as in the perceptual judgment 'this cow is brown', what is asserted is the identity of the universal 'cowness' with the individual. And when the universal is referred to in the character of the individual as in the judgment 'this variegated cow cannot be that brown cow', what is asserted is the difference between the universal 'cowness' and the particulars.[26] In other words, when by the word 'cow' reference is made to the universal character, the individual and the universal are apprehended as identical; and when by that word reference is made to an individual, the two are apprehended as different. Such a view, according to Pārthasārathi, successfully avoids the alleged contradiction.

Pārthasārathi anticipates here an objection from the side of the 'difference' view. It might be argued that the apprehension of identity of two different things is immpossible. The cognition of things in their unique character (*vilakṣaṇarūpa*) is the cognition of difference; and the cognition of them shorn of their uniqueness (*avilakṣaṇasvarūpa*) is the cognition of their identity. How can both the cognitions arise with regard to the same things? The occurrence of one rules out the possibility of the other. If the universal and the individual are cognised in their uniqueness, then the cognition of identity between the two is impossible. And if they are cognised as identical, then it only means that either the universal or the individual remains uncognised. In any case, there can be no cognition of identity between the two; there may be absence of cognition of one or the other. Hence, it is inadmissible that the universal and the particular are apprehended as both identical and different.

Pārthasārathi meets the above objection by analysing the cognitions of identity and difference. He points out that the cognition of *difference* does not merely consist in the cognition of two different things, for the former fails to arise even when the latter occurs. When a thing is perceived for the first time both its class-essence (*jāti*) and its individuality are perceived, and yet their difference is not

26. ŚD, p. 395.

apprehended. Later when another individual of the same class is perceived and assimilated with the previously perceived individual and also differentiated from it, the difference between the universal and the individual becomes cognised. Similarly, when we perceive an indivi-dual at a distance and, due to some similarity, are reminded of a person whom we had known in the past, we are put in doubt whether we are perceiving the same person or someone else, while, in fact, we are perceiving a different person altogether. Hence, it is wrong to hold that the cognition of difference is the same as the cognition of two different things. Similarly, the cognition of identity, too, does not consist merely in the cognition of the same thing. Even on perceiving the same thing we may not be sure that we are perceiving the same thing. Therefore, just as cognition of 'difference' is not the same as the cognition of 'differents' so also the cognition of 'identity' is not the same as the cognition of the 'identical'. It follows that when things are cognised as 'different', it is the cognition of their difference; and when they are cognised as 'the same', it is the cognition of their identity. We have both the kinds of cognitions with regard to things. When we cognise different individual cows as 'cow', we are apprehending the identity of the individuals with the universal 'cow'. And when we differentiate between the individual cows as 'this cow is not that cow', we are apprehending the difference between the universal and the individual. Hence, Pārthasārathi maintains, there is nothing incongruous about his position.[27]

The advocates of the 'difference' view bring forward another objection against the 'identity' view. The universal, by hypothesis, is common and eternal, while the particular is just the opposite of these. How can the two be identical? One and the same thing cannot be both common and non-common, eternal and non-eternal. If it could be so, then anything might be anything. The universal may be non-eternal, and the individual may be eternal. Pārthasārathi replies that this is no objection to his theory at all. A thing has manifold characters; it is eternal in certain character and also non-eternal in certain other character The universal as identical with the individual is non-eternal, and the individual as identical with the universal is eternal. There will be contradiction if eternality and non-eternality were asserted in the same character. The universal as universal is eternal, and the particular as particular is non-eternal. So there is no

27. Ibid., pp. 397-98.

contradiction in asserting the eternality of the individual in the form of universal, and non-eternality of the universal in the form of individual.[28]

4. *The Prābhākara view of universals*

It is not necessary to discuss here the Prābhākara theory of Universals in detail, for it is substantially the same as that of the Naiyāyika. There is, however, one point of difference which, though not fundamental, may yet be regarded as significant. Like the Nyāya, the Prābhākara also regards the universal as different from the individual. It is said to be perceived due to the repetition of the same form in our experience.[29] The point of difference between the two pertains to the conception of *samavāya* which is admitted by both as the relation between the universal and the individual. Unlike the Nyāya-Vaiśeṣika, the Prābhākara regards the relation (*samavāya*) between the universal and the individual as non-eternal.[30] According to the former, *samavāya* must be regarded as eternal, since whatever is non-eternal, i.e., is produced, necessarily has three-fold causes, viz., inherent, non-inherent and efficient. *Samavāya* can have neither an inherent cause nor a non-inherent cause, since both of them presuppose its existence. Hence, *samavāya* cannot be said to be non-eternal. The latter, on the other hand, distinguishes between two kinds of *samavāya*, eternal and non-eternal. The *samavāya* between two eternal things, e.g., *ākāśa* and its magnitude (*mahattva*) is eternal. But that between two non-eternal things, e.g., whole and part, and between an eternal and a non-eternal thing, e.g., the universal and the individual, is non-eternal. In these latter cases *samavāya* is born of the causal factors of either of the relata. Thus according to the Prābhākara, *samavāya* differs with the relata; in this it is similar to conjunction.[31]

Why does the Prābhākara, as opposed to the Nyāya-Vaiśeṣika, regard the relation between the universal and the individual as non-eternal? The reason seems to be that, for the Prābhākara, no relation having a non-eternal relatum can legitimately be regarded as eternal. If the

28. nānākāraṁ hi tadvastu kenacid ākāreṇa nityatvādikaṁ kenacit ca anityatvādikaṁ bibhran na virotsyate. jātirapi vyaktirūpena anityā vyaktirapi jātyātmanā nityeti nātra kācid aniṣṭāpattiḥ. Loc. cit.

29. jātir āśrayato bhinnā pratyakṣajñānagocarā,
pūrvākārāvamarśena prabhākaragurormatā. PP, p. 64.

30. Ibid., p. 91.

31. See *Nyāyasiddhi* on PP, p. 92.

relation between the universal and the individual is eternal, then the former should be perceived even after the latter is destroyed. The fact that it is not so perceived, proves that the relation between the two is not eternal. According to the Prābhākara, the destruction of *samavāya* following the destruction of the individual is the cause of the non-perception of the universal, while according to the Nyāya, the destruction of the individual alone is the cause of the said non-perception.[32] The Prābhākara admits that *samavāya* is an intimate relation between inseparable things as distinguished from conjunction (*saṁyoga*). But he maintains that it is absurd to regard it as existent even after one of the relata is destroyed.

There is another point of difference between the Nyāya-Vaiśeṣika and the Prābhākara relating to the cognition of the universal. This point is closely connected with the different conceptions of *samavāya* held by them. For the Nyāya-Vaiśeṣika, *samavāya* is the cause of the notion of 'constitutive locus' (*ihapratyaya*).[33] He, therefore, uses such expressions as 'cowness is in the cow' (*iha gavi gotvam*) or 'the pot has potness' (*ghaṭe ghaṭatvam*) in order to express the cognition of the universal. But the Prābhākara does not admit the above expressions as legitimate, because, for him, both the universal and the particular are the contents of one and the same cognition. Śālikanātha points out that the relation of the universal to the individual, viz., *samavāya*, must be distinguished from the relation of 'containing' (*iha*). The latter is apprehended where two things are first cognised separately and then one is found to be 'contained' in the other. But such is not the case as regards the cognition of the universal. The universal is never cognised without the cognition of the individual. It is always cognised as inherent in the individual, which is impossible without the cognition of the latter. Thus the universal and the particular being cognised by one and the same sense-organ and being the contents of one and the same cognition (the universal being included in the cognition of the individual), it must be admitted, Śālikanātha argues, that there are no separate cognitions of the two. Consequently there can be no cognition of the universal as 'contained' in the individual.[34]

---

32. PP, p. 93; cf, *Pūrva-Mīmāṁsā*, pp. 71-72.
33. See VS, VII, ii, 26-28; also PPB, p. 14.
34. bhedavādaḥ punar asmākam api sammata eva na ca tatra ihapratyayāpattir doṣaḥ. pratītya hy ādhāram ādheyaṅ ca sambandhaṁ pratīyāt sarvañca rūpaṁ rūpigrahaṇam antareṇa na pratīyate. ataḥ samānendriyagrāhyatayā jātirapi vyaktipratyayānupraveśinīti na iha pratyayasaṁbhavaḥ. PP, pp.93-94.

The relation of substance and attribute (*dharmi* and *dharma*), according to the Prābhākara, must be distinguished from that of the support and the supported (*ādhāra* and *ādheya*). The individual is related to the universal as substance to its attribute. It is, therefore, wrong to regard it as the support of the universal.[35]

5. *Criticism of Kumārila's view*

Despite their differences, as discussed above, the Nyāya-Vaiśeṣika and the Prābhākara unite in rejecting Kumārila's view of identity-in-difference (*bhedābheda*) between the universal and the particular. Śrīdhara poses the question: are the cognitions of the universal and the individual identical or different? If the former, then they are not two but one, since the things of which cognitions are identical cannot be regarded as different. And if the latter, then Kumārila's theory stands self-refuted, since the difference of cognitions cannot be sustained without admitting the difference of objects.[36] According to the Naiyāyika, difference of cognitions is incompatible with the identity of objects. There can neither be any identity of differents, nor can there be any cognition of such an identity. How, then does the Naiyāyika explain the identity of the universal and the individual expressed by the perceptual judgment 'this is cow'? Śrīdhara holds that the said identity expressed by such judgments is not real. The universal and the individual are different, but due to the power of *samavāya* between them, they appear as indistinguishably united like iron and fire in a red-hot iron ball.[37] The argument that the universal and the individual are identical because one is never cognised without the other has, according to Śrīdhara, no force, since it does not prove that the two are not different. Besides, the cognition of one excluding the other is a matter of ordinary experience. From a distance we may perceive only the individual and not its determinate class; and again we may erroneously perceive 'silverness' in something which is not silver. These considerations, according to Śrīdhara, conclusively establish that the universal is different from the particulars in which it subsists.[38]

---

35. See *Nyāyasiddhi*, p. 94.
36. viṣayātiśayamantreṇa pratyayātiśayānupapatteḥ. NM, pt. I, p. 314; also see NK, p. 316 & NM, pt. I, p. 311.
37. NK, p. 316
38. Ibid., cf. NM, pt. I, p. 311.

The Prābhākara also, like the Naiyāyika, rejects the identity-in-difference view of Kumārila. Śālikanātha maintains that the universal is always cognised as something different from the particular. Besides, he argues, two contradictory characters of identity and difference cannot belong to one and the same thing. The universal cannot both be identical with and different from the individual. The two are cognised as different, therefore, they must be admitted as such.[39] Although the Prābhākara agrees with the Naiyāyika in his denial of the identity of the universal and the individual, yet he does not accept the latter's analysis of the perceptual judgment 'this is cow'. For the Naiyāyika, this judgment, rightly understood, means that 'this has cowness' or 'this supports cowness'. The apparent identity between the individual and the universal alleged to be expressed by this judgment can be removed by this explication. The Prābhākara, on the other hand, does not accept this analysis. For him the relation between the individual and the universal, as we have seen, is not the same as that between the support and the supported. Hence the judgment 'this is cow' cannot be analysed into the forms stated above. This judgment, according to him, really expresses an intimate relation (*samavāya*) between two different things, the individual and the universal, a relation which is not reducible either to identity or to the relation of the support and the supported.

6. *Concluding remarks*

The Mīmāṁsā theory of universals is evidently as realistic as that of the Nyāya-Vaiśeṣika. The universal is conceived in it also as an eternal entity existing independently of the cognising mind. The Nyāya and

---

of a thing, then how do they co-exist in the same substratum? And if their absolute difference is not a bar to their co-existence, then why do 'cowness' and 'horseness' not co-exist ? Udayana answers that co-existence presupposes numerical difference. What is asserted is that things related to common substratum are numerically different. This does in no way imply that all numerically different things co-exist. Some things co-exist and others do not. It might again be asked, why is the relation of co-existence true in the case of some things and not others? Such a question, according to the Naiyāyika is illegitimate. The ultimate natures of things discovered in uncontradicted experience are unquestionable. We perceive 'cowness' co-existing with the individuality of cows and not with 'horseness'. This is the ultimate nature of things. No amount of *a priori* reasoning can disprove what is an experienced fact. See ĀTV, pp. 170-81.

39. PP, p. 93.

the Prābhākara school of Mīmāṁsā are agreed on the point that the universal, though inseparably related to the particular by inherence, is yet absolutely different from it. The Bhāṭṭa school of Mīmāṁsā, on the other hand, maintains that the absolute difference between the universal and the particular is contrary to experience. The universal and the particular, it is argued, are both identical and different as expressed by the perceptual judgment 'this is that'. Kumārila has maintained also that the universal cannot be identified with similarity, since in our cognitions of things as 'cow', 'horse', 'pot', etc., we cognise different individuals as 'the same' and not as 'similar'. Besides, similarity being always similarity in certain respect, it presupposes identity which is a universal. It is also maintained that the question of total or partial subsistence of the universal in the particular is illegitimate, since the universal being, by hypothesis, impartite, such a question cannot be raised at all. The relation of the universal and the individual is held to be *sui generis* which cannot be equated to either total or partial subsistence. This relation (identity-in-difference) is said to be a perceptual fact which needs no validation. Let us examine briefly these contentions of the Mīmāṁsaka.

Kumārila and his followers criticise the Nyāya and the Prābhākara theory of *samavāya* posited as the relation between the universal and the particular. The main argument is that the conception of two absolutely different things inseparably related by a relation external to them is quite unintelligible. But if the Nyāya conception of *samavāya* is unsatisfactory, is the Mīmāṁsā conception of 'identity-in-difference' satisfactory? The universal, according to the Mīmāṁsaka, is an eternal and unchangeable entity as contrasted with the particular which is non-eternal and constantly changing. If the difference between the universal and the individual is real, then it is not intelligible how the two can also be identical. Either the two are not different, or they are not identical. Unless we change the meanings of 'identity' and 'difference' so as to remove their mutual incompatibility, we cannot assert both of them together.

Pārthasārathi has maintained that the universal and the particular must be regarded as both identical and different because they are so apprehended in uncontradicted experience. The perceptual judgment 'this is cow' expresses both identity and difference between 'this' and 'cow'. But this seems to be unacceptable. If the perceptual judgment 'this is cow' means that 'this' and 'cow' which are different entities are also identical, then it is manifestly self-contradictory.

Pārthasārathi has argued that what is expressed by the judgment 'this is cow' is the felt identity of 'this' and 'cow'. But since 'this' and 'cow' have different meanings, they are also apprehended as different. This clearly means that the knowledge of the difference of 'this' and 'cow' is obtained from a source other than the perceptual experience. This would defeat the Mīmāṁsā contention that the difference of the particular and the universal is a perceptual fact.

Thus, if the identity and difference of the particular and the universal are the contents of one and the same perceptual experience, then it is self-contradictory. And if they are the contents of two different perceptual experiences, both of them connot be true. The Naiyāyika is perfectly right in criticising the Bhāṭṭa conception of 'identity-in-difference', though his own view of absolute difference between the universal and the particular is not free from difficulties. He is, nevertheless, quite consistent in denying that the two are ever perceived to be identical. The Bhāṭṭa wants to retain the realism of the Nyāya and also avoid the difficulties inherent in the latter's conception of *samavāya* which is an external relation. He therefore denies absolute difference between the universal and the particular and asserts a natural relation (*tādātmya*) between them. He wants to avoid the assertion of both absolute identity and absolute difference, because the former would annihilate either the universal or the plurality of particulars, and the latter result in a non-relation between them. At the same time he wants to retain the eternal unchangeable universals as the meanings of eternal words. All this results in the theory of 'identity-in-difference' between the universal and the particular which, as we have found above, is not quite tenable.

Kumārila has maintained that the universal cannot be identified with similarity because identical conceptions, such as 'cow', 'pot', 'blue', etc., could be based on identity and not on similarity. Moreover, he maintains, similarity being always partial identity, it presupposes the universal. Both these contentions would be controverted by the opponents of extreme realism. The Jaina, as we shall see, maintains that the universal is nothing but similarity (*sadṛśapariṇāma*). Also, for him, similarity does not necessarily involve identity. Similarly, the Viśistādvaitin also maintains that our identical conceptions of things are based on close resemblance (*sausādṛśya*) amongst them. Even the Prābhākara who distinguishes the universal from similarity like Kumārila, does not accept the latter's contention that similarity is partial identity. Similarly, the

Western conceptualists who accept objective similarity as the basis of abstract concepts deny that there is any identity involved in it. Obviously there are two important questions involved here: (a) Does similarity necessarily involve identity? and (b) can similarity be the basis of identical conceptions? The consideration of these questions must be deferred for the present.

Another contention of Kumārila and his followers is that the question whether the universal subsists in the particular wholly or partially cannot legitimately be raised because the universal is, by hypothesis, an impartite entity. The relation of the universal to the particular is said to be uniquely apprehended in valid perceptual experience. This unique relation, according to the Mīmāṁsaka, is neither absolute identity nor absolute difference, but identity-in-difference. Now, how are we to understand this assertion? Does it mean that the universal is partially identical with and partially different from the particular? Such an interpretation is ruled out, since the universal is *ex hypothesi* impartite. Does it then mean that identity and difference of the universal and the particular are relative to our thought? This too is ruled out, since it would make the relation between the two conceptual, which would be contrary to the fundamental realism of the Mīmāṁsaka. Can we, then, understand the above assertion to mean that the universal is identical with the particular in certain respects and different from it in others? If so, then the respects in which they are identical and those in which they are different must be specified. All that we are told is that the individual is identical with the universal as universal and different from it as the individual. But this is precisely the question. How is the individual which is different from universal also universal? We are not enlightened on this question by the Mīmāṁsaka.

All these difficulties concerning the relation between the universal and the particular arise because the former is conceived by the Nyāya and the Mīmāṁsā as an entity existing in its own right, though depending for its manifestation on the latter. If the universal is conceived as an entity different from the particular, then the problem of its relation to the latter would always defy explanation. The difficulties inherent in the Nyāya-Mīmāṁsā realism is well exposed by the Buddhist nominalist who denies the existence of the universal altogether. We may proceed to consider his criticism presently.

CHAPTER IV

THE BUDDHIST CRITICISM OF REALISM AND THE REALIST REPLY

I. *THE BUDDHIST CRITICISM*

1. *Universal a thought-construction*

The severest attack on all forms of realism comes from the camp of the Buddhist nominalist who refuses to recognise the reality of universals altogether. He maintains that universals are subjective contructions capable of being associated with names. They are not real entities subsisting extramentally as the realist assumes. The universe, in his view, is a flux of momentary particulars; there is nothing identical or similar in it. Identity and similarity are nothing but fancies of our imagination. There is no recurrence in reality, for the momentary particulars (*svalakṣaṇas*) constituting it are non-repetitive.[1]

Dharmakīrti distinguishes between two kinds of objects: *svalakṣaṇa* and *sāmānyalakṣaṇa*. The former is the absolute particular, the point-instant, and the latter is the universal (*sāmānya*).[2] These two are said to belong to different orders of existence. The distinction between the two is based on several grounds. Firstly, the particular has causal efficiency, while the universal does not. Our pragmatic ends are fulfilled by the particulars and not by universals. Secondly, the particular is different, while the universal is identical. One and the same thing cannot be both identical and different, as the two, identity and difference, are incompatible. Thirdly, the particular is indeterminate, while the universal is determinate. And lastly, the cognition of the particular depends solely on the particular, while that of the universal depends on mental activity in the form of comparison, recollection of the conventional name, etc. Subjective activity is

1. See TS, 2-3; TSP, pp. 11-12.
2. PV, II, 1-2.

necessary for the cognition of the universal, while it is not only unnecessary, but also contrary to the cognition of the particular.[3]

According to Dharmakīrti, causal efficiency is the criterion of reality. The particular is an existent (*sat*) because its cognition cannot arise without it. But such is not the case with regard to the universal. The cognition of the universal does not depend on the existence of the universal, but on the activity of mind. The universal, therefore, is only empirically real (*saṁvṛtisat*), i.e., has only an imaginary existence (*kalpanāmātravyavahāryatvāt*).[4]

Dharmakīrti accepts the Mādhyamika view that causality is not ultimately true; it has only empirical validity. The causal relation is not perceived but imagined on the basis of the constant succession of phenomena.[5] Hence, the definition of the real as causally efficient is valid only from the empirical point of view; ultimately the notion of causality is not applicable to the real at all. But the universal, according to Dharmakīrti, has no causal efficiency even empirically, since its notion is explicable without assuming its existence. The sensation of colour, for instance, does not arise without an existent colour, but the idea of the universal does arise even without an existent universal. In other words, the universal, according to the Buddhist, is not an object of perception, but that of conception. Its notion arises purely due to subjective activity consisting in the revival of past impressions (*saṅketasaṁskāraprabodha*).[6]

Although Dharmakīrti repudiates the existence of the universal as an external thing, he recognises its reality as an idea (*jñānākāra*). But, as an idea, he points out, it is not a universal. All ideas as states of consciousness are particulars. An idea is said to be a universal when it is regarded as an attribute common to numerous particulars. It is in this form that the universal is denied reality. The Buddhist denies externality of the universal, and not its reality as a particular idea.[7] It is noteworthy that external reference of ideas is not

3. yatra viṣayavyatiriktanimittasadbhāve bhavati buddhistatsāmānyam yatra tu na bhavati tat svalakṣaṇam. PVV, II, 2.
4. See PV, II, 3, and PVV on it.
5. Ibid., II, 4.
6. Ibid., 5-6.
7. tathā jñānākāratayā sāmānyasyāpi svalakṣaṇatayā iṣṭatvādadoṣaḥ artharūpatvenādhyavasīyamānajñeyarūpatvena samānatā na tu budhyākāratvena. PVV, II, 9-10.

regarded as illusory in every case. The ideas of sensation are said to refer truly to particular point-instants external to mind, since they cannot arise without the existence of the latter. But the external reference of general ideas is said to be illusory, because, it is explainable, according to the Buddhist, purely on the basis of subjective activity without assuming the reality of the universal.

2. *Refutation of the realist theory of general cognition*

The realist has argued that general cognitions, e.g., 'this is cow', or 'this is red', imply the existence of the corresponding universals 'cowness' and 'redness' as subsisting in particular cows and red patches. These cognitions being distinct from the particular cognitions, their objects must also be distinct from the particulars. The particular as such cannot explain the idea of unity or identity. The Buddhist rejects the above contention of the realist. He maintains, on the contrary, that the idea of unity is perfectly explainable without assuming the existence of the universal outside the mind. The particular causally efficient things may themselves be regarded as the basis of the notion of unity. But how, it may be asked, can absolutely different particulars serve as the basis of an identical conception? If the individual cows, for instance, have nothing in common, how are they identically cognised as 'cow'? The Buddhist answers these questions on the basis of certain analogies. Dharmakīrti gives the example of colour-cognition to show how different things produce an identical effect.[8] The cognition of colour, even according to the realist, involves four factors, viz., the object (colour), light, the organ of vision, and the cognising mind. These factors have nothing in common and yet they contribute towards the production of an identical effect, viz., colour-cognition. Similarly, different particulars having nothing in common may be supposed to produce an identical cognition. Another example given by the Buddhist is that of medicines. Different medicines, or herbs, are seen to produce an identical cure. These medicines do not have any cognisable unity embracing them all, and yet they succeed in producing an identical effect. In the same way, different particulars devoid of any uniting principle, may produce a synthetic cognition.[9]

8. pratyāsattirvinā jātyā yatheṣṭā cakṣurādiṣu,
jñānakāryeṣu jātirvā yathānveti vibhāgataḥ. PV, II, 47, and PVV thereon; cf. Ap. Sid. p. 12.
9. TS, 723; TSP, p. 40; PV, III, 72-73.

Now, a couple of important questions arise here: Does not the identity of effect in the above example imply the identity of causal efficiencies of the different medicines? Again, does not the acceptance of these identities amount to the surrender of the Buddhist position? The Buddhist denies that the causal efficiencies of the different medicines are identical. Some are more effective, some are less; some act more speedily than others; some are effective independently, while others act only when mixed with some other materials. These diverse causal efficiencies cannot be regarded as determined by an identical nature. Similarly, the effects produced by these medicines are also not identical. The cures produced by different medicines vary in the degree of efficacy and duration.[10] Thus, the Buddhist denies identity on both the sides; there is real identity neither of causes, nor of effects. All identity is merely apparent. Even the identity of general notion produced by different particulars is apparent and not real.[11]

The realist objects that if synthetic cognitions can be produced by particulars having no unity at all, then any cognition may be produced by anything. The cognition of 'cow', for example, may be produced by horses, since all particulars as particulars are non-different. Would it not annihilate all genuine knowledge? The Buddhist answers this question by posing a counter question to the realist. How does the realist explain the subsistence of 'cowness' in the individual cows only and not in horses, when each individual cow is as different from the other as it is from a horse? The only explanation he can give is that it is the nature of particular cows and not of horses to manifest 'cowness', due to which 'cowness' subsists only in the former and not in the latter. The Buddhist argues that if the ultimate explanation rests on the nature of particulars then the same nature may be supposed to produce identical cognition also. Different cognitions arise due to different natures of the particulars. What is the need of assuming universals?[12]

It must be pointed out here that the particular, according to the Buddhist, is not the direct cause of general cognition as it is of sensation. The particular is only an indirect cause, the direct

10. Ibid., 724-26; TSP, pp. 40-41, PVV, III, 72-75.
11. For a detailed discussion on this point see the chapter on the Buddhist Nominalism.
12. See PVV, II, 47; cf. Ap. Sid., p. 13.

cause being the recollection of the conventional name. It is established by convention that terms such as 'cow', 'horse', etc., should be applicable to things serving such diverse purposes as yielding milk, carrying load, etc. Unless these conventional names are known and recollected, the corresponding general cognitions would not arise even after the perception of the particulars. And if they did, there would be no justification for verbal conventions at all. Hence, the invariable relation between the recollection of the conventional name and the corresponding general cognition proves that it is the former and not the universal which is the cause of the latter.[13]

Does the Buddhist mean that there is no apprehension of 'the same' without the recollection of the conventional name? It would be obviously absurd to hold such a position. What the Buddhist seems to mean is that an explicit judgment of the form 'this is cow', 'this is man', etc., cannot arise without the recollection of the conventional name. But so far as the apprehension of 'the same' is concerned, it can arise even without its recollection. In such cases, as Dharmakīrti clearly states, the synthetic cognition is determined by the momentary particulars themselves.[14]

The Buddhist repudiates the existence of the universal on another ground. He argues that if we introspectively analyse our general cognitions, we find nothing corresponding to the realist's universals. The content of a general cognition is found to have colour, shape, etc., none of which belong to the universal of the realist's conception. And if there can be something in the cognition which is not in the object producing it, then the consequences would be fatal to the realistic position. Anything, in that case, might be the cause of any cognition. Hence, the realist's conception of the universal as the cause of general notions does not stand to reason.[15]

The Buddhist further argues that the realist's argument for the existence of universals as the basis of general concepts loses all its force when he himself admits the existence of concepts which

---

13. hetāvādye' pi vaiphalyaṁ samayābhogabhāvitā,
teṣāmiṣṭaiva saṁsargī so'nvayavyatirekavān. TS, 732, also see 27-29, 773 f; TSP, pp. 240 f., and 251. Cf. Ap. Sid., p. 12.
14. yāpyabhedānugā buddhiḥ kācidvastudvayekṣaṇe,
saṅketena vinā sārthapratyāsattinibandhanā. PV, II, 46.
15. See TS, 735-39; TSP, p. 243.

are not based on the apprehension of universals. The concepts of 'cook', 'teacher', 'universal', 'negation', etc., are not recognised by the realist as corresponding to universals (*jāti*). If these concepts can arise without universals, then what justification is there for assuming universals in the case of other concepts, such as 'cow', 'man', 'substance', etc.? One and the same explanation may hold good in both the cases. Particulars themselves, by their own nature, might be admitted as the causes of general concepts.[16]

The realist, however, maintains that a definite cognition cannot be accidental. The general idea, which is different from a particular idea, must be due to a different cause. This cause may not be a universal in all cases. But even in those cases in which the universal is denied, the concept is not without an objective basis. The concept of 'cook', 'universal', etc., are not admitted to be based on universals because of certain logical reasons. Nevertheless, they correspond to certain general characteristics possessed by things.[17] The Buddhist, on the contrary, maintains that all concepts, without exception, are explainable without assuming universals or general characters. Besides, no general character common to numerically different particulars is discoverable or logically defensible.[18] Particular things together with the memory of the conventional name are sufficient to account for all general cognitions. The realist would agree that perception of the individual and the recollection of the conventional name are necessary conditions of all definite cognitions. But the Buddhist insists that they are also sufficient, as nothing else is required to explain the definite cognitions of things.[19]

Śāntarakṣita advances another argument to prove the above point. He argues that no causal relation can be said to hold between universals and general cognitions. A causal relation is said to exist where there is positive and negative relation (*anvayavyatireka*) between two facts. If the cause exists, the effect must arise and conversely, if the effect does not arise, the cause must be non-existent. Now, if the universal is said to be the cause of general cognition, then the latter must always arise, since the universal is by hypothesis eternal. But this being not the case, no

16. TS, 748-49.
17. See NV, p. 317.
18. See PV, III, 156-58; cf. SDD, p. 94.
19. See TS, 764-65; TSP, pp. 257-58.

invariable positive relation can be said to hold between the universal and general cognition. Similarly, there can be no negative relation either, since from the non-occurrence of a general cognition we cannot infer the non-existence of the corresponding universal, for it is by assumption eternal. Hence, in the absence of a valid causal relation between the universal and general cognition, the assumption of the former as the cause of the latter is absolutely unwarranted.[20]

3. *Difficulties in the realist theory of universals*

Dharmakīrti draws our attention to some serious problems arising out of the realist's conception of universals as real entities identically subsisting in numerically different particulars. He holds that if the universal is regarded as a real entity, then its relation to the plurality of particulars becomes unintelligible. He first raises the question whether the universal is confined to its own particulars, or is ubiquitous? In the former case, it is unintelligible how a new-born thing becomes related to its universal (*jāti*). The universal being eternal it cannot be born with the thing. It being inactive by hypothesis it cannot be said to migrate from its present locus to the new-born thing. And even if such migration be admitted for argument's sake, the particular from which the universal migrates would be bereft of its class-essence. This would also imply that the new born thing which becomes related to its universal remains without it at least in the first moment of its existence. Again, the universal being impartite by assumption, it cannot be said to remain partially in the original locus and partially migrate to the new-born thing. Thus all the above alternatives being impossible, it is unintelligible how the universal, which is confined to its own substrates, becomes related to a new-born thing. If to avoid this difficulty the other alternative is accepted, i.e., if the universal is regarded as a ubiquitous entity, then its non-perception in empty space becomes unexplainable.[21]

20. Ibid., also see TS, 777, TSP, p. 252; cf. SDD, pp. 96-97.
21. na yāti, na ca tatrāsīdasti paścānna cāṁśavat,
jahāti pūrvaṁ nādhāramaho vyasanasantatiḥ.
anyatra vartamānasya tato' nyasthānajanmani,
svasthānādaclato' nyatra vrttirayuktimat.
yatrāsau vartate bhāvastena sambadhyate' pi na,

Apart from the above, Dharmakīrti points out other difficulties in the realist's conceptions of the universal and its relation to the particular. The universal is conceived by the realist as an entity identically subsisting in all its particular substrates. Now, if different individuals have an identical essence, it would mean that they are both different and non-different, which is logically untenable. The problem is that the concept of universal has no meaning unless particulars are recognised as mutually different. But if particulars are mutually different, how can they have an identical essence? A self-identical thing cannot have contradictory natures, since they imply difference of things. The realist asserts that numerically different individuals have an identical universal pervading all of them. Dharmakīrti asks: is the universal identical with or different from the individual? In the former case, either the universal will cease to be a common attribute or the individuals will cease to be different. In either case the concept of universal would become meaningless. If, to avoid this consequence, the universal is regarded as different from the particular, then their relationship becomes inexplicable.[22] The Nyāya-Vaiśeṣika postulation of inherence (*samavāya*) does not help, since, being external to the terms it is supposed to relate, it fails to perform its assigned function.[23] In the Buddhist view, all relations are reducible to two: identity and causality. If the relation between the universal and the particular is not that of identity, can it be that of causality? The Buddhist denies that an eternal entity can ever be a cause. It can neither be a cause nor an effect. Hence it is a non-entity.[24]

The difficulties of the realist position, the Buddhist maintains, can be avoided by regarding the universal as a thought-construction (*apoha*). The question of the relation of this thought-construct to the particulars would not arise at all, as it is a non-entity. The problems discussed above arise only when the universal is conceived as a real identity subsisting in different particulars. But if it is

---

taddeśinañca vyāpnoti kimapyetanmahādbhutam. PV, III, 151-153, also see ibid., 154-55. Cf. TS, 806-7, and TSP, pp. 260-61.

22. See PV, II, 41-42 and PVV thereon. Cf. ibid., II, 25, and III, 135. Cf. The criticism of Ideas in Plato's *Parmenides*.
23. See Ap. Sid., p. 14.
24. See PVV on PV, II, 42.

regarded as a conceptual identity constructed for empirical purposes, no difficulty arises at all. As a matter of fact, universality for the Buddhist is the sign of unreality. Whatever is conceived as universal or common must necessarily be regarded as unreal.[25] Similarly, eternality also is the sign of unreality. In the Buddhist view, whatever is real is perishable; hence, whatever is eternal, the universal in the present case, is necessarily unreal.[26]

To put the matter briefly, the universal, according to the Buddhist, has no real nature. The conception of universal or of things having 'general essence' is a transcendental illusion originating from the beginningless dispositions of the human mind.[27] All general cognitions, therefore, are ultimately illusory. Not only there is nothing universal in the external world, but also there is nothing universal in the mental world. All cognitions, or ideas, as states of mind are particular and momentary.[28] The universal is thus neither an external nor an internal fact. It has no place in the scheme of reality. However, since the universal is commonly believed or judged to be real and forms the basis of our pragmatic activity, it may be regarded as empirically real (*sāṁvṛta*). But from the ultimate point of view, it is a fiction pure and simple.[29]

4. *The Buddhist explanation of recognition*

The absolute denial of identity in reality by the Buddhist gives rise to an important question, viz., how is recognition to be explained in his view? Recognition is of two kinds: (i) the cognition of an individual as 'the same' and (ii) the cognition of an individual as of 'the same kind'. Both these kinds of recognition, according to the realist, presuppose identity. An individual is recognised as 'so and so' because of personal identity, and a thing is recognised as of 'the same kind' because of an identical class-essence. The Buddhist, on the other hand, denies both these kinds of identity. There is neither any identity running through the individuals

25. tasmāt samānataivāsmin sāmānye 'vastulakṣṇam. Ibid., II, 43.
26. vastumātrānubandhitvād vināśasya na nityatā. Ibid., II, 44.
27. tasyām rūpāvabhāso' yaṁ tattvenārthasya vā grahaḥ,
bhrāntiḥ sā anādikālīnadarśanābhyāsanirmitā. Ibid., II, 29.
28. na hi buddhyākāraḥ sāmānyamuktaṁ svalakṣaṇatvāt. PVV, II, 31,' 32; also see PV, III, 70.
29. tasyā abhiprāyavaśāt sāmānyaṁ satprakīrtitam,
yayā tayopakalpitaṁ tadasat paramārthatah. PV, III, 69, and PVV thereon.

cognised at different times, nor any identity common to different particulars constituting a class. How, then, does he explain recognition? Dharmakīrti maintains that recognition is perfectly explainable without assuming identity. Difference of particulars is no bar to recognition. If it were a bar, then there could be no recognition even on the assumption of identity. Recognition invariably refers to the individual. If individual differences were opposed to it, there could be no recognition at all. Hence it must be admitted that inspite of mutual differences of individuals, they may be recognised as 'the same'.[30]

But the point is not whether the difference of the individual is a bar to recognition, but whether there can be recognition without some kind of identity. Even if it be granted, the realist would urge, that individual differences are not opposed to recognition, the question still remains whether there can be the cognition of 'the same' without there being an identity running through the individuals? Dharmakīrti answers that in recognition there is no apprehension of identity but only of similarity. No continuous identity like the thread running through the beads is ever apprehended. What is apprehended is similarity which is based not on any positive identity but on the nature of individuals themselves.[31]

But does not similarity imply identity? It would be urged that if different individuals are cognised as similar, there must be something identical in them. Without some kind of identity, there could be no apprehension of similarity at all. The Buddhist maintains that similarity is not identity. The notion of similarity with regard to different particulars arises because of their similar causal efficiencies.[32] But this is only substituting one similarity for another similarity. The question is: can there be similarity at all without identity? Dharmakīrti's answer is that all identity is only conceptual. Because of identical conceptions repeated over and over again, their causes, the particular cognitions, are supposed to be identical. And because of this supposed identity of cognitions,

---

30. See ibid., III, 97-101.
31. pratibhāso dhiyā bhinnaḥ samānā iti tadgrahāt. Ibid, III, 106.
na hi bhūtakaṇṭhavadekaṁ sāmānyaṁ sarvānuyāyivyaktivyatiriktaṁ pratibhāti. kintu gaurgauriti sāmānyamavasīyate tacca bhedādhiṣṭhānameva. PVV on the above.
32. na khalu samatvam ekatvaṁ kintvekakāryatāsādṛśyam. PVV, III, 107.

their causes, the external particulars, are assumed to be identical.[33] There is no real identity anywhere. Neither the particulars nor their cognitions are identical. Identity exists only in conception, not in reality.

Thus, the similarity of causal efficiencies referred to above does not involve any real identity. It only means, according to the Buddhist, 'the negation of the opposite causal efficiency'.[34] For the purposes of common discourse we make use of one and the same verbal symbol for referring to the different things which are similar in the above sense, but this in no way implies positive similarity or identity.[35] The notion of identity arises by neglecting the mutual difference of particulars and by projecting in its place a common form which is nothing but 'the negation of the opposite' The cognition of an individual as 'man', for example, neglects the difference of the present individual from other human beings and projects a unity of the form of 'the negation of non-man'. There is no positive identity or similarity corresponding to the concept 'man'. It is a negative or conceptual unity for which the term 'man' stands. The belief in an objective identity, or the universal, arises due to the confusion between the imagined and the real.[36] All empirical knowledge (*saṁvṛti*), according to Dharmakīrti, is of this nature. It consists in omitting real difference and projecting in its place a conceptual identity of the form of 'the negation of the opposite'.[37]

The realist, according to the Buddhist, is mistaken in regarding what is a subjective construction as an ontological fact. The absurdity of such an assumption has already been exposed. Our general notions, according to Śāntarakṣita, appear in succession, are synthetic and are produced and destroyed. They cannot be said to be due to the eternal and ubiquitous universals of the realist conception. All synthetic concepts, without exception, are

33. ekapratyavamarśasya hetutvād dhīrabhedinī
ekadhihetubhāvena vyaktīnāmapyabhinnatā. PV, III, 108.
34. tasmāt tatkāryatāpīṣṭā 'tatkāryādeva bhinnatā. Ibid., 140.
35. Ibid., 141.
36. See PVV, II, 10.
37. ekārthapratibhāsinyā bhāvānāśritya bhedinaḥ,
rūpaṁ pareṣāṁ vyāvṛttam sā dhīḥ saṁvṛtirucyate.
tayā saṁvṛtanānātvāḥ saṁvrtyā bhedinaḥ svayam,
abhedina ivābhānti bhedā rūpena kenacit. PV, III, 67-68.

For a detailed discussion of the Buddhist theory of concepts, refer to the chapters X and XI.

constructs having no objective basis. Our mind through its natural capacity for creation projects its own ideas outwardly and views them as self-existing entities.[38]

The main points made by the Buddhist in his criticism of the realist doctrine of universals may be summed up as follows: (1) The ultimately real is the fleeting momentary particular (*svalakṣaṇa*) which is absolutely discrete and disparate. (2) The universal is not an entity belonging to the same order of existence as the particular. It is a category of thought and not a thing. The realist commits the mistake of confusing two different orders of existence: the empirical and the ultimate. (3) Identical cognitions do not imply real universals. They are explainable on the basis of particular existents and the naturally constructive mind. (4) The assumption of real universals pervading different particulars is fraught with insoluble difficulties. These difficulties can be avoided only if universals are regarded as thought-constructs. (5) No identity or similarity is given. The universal is not a perceived fact. (6) All notions of identity are negative; they arise by neglecting the mutual difference of particulars and by differentiating them from their opposites.

II. *THE REALIST REPLY*

1. *Universals are real entities*

The realist vehemently opposes the Buddhist view that universals are subjective fictions. Such a view, he maintains, is supported neither by experience nor by logic. Our experience, on the contrary, vouches for the reality of universals and logic supports it. It is indisputable that we cognise general characters in different individuals, which synthesise them into a class and differentiate them from others. If there are no universals, then each individual thing should be apprehended as a unique particular having no community of nature whatever with other things. This would do away with all genuine basis for classification and generalisation. Also there will be no reason why a term, e.g., cow, should be used to refer to certain things only and not others. The Buddhist view would thus result in the impossibility of all knowledge and complete anarchy in the use of words.[39]

38. See TS, 810-11; TSP, p. 262.
39. See NK, p. 317.

The Buddhist has maintained that class-notions originate from verbal conventions set up by the common consent of the people. This, the realist points out, is like putting the cart before the horse. Verbal conventions must be admitted to be ultimately based on experience. They arise from the experience of common features which synthesise things into classes and function as the principles of differentiation amongst them. The conventional designation of things cannot be explained without admitting the apprehension of general characters. The name given to a class of things may be arbitrary, but the class itself is not. Thus the convention which follows the apprehension of universals cannot be made the basis of general notions.[40]

Similarly, the Buddhist contention that class-notions are based on similar causal efficiencies of things is, according to the realist, also untenable. Causal efficiencies cannot be similar unless determined by a common nature.[41] Cows, for instance, give birth only to calves and not to foals. They produce cognitions different from those of horses, camels, etc. These causal potencies of individual cows cannot be explained except on the hypothesis of a common nature. The unity of the natural class of 'cows', Śrīdhara maintains, cannot be said to consist in such causal efficiencies as of producing milk, etc., because, in that case, all milk-giving creatures should form one natural kind. This would abolish the difference among species, such as cows, buffaloes, etc. Consequently, cows should be able to give birth to buffaloes and *vice versa*. Moreover, if the causal efficiency of giving milk is held to be the basis of the class-unity of cows, then we shall have to deprive that creature of the name 'cow' which has ceased to give milk.[42]

Jayanta argues that the Buddhist conception of universals as fictions of thought would render inference and verbal knowledge impossible. Inference depends on the relation between universals, and so does verbal knowledge depend on the relation of words to universals. Particulars by themselves cannot be the basis of inference, since no universal relation can be apprehended among

40. Ibid.
41. Ibid. Jayanta points out that, in the Buddhist view, the causal efficiencies of different particulars being different, they cannot be regarded as the basis of identical cognition. See NM, pt. I, p. 314.
42. NK, p. 318.

innumerable particulars belonging to different times and places. Similarly, words cannot be related to innumerable particulars differing in place and time in the absence of universals. Consequently, the meaning of words can never be established. The communication of thought and knowledge by means of words would become impossible. Thus, the denial of universals would result in the annihilation of all knowledge and practical activity.[43]

2. *General cognitions imply universals*

It is a fundamental contention of the realist that definite cognitions cannot be accidental.[44] We have a definite cognition of the general character apart from that of the individual objects. These cognitions are different in character and content. This difference cannot be explained except on the ground of difference in their objects.[45] This can be illustrated in the case of the cognition of colour. The cognition of 'blue' for example, with regard to a number of things, viz., a piece of cloth, a piece of skin and a blanket, is based on something distinct from the objects themselves. In the same way, the cognition of general character must be based on something other than the particular things. Uddyotakara rejects the suggestion that the basis for general cognitions may be found in the similarity of shape, or form, of particular things. The physical shape of a particular is not a common property; it is as particular as the thing to which it belongs. And if it is regarded as a common property, then it is nothing different from the universal. The quarrel, in that case, is only about names and not about facts.[46]

The realist thus rejects the Buddhist contention that particulars by their own nature produce general cognition. The genesis of general cognition cannot be explained without accepting the reality of general character. Pārthasārathi answers Dharmakīrti's question raised in this context as to why a specific universal subsists in a determinate group of individuals and not in others. According to him, this is determined by the causal factors producing the individuals. Particular cows, for example, are so determined by their causal factors that they belong to the class 'cow' (*gotva-jāti*) alone and not to any other class.[47] These causal factors again

43. NM, pt. I, p. 302. See for a detailed discussion on this point Chapter XI.
44. viśeṣapratyayānām anākasmikatvāt. NV, p. 316.
45. viṣayātiśayavyatirekeṇa pratyayātiśayānupapatteḥ. NM, pt. I, p. 314.
46. NV, p. 316.
47. ŚD, p. 407.

are united in a class (*jāti*) otherwise the unity of their effects cannot be explained. The unity of these causal factors is determined by their own causal factors which again must be united in a class. It may be objected that this line of argument leads to infinite regress. Pārthasārathi, however, does not consider it a defect. Such successive generation determined by the unity of causal factors is exemplified in the realm of nature. A bamboo-seed by virtue of its class-nature produces by successive generation, a bamboo tree which in turn, determined by its own class-nature, produces other bamboo-seeds which belong to the same class as the original seeds. No beginning or end can be traced in this process of successive generation. The fact it exemplifies is the unity of class determining the successive stages of generation. Hence, the reality of the universal is impossible to deny. If particulars are said to produce general cognitions by their own nature, then this nature must be a universal and not a particular.[48]

The Buddhist contention that general notions are formed by neglecting the mutual difference of particulars and by 'excluding their opposites' is rejected by Pārthasārathi as logically unsound. 'The exclusion of the opposite' presupposes a positive universal. Unless the universal 'cow' is admitted, there can be no 'exclusion of non-cow'. The question is, how are we to determine what is 'non-cow', or the 'opposite' of particular cows, if the universal 'cowness' is not recognised? It cannot be determined individually (*prātisvikena rūpeṇa*), as individuals are innumerable. And unless 'non-cow' is determined, the general notion of 'cow' which, according to the Buddhist, is based on 'the negation of non-cow' cannot arise at all. This would mean the impossibility of the general cognition of 'cow'. To avoid this absurd consequence, the universal 'cowness' must be admitted. Once it is admitted, 'the negation of non-cow, would also become possible. Moreover, the universal cannot be identified with 'the negation of the opposite' because it is felt as positive and not as negative.[49]

The Buddhist has argued that when some general notions, such as 'cook', 'negation', 'universal', 'forest', etc., are admitted by the realist as having no reference to existent universals, then why not

48. Ibid., pp. 408-9.
49. Ibid., pp. 410-11. For a detailed discussion on this topic see chapters X and XI.

admit other notions, such as 'cow', 'man', 'jar', etc., also to be of the same kind? Uddyotakara has anticipated and answered this question from the Nyāya point of view. Udayana also has met this objection by his theory of '*jātibādhakas*'.[50] The general answer given by the realist to the above question is that the universal (*jāti*) is to be admitted only where its cognition is distinct from the cognition of the individual.[51] In the case of 'cook', for example, there is no cognition of 'cookness' apart from the individual cook, just as we have cognition of 'cowness' apart from this or that cow. The notion of 'cook' merely refers to the act of cooking performed by certain individual human beings. If 'cookness' were a universal, then we should be able to cognise an individual as 'cook' as soon as we see him. Similarly, in the collective notion of 'forest' we have no cognition of 'forestness' over and above the cognition of individual trees. If 'forestness' were a universal then we should call each individual tree as 'forest'. In the case of negation, or non-being, also, 'non-beingness' is not recognised as a universal because the inherence of a universal by definition is not possible in a negative entity. The notion of 'negation', therefore, refers to an unanalysable characteristic (*akhaṇḍopādhi*). Also there is no cognition of negation as such, but only of this or that negation. Hence, there being no distinct cognition of 'non-beingness' apart from the cognitions of particular negations, it is not recognised as a universal.[52]

Similarly in the case of universals no 'universality' is apprehended as a distinct character. The notion of 'universal', according to Uddyotakara, refers to the fact of the inherence of universals in several particulars. The universal 'cowness' inheres in many individuals, and so do other universals. It is this similarity among universals in respect of inherence in several particulars, which generates the notion of 'universal'. This notion refers to the diverse universals themselves and not to any universal over and above them.[53] Besides, it has already been shown that the assumption

50. See chapter II.
51. viśeṣapratyayānām anākasmikatvādityasya hetoḥ piṇḍapratyayavyatiriktasya pratyayasya nimittāntarādutpāda ityayam arthaḥ na punaḥ sarvo 'nuvṛtti-pratyayaḥ sāmānyādeva bhavatīti. NV, p. 317.
52. See the section on '*jāti* and *upādhi*' in chapter II.
53. yathā gotvam anekārthasamavāyi tathā aśvatvādītyanekārthaistatsamavāyasya samānatvāt gotvādiṣvanuvṛttipratyaya iti. NV, p. 317.

of 'universality' as a universal synthesising diverse universals would lead to infinite regress.[54]

The Buddhist has argued that the notions of 'cow', 'man', etc., may also be regarded as similar to the notion of 'universal' referring to the particular things and not to universals. Kumārila answers that there is an important difference between the general notions of 'cow', etc., on the one hand, and that of the 'universal', on the other. In the former case, the general notion is determined by the common character subsisting in different particulars. When we perceive cows, we perceive also their identical character, distinct from their individual differences, uniformly subsisting in all of them. This is the basis of the general notion of 'cow' which cannot be denied without contradicting experience. Whereas in the latter case, the general notion of 'universal' is not determined by an identical character subsisting in universals but by the fact of their being extraordinary causes of identical conceptions.[55] Thus the realist is radically opposed to the equation of such general notions as 'cow', 'man', etc., with those of 'cook', 'negation', 'universal' and so on. The fact that some notions arise without corresponding universals does not imply that all notions arise in the same manner. The verdict of uncontradicted experience cannot be denied. Experience, according to the realist, proves that while some general notions arise without the corresponding universals, there are others which have an indubitable reference to existent universals.[56]

3. *Difficulties raised by the Buddhist answered*

The Buddhist has argued that if the universal is a ubiquitous entity different from the individual, why is it not perceived separately from the latter? The realist replies that it has no medium of manifestation outside the individual. The universal depends on the individual for its manifestation and cognition. It is for this reason that it is not perceived separately from the latter. But this fact cannot be made the ground for denying reality to the universal.[57] Ultimate natures of things attested by experience are unquestionable. It is indisputable, according to Udayana, that the

---

54. See the section '*jāti* and *upādhi*', chapter II.
55. tasmādekasya bhinneṣu yā vṛttistannibandhanaḥ, sāmānyaśabdaḥ sattādāvekadhīkaraṇena vā. ŚV, *ākṛti*, 24.
56. See NM, pt. I, p. 314.
57. See PP, p. 95; cf. ŚD, p. 402.

universal is felt as distinct from the individual. Its difference from the latter is proved by the fact that it is felt as the *same* in all individuals. It is, therefore, wrong to assert that the universal is identical with the individual. It is invariably felt as different and yet intimately related to the latter.[58]

The dependence of the universal on the individual for its cognition, according to Udayana, is not incompatible with its self-existence. Universals are self-existent entities; individuals only manifest their being. The existence or non-existence of the individual has no effect on the being of the universal. The universal has a self-being independent of the individual; it depends on the latter only for its relation to it.[59] It may be urged that the relation of the universal and the individual, viz., inherence, being by hypothesis eternal, the former should always appear as related. The Naiyāyika would answer that a relation in order to be felt requires two terms. The inherence of the universal in the individual, though eternal, is not felt in the absence of the other term, the individual.

The relation of inherence (*samavāya*), the Naiyāyika cautions, should not be regarded as analogous to the relation between two separable things. The universal is not 'in' the individual just as an apple is 'in' the basket. When the universal is said to inhere in the individual, what is meant is that the two are inseparably related. Inherence is the basis of the conception of one thing abiding in another.[60] It is not a relation existing between separables; it is a relation existing between distinct but inseparable entities. Also, the inherence of the universal in the individual does not bring about any change in the former. The universal is eternal and changeless entity; it remains unaffected by its relation to the particular.

It might be argued that a relation is conceivable between things which are separate, but to talk of relation between inseparable entities is a contradiction in terms. Things which are inseparable must be regarded as identical. The Naiyāyika maintains that a

58. ĀTV, pp. 175-76.
59. svarūpasattvāsattvayordvitīyānapekṣatvāt sambandhatvāsambandhatve tu dvitīyāpekṣe. Ibid., p. 179.
60. vṛttiḥ samavāya itīhapratyayahetutvāt. NV, 318.

relation presupposes distinctness of the terms related and not their separateness. The cognitions of the universal and the particular are distinct; this implies that their objects are also distinct. These objects, the universals and the particulars, are never found separately. On the contrary, they are invariably found to be inseparably united. These facts of experience must be taken into account while determining the nature of the relation between the universal and the particular. This relation must fulfil two conditions: (1) it must relate two distinct entities and (2) it must signify their inseparability. Such a relation can only be inherence (*samavāya*). It is, by definition, the relation between two distinct but inseparable entities.[61]

A question has been raised whether the universal subsists in the particulars wholly or partially. It has been argued that both these alternatives are impossible. If the universal subsists wholly in one particular it cannot subsist in other particulars. And if it is said to subsist partially in each particular, then no particular will be a complete instance of it. Moreover, possession of parts would not be compatible with the eternality of universals. Uddyotakara answers that the alternatives raised in this objection are not admissible at all, for the universal is not conceived as a composite entity possessing parts. Hence, the question whether it subsists in the particulars wholly or partially is illegitimate, since it presupposes compositeness which is denied by definition. Further, this question cannot be raised against the theory which maintains that one (universal) subsists in many (particulars), because both the alternative forms of the question involve contradiction.[62] To ask whether one (universal) subsists in each of the diverse particulars 'wholly' is self-contradictory, because it becomes a case of many subsisting in many and not of one subsisting in many. Similarly, to ask whether one universal subsists in many particulars 'partially' is also self-contradictory, because this too, like the previous one, is a case of many subsisting in many and not of one subsisting in many. Hence, both the alternatives of the question being self-contradictory, it cannot be accepted as a legitimate objection.[63]

61. pratītibhedād bhedo 'sti deśabhedastu neṣyate,
tenātra kalpyate vṛttiḥ samavāyaḥ sa ucyate. NM, pt. I, p. 312.

62. ekam anekatra vartata iti pratijānāno nānuyoktavyaḥ. ubhayena vyāghātāditi. NV, p. 318.

63. See TT, p. 477.

Uddyotakara obviously finds a logical escape and does not face the real question at all. It may not be legitimate to ask whether the universal subsists in the particular wholly or partially, because it is by definition impartite. But it is perfectly legitimate to ask how does the universal which is a self-identical non-composite entity subsist in infinite number of particulars at the same time? Jayanta's answer to this question is more straightforward. He maintains that this question cannot be raised against what is a fact of uncontradicted experience. The universal is seen to be fully manifested in each individual. This perceptual fact does not stand in need of being substantiated by any other evidence. An uncontradicted perceptual experience is ultimate. The universal is perceived to be fully manifested in each and every of its particular instances simultaneously. This evidence of experience cannot be set aside by any amount of reasoning.[64]

Similarly, the difficulty raised by the Buddhist concerning the relation of a new-born thing to its universal is also answered by the realist. The universal is neither born with the thing nor does it migrate to it from elsewhere. The new-born calf, for example, is born with the realtion to its class-essence (*jāti*) due to its own causes. The universal 'cowness' is not born with it, nor does it migrate to it from some other cow, for the former is, by definition, eternal and inactive. The birth of an individual and its relation to its class-essence are simultaneous. The individual is never without its class-essence even for a moment. Prior to its relation with the universal 'cowness' the calf does not exist at all. If the Buddhist persists in asking 'how is it so?', then, Jayanta argues, the same question may be raised in his position also. How does he explain the problem in his doctrine of *apoha*? How do a brown ox and a black cow eating green grass produce a white calf. The 'how' of such questions is unanswerable. We can do nothing but to accept the evidence of uncontradicted experience. Just as colourless things are never seen, so also objects devoid of class-nature are never experienced. There can be no 'why' and 'how' in these matters. The sole evidence is experience which attests the fact that everything is born with its class-nature (*jāti*) just as it is born with its individuality.[65]

64. See NM, pt. I, pp. 311-12; cf. PP, p. 94.
65. Ibid., p. 313; cf. NV, pp. 318-19. Also cf. svakāraṇānniṣpadyamānā vyaktirjātiviśesātmanā sambaddhaivotpadyata iti na doṣaḥ. ŚD, p. 400.

Pārthasārathi maintains that the Buddhist objection concerning the relation of a new-born thing to its universal is based on the confusion between the nature of conjunction on the one hand and that of identity (*tādātmya*) or inherence (*samavāya*) on the other. The nature of the latter relations must be distinguished from that of the former. Conjunction requires movement in space. A pot, for example, which is brought to, say, place A from place B, becomes successively conjoined with different points of space in the course of its movement and finally becomes conjoined with place A. But the relations of identity and inherence do not require any such spatial movement. The individual becomes related to the universal, whether by identity or by inherence, due to its own causal factors. There is no ground for maintaining that identity and inherence have the same nature as conjunction. Things have their peculiar natures which are unquestionable.[66]

Pārthasārathi answers also the Buddhist argument that the universal has no existence, since, being eternal, it cannot produce its own cognition. If eternal entities could produce their own cognition, then it should never cease. The fact that we have no ceaseless cognition proves that eternal entities have no causal efficiency and, for that reason, no existence. Pārthasārathi answers that the above conclusion would follow only if the Buddhist dictum that 'existence is causal efficiency' is accepted. But there is no reason why it should be accepted at all. No doubt causal efficiency can belong only to an existent. But it is not evident why every existent must be causally efficient all the time. Also it is not necessary that every existent must produce its cognition. There may be existent things which are not known at all. Moreover, certain existents may not have causal efficiency by themselves, but they may produce their effects in association with auxiliary causes. A seed, for example, does not produce a sprout by itself, but in collaboration with soil, water, etc., it succeeds in producing the latter.[67] In the same way, the universal, though causally efficient, does not produce its cognition by itself but through the individual. The individual is an essential condition for the cognition of the

---

66. tādātmyasamavāyayostvanantaradeśamanapekṣyaiva svakāraṇato niṣpattiḥ. na hi yaḥ saṁyogasya svabhāvaḥ sa eva tādātmyasya samavāyasya vāṅgīkartavyaḥ, pramāṇābhāvāt, vilakṣaṇasvabhāvatvād bhāvānām. ŚD, p. 401.
67. Ibid., pp. 578-79.

universal. This explains also why the cognition of the universal is not ceaseless. It arises when the individual is perceived, and it ceases to be when our attention is withdrawn or diverted from it.[68]

Pārthasārathi rejects the Buddhist view that cognitive relation is causal in nature.[69] According to him, to be perceived is not necessarily to be the cause of perception, but to be the content of perceptual cognition.[70] The Buddhist advocates the causal nature of cognitive relation in order to support his other tenet, viz., that things lend their forms (*ākāra*) to their cognitions. Pārthasārathi argues that the forms of cognitions may be explained even otherwise. They may be due to 'internal dispositions' (*samanantarapratyaya*). The different forms of cognitions do not necessarily imply external causes. We do cognise in the state of dream various forms due to internal dispositions without there being real objects. Similarly, in the waking state also, our cognitions may have forms without there being external objects to produce them. Thus the Buddhist need not assume cognitive relation to be causal in nature in order to account for the forms of cognitions. Consequently, there is no ground to suppose that to be perceived is to be the cause of perception.[71]

Pārthasārathi has emphasised two points in the foregoing arguments. Firstly, the universal is not devoid of causal efficiency as the Buddhist thinks, for it produces its cognition through the individual. And, secondly, even if it be admitted that the universal is causally non-efficient, it does not follow that it is non-existent, or that it is not an object of valid cognition. To be an *object* of cognition, according to Pārthasārathi, is not the same as to be the *cause* of cognition.[72] An object must be accepted as existent if it is the content of a valid cognition, no matter whether it is the cause of that cognition or not. The universal is definitely apprehended as the content of such cognitions as 'this is cow', 'this is pot', and so on. Hence it must be accepted as a real entity.[73]

68. Ibid., p. 406; cf. PP, p. 87.
69. na ca hetulakṣaṇaṁ grāhyatvam. Loc. cit.
70. jñānajanyaphalabhāgitvam. Loc. cit.
71. Ibid., p. 187.
72. Cf. yastu yataḥ pratīyate sa tasya viṣaya iti sārvalaukikam. PP, p. 88.
73. Śālikanātha defends the validity of the cognition of universal from his own point of view. He maintains that every cognition is intrinsically valid, i.e., it does not require another cognition to validate it. Even the erroneous cognition

The main points of the realist answer to the Buddhist criticism may be summarised as follows: (1) If real universals are not admitted, there can be no genuine class-distinctions. Also there will be a complete anarchy in the use of words. (2) Conventions with regard to the use of words are not made arbitrarily; they presuppose the apprehension of universals. (3) If existence of universals is not admitted, there can neither be any knowledge (perceptual or inferential) nor any verbal communication. (4) The Buddhist concept of universal as 'the exclusion of the other' becomes unintelligible unless the existence of positive universals is admitted. (5) The universal is apprehended as distinct from the individual, not as separate; it is self-existent, though depending on the individual for its manifestation. (6) The universal is apprehended as wholly revealed by each individual instance. This is the nature of things given in valid experience which is unquestionable.

4. *Concluding remarks*

The realist has tried to vindicate his position quite forcefully against the criticism of the Buddhist. He is right in so far as he asserts the objectivity of general features implied by our knowledge of things. But his conception of universals as eternal entities having a being of their own is hardly defensible. Firstly, no such entity distinct from the particular is ever apprehended; secondly, no such entity is necessarily implied by our identical cognitions; and thirdly, the assumption of the universal as a distinct entity entails, as the Buddhist rightly points out, all sorts of difficulties concerning its relation to the individual. The realist has not been able to answer these difficulties adequately, except by falling back upon the dogmatic argument that the nature of things is unquestionable.

The universal, in our view, can be said to be real only as a feature of the individual which reveals it. It has no being distinct from that of the individual, that is, it has being only as its

---

is felt as valid, as is proved by the activity it generates. A cognition depends on something external to it only for its generation and not also for its validity. So, even if universals, being eternal,be regarded as causally non-efficient, the validity of their cognition cannot be denied. (tenotpattimātra eva vijñānasya parāpekṣā, na prāmāṇye 'rthāvyabhicāralakṣaṇe. .....ato nityāyāmapi jātau bhavatyeva pratyakṣasya prāmāṇyam. PP, p. 89.

individual instances. We may distinguish the universal from the particular in thought and even talk about it in abstraction from the latter, but this does not imply that the universal is a thing in its own right. Our identical cognitions refer to the universal features of things; similarly, our differentiating cognitions refer to their distinctive features. The objects of these cognitions are no doubt distinguishable, but they can in no way be regarded as distinct. The realist uncritically assumes that the universal as the object of identical cognition, as distinguished from the particular which is the object of differentiative cognition, has a being of its own. Such an assumption seems to be warranted neither by experience nor by reason. The universal and the particular are never apprehended as two different things, like a cow and a horse, nor is the one apprehended without the other. The assumption of the universal as a distinct entity is also not required to explain our identical cognitions of individual things, since they are explainable on the basis of universal features revealed by the latter. Thus, both the extreme positions, that of the Nyāya and the Mīmāṁsā on the one hand and that of the Buddhist on the other, are untenable. Just like the universal entities of the realist, the absolute particulars of the Buddhist also are sheer abstractions. The untenability of both these positions would become more and more apparent as we proceed through our discussion.

It may be pointed out in passing that the Buddhist also recognises the distinction of universals from pure fictions when he calls them natural (or transcendental) illusions. Universals, for him, are subjective in a deeper sense, in the sense of being *a priori* or natural constructions of the human mind, and not in the superficial sense in which dreams, ordinary illusions and imaginary objects are subjective. In other words universals, for the Buddhist, are not arbitrary constructions of the individual minds as such, but the products of the natural tendency for conceptual construction inherent in them. It is for this reason that he calls universals as empirically real (*saṁvṛtisat*). This distinguishes universals from the imaginary objects on the one hand, and the ultimately real particulars (*svalakṣaṇas*) on the other. From the ultimate point of view, however, universals for the Buddhist, are indistinguishable from the imaginary objects. It is evident that the hypothesis of the innate constructive tendency of the human mind is vital to the Buddhist epistemology. Being wedded to the ontology of absolute particulars having no generality or similarity, he cannot explain general cognitions, common understanding of ideas and the usage of words without this hypothesis. We shall return to a detailed discussion of the Buddhist view and the realist criticism of it in a subsequent chapter.

We now proceed to the controversy between the realist and the Buddhist over the nature of perception and that of the object given in it. The Buddhist maintains that what is given in sense-perception is the absolute particular; no universals are ever perceived. The realist, on the contrary, maintains that universals as well as particulars are given in perception. As this issue is intimately connected with the question of universals, we propose to take it up presently.

CHAPTER V

ARE UNIVERSALS PERCEIVED?

I. *THE BUDDHIST POSITION*

The radical opposition between the realist and the Buddhist nominalist over the question of universals may be regarded as originating from their extremely opposed views concerning the nature of sense-perception. The realist holds that both the general as well as particular features of things are apprehended in sense-perception. The Buddhist, on the contrary, maintains that the particular alone is perceived and the universal is a thought-construct projected outside by the faculty of understanding. The issue between the two calls for a detailed consideration of the rival contentions, for the question whether universals are perceived or not is of vital importance to any theory of universals.

1. *The Realist's view of Perception*

The Naiyāyika maintains that the universal is a perceptual fact. The cognition of the universal is born of sense-object contact. Although what is in direct contact with the senses is a particular, yet the universal is invariably cognised as inherent in it. There is no knowledge worth the name which does not have universal as its content. A perceptual cognition, according to the Naiyāyika, takes note of three elements: the substantive (*viśeṣya*), the adjective (*prakāra*) and the relation (*sambandha*) between the two. A cognition which does not contain all these three elements is not psychologically felt. Thus, a felt cognition, for the Naiyāyika, is always determinate, i.e., its content is always a determinate particular. He admits the existence of indeterminate cognition also, not because it is a felt fact, but because it has to be assumed due to logical necessity. A determinate cognition takes note of the relation between the substantive and the adjective, the 'this' and the 'that'. This logically presupposes the apprehension of the relata in a non-related manner. This apprehension cannot be determinate or relational, as such an assumption would lead to infinite regress. Indeterminate knowledge is thus accepted only as a logical necessity. The Naiyāyika does not believe in the possibility of a felt knowledge which has for its content an undetermined object. The object, whatever it is, must be felt as determined by the character qualifying it. The character qualifying or determining the object of cognition may be a universal (*jāti*) or an *akhaṇḍopādhi.*[1]

The Naiyāyika further maintains that both the coordinating and differentiating characters of an object are apprehended in indeterminate perception, but this apprehension is not definite or distinct. A definite cognition of the general and particular characters arises only after the object perceived is compared and contrasted with other objects. That is, at the indeterminate stage, all the features of an object are apprehended in their own nature without any reference whatever to their coordinating or differentiating characters.[2] At the subsequent determinate stage, the data received in indeterminate apprehension find a systematic and definite shape. Indeed, for the Naiyāyika, the indeterminate and the determinate are two consecutive stages of one and the same process of perception. The universal is perceived in both the stages. It is apprehended in its own nature at the indeterminate stage, and subsequently perceived as the coordinating principle in the determinate cognition.

2. *The Buddhist view of Perception*

Of the two forms of perception admitted by the Naiyāyika, the Buddhist recognises only the indeterminate one as valid. Dharmakīrti defines perception as 'the direct sense-apprehension free from conception and error.'[3] Perception, for the Buddhist, is the bare sensation in which the absolutely unrelated particular (*svalakṣaṇa*) is given. It is absolutely free from all forms of mental activity involving interpretation or understanding of the given data. In the

1. See the section on '*jāti* and *upādhi*' in chapter II for greater detail on this point. Also see NSM, pp. 186-87; VS, I, 5; *Upaskāra* on VS, VIII, i, 5, 6 and 9. Also cf. NK, p. 189.
2. nirvikalpakadaśāyāṁ ca piṇḍāntarānusandhānābhāvāt sāmānyaviśeṣayor anuvṛtti-vyāvṛttidharmau na gṛhyete tayoragrahaṇānna vivicya grahaṇam, svarūpa-grahaṇaṁ tu bhavatyeva tasya anyānapekṣatvāt. NK, p. 189. Cf. ŚV, *pratyakṣa*, 118-20.
3. tatra kalpanāpodham abhrāntaṁ pratyakṣam. NB, I, p. 11.

determinate cognition, on the contrary, there is subjective elaboration of facts envisaged in sensation. The data of sensation are comprehended under a general form, classified and named. Thus the latter, according to the Buddhist, cannot be regarded as genuine perception, since it involves conception. The universal which is associated with the particular in the determinate cognition is not a sense-datum, an existent fact, but a thought-construct superimposed on the particular by the understanding.[4]

3. *The universal not a percept*

The universal, Dharmakīrti argues, cannot be regarded as a percept, since no sensible quality is the content of its idea. It is never perceived with or without the particular. It is perceived only as a word (*śabda*), whether as a sound or as a written mark; hence it is merely a name and nothing else.[5] Dharmakīrti severely criticises the Nyāya view of determinate perception in which the particular is said to be apprehended as qualified by the universal. He maintains that no clear conception of such a relation between the particular and the universal is possible. In the case of such cognitions as 'the man with the stick', both the relata and the relation are distinctly apprehended. But no such clear apprehension is available in the case of the qualified cognition of a particular. The particular, the universal and their relation as substantive and adjective are never apprehended distinctly. Hence, no determinate perception of the particular as qualified by the universal is admissible. Also the particular being, by definition, indeterminate, it cannot be an object of determinate cognition.[6]

One might ask, if the Buddhist does not accept the universal as a perceived fact, how does he explain the existence of general ideas (*anvayivijñāna*)? Dharmakīrti answers that even though general ideas may be admitted to exist, they cannot be said to correspond to universals. The content of a general idea is a particular word (*śabda*),

---

4. PV, III, 57.
5. PV, II, 48-49, and PVV thereon.

Paṇḍita Aśoka argues that whatever is said to have perceptual character (upalabdhilakṣaṇaprāpta) and yet is never perceived, must be regarded as non-existent. The universal is defined by the realist as perceivable, and yet it is never perceived; therefore, it has no being. SDD, pp. 97 ff.

6. Ibid., II, 145-46.

a particular colour (*varṇa*) and a particular figure (*saṁsthāna*). The universal, in the realist view, is not admittted to have any of these elements. Hence, it cannot be admitted as the cause of general idea.[7] Further even if the content of general idea is admitted to be general, Dharmakīrti argues, it cannot be accepted as a perceptual datum. The reason is that while the content of a general idea is hazy or non-vivid (*asphuṭa*), that of a percept is vivid (*sphuṭa*). If the content of general idea is said to be a percept, it would amount to saying that it is both vivid and non-vivid, which is self-contradictory. Moreover, if the content of one and the same idea is said to be both vivid and non-vivid, the distinction of concept and percept would be abolished. It would amount to the assertion of the absurdity that a concept may be sensuous and a percept may be non-sensuous. Hence, neither the universal nor the content of a general idea can be regarded as a perceived fact.[8]

Dharmakīrti rejects the realist's argument which seeks to prove that the apprehension of the universal is presupposed by every determinate cognition of things. The argument runs like this : The determinate cognition of a thing as qualified by its attributes presupposes the cognition of the attributes as, for instance, the cognition of 'the man with the stick' presupposes the cognition of the stick. The cognition of 'cow' is such a determinate cognition. Therefore, it presupposes the cognition of the attribute 'cowness' which is a universal. This argument, according to Dharmakīrti, fails to prove the apprehension of the universal as distinct from the particular, since no attribute is ever apprehended in this manner. Also the example given is not adequate to prove the realist's point. All judgments being relational (*sāṁvṛta*), they cannot be regarded as originating from the apprehension of the non-relational thing (*svalakṣaṇa*). They must, therefore, be due to the apprehension of things in relation. In the given example, the judgment, viz., 'the man with the stick', is not due to the apprehension of the 'stick-particular' (*svalakṣaṇa*), but due to the apprehension of 'the stick in relation with the man', otherwise the said judgment should arise with regard to any human being. Now the apprehension of 'the stick in relation with the man' may produce the judgment 'the stick with the man',

7. yadapyanvayi vijñānaṁ śabdavyaktyavabhāsi tat, varṇākṛtyakṣarākāraśūnyaṁ gotvaṁ hi varṇyate. PV, II, 147. Cf. PVV on the above, and SDD, p. 99.
8. Ibid., II, 148, and PVV thereon.

just as it produces the judgment 'the man with the stick'. This shows that the substance-attribute relation between the man and the stick is purely imagined. Hence, this example cannot be cited to prove the reality of substance-attribute relation between the particular and the universal.[9]

The Buddhist further points out that the major premise of the realist's argument is also not established. The realist himself admits the possibility of determinate cognitions which do not presuppose the cognition of universals, as no universals are admissible in those cases. For example, the cognition of all the categories as 'things' (*padārtha*), or that of a group of houses as 'city', arises without any preceding cognition of 'thinghood' or 'cityness', since no such universals are recognised by the realist. In the event of the major premise itself being unestablished, the conclusion based on it cannot be accepted as proved.[10]

Now, if the universal is an unproved assumption, how does the Buddhist explain general ideas of things? Dharmakīrti maintains that particular things, though mutually different, produce general ideas by their own nature. And it is because of general ideas that particular things are regarded as identical.[11] But this identity is nothing but pure imagination. The existence of general ideas does not prove the existence of universals. The object of general idea, according to the Buddhist, is 'the negation of the opposite'. This is the only basis of the synthesis of particulars. Wherever there is an identical idea with regard to different particulars, those particulars are regarded as having a unity. This however should not be taken to imply the actual existence of universals.[12]

4. *Determinate cognition not perceptual*

The crux of the whole matter is that, according to the Buddhist, sense-cognition must be radically distinguished from the cognition involving subjective activity. The cognition of the universal never

9. anumānañca jātyādau vastuno nāsti bhedini,
sarvatra vyapadeśo hi daṇḍāderapi sāṁvṛtāt. PV, II, 154; also see PVV on it.
10. PVV, II, 155; cf. Ap. Sid. pp. 15-16; and also JN, p. 234.
11. vastudharmatayaivārthāstādṛgvijñānakāraṇam,
bhede' pi yatra tadjñānāttān tathā pratipadyate. PV, II, 161.
12. See PVV, II, 161.

arises immediately after sense-object contact. It arises only after the present data of the senses are associated with those of the past and the conventional name is recollected.[13] In other words, the universal is cognised only when the object seen in the past is remembered and related to the present object. The cognition of the universal is thus a product of the relation of the remembered and the perceived. This relation, according to the Buddhist, is not a given fact, but a work of the understanding. To put it precisely, the universal, according to the Buddhist, is not perceived, but 'conceived' and conception is not the function of the senses but that of the understanding. This is proved also by the fact that when the attention of a person is diverted elsewhere, there is no conception inspite of the sense-cognition of the object.[14] Understanding, therefore, must be admitted as a faculty of cognition distinct from the senses. It is mind's spontaneous activity subsequent to the function of the senses. If the universal were an external fact like the particular, then its cognition would have been produced immediately after the sense-object contact. But the fact that it does not so happen, proves that it is not an external entity. The cognition of the universal is always indirect; it is mediated by subjective activity. If it is confused with perception which is always direct, then the distinction between direct and indirect cognitions would be completely annihilated.[15]

Dharmakīrti advances another argument against the realist's contention that universals are perceived facts. He argues that, since names are not given in sensation, whatever is associated with names, or expressed through words, is not an object of perception but that of imagination.[16] This means that all articulated or determinate knowledge is non-perceptual. This also means that, if no origin of knowledge other than the external world is admitted, all cognitions worth the name would have to be regarded as unutterable. The Buddhist, therefore, maintains that understanding must be recognised as a separate source of knowledge having as its object utterable essences (universals) as contrasted with the unutterable particulars

13. tatsaṅketamanaskārāt sadādipratyayā ime,
jāyamānāstu lakṣyante nākṣavyāpṛtyanantaram. TS, 729; also see TSP, p. 240; cf. PV, II, 45.

14. anyatra gatacittasya vastumātropalambhanam,
sarvopādhivivekena tata eva pravartate. TS, 731; TSP, p. 241.

15. See TSP, p. 240; cf. BL, pt. I, p. 150.

16. abhilāpasaṁsargayogyapratibhāsapratītiḥ kalpanā. NB, I, p. 13.

(*svalakṣaṇas*) constituting the external world. It is because of the failure to notice the difference between these two kinds of objects that the imagined universal is mistaken to be a perceived fact. This failure, according to the Buddhist, is due to the fact that the particular thing and the utterable universal are cognised in one sweep, so that the two are felt as an inseparable whole.[17]

The main points of the Buddhist argument against the perceptibility of the universal may be summarised thus. The universal is not a perceived fact because: (a) its cognition depends on the activity of thought and revival of past impressions; (b) it has no sensible quality; (c) it is never apprehended distinctly from the particular; (d) its idea is not vivid like a sense-datum; (e) its cognition is always indirect; and (f) it is associated with words which are not given in sensation. Besides, the Buddhist has also argued that the perception of the universal is not proved even indirectly. It is required to explain neither general ideas nor qualified cognitions. Hence, the Buddhist declares universals to be pure fictions of imagination.

II. *THE REALIST'S CRITICISM*

1. *Universal a perceived fact*

The realist vigorously attacks the Buddhist contention that the universal is not a perceived fact at all. Jayanta asserts that the universal, like the particular, is apprehended in uncontradicted and indubitable sense-experience.[18] Pārthasārathi argues that we have such cognitions as 'this also is a cow', 'this also is a tree', and so on. These cognitions, which are undoubtedly perceptual, are synthetic (*anuvṛttākāra*) and they arise inspite of the spatial, temporal and other differences amongst the particulars. These uncontradicted perceptual cognitions indubitably prove that things have both particular and universal characters. In the face of such a strong evidence it is futile to deny the perceptibility of universals.[19]

The realist disputes also the distinction made by the Buddhist between the objects of indeterminate and determinate cognitions.

---

17. ekasmin jñāne' bhidheyākārasyā' bhidhānākāreṇa saha grāhyatayā śīlanam. NBT, p. 13.
18. nāpi jātyāderasattvam indriyārthasannikarṣotpannabādhasandeharahitapratyaya-gamyatvāt, svalakṣaṇavat. NM, pt. I, p. 309.
19. See ŚD, pp. 386-87.

There is no valid ground for supposing that indeterminate cognition, or pure sensation, apprehends bare particulars, while determinate cognition apprehends pure universals (thought-constructs from the Buddhist point of view). For the realist, the objects of both the kinds of cognitions are the same. The difference being only that while pure sensation is indefinite, determinate cognition is definite. But, as regards the perceptual character and the object, there is absolutely no differene between the two.[20]

Jayanta maintains that the issue between the realist and the Buddhist concerning what is really given in pure sensation can be decided only by considering and analysing the consequences following upon it. Our experience attests that sensation is followed by determinate cognition which apprehends both general as well as particular features of the thing. If sensation apprehends only the all-exclusive particular, as the Buddhist holds, then how does the general feature enter into the subsequent determinate cognition at all? The Buddhist has explained that the cognition of the general character arises due to the recollection of the conventional name. But this, Jayanta points out, is contrary to experience, since the cognition of the universal is seen to arise even without the knowledge of the conventional name. When a South Indian, for instance, who has never seen or heard of a camel, comes to the north and observes a row of camels, he surely cognises their identity of class even though he is ignorant of the conventional name by which the animals are referred to.[21] As a matter of fact, verbal convention follows upon the apprehension of general character and not precedes it. Moreover, memory and recognition cannot be explained without accepting the perceptibility of the universal. On perceiving the present cow we are reminded of the cow seen in the past and there arises the cognition of 'the same'. If the universal is not perceived, why should we be reminded of the past cow on perceiving the present one? The only plausible answer, according to Jayanta, is that we perceive in the present cow the same general character of 'cowness' which we had perceived in the past one. This also explains the recognition of 'the same'.[22]

20. See NM, pt. I, pp. 309 f.
21. paśyatynugataṁ rūpam avijñāte' pi vācake,
dākṣiṇātya ivākasmāt paśyannuṣṭraparamparām. Loc. cit.
22. Op. cit., p. 310.

The Buddhist has argued that the universal is not apprehended directly like the particular. The general notion is not a simple idea arising directly out of sense-object cantact. The cognition of the universal depends on the operation of the intellect in the form of comparing and contrasting. This shows that the universal is a thought-construct and not a percept. Jayanta asks, if the universal is not apprehended immediatly, is the particular so apprehended? The answer cannot but be negative, because the apprehensions of both the universal and particular characters are relative to the apprehensions of more than one thing. Operation of the intellect is common to the apprehensions of both identity and difference. The Buddhist, therefore, cannot legitimately recognise one as genuine perception and relegate the other to the realm of thought-constructions.[23] If the particular is admitted to be given in sense-apprehension, there is no reason whatever to think otherwise in the case of the universal. The Buddhist might maintain that sensation apprehends the bare unrelated thing (*artha* or *vastu*) without any reference to generality or particularity, for the apprehensions of both involve the operation of thought. In this position, Jayanta argues, the cognitions of both identity and difference would go unexplained. Neither identity nor difference can be regarded as a given fact. Such a position is opposed to reason and experience. As a matter of fact, Jayanta maintains, the thing devoid of general and particular characters is never experienced.[24] At the stage of sensation their apprehensions are not clear and distinct, but at the stage of determinate cognition, when the intellectual operations of comparing and contrasting have taken place, the definite cognitions of both the general as well as the particular characters arise. To assert either that the nature of the thing is exclusively particular or that it is exclusively

---

23. samānavṛtyapekṣatvāt sāmānyasyānupagrahe,
viśeṣo'pi hi mā grāhi vyāvṛttim sa hi cekṣate. Ibid.

24. Loc. cit. Śālikanātha maintains that the universal is perceived along with the particular even when the latter is perceived for the first time. Only its universality (*anuvṛtti*) is not apprehended owing to the non-perception of the other individuals of the same class. The apprehension of a thing without the apprehension of its attribute, according to Śālikanātha, is not unintelligible (agrahaṇe'pi ca dharmasya dharmiṇo grahaṇaṁ nānupapannam). When the other individuals of the same class are perceived the recognition of 'the same' arises and the universality (*anuvṛtti*) of the universal (*anuvṛtta*) becomes cognised. PP, p. 90.

universal is, according to Jayanta, to display the ignorance of the real natures of things.[25]

The Buddhist might object that two contradictory characters of generality and particularity cannot belong to a self-identical thing. Jayanta maintains that they are not contradictory characters, since they are apprehended as co-existing in a valid perceptual experience. If they were opposed to one another, they would never have been perceived together in the same locus. The perception of their co-existence cannot be an illusion because it is never sublated by subsequent experience, like the erroneous cognition of silver in the shell. Hence, there is no incompatibility between the particular and the universal, as they go together without any conflict or opposition.[26]

The main point of dispute between the realist and the Buddhist is whether the determinate cognition in which the universal is distinctly apprehended is a case of perception or not. The Buddhist denies that determinate cognition is perceptual, because it involves the operation of thought and memory. The realist, on the other hand, maintains that these operations do not make the determinate cognition non-perceptual. While, for the Buddhist, the indeterminate sensation and the following determinate cognition are opposed to one another as perceptual and non-perceptual, for the realist they are two stages of the same process of perception of an object. They are opposed to one another only as indistinct and distinct. Hence, the question whether universals are perceptual facts is inseparably linked with the question whether determinate cognition of a thing following upon its indeterminate cognition is perceptual. It is on the answer to the latter question that the answer to the first depends. We have discussed the Buddhist position on this question in previous sections. Let us now consider the realist's position in some detail.

2. *Determinate cognition perceptual*

The Buddhist has maintained that the indeterminate sensation and the determinate cognition being opposed to one another, the latter is not a case of perception. Vācaspatimiśra points out that this conclusion would follow only if the Buddhist doctrine of

25. vastuno'ṅgīkṛtā prājñairata evobhayātmatā,
yau brūtastvekarūpatvaṁ tāvubhāvapi bāliśau. NM, pt. I, p. 311.

26. parasparavirodho 'pi nāstīha tadavedanāt,
ekabādhena nānyatra dhīḥ śuktirajatādivat. Ibid., p. 311.

momentariness is accepted. If every object is considered as a string of events and the momentary particular alone is recognised as real, then the Buddhist's conclusion would be inescapable. But the realist, who refuses to admit the doctrine of momentariness, is not obliged to accept his conclusion. The realist believes in the world of stable objects possessing a variety of attributes. These enduring objects are, for him, ulimately real and their contents are expressible by connotative names. These objects produce both the indeterminate and the determinate perceptions and, hence, there is no incompatibility between the two. It is wrong to hold, according to Vācaspati, that a sense-perception is always unutterable; it is, indeed, true with regard to the indeterminate perception, but not with regard to the determinate perception which is always expressible in words.[27]

The realist of course admits that names are not discovered in the external world. But this does not prevent names from referring to the external things. There is, according to Vācaspati, a conformity between the external reality and the structure of language.[28] Again, connotative names, though referring to external things, do not affect their perceptions in anyway. Determinate perceptions never represent external objects as identical with their names.[29] The name, if it is known, is almost invariably brought to memory, but it does not in the least help to generate the determinate perception. Otherwise, infants and dumb-deaf persons should not have definite perceptions arising from their sensations, since they cannot remember the conventional names. So the name is something arbitrary or accidental; it is not intrinsic to the determinate perception at all.[30] The name recollected, Vācaspati maintains, does not distort perception; it stands apart from the thing named and is incapable of hiding its sensible aspect.[31] Thus the recollection of the conventional name of an object, in the view of the realist, does not produce a break in the operation of the senses and of the external objects as the Buddhist assumes. They generate

27. TT, p. 137.
28. yathā ca bhede'pī teṣām tadavācakānāṁ sāmānādhikaraṇyam. Loc. cit.
29. Op. cit., p. 138.
30. śabdastu sampātāyāto na niveśayatyātmānamindriyaje vikalpe. Ibid.
31. saṁjñā hi smaryamāṇāpi pratyakṣatvam na bādhate,
saṁjñinaḥ sā taṭasthā hi na rūpācchādanakṣamā. Loc. cit. Also cf. NK, p. 192.

both the primitive indeterminate perception and the subsequent complex determinate cognition.

Vācaspati argues further that determinate cognition cannot be denied perceptual character merely because it depends on the aid of memory. The cause of anything is always complex. The cause of determinate perception is the complex of sense-object contact and memory. Sense-object contact is the principal cause, while memory is the accessory cause; the two together produce the determinate perception of an object.[32] If the doctrine of complex causality is not admitted, then the generation of indeterminate perception also cannot be explained. The object and the senses by themselves cannot produce the indeterminate perception. At least four factors are required for a visual sensation to arise : senses, the object, light and the aroused attention. The determinate perception requires one more factor, viz., memory. If the fully qualified percept does not arise in the first moment, it is because memory has not yet cooperated. It does not mean that determinate cognition is not born of sense-object contact at all. If the seed in the granary, for example, has not yet produced the sprout, it does not mean that it will never produce it. Nothing can prevent it from producing the sprout later when soil, sun, moisture and all the totality of causes and conditions have cooperated.[33]

3. *Refutation of the Buddhist arguments for momentariness*

The Buddhist, however, would not agree that the seed producing sprout and the seed not producing it are one and the same. The seed, according to him, is a string of events. The law of contradiction prevents us from regarding the same thing as both producing and not-producing. Therefore, the seed in the granary is completely different from the seed producing sprout. We regard the two seeds as identical, but this identity, according to the Buddhist, is a thought-construction and not a fact. Similarly, the object producing sensation

32. Op. cit., 138. Vācaspati points out that the Buddhist has himself admitted the dictum that causes of phenomena are always complex. He quotes the following passage, which is probably from Dignāga, not yet identified : 'na kiñcidekam ekasmāt sāmagrayāḥ sarvasambhavaḥ'. That is, 'Nothing is produced from a unique cause; every single thing arises from some totality of causes and conditions'. Loc. cit. Also see BL, Vol. II, n. 7, p. 278.
33. See TT, pp. 138-39; NM pt. I pp. 95–96; and NK, p. 191; ĀTV p. 183.

cannot be the cause of the determinate cognition, because the latter is not produced in the same moment as the former. If the object could produce the determinate cognition, it should have done so in the very first moment. It would be contradictory to assert that the object is both capable and incapable of producing a qualified percept. When incompatible, or mutually exclusive, attributes are assigned to a thing, it cannot represent a unity, otherwise the whole universe would be one.[34]

The Buddhist argues further that the objects of indeterminate and determinate cognitions must be regarded as different, because it would be a contradiction to assert that a single object resides in two different space-times (*deśakāla*). A difference in space-time means a difference in the object. For example, when a ruby is perceived, all non-rubies are excluded, otherwise the presence of the ruby would not be determined. Similarly, when a thing is located in a former space-time, all other space-times, including the presnt one, are excluded. Thus the same thing cannot be located in a subsequent space-time also. This shows that the object of simple sensation and that of the subsequent determinate cognition are different, since location in one space-time makes the thing radically different from the thing located in another space-time.[35]

The whole argument of the Buddhist is purported to prove that every moment is an object apart and, therefore, the object of sensation and that of determinate cognition cannot be one and the same. Udayana advances an extremely subtle dialectic against the Buddhist doctrine of momentariness.[36] His main argument is that if everything in the world is unique and momentary, no universal relations would be possible. In the absence of such relations no inference could be valid. This consequence, Udayana argues, is not desirable even for the Buddhist because, unless the validity of inference is established, the doctrine of momentariness itself cannot be proved. All the reasonings of the Buddhist in support of momentariness are inferential in nature. Therefore in the event of inference itself being invalid his arguments would fail to prove his point. The Buddhist cannot say that momentariness is a perceptual

34. na ca viruddhadharmasaṁsarge 'pyekatvam. trailokyasyaikyaprasaṅgāt. TT, p. 140.
35. Ibid.
36. See Kus., pt. I, pp. 184 ff.

fact, because he does not admit determinate cognition to be a case of genuine perception. The cognition of momentariness, if at all perceptual, must be determinate, since it involves judgement. The Buddhist cannot say that the momentary nature of things is known indeterminately, because, in that case, he cannot make any assertions about it. Moreover, indeterminate perception is not a felt fact; it can only be inferred from the determinate perception as a logical implication. If the validity of the determinate perception is not admitted, nothing can be said about the content of indeterminate perception. Hence, the Buddhist has to face the following predicament: If momentariness is held to be true, inference and determinate perception become invalid; and if the latter are invalid, momentariness cannot be proved. The Buddhist, Udayana maintains, has no way out of this impasse unless he gives up momentariness as a false doctrine.[37]

Vācaspatimiśra refutes the Buddhist contention that every point of space-time makes a different object, thus converting the existence of the object into a string of events. It is true, he says, that when we perceive the ruby, we at the same time negate the non-rubies, because, all entities contain the negations of their opposites by implication. But the question is, why are topazes and all the other precious stones negated when the ruby is perceived? The Buddhist would reply that it is because they are necessarily included in the non-rubies. But why are they necessarily included in the non-rubies? The Buddhist will have to say that their identity with the rubies has never been apprehended. It would thus follow that if identity is apprehended, there would be no necessary exclusion. The ruby which is apprehended as identical through different space-time in a perceptual cognition cannot, therefore, be divided into different events appearing in succession. The two space-times may be admitted to be different, since they have never been apprehended as being one and the same. But ruby is a thing apart from the two points in the space-time in which it is alternately located. If the two space-times are different, it does not follow that the ruby located in them is also different. Such a contention would lead to the over-absurdity that there is nothing

37. na vaijātyaṁ vina tatsyān na tasminnanumā bhavet,
vinā tena na tatsidhhiḥ nādhyakṣaṁ niścayaṁ vinā. Op. cit., p. 184; also see pp. 184-7, and 196.

identical or similar in the universe.[38] Hence, the right view, according to Vācaspati, is that all the functions of our cognition, without exception, have their origin in our sensibility. They may be determinate or indeterminate, but they invariably refer to one and the same object. Therefore, the determinate cognition arising after sense-object contact must be recognised as perceptual.[39]

4. *Some more objections answered*

The Buddhist maintains that determinate cognition cannot be regarded as sense-perception, because sensation is always unutterable. It is argued that if sensation could be conveyed through words, then one should know what heat is from the word 'heat', just as one knows it from sensation. Vācaspati points out that this argument of the Buddhist misses an important distinction. There is absolutely no incongruity in holding that sensations are utterable. As a matter of fact, sensation of heat and its name refer to one and the same thing, but the reactions they produce are quite different. This is because the causation of the two, the sensation and the name, are quite different. The sensation is a direct cognition, while the name is an indirect suggestion. Therefore, the sensation of cold does not disappear from the mere idea of heat suggested by its name, since for that an actual connection with heat is indispensable.[40]

Dharmakīrti, in one of his most famous Kārikās, argues that if determinate cognition is the perception of the real thing which, in the realist view, is the support of various attributes (qualities and universals), then all its attributes must be perceived simultaneously. The function of supporting attributes of a self-identical indivisible thing must be identical. Hence, the cognition of the thing (substance) as the support of one attribute must necessarily include the cognition of all its attributes.[41] But since this is contrary to our experience,

38. tasmāt pūrvāparadeśakālau tatsambandhau vā kāmaṁ bhidyeyātāṁ parasparābhāvāvinābhāvāt. tayorekadāpi tādātmyenāpratibhāsanāt na tu tadāliṅgitasvabhāvaḥ padmarāgamaṇistasya tābhyām, anyatvāt, na ca anyabhedo' nyabhedamāpādayati atiprasaṅgāt. TT, p. 141.

39. tasmād indriyārthasannikarṣalabdhajanmāno vikalpā darśanavyāpārā nānya iti yuktam utpaśyāmaḥ. Ibid.

40. Ibid., p. 142.

41. ekopakārake grāhye' dṛṣṭāḥ tasminna santi te,
sarvopakārakaṁ hyekaṁ tadgrahe sakalagrahaḥ. PV, III, 54, Also see verses 51-53.

determinate cognition cannot be regarded as the perception of the thing at all. Replying to this argument, Vācaspati points out that it assumes the identity of the thing with its attributes. Whereas, in his view, the substance is characterised by its attributes, but neither the attributes nor their relations to the substance are identical with the substance. All are different unities.[42] Every attribute, according to him, is cognised in accordance with the special conditions of its perceptibility. The conditions under which different attributes characterising the thing are perceived are not identical. The realist never admits that the attributes and the relations are supported by the substance in its one supporting essence so as to be included in one unity. Hence, the Buddhist argument does not affect the realist position at all. Besides, Vācaspati urges, if what is related to the substance is nothing over and above the substance, if it is the substance itself, then there can be in the world no relations at all, since a thing cannot be related to itself.[43]

5. *Defence of substance-attribute relation*

It is clear from the above that for the realist relations are as real as the terms they relate. Between two related terms there is a third unity in the form of the relation itself. But this third unity does not require another relation to relate it to the terms, because, such a process would involve *regress ad infinitum.* The relation of this third unity to the terms is said to be 'natural' (*svabhāvasambandha*) which is the same as the relation of 'qualification and qualified' (*viśeṣaṇaviśeṣyabhāva*). The 'natural realation' is such that it relates two entities without itself being a separate entity. Other examples of this relation are those which obtain between negation and its locus, and between *subject* and *object.*[44] One of the chief reasons why the realist insists on the stability of the objects of experience is that he admits the reality of relation. On the other hand, the Buddhist, who reduces the existence of things to a stream of momentary events, divides the relations into real (*vāstava*) and logical (*kalpita*). The former is the relation of causality obtaining betweeen the successive moments and the latter includes

42. svabhāvo hi dravyasyopādhibhir viśiṣyate na tūpādhayo vā tairviśiṣṭatvaṁ vā tasya svabhāvaḥ. TT, p. 142.
43. na ca yatsvabhāvasambandhi sa svabhāvaḥ, tathā satyasambandhitvameva syāt na hi tadeva tena saṁbadhyate. Ibid., p. 142.
44. See NSM, pp. 65-68.

the relation of things with attributes and motion. All *logical* relations, according to the Buddhist, are superimposed on reality by the productive imagination. He never accepts that relations are perceived by the senses. Even causality as a relation is for him a construction of thought; only its terms, the moments, are real.[45]

Thus the difference between the realist and the Buddhist is radical. The realist insists that the determinate cognition apprehending substance, attribute and their relation cannot be denied perceptual character. The universal is, therefore, a perceived fact cognised as an attribute different from the particular in which it subsists. The perception of the universal as a distinct entity cannot be regarded as an illusion, because it is never contradicted by subsequent experience.[46] The Buddhist, on the other hand, maintains that if substance and attribute are regarded as distinct realities, the one characterised by the other, they cannot be included in one presentation, since two separate entities are always perceived in two separate presentations. Vācaspati argues that if substance and attribute were apprehended in two separate cognitions, then the relation of qualification and qualified (*viśeṣaṇaviśeṣyabhāva*) between them would not be possible. An independent cognition either of substance or of attribute would not be able to determine its own object, because, *ex hypothesi,* they know nothing about one another. Hence, there must only be one qualified percept corresponding to a characterised substance.[47] The difference of substance and attribute, according to the realist, is not a bar to their unitary cognition, since they are so related that they are capable of being perceived in one presentation.

Śrīdhara repudiates the Buddhist contention that substance-attribute relation is logical, or constructed, since the real is something unique and indivisible. He maintains that no construction is involved in the cognition of substance as characterised by its attributes. It is true that the determinate cognition of a thing involves the operation of thought (*vicāra*). We first apprehend substance, attribute and their relation in an indeterminate manner, and after deliberations, apprehend them in their real order and express them in the form of a determinate judgment. Nevertheless, all thinking is not construction.

---

45. Cf. BL., Vol. II, p. 69, and n. 3, pp. 287 f.
46. jātir jātimato bhinnā guṇī guṇagaṇātpṛthak,
tathaiva tatpratīteśca kalpanoktirabādhikā. NM, pt. I, p. 96.
47. TT, p. 142.

It may very well be directed towards understanding of facts and their relations. As a matter of fact, according to Śrīdhara, thought and memory are accessory causes of the definite cognitions of things. So the perception of substance as qualified by its attributes cannot be denied validity merely because it involves thought and memory.[48]

The Buddhist, however, denies that the categories of substance, attribute and relation are apprehended in sense-perception. The senses, which do not think but only react, are incapable of putting together the complicated edifice of the categories. This function, according to the Buddhist, belongs to reason which is not limited in its objects like the senses. Vācaspati asks, if reason or mind does not apprehend what is present, i.e., if it is confined to the past impressions, how can it be said to be unlimited in its objects? In the Nyāya view, the mind, although not limited in its objects like the senses, is nevertheless by itself just as unconscious as all the senses are. It does not think because it is not conscious. Consciousness belongs to the soul which is the receptacle of all the cognitions and of all the impressions (*saṁskāras*) which are left behind by them in our experience. The soul puts on record every sensation, and arranges past experience in right combinations.[49] It is, indeed, the soul that at first in a sensation throws a glance at the indistinct object, the actual possessor of those attributes which are not noticed distinctly in the first moment. It then awakens the dormant traces of former experience and creates a recollection of formerly experienced things. Armed with this reaction it creates, but again necessarily through the medium of the senses, the judgment such as 'this is a cow'.[50] Therefore, according to Vācaspati, it is wrong to hold, as the Buddhist does, that our reason is autonomous in creating categories. In his view, there is absolutely no construction involved in our apprehensions of the various categories. The categories are, indeed, realities apprehended as they are in the objective world.

Vācaspati agrees with the Buddhist that it is impossible to distinguish

---

48. See NK, p. 193 f; cf. ĀTV, pp. 182-83.
49. yadi pūrvakaṁ vijñānaṁ manaḥ kathaṁ sarvaviṣayatā? asmākantu sarvaviṣayamapi acetanatayā na vicārakam, tasmād ātmaiva. sakala-jñānatajjanitavāsanādhārah smartā ca pratisandhātā ca. TT, p. 143.
50. sa khalvindriyārthasannikarṣād ālocya jātimantaṁ sammugdham artham udbuddhasaṁskārasamupajātapūrvapiṇḍānusmṛtisahāyaḥ prāgeva cakṣuṣā vikalpayati gaurayam iti. Ibid., p. 143.

in a single presentation two different parts, the one causing the other, or the one entailing the existence of the other, but inasmuch as the one suggests the existence of the other, the single cognition of substance with its attribute is possible. There is in every percept an element of sensation and an element of former experience. They are as though the one characterised by the other. Both these elements together produce the qualified percept. This is the sort of efficient production admitted by the Naiyāyika, not the causation between two parts of an individual presentation.[51] The circumstance that both the parts are not grasped in full at the first moment of sense-cognition is, according to Vācaspati, irrelevant. Nothing warrants us to expect that whatever exists must be apprehended in full at the first moment. If only one aspect of reality is seized at first and it is fully grasped in a subsequent moment, this does not imply that the latter cognition is erroneous. The full determinate cognition is produced by two factors, sensation and memory, as has already been pointed out. It is a sense-perception nevertheless, since, although representing a latter stage, it is also produced by sense-object contact. According to Vācaspati, the circumstance that a part is cognised later does not make it an 'other' thing. Things possess duration, and during the time their existence lasts they gradually unfold their characteristics by successively combining with the totality of causes and conditions which create together a stable result.[52]

Vācaspatimiśra therefore urges that a better explanation of our empirical knowledge would be possible if the Buddhist, instead of trying to prove the ideality of universals, bestowed his efforts to prove their reality and amenability to the senses. If he does so, he would certainly succeed in proving with clear evidence that substance and its attributes really exist and are apprehended by our senses; they are not constructed by our imagination. Otherwise the Buddhist has nothing left for except to imagine a stream of pure sensations corresponding to momentary particulars upon which our productive reason builds the edifice of categories.[53]

The main points of the realist's arguments in defence of his view

51. tenaikavijñānavedyatve yadyapi jñāpyajñāpakabhāva upakāryopakārakabhāvo nāsti tathā' pi tadarthālocanānugatasmaraṇayor viśeṣaṇaviśeṣyabhāvāvagāhi vijñānaṁ pratyutpādakatvamevopakārakatvamasti. Ibid., p. 143.

52. Ibid.

53. Ibid., p. 142.

that universals are perceptual facts may be recapitulated as follows : (1) Determinate cognition in which the universal is definitely apprehended cannot be denied perceptual character. (2) No radical distinction between sensation and determinate cognition can be made. They may be distinguished as indistinct and distinct. (3) If perception were confined to pure indeterminate sensation, there could neither be any idea of the universal, nor of particular; neither of identity nor of difference. (4) Things are not bare particulars; they possess general characters which are perceived along with them. (5) The conventional designation of things itself depends upon the apprehension of the universal. The universal is apprehended even without the knowledge of the conventional name. (6) The revival of memory itself cannot be explained without the perception of the universal. (7) The presence of memory as an indispensable factor does not make determinate cognition non-perceptual. (8) The doctrine of momentariness of things itself being unproved, the Buddhist conclusions based on it cannot be accepted as valid. (9) Substance, attribute and relation are not categories of thought but real things apprehended in valid perceptual experience.

6. *Concluding remarks*

The whole controversy between the Buddhist and the realist concerning the perceptibility of the universal evidently originates from their radically opposed metaphysical points of view. For the Buddhist, whatever exists is momentary; there is neither any identity nor any repetition. For the realist, on the contrary, things have duration and they possess identical attributes. There is indeed no meeting point between these two opposed philosophies. Vācaspati has therefore rightly remarked that if the premise of the Buddhist, namely, the doctrine of momentariness, is granted, all his conclusions which logically follow from it must also be granted. This is the reason why Vācaspati and Udayana reject the doctrine of momentariness as an unproved assumption. Anyway, it is quite evident that if there were no identity, duration and repetition in the world, there could be no conceptual knowledge. And even if we came to possess such a knowledge, it would be completely erroneous. Only immediate intuitions or sensations which were unadulterated by thought would be free from error. Thought and speech would be completely divorced from reality. These conclusions make us strongly suspicious about the premises from which they follow. They evidently fail to do justice to our empirical knowledge.

It seems undeniable that we discover repetitions in the world. The same colours, shapes, etc., repeat over and over again in our experience. It is true that these discoveries involve more than pure sense-awareness. They involve mental activity in the form of recollection, assimilation, differentiation, etc. It will, threrefore, be more appropriate to say that we 'observe' or 'notice' repetitions in the world. Observation is systematic watching with a view to discovering facts. If perception means observation and not bare sense-awareness, then we certainly discover recurrent qualities in our perceptual experience of things.[54] These qualities are universals, because they are recurrent. We observe these qualities repeated singly as well as in groups. In the same way, we observe certain spatial and temporal patterns or arrangements repeated over and over again in our experience. For example, we observe things as 'preceding' or 'succeeding' one another, as one 'beside' the other, as one 'on top of' or 'inside' the other and so on. These relations also are universals, because they are recurrent. They are independent of the mind, because things would be related in these ways whether anybody thinks about them or not.[55]

In addition to the universals of quality and relation described above, we discover another important type of relational universal, namely, similarity. We observe that two shades of blue, e.g., 'sky-blue' and 'royal blue', resemble one another. We also observe that they

---

54. Both in our recognition of a quality and in the observation that two or more things have the same quality, memory disposition is invariably present. In other words, both the cognition and recognition of the universal involve memory, not in the sense of conscious recollection, but in the sense of a disposition. Similarly, in our discovery of a universal, 'abstraction' in the sense of 'singling' or 'isolation' is also present. We concentrate upon a quality in noticing that two or more things have the same quality. In this sense it would be true to say that we abstract even when we perceive a quality, for we isolate it for observation. But it is necessary to distinguish this kind of abstraction from the other kind, namely, construction of an abstract concept. The common quality, or the universal we are discussing, is not a construction of thought, but a discovered fact, though it involves thought in the sense of abstraction we have pointed out above. The Buddhist believes that the presence of memory and thought in the apprehension of the universal necessarily implies that it is a construction and not a discovery. But, as the Naiyāyika has pointed out, there seems to be no valid reason to think so, unless we believe with the Buddhist that thought is always constructive and it is incapable of apprehending the real.
55. See Russell : *The Problems of Philosophy*, pp. 97-98. cf. H.H. Price : *Thinking and Experience*, pp. 1 ff.

resemble one another more closely than any of them does to a shade of green. Similarly, we observe resemblances amongst things, individuals, situations and so on. It might be objected that resemblance is not an independent relation; it is always identity in certain 'respect'. If this contention is true, then the 'respect' in which two colours or two things resemble must always be discoverable. Where it is not discovered, no resemblance could be observed. But it seems true that we observe resemblances between things and qualities without being able to specify the 'respect' in which they are identical.[56] Anyway, this issue need not engage us here, since we are going to take it up for a detailed consideration in a later chapter.

It is however necessary to emphasise that the identities and similarities discovered in our experience of things are not in any way mental constructions as the Buddhist maintains. They are objective, since they are the characteristics of things—qualities and relations—discovered by us through observation. Nevertheless, the Buddhist is right in so far as he denies that the universals of the Nyāya-Vaiśeṣika or the Mīmāṁsā conception are observed facts. The realist seems to be quite wrong in holding that the concepts of 'cow', 'man', 'jar', etc., correspond exactly to real universals discovered in perception. Inspite of our best efforts we fail to discover 'cowness', 'manness', 'jarness', etc., in our experience of cows, men and jars. These concepts, and others like them, are in some way workings of the mind. Nevertheless, they are not without objective basis. They arise out of our observations of recurrent characteristics, or similarities. They are not purely arbitrary constructions of thought like that of 'unicorn' or 'square-circle'. They are concepts suggested and determined by our experience of things.

Thus we find ourselves in disagreement with the positions of both the Buddhist and the realist. Against the Buddhist we maintain that the world we experience presents repetitive features which are universals. Against the realist we maintain that the universals (*jāti*) of this conception are not observed facts. We maintain also that thought is not idle in the discovery of universals. It is implicit in our observations of recurrent characteristics and similarities. But such participation of thought does not entail construction or projection of something which is not given. In fact the experience of recurrent

56. Cf. Aaron, R. I., *The Theory of Universals*, pp. 234 f. Also see B. Blanshard : *Reason and Analysis*, pp. 415 f.

features is the original source of our basic empirical concepts on which thought operates. Therefore, these basic concepts themselves cannot be regarded as thought-constructions. If the experience of recurrence is denied, there would be no recognition. And if there was no recognition, we could not come to possess any empirical concept.[57] Thought, in that case, would be impossible. And even if it became possible by means of *a priori* concepts, it would have nothing to do with the experienced world.

57. As Price says, "Recognition, then, is the first stage towards the acquisition of a primary or basic concept. It is, therefore, the most fundamental of all intellectual processes. Without it, we should acquire no basic concepts; and without basic concepts, we should not be capable of thinking at all". Op. cit., p. 35.
Price further points out that recognition is 'preverbal'. One recognises the universal prior to making use of words. Not only this, recognition is logically presupposed by the use of words. One could not use the word 'cat' in one's recognition of cats unless one already recognised the mark or the sound 'cat' as itself an instance of the word. Op cit., pp. 37-38.

CHAPTER VI

THE JAINA THEORY OF UNIVERSALS

The extreme realism of the Nyāya and the Mīmāṁsā was controverted not only by the Buddhist nominalist but also by the Jaina who tries to steer clear of both the extremes of realism and nominalism. The Jaina position on universals is usually described as conceptualism, but our exposition of this view would reveal that it is difficult to glean out a single coherent view from the writings of different Jaina thinkers. All the three traditional views, viz., realism (of the moderate variety), conceptualism and nominalism are represented in the Jaina thought. It would therefore be quite pertinent to ask which of these views is compatible with the fundamental standpoint of the Jaina.

1. *The nature of the object of knowledge*

The object of valid knowledge, according to the Jaina, is of the nature of both universal and particular.[1] There is nothing which is known as purely universal or purely particular. One and the same thing being the source of both general as well as particular cognitions, it must be regarded as having both universal and particular natures. When, for example, we perceive a cow, we apprehend its unity with other cows and also its difference from non-cows. Similarly, when we perceive a cow with some particular character, we nevertheless cognise it as 'cow'. Thus, the two—the universality and the particularity—are always found in one. As Malliṣeṇa asserts, the universal and the particular are never apprehended separately by anyone at any time.[2] The Jaina argues this point also from the pragmatic point of view. What satisfies our practical purpose is the concrete thing having both universal and particular nature. The universal is the stable element persisting through the changing modes which are particulars. Things having this dual nature are the genuine objects of desire.[3] Change and stability, according to the Jaina, are not incompat-

1. sāmānyaviśeṣātmā tadartho viṣayaḥ. PMS, IV, I; cf. PNT, V, I.
2. SM, pp. 101-2; cf. ST, V, 2.
3. pūrvottarākāraparihārāvāptisthitilakṣaṇapariṇāmena arthakriyopapatteśca. PMS, IV, 2.

ible with one another. On the contrary, they are so intimately related that one does not exist without the other. There is no mode without stable substance, nor is there any substance without changing modes. Substance is the unity running through the different modes. Every object of valid cognition is 'universal-particular'. The one without the other is an abstraction having no basis in experience.[4]

2. *Identity of Existence*

All things, according to Samantabhadra, are united in a common existence. Things might differ as substances, qualities and so on, but they are all identical so far as their existence is concerned.[5] Unity and difference, according to the Jaina, are not opposed to one another. Their intimate relationship is supported by both experience and reason. The opposition between them arises only when they are regarded as absolute. Absolute unity or absolute difference has no foundation in reality. Thus the unity of existence advocated by Samantabhadra is not an absolute unity, but a *unity-in-difference.* The universal 'existence' is not unaffected by the individual differences. In so far as it is identical with the individuals, it is manifested differently by different individuals. It is conceived by the Jaina as a dynamic unity as opposed to the Nyāya conception of it as an eternal changeless universal.[6] Samantabhadra maintains that things do not differ in respect of existence, but only as this or that instance of existence. If things are held to differ in respect of existence, then both knowledge and its object would become unreal.[7] If knowledge differs from its object in respect of existence, then it must be regarded as non-

4. See SR, V, 2; PKM, p. 466; ST, V, 1 and 2.
5. satsāmānyāttu sarvaikyaṁ pṛthagdravyādibhedataḥ. ĀM quoted in JPN, p. 296.
6. The universal, for the Jaina is not an eternal changeless unity unaffected by the plurality of its substrates. The common universal is also non-common, one as well as many. It is identical with as well as different from its substrates. This is true not only of 'existence-universal', but of all universals, such as 'substancehood', 'manhood', 'cowness', etc.

   Sattaikā yugapad anekatra vartāta ityapyasiddham, tadanantaparyāyatvasādhanāt svaparyāyebhyo 'tyantabhedāsiddheśca dravyatvādisāmānyamapi naikam anaṁśam anekasvavyaktivṛtti....... tasyāpi svāśrayātmakatayā kathañcit sāṁśatvānekatvapratīteḥ. AS quoted in JPN, p. 398.
7. sadātmanā ca bhinnaṁ ced jñānaṁ jñeyād dvidhāpyasat. Loc. cit. Cf. ST, V, 1.

existent. And if knowledge is non-existent, then there is no evidence for the existence of objects. Also, knowledge presupposes the unity of *subject* and *object*. This unity consists in their common existence irrespective of their mutual differences.

The Jaina propounds a pluralistic metaphysics in which things are systematically related from the lowest to the highest. They are united in various categories or classes, and these again are united in the highest universal 'existence'. The aspect of unity, for the Jaina, is as real as that of diversity. Mere classification of particulars under different categories unrelated with one another would not constitute a satisfactory ontology. This would only substitute a plurality of unrelated categories for the plurality of things. Hence, a unity higher than the categories has to be recognised. This unity, according to the Jaina, is the unity of *existence*. From the point of view of *modes* there is infinite plurality of things, and from the point of view of *existence* everything is one. This view of reality alone is attested by experience. The Buddhist and the Advaitist, who advocate the modal and the substance view respectively, are guilty of having a partial view of reality. The right view, according to the Jaina, consists in recognising both unity and diversity as equally real aspects of the universe.[8]

3. *Arguments for the reality of the universals*

The Jaina argumens for the reality of the universal are hardly different from those of the Nyāya and the Mīmāṁsā. The reality of the universal, Prabhācandra argues, is undeniable, as it is attested by uncontradicted experience.[9] If the reality of the universal given in uncontradicted experience is denied, then the reality of particulars also becomes questionable. Experience cannot be summoned to prove the reality of one and deny the reality of the other. The unerring objective reference of our cognitions proves the reality of both universals and particulars. If there were no universals, there could be no rational activity, since all rational activity depends upon the apprehension of the universal. Prabhācandra argues like the Naiyāyika for the difference of the universal from the

8. Cf. JPN, pp. 301-2.
9. gaurgauḥ ityabādhitapratyayaviṣayasya sāmānyasyābhāvāsiddeḥ. PKM, p. 467.

particular. The difference of general and particular cognitions, he maintains, necessarily implies the difference of their objects. The two cognitions would be indistinguishable if their contents were identical.[10] Moreover, the general and the particular cognitions have different forms: one is co-ordinative and the other is differentiative. This difference of form cannot be accounted for without admitting the difference of objects. Further, general cognitions cannot be said to arise without external universals, since their contents are felt as spatio-temporally determined.[11] Particulars as particulars, i.e., as shorn of all general features, could not account for different general cognitions. Besides, the view which denies universals altogether would have to admit the possibility of any particular giving rise to any general cognition. To avoid this absurd consequence the reality of universals must be granted.[12]

4. *The two kinds of universals*

As opposed to the Nyāya and the Mīmāṁsā, the Jaina distinguishes two kinds of universals. One is the *general* feature possessed by things serving as the basis of general conceptions, and the other is the *substantial identity* running through the successive modifications of a thing. The former is called horizontal or crosswise universal (*tiryak sāmānya*), and the latter vertical universal (*ūrdhvatā-sāmānya*).[13] The general conceptions of 'cow' 'tree', 'man', etc., refer to the former, and the notions of substantial identity, e.g., of 'gold' as underlying the successive modifications of it in the form of different ornaments, refer to the latter. It may be noted here that some later Jaina thinkers (Prabhācandra, Vādideva and others) regard the horizontal universal as 'similarity of development' (*sadṛśapariṇāma*).[14] 'Cowness', for example, is nothing but the similarity of individual cows. This conception of universal is different from the Nyāya-Mīmāṁsā conception of it as an identity. It is also different from the conception of the universal as 'relative identity' held by Samantabhadra. We shall return to the discussion of these differences in a later section.

10. Ibid.
11. na cānugatapratibhāso bahissādhāraṇanimittanirapekṣo ghaṭate; pratiniyatadeśakālatayā tasya pratibhāsābhāvaprasaṅgāt. Ibid., p. 468.
12. Ibid.
13. PNT, V, 4-5; cf. PMS, IV, 3-4.
14. See SR, p. 729; PKM, p. 467.

5. *Criticism of the Buddhist and the Nyāya views*

The Jaina makes use of all the arguments of the Nyāya and the Mīmāṁsā for refuting the Buddhist nominalism. Prabhācandra argues that 'the negation of the other' (*apoha*), which the Buddhist substitutes for positive universals, would not be possible if things had no positive similarity. The notion of the 'other' logically presupposes a positive class-concept based on the similarity of things.[15] The Jaina rejects the Buddhist contention that things are absolute point-instants as contrary to experience. If things were absolute point-instants having no similarity, then they could not be apprehended as similar.[16] The fulfilment of pragmatic activity inspired by such apprehensions is enough evidence for their objectivity. The Buddhist contention that absolutely dissimilar particulars produce an identical conception, just as different herbs produce an identical cure, proves, according to the Jaina, the contrary point. It proves that the herbs possess similar efficiency, otherwise any herb could be regarded as cure for any disease. Moreover, if general cognitions are said to arise without real similarity, then particular cognitions also may be said to arise without real difference. If the latter are admitted to have positive basis, then there is no reason for denying the same in the case of the former. If no universal is recognised as the basis of our class-notions, then all class-distinctions would become completely arbitrary.[17]

Dharmakīrti has maintained that there is an illusion of identity of individuals because their indeterminate sense-apprehensions are erroneously regarded as identical. And the latter error arises because the indeterminate sense-apprehensions produce an identical judgment (*ekapratyavamarśa*).[18] Prabhācandra argues that the whole process described by Dharmakīrti is completely unconvincing. It is unintelligible how indeterminate sense-apprehensions, each of which is unique in itself, cooperate to produce an identical judgment. Even if this be granted for argument's sake, there will be the contingency of any set of indeterminate apprehensions producing any synthetic judgment, since the former, in the Buddhist view, are all alike in being unique and

15. sarvathā samānapariṇāmānādhāre vastunyatatkāryakāraṇavyāvṛtterevāsaṁbhavāt. PKM p. 469.
16. SR, p. 728.
17. tato rūpādipratibhāsasyevā 'nugatapratibhāsasyāpyālambanaṁ kalpanīyamityasti vastubhūtaṁ sāmānyam. SR, p. 730; cf. PKM, p. 469.
18. PV, III, 108.

dissimilar. So the indeterminate sense-apprehensions of individual horses, for instance, may be said to produce the synthetic judgment of 'cow'. To avoid this absurdity, some kind of relationship amongst indeterminate sense-apprehensions, which accounts for their production of a specific synthetic judgment, will have to be admitted. This relationship, according to the Jaina, can be nothing but the possession of a similar form which is ultimately derived from the similarity of individuals. But, since the Buddhist does not admit any positive similarity amongst particulars, his account of the genesis of synthetic judgments fails to be satisfactory.[19]

The Jaina is as opposed to the Nyāya realism as he is to the Buddhist nominalism. He agrees with the Nyāya that general cognitions have valid objective reference. But this, according to him, does not prove the existence of eternal class-essences (*jāti*). Not only the Nyāya universals are unnecessary to explain general cognitions, they are also not in conformity with reason and experience. Prabhācandra attacks the Nyāya view by making use of all the arguments in the Buddhist armoury. The universal, he argues, cannot be eternal and ubiquitous. An eternal and ubiquitous universal is a non-entity, as it can have no causal efficiency.[20] If the universal is eternal, it cannot be said to depend upon the individual for its cognition. Dependence implies change which is incompatible with eternality. Further, if the eternal universal is said to be causally efficient, then not only it should be able to produce its own cognition independently of individuals, but also produce it eternally. The causal efficiency of an eternal entity cannot be non-eternal. And if the eternal universal is said to be causally non-efficient by nature, then it can never be cognised even with the help of the individuals. Hence, the eternal universal of the Nyāya, Prabhācandra argues, is a fiction, since the real by definition is that which produces an effect.[21]

Prabhācandra further maintains that the universal cannot be a pervasive or a common attribute. If the universal is conceived as an identity common to manifold individuals, as is done by the Nyāya, then it is

19. See PKM, pp. 469-70; cf. SR, pp. 730-31.

The Jaina, it may be noted, does not recognise indeterminate sense-apprehensions, since they are not known at all. So the production of synthetic judgments via indeterminate sense-apprehensions is not admissible to him. See SR, p. 731.

20. taccā 'nityāsarvagatasvabhāvam abhyupagantavyam; nityasarvagatasvabhāvatve' rthakriyākāritvāyogāt. PKM, p. 470.

21. ajanakasvabhāvaṁ ca sāmānyaṁ kāryasya ityavastutvāpattir nityaikasvabhāva-sāmānyasya, arthakriyākāritvalakṣaṇatvād vastunaḥ. Ibid., p. 471.

impossible to explain how an identical attribute is simultaneously present in numerous substrates. The universal being, by hypothesis, impartite it cannot be said to be present in each individual partially. And if it is said to be present wholly in each of its substrata, then such subsistence becomes completely unintelligible.[22]

6. *The Jaina conception of the universal*

According to Samantabhadra and Vidyānanda the universal can be regarded neither as absolutely identical with the particular, nor as absolutely different from it. In the former case, there will be either only universal or only particular. In the latter case the relation between the particular and the universal as substance and attribute would become unintelligible. Hence, the right view must steer clear of both these extremes.[23]

Samantabhadra and Vidyānanda advance a theory of *relative universals* in place of the Nyāya theory of *absolute universals*. Vidyānanda maintains that the relative character of universals is established even on the Nyāya view.[24] The lower universals (*aparasāmānya*), according to the Nyāya, are the bases of both co-ordination and differentiation. This means that one and the same universal is both general and particular. Its generality and particularity are, of course, relative. This, according to the Jaina, is the nature of all universals. Indeed, in the Jaina view, there are neither absolute universals nor absolute particulars. Generality and particularity are neither two mutually opposed realities nor two related realities; they are only related aspects of a single reality. The relative character of the universal and the particular implies that their relation can be regarded neither as absolute identity nor as absolute difference. The two must be regarded as relatively identical and relatively different. As aspects they are

22. See PKM, pp. 472 f.
23. See ĀM, st. 61 and 62.
Vidyānanda maintains that the universal and its substratum are identical because they belong to an identical space. Things which are different belong to different space: kāryakāraṇayorguṇaguṇinoḥ sāmānyatadvatostādātmyamabhinnadeśatvāt. yayoratādātmyaṁ na tayorabhinnadeśatvam. yathā sahyavindhyayoḥ. AS, p. 213. Cf. ekāntabhede viśeṣaṇaviśeṣyabhāvānupapatteḥ karabharāsabhayorivā dharmadharmivyapadeśābhāvaprasaṅgācca. SM, p. 11. ekāntābhede vānyatarsyāsattvaprasaṅgaḥ. Ibid., p. 12.
24. AS, p. 218.

different, but as aspects of one and the same thing, they are identical. This view, according to the Jaina, besides safeguarding the reality of both the universal and the particular, succeeds also in explaining the relation between the two in a satisfactory manner. The Nyāya view of absolute difference between the universal and the particular completely fails to explain their relation. The postulation of inherence (*samavāya*) does not help, because, as a thing external to the terms, it fails to relate them.[25] The Jaina view of relation between the universal and the particular, it is claimed, escapes the above difficulties. The relation of relative identity and relative difference, according to Vidyānanda, is unique and unanalysable (*aśakyavivecanatvāt*). It is akin to the relation of subject and object in a cognition. So the questions of total or partial subsistence of the universal in the particular cannot be raised in this view.[26]

There is one Jaina writer named Abhayadevasūri, the commentator on *Sanmati Tarka,* whose view on universals is quite opposed to the one we have been discussing above. His view, as will be presently seen, is quite indistinguishable from that of the Buddhist. He maintains that apart from the particulars, no universal is ever apprehended in perceptual experience.[27] General cognitions, according to him, do not apprehend universals, but fleeting particulars which generate them.[28] It is not necessary to postulate universals in order to explain general cognitions. Particulars themselves may be regarded as their cause, just as they are of

---

25. Ibid., p. 221; cf. SM, p. 11.

Samantabhadra maintains that the Nyāya view logically leads to the unreality of all the three—the universal, the particular and their relation (*samavāya*). Since *samavāya* fails to relate, there is nothing else in the Nyāya view to relate all these three to the 'existence'-universal. Consequently all the three are reduced to non-entities.

sarvathānabhisambandhaḥ sāmānyasamavāyayoḥ,
tābhyāmartho na sambaddhastāni trīṇi khapuṣpavat. ĀM, st. 66.

26. nanvevamapi vṛtterdoṣo yathopavarṇitaḥ syādvādināṁ prasajyate iti cennāyaṁ prasaṅgo 'nekānte, kathañcittādātmyādvedyavedakākārajñānavat. AS, p. 316.

Vidyānanda here refers to the difficulties raised in the Nyāya view of absolute difference between the universal and the particular, namely, whether the universal subsists in the particular wholly or partially, how does it subsist at the same time in different individuals, and so on. These difficulties, according to him, do not arise in the Jaina view, because it denies both absolute identity and absolute difference between the universal and the particular.

27. śābaleyādivyatirekeṇa aparasya anugatākārasya akṣajapratyaye sāmānyasya apratibhāsanāt. TBV, p. 689.

28. anugatākārabuddheravyāpakakṣaṇikaśābaleyādipadārthaprabhavatvāt tadgrāhakatvameva na sāmānyagrāhakatvam. Ibid., p. 692.

particular cognitions.[29] There is no contingency, according to Abhayadeva, of any particular generating any cognition, since particulars are endowed with definite efficiencies. The cognition of cow, for example, can be generated by certain particulars alone and not by all. The causality of a thing is established on the basis of its invariable relationship with the effect. The causal efficiency of particulars is proved in the case of particular cognitions. So, they should be legitimately regarded as the cause of general cognitions also. The universal, of which causal efficiency is never known in any instance, cannot be regarded as their cause.[30] Abhayadeva considers it a gross superstition to believe that a general notion necessarily implies a general cause. Our notions of imaginary things, and of things unborn or destroyed, prove that we can have general notions even without any real universals corresponding to them. And if by the universal is meant only some kind of unity determining general notions, then it may be admitted as an imagined unity of the form of 'the negation of the opposite'.[31]

It is quite obvious that Abhayadevasūri is to a great extent influenced by Dharmakīrti and Śāntarakṣita whom he quotes profusely in his criticism of the realist theory of universals. He does not seem to accept even the theory of relative universals, or that of similarity (*sadṛśapariṇāma*) advocated by the other Jaina thinkers. For him the particular alone is real and the universal is pure imagination. This is pure and simple nominalism. The absolute denial of the reality of universal by Abhayadeva is evidently incompatible with the fundamental non-absolutistic stand-point of the Jaina.

Apart from the two mutually opposed views discussed above, there is a third view advocated by such eminent Jaina thinkers as Prabhācandra and Vādidevasūri. This view, as we have already indicated, may be described as 'the similarity theory'. According to this view, similarity of individuals (*sadṛśapariṇāma*) is the only positive basis of general cognitions. What is discovered in perceptual experience is only similarity, and it provides sufficient basis for our general notions. This similarity, according to Prabhācandra, being identical with the individual, is non-eternal, non-

29. kecid bhāvāḥ-prakṛtyaiva ekākāraparāmarśahetavo bhaviṣyantīti na tadarthaṁ sāmānyaprakalapanaṁ yuktam. Ibid.
30. Ibid., p. 689.
31. atha sāmānyena ekanibandhanatvamātraṁ sādhyate tadā siddhasādhyatā vijātīyavyavacchedena kalpitaikā 'govyāvṛttinibandhanasya iṣṭatvāt. Ibid., p. 696.

pervasive and manifold just like other qualities.[32] Eternal and pervasive universals of the Nyāya are not only unnecessary, but are also contrary to experience and reason. Prabhācandra points out that even the Nyāya has to admit the existence of general notions, e.g., of 'universal', 'negation', 'cook', etc., which do not correspond to eternal and pervasive class-essences. Therefore there is no reason why the same may not be true in the case of all general notions.[33]

It is noteworthy that 'similarity' for Prabhācandra, though a universal (*sāmānya*), is not an identical character common to similar individuals. He maintains that the universal 'similarity' is as manifold as the dissimilar particulars which it characterises.[34] The concept of 'cow', for example, corresponds to the similarity of individual cows, but this similarity, as the character of each individual cow, is as diverse as the cows themselves. This is said to follow from the relative identity of the universal with the particular. The similarity which is identical with one particular cannot be an attribute of another. The relative difference of the universal 'similarity' from the particular does not make it a common attribute but only serves to distinguish it from its substratum.[35] The non-common character of the universal is said to be not opposed to its universality. Just as colour does not cease to be an attribute because of its identity with substance, so also the universal does not cease to be a universal because of its identity with the particular. Similarity and dissimilarity, according to Prabhācandra, are properties of things just like other properties. The only difference is that they are relative properties (*parāpekṣa*) as distinguished from colour tastes, etc., which are non-relative (*parānapekṣa*) properties. Just as colour, taste, etc., generate their specific cognitions, so also similarity and dissimilarity produce, respectively, general and particular cognitions. General cognitions, according to Prabhācandra,

32. anugatapratyayasya ca sadṛśapariṇāmanibandhanatvaprasiddheḥ. sa cānityo' sarvagato' nekavyaktyātmakatayā' nekarūpaśca rūpādivatpratyakṣata eva prasiddhaḥ. PKM, p. 474.

33. See op. cit., pp. 476 f.

34. vibhinnaṁ hi prativyakti sadṛśapariṇāmalakṣaṇaṁ sāmānyaṁ visadṛśa-priṇāmalakṣaṇaviśeṣavat. Op. cit., p. 479.

35. Ibid. The unity of the universal and the particular, according to Yaśovijaya, an eminent Jaina thinker of the later period, is a simple case of co-incidence. The universal is different from the individual, and the identity of the two consists in the fact of both the universal and particularity being co-incident in the same substratum. (so 'pya bhedaḥ pravibhaktapradeśatvarūpabhedābhāvarūpatvāttathā ca jātau vyakteranyatvarūpo bhedo 'nanyadeśatvarūpo 'bhedaśca ityubhayamapyaviruddham). *Nyāyakumudacandra*, p. 272, quoted in JPN, p. 307.

imply only specific properties of things, other than their particularities, which explain their origination. They do not imply, as the Nyāya believes, an identical universal common to diverse particulars. Besides, the Nyāya conception of the universal, as has already been shown, is untrue to experience and unsupported by reason.[36]

It might be urged that in the absence of identical characters common to different individuals, we could not come to possess identical concepts with regard to them. Prabhācandra denies that the existence of identical concepts implies objective identities common to diverse particulars. He distinguishes between two kinds of identity : primary (*mukhya*) and secondary (*upacarita*). In the case of the self, the identity is primary or ontological; but in the case of the universal, it is only secondary. There is no real identity corresponding to our general notions. Similarity of individuals is the only ontological basis of our class-concepts.[37] Prabhācandra further adds that it is because of the identical concept and the identical name corresponding to similar individuals that we come to regard their *similarity* as *identity*. The universal is an identity only as a concept; ontologically it is only similarity of particulars irreducible to identity.[38] Thus, according to the Jaina, there is nothing identically the same in similar individuals. Their similarity is ultimate and unanalysable.

Prabhācandra anticipates here an objection to his 'similarity-theory' of universals. It might be asked, if all general notions depend on objective similarity, then what about the notion of 'similarity' itself? There are, according to the above theory, innumerable similarities pertaining to each class-notion. Therefore the question arises, are these similarities again similar to each other, or not? If they are not, then there could be no general notion of similarity, i.e., the various similarities could not be referred to by one and the same word 'similarity'. And if they are, then there will be a 'similarity' of similarities. Now this second similarity, being also called 'similarity', must be, for the same reason, similar to the first one. Therefore there will be a third similarity of the first and the second similarities. This process obviously leads to infinite regress. If, to avoid this consequence the second similarity is dispensed with, i.e., if

36. Op. cit., p.480.
37. Op. cit., p. 481. Vidyānanda also clearly says that the Jaina does not regard similarity as an identity simultaneously pervading numerous individuals. The said identity is only conceptual: na hi vayaṁ sadṛśapariṇāmamanekavyaktivyāpinaṁ yugapadupagacchāmo 'nyatropacārāt. TBV, p. 320, quoted in JPN, p. 304.
38. See PKM, p. 481. Cf. tasmādabheda ityatra samabhāvaṁ pracakṣate. *Nyāyaviniścaya* of Akalaṅka, p. 206 quoted in JPN, p. 303.

no similarity corresponding to the notion of 'similarity' is said to be required, then the first similarity, i.e., the similarity of individuals, has no *raison d' etre.* If the notion of 'similarity' without real similarity is possible, then the same may be true of all other concepts. Prabhācandra's answer to the above objection is that things have determinate capacities. A pot, for example, requires to be illumined by a lamp in order to be perceived in darkness, but the lamp itself does not require to be illumined by another lamp. In the same way, the general notions of things could not arise if there were no objective similarities, but the general notion of 'similarity' itself does not stand in any such need. Similarities of individuals, according to Prabhācandra, do not only produce general notions about individuals, but also the general notion about themselves. Just as ultimate particulars for the Buddhist (and also for the Vaiśeṣika) are self-differentiating entities, so are similarities for the Jaina ultimate self-co-ordinating characteristics of things.[39]

The 'similarity theory' of universals expounded above is not acceptable to all the later Jaina thinkers. Vimaladāsa, the author of *Saptabhaṅgī Taraṅgiṇī,* maintains that the universal cannot be absolutely diverse like particulars.[40] If the universal, which is the principle of unity of particulars, is regarded as a non-common character, then it will be indistinguishable from particularity. This would also render the unity of existence impossible. Samantabhadra, as we have seen, considers all entities identical in respect of existence, though they differ as particular instances of it. In the same way, Vimaladāsa also regards the universal 'existence' as an 'identity-in-difference': identity in itself and diverse as manifested in particular instances.[41] The same holds true with regard to all universals. The Jaina, according to Vimaladāsa, denies universals only as absolute identities different from individuals, as such entities are not attested by experience. But universals as aspects of particulars, relatively identical with them, are admitted by him. It is meaningless to call something universal if it is as diverse as particulars. Such a view would be indistinguishable from that of the Buddhist. The rejection of the Buddhist view by the Jaina as a partial

39. Ibid., cf. pp. 731 f.
40. The problem for Vimaladāsa arises in connection with the universality of 'sevenfold predication' (*saptabhaṅgī*). He obserevs that the totality of existence could be determined as one and many, which the universality of the law of 'sevenfold predication demands, only if the particulars were possessed of a common existence as the fundamental element of their individuality. Cf. JPN, p. 309.
41. sattāsāmānyamekamanekātmakameva siddhānte svīkṛtam. sattvaṁ hi vyaktyātmanā 'nekamapi svātmanaikaṁ bhavati. SBT, p. 77.

view of diversity (*pṛthaktvaikāntapakṣa*) would have no meaning if he himself advocated a similar view.[42]

The denial of the universal (similarity) as an identical character common to diverse individuals by Prabhācandra and others should be understood, according to Vimaladāsa, as the denial of it as an absolute identity and not also as relative identity. His own view in this regard is that similarity cannot be an ultimate characteristic of things. Similarity is always similarity in certain respect. Things could not be called similar if there was nothing common to them. In other words, similarity, for Vimaladāsa, is always partial identity.[43] In this he entirely agrees with the Nyāya. The concept of similarity, in his view, is derived from the fundamental concept of identity-in-difference.

7. *Comparison with the Viśiṣṭādvaita view*

The Jaina view of universals as similarity resembles the Viśiṣṭādvaita conception of universals very closely. For the Viśiṣṭādvaitin also, as for the Jaina, the universal is similarity (*sādṛśya*) of things. The universal in composite objects, according to him, is nothing but close resemblance (*sausādṛśya*, or *atyantasādṛśya*) between various arrangements of parts (*avayavaracanābheda*).[44] He maintains that when similarity of parts can serve as the foundation of general notions, the assumption of a separate category of universals over and above it is quite gratuitous.[45] It might be argued that if the similarity of parts, e.g., of cows, is a common attribute of all cows, then it is nothing different from the universal 'cowness'; and if it is not a common attribute, then it is not legitimate to regard it as the basis of the identical notion of 'cow'. The Viśiṣṭādvaitin answers that even though a part (dew-lap, etc.) is not a common property, yet the parts of each cow have 'rivals', or 'equals' (*pratidvandvī*) in the parts of other cows by nature. This mutual 'rivalry' or 'equality' of parts is what is meant by the word 'similarity'. This rivalry is natural; it is without any external determination.[46] Facts must be admitted as they are apprehended. The parts of a cow are found to have 'rivals' only in things having dew-lap, etc.,

42. Ibid.
43. anekavyaktyanugatasyaikadharmasyānaṅgīkāre sādṛśyameva durvacanam, yatastadbhinnatve sati tadgatabhūyodharmavattvaṁ sādṛśyam. Ibid., p. 78.
44. TMK, V, 116; SS, p. 313.
45. TMK, V, 117; SS, p. 313.
46. yadyapyekaikasthaṁ sāsnādidharmasvarūpam, tathā' pi tat nirupādhiniyataiḥ — svabhāvato niyataiḥ taistaiḥ sāsnādibhir anyaniṣṭhaiḥ sapratidvandvikaṁ syāt. idamevānyo 'nyasapratidvandvikaṁ rūpaṁ sādṛśyaśabdavācyam abhidhīyate. SS, p. 314; TMK, V, 119.

and not in things having manes. Manes, etc., have rivals only in horses. Thus, in his view, the Viṣiṣṭādvaitin claims, there is no contingency of confusion of classes. The close resemblance of parts attested by valid experience supplies the necessary and sufficient foundation for general notions and classifications.[47]

One might ask if the universal is identified with the close resemblance of parts, then how can the general notions of non-composite objects, like qualities, souls, etc., be explained? The Viśiṣṭādvaitin replies that the nature of things alone is the determinant everywhere.[48] In the case of non-composite objects, therefore, the objects themselves, by virtue of their mutual and natural 'rivalry', become the foundations of general notions. One cannot refuse to recognise the rule of the nature of things. Even the Naiyāyika who admits class-essences (*jāti*) has ultimately to acknowledge this rule in order to explain why certain things alone are the substrates of certain class-essence, not others. If this rule is not recognised, there is no escape from infinite regress. Thus, in the case of composite objects the specific structure of their parts is the basis of their general notions. In the case of non-composite objects, like qualities, etc., on the other hand, the objects themselves by their very nature become the foundations of general conceptions.[49]

It is significant to note that similarity (*sādṛśya*) for the Viśiṣṭādvaitin is not a separate category as it is for the Prābhākara. It is, according to him, included in the category of quality. He maintains that if separate categories are postulated for minor differences, then each quality included under the category of quality would have to be regarded as a separate category. So, if mutually diverse properties of things can be synthesised under the category of quality, then similarity may also be included under it, as it is also a property of things—a property which is the foundation of their general conceptions.[50]

Thus the universal for the Viśiṣṭādvaitin is the natural similarity of things. It is not an identical and eternal class-essence as conceived by the Nyāya, but close resemblance manifested by the particulars. It is noteworthy

---

47. Loc. cit.
48. ṭattadvastusvabhāvaniyama eva sarvatra niyāmakaḥ. SS, p. 315.
49. tena sasaṁsthāneṣu vastuṣu saṁsthānabheda eva vyavahāraniyāmakaḥ guṇādiṣu tattad asādhāraṇalakṣaṇameva tattadvyavahāraniyāmakam. Ibid.
50. See TMK, V, 120, SS, pp. 314-15.

that, like the Jaina, the Viśiṣṭādvaitin does not assert the similarity of a class of individuals to be a non-common feature. It is, for him, a universal, though a universal of a special kind. It is not a universal as identical class-essence, but universal as close resemblance. This resemblance, according to him, is an ultimate and unanalysable characteristic of things by virtue of which they fall into natural classes. In his conception of resemblance as the basis of class notions, the Viśiṣṭādvaitin comes very close to the Western conceptualists. However, the latter would not accept his notion of resemblance as a universal.

8. *Concluding remarks*

Our exposition of the Jaina view of universals reveals that there is no one single theory advocated by all the Jaina thinkers. In the course of our inquiry we have come across three distinguishable views. The first is represented by Samantabhadra, Vidyānanda, Malliṣeṇa and Vimaladāsa, for whom the universal is an identity-in-difference. It is the universal character of the particular which unites it with other particulars. The universal is, in this sense, a unity common to all the particulars it characterises. But, as an aspect of the particular, it is also identical with each particular. Thus the universal and the particular, according to this view, are relatively identical and relatively different. In the former character, the universal differs with each individual, but in the latter character, it serves as the principle of synthesis of diverse particulars. This view may be described as moderate realism as contrasted with the extreme realism of the Nyāya-Vaiśeṣika and the Mīmāṁsā. It rejects the conception of universals as eternal class-essences advocated by the latter. Also it is in complete conformity with the fundamental realistic and non-absolutistic stand-point of the Jaina.

The second view which we have considered is represented by Abhayadevasūri, who does not recognise the universal in any form. The universe, for him, is composed of particulars having nothing in common with one another. There is no generality whatever corresponding to our concepts. The universal is recognised by Abhayadeva neither as an aspect of the particular, nor as similarity (*sadṛśapariṇāma*). It is according to him, an imaginary construction, or *apoha*. Evidently, Abhayadeva was considerably influenced by the Buddhist criticism of realism. His view of universals is indistinguishable from the Buddhist nominalism which was rejected by other Jaina thinkers as a partial view of reality. The total denial of identity by Abhayadeva is radically opposed to the fundamental Jaina stand-point of non-absolutism.

The third view is represented by Prabhācandra, Vādidevasūri and others for whom the universal is 'similarity' (*sadṛśapariṇāma*) of particulars. It is conceived as an ultimate and unanalysable feature of things, which is neither itself an identity common to different particulars nor does it involve any identical element. 'Similarity' as the character of similiar things is said to be as diverse as the things themselves. There is no identical character common to different particulars corresponding to our concepts. All concepts correspond to 'similarity' which is a non-common character of things. The identity of a concept, on this view, would be, by implication, a pure fabrication of the mind. This is pure conceptualism. The important question is whether it is compatible with the fundamental non-absolutistic stand-point of the Jaina.

The most fundamental principle of the Jaina ontology is identity-in-difference. Unity and diversity are relative aspects of every real thing. The Jaina is radically opposed to an unmitigated diversity as he is to an absolute identity. All diversity, according to him, involves relationships which form the bases of the unity of the universe. The unity of reference which our concepts have is not absolutely baseless. It corresponds to an objective unity which is an aspect of concrete things. The similarity view advocated by Prabhācandra denies that things have any unity. Even their similarity is said to be diverse. It is not regarded by him as relative identity of particulars. He clearly says that the unity attributed to similarity is not real, but only conceptual. Thus the conceptualism of Prabhācandra is a repudiation of the basic stand-point of the Jaina. However, according to Vimaladāsa, the denial of unity by Prabhācandra and others should be understood as the denial of absolute unity and not also of relative unity. But, in view of the clear statements of Prabhācandra, we find it difficult to agree with him.[51] Now, the question is, why did these thinkers deviate from the original Jaina position ? Did they find it defective, or were they frightened by the onslaughts of Buddhism ? Dr. Satkari Mukherjee thinks that some later Jaina thinkers were led to surrender their realistic position owing to the severe attacks of the Buddhists on all forms of realism. They were not as tenacious and determined as the Naiyāyikas and the Mīmāṁsakas who stuck to their realism to the last.[52] In any case, it is not intelligible why Prabhācandra does not recognise the universal (*similarity*) as relative identity when he recognises substantial unity in the case

51. See PKM, pp. 480-81.
52. See JPN, p. 305.

of a thing undergoing successive modifications (*ūrdhvatā-sāmānya*) and also accepts the real unity of the self through its successive states.

Thus, out of the three views distinguished above only the first is consistent with the fundamental Jaina position, and the other two are opposed to it. Now we may briefly examine these views in themselves. According to the first view, the universal is a relative identity, or identity-in-difference. The relation of the universal to the particular also is relative identity (*kathañcittādātmya*). Now, how are we to understand this notion of relative identity? The Jaina has explained that the universal considered in itself is an identity, but as one with the particulars it is also diverse. By the same logic, the universal considered in itself is different from the particular, but considered as an intimate aspect of the latter, it is identical with it. Identity and difference, according to the Jaina, are not to be asserted categorically. What this explanation means is that the universal is both one and many, that it is both identical with and different from the particular. Does not this assertion involve self-contradiction? The Jaina maintains that there is no contradiction because identity and difference are asserted from two different points of view. If this is so, then both identity and difference would be relative to thought and not real. The Jaina however would not accept this, since identity and difference for him are real relational characteristics of things. The said contradiction might be sought to be removed by maintaining that the universal and the particular are identical in one character and different in another, just as two oranges are identical in colour and different in size. In that case, the characters in which the universal and the particular are identical and different must be specified. What the Jaina has said is that the universal in itself is a unity different from the particular, but as the intimate aspect of particulars it is diverse. This amounts to saying that the universal in its own character is a unity different from the particular and in the character of the 'other' (i.e. particular) it is diverse. But how can the universal be both itself and the other (the particular)? To say that the particular is not absolutely an 'other' begs the question, since the very issue is the relative identity of the universal and the particular. Thus we fail to see how the Jaina view can escape self-contradiction. The Jaina, however, tries to avoid explaining the above difficulties by maintaining that relative identity of the universal and the particular is an ultimate and unanalysable relation.

As regards the second view, namely, that of Abhayadeva, we need not say anything here, as it is not different from the Buddhist nominalism which we are going to consider later. We must however, consider the third view, namely, the 'similarity view' of the later Jaina writers. Similarity (*sadṛśapariṇāma*), according to this view, is the general character of things by virtue of which they are cognised as belonging to an identical class. Cows, for example, are united in one class and are referred to by the same name 'cow' because they have similarity to one another. This may be granted, for it is quite reasonable to hold that generic concepts, such as 'cow', 'man', 'colour', etc., are based on similarity of things. But difficulties arise when we consider the Jaina conception of similarity itself. It has been maintained that similarity is a non-common character. This would mean that similarity, for the Jaina, is a quality or an attribute and not a relation, for if it were a relation, it could not be non-common. Now, if similarity, as the Jaina says, is a non-common or a non-recurrent character of things, then we fail to understand how it can be called a universal (*sāmānya*), and how it can be regarded as the basis of general conceptions. If similarity of cow 'A', for example, is numerically different from the similarity of cow 'B', then identical designation of them as 'cow' becomes unintelligible. Similarity is held by the Jaina to be the general aspect of things as contrasted with their dissimilarity. But if the similarity of each individual cow to another is as non-common a character as its dissimilarity, then in what way is it distinguishable from the latter? Either similarity is not a universal, or it is not a non-common character. The Jaina conceptualist wants to have similarity as a universal but does not want to admit it as a common character. This, in our opinion, is an impossible position.

Further, similarity as a self-contained attribute of each member of a class is completely unintelligible. If similarity of A to B is different from the similarity of B to A, then how can they be called similar at all? The Jaina, therefore, would have to admit that one and the same similarity is repeated in each individual member of a class. In other words, the Jaina must recognise similarity as a transitive and symmetrical relation like identity. Only as such a relational characteristic recurring in each member of a class, it can serve as the basis of general notions. That is to say, similarity must be recognised as a relational universal.

The Jaina might hold with the Western conceptualists, that similarity is not a universal at all. It is neither an identity nor does it involve any identity.[53] How, then, are the similarities, e.g., of the various pairs of cows

53. This is the view of the Prābhākara also. Similarity for them is a category of reality, which cannot be identified with any of the categories of the Vaiśeṣika. It is the object of the cognition 'this is similar to that'. It is neither a relation nor a universal. The Prābhākara recognises similarity as an attribute of things by virtue of which they

related? It may be said that these similarities are not the same but similar, and in this manner general notions may be explained without assuming the universal. But this explanation involves a serious difficulty. If similarities of the various pairs of cows are not the same but similar, then how is the second similarity related to the first similarities? Is it identical with them, or similar to them? This question arises because one and the same word 'similarity' is used for both of them. If it is identical with them, then it amounts to the admission of a universal. And if it is said to be similar to them, then the same question would arise with regard to this similarity too. This position would thus lead to infinite regress. This third conclusion would of course be controverted by the protagonists of the 'resemblance theory'. We shall return to this subject in a later chapter.

---

are cognised as similar. But it is not recognised as the basis of general notions as is done by the Jainas. (anuvṛttapratyayanimittatvābhāvācca na sāmānyam. samavāyastu sambandharūpa iti na tatra sādṛśyāntarbhāvaḥ). PP, p. 268.

CHAPTER VII

THE ADVAITA VIEW OF UNIVERSALS

The extreme realism of the Nyāya and the Mīmāṁsā is rejected also by the Advāita. The Ādvaitist approaches the question of universals from the stand-point of absolute identity. The ultimate reality, according to him, is the self-identical indeterminate Brahman, the Existence itself, and all diversity is merely the phenomenal appearance of it. The empirical objects are determinations, in names and forms, of the fundamental identity of Existence. For the Advaitist, Existence alone is universal in the real sense of the term, because it is the immanent essence of all that appears to exist. He does not recognise the universals (*jāti*) of the Nyāya conception, for the acceptance of a plurality of eternal and ubiquitous universals would be radically opposed to his fundamental non-dualistic stand-point. The universals of the Nyāya, according to him, are neither ultimately nor empirically real. The ultimately real is the universal Existence appearing as diverse particulars, and the empirically real are those particulars themselves. The universal of the realist does not find any place in this scheme of reality. The Advaitist does not consider it necessary to postulate eternal class-essences (*jāti*) in order to explain general cognition and designation of particular things. These, he maintains, are explainable on the basis of the universal Existence, the empirical particular and the principle of primordial nescience (*mūlāvidyā*).

1. *The universal Existence and the empirical particular*

We have already noted in the second chapter that Existence for the Advaita is not universal in the sense of 'class-essence' (*jāti*) as the Nyāya and the Mīmāṁsā conceive it. It is universal not as a predicate, but as the subject of all predicates. It is the ultimate substratum of everything that enters our consciousness. All objects are therefore predicates or determinations of the foundational Existence. The Advaitist maintains that in our cognitions of things as 'existents' (*sat*) it is the universal Existence which is identically felt. But our empirical consciousness, owing to the force of nescience, determines it in diverse names and forms. These determinations are by their very nature illusory (*kalpita*), since, as Madhusūdana Sarasvatī says, they introduce difference where there is identity.[1] The self-identical Existence, is diversified into mutually exclusive things. This mutual exclusion or difference is what constitutes the illusoriness of empirical objects. To take an analogy given by the Advaitist, empirical objects are like reflections of the self-identical moon on different waves of water. If a person considers these reflections as different moons, he is certainly deluded. The illusoriness of the diversity of moons is proved also by the fact that all of them are identically cognised as 'moon'.[2] In the same way, the Advaitist argues, all empirical objects being the determinations of Existence and identically apprehended as 'existents', their mutual difference in which their exclusive being consists is illusory.

It must be mentioned here that when the Advaitist calls empirical objects as illusory (*kalpita*), he does not mean that they are to be equated to pure fictions like 'hare's horn', or 'sky-lotus'. What he means is that these objects are subject to cancellation when true knowledge is born, or that they are apprehended where they are really not.[3] If they were pure non-entities, they would not even appear. The Advaitist distinguishes empirical objects also from the objects of illusion, such as rope-snake, shell-silver, etc., which occasionally appear in our consciousness. The former belong to a higher level of existence than the latter, since they are objects of common experience as distinguished from the latter which are wholly private. This distinction is strengthened by the fact that the latter are cancelled by true empirical knowledge, while the former are not. However, this distinction of empirical objects from the illusory, according to the Advaitist, does not in the least mitigate their ultimate illusoriness. Empirical objects are said to belong to a higher level of existence than the illusory only from the epistemological

---

1. ata eva ghaṭādayaḥ svānugatapratibhāse vastuni kalpitāḥ vibhaktatvāt, yathā sarpamālādikaṁ svānugatapratibhāse rajjvā idamaṁśe vibhajyate, evaṁ brahmaṇyanugacchati ghaṭādikaṁ vibhajyate san ghatah san pata iti ānandabodhoktamapi sādhu. Ad. Sid., p. 316.
2. See Ad. Sid., pp. 316-18.
3. kalpitatvaṁ jñānanivartyatvaṁ svābhāvavati jñeyatvaṁ vā. *Laghucandrikā*, p. 316.

stand-point. From the ultimate or ontological stand-point, however, both of them are equally appearances of Existence. Empirical objects are also cancelled by the true knowledge of the identity of Existence, just as the illusory objects are cancelled by the true empirical knowledge. It is from this point of view that the Advaitist calls empirical objects as illusory (*kalpita*).

The Advaitist has maintained above that in our cognitions of things as 'existents' what is really cognised is the universal Existence, Brahman itself. But how, it may be asked, can Brahman which, according to the Advaita view, is indeterminate (*rūpādihīna*), is concealed by the original nescience as long as the phenomenal world lasts (*āsaṁsāramajñānāvṛta*) and is knowable only through the scriptural testimony (*śabdaikagamya*) be regarded as the object of such cognitions as 'pot exists', 'cloth exists', and so on ? This being evidently impossible, the objects of these cognitions must be admitted to be the particular determinate existences of things, just as in the cognition of a pot as 'perishable', the object is admitted to be the non-eternality of the particular pot. The Advaitist replies that Brahman as Existence is not concealed by the original nescience (*mūlājñāna*), but by the particular modes (*avasthā*) of it determined as 'pot', etc. (*śaktyajñāna*). Hence, when the veil of this nescience is removed by the sense-cognition there remains no obstacle in the way of the apprehension of universal Existence in our cognitions of the existence of particular things.[4] But how, it may be asked again, can Brahman which is said to be devoid of all qualities, including the sensible ones, be an object of sense-cognition at all? The Advaitist answers that the objects of specific sense-organs alone depend upon sensible qualities for their perception. But Brahman as Existence being apprehended by all the senses, it does not stand in any such need.[5]

Thus, Existence, according to the Advaitist, is the universal essence of all that appears to exist. It is uniformly apprehended as the 'being' of all empirical objects. The relation of Existence to empirical objects is, therefore, very intimate, viz., that of non-difference. The latter are

---

4. yataḥ sadātmanā na brahmaṇo mūlājñānenāvṛtatvam, kintu ghaṭādyavacchinna-śaktyajñānenaiva, tathā ca cakṣurādijanyavṛttyā tadāvaranabhaṅge sati 'san ghaṭaḥ' ityatra brahmaṇaḥ sphuraṇe bādhakābhāvāt. Ad. Sid., p. 318.
5. Ibid. The Advaitist points out further that the perceptibility of 'existence' by all the senses is accepted also by the Nyāya and the Mīmāṁsā. See Ad. Sid., and *Laghucandrikā*, p. 318.

the forms in which the universal Existence or Brahman appears in our consciousness. It is due to the immanence of the universal Existence in particular objects of experience that they are known and referred to as 'existents'. Now the question is, how does the Advaitist explain the general conceptions of things as 'cow', 'pot', etc.? If Existence is the only universal, as the Advaitist holds, then he is required to explain how we come to possess different class-concepts and how we make use of different class-names. The Advaitist answers these questions from his stand-point of absolute identity, rejecting the realist theory of universals as logically untenable. We would consider his criticism of the realist theory before discussing his answers to the above questions.

2. *Criticism of the realist theory of universals*

Citsukhācārya and Śrīharṣa advance a very subtle dialectic against the realist conception of universals. Their main contention is that the realist can neither formulate a satisfactory definition of the universal nor can he explain the relation of the universal to the particular in an intelligible manner. They examine five alternative definitions of the universal which the realist might advance and reject all of them as untenable. The realist might define the universal as (i) that which is the cause of general cognition, or (ii) that which is proved by general cognition, or (iii) that which is common, or (iv) that which is eternal and common, or (v) that which is an eternal unity inherent in many.[6] The Advaitist finds all these definitions to be logically indefensible.

(i) The definition of the universal as the cause of general cognition is too wide, since the cause of general cognition being complex, it includes several factors other than the universal, such as the cognitive apparatus and the co-existing qualities, etc. The present definition would apply to all these causal factors which are not admitted by the realist to be universals.[7] The realist might explain that by the term 'cause' he means the peculiar or the extraordinary cause and not the factors common to all cognitions. Such a cause is the universal and nothing else. Śrīharṣa points out that even after this explication the

6. tathā hi kimidaṁ sāmānyam? kimanuvṛttapratyayakāraṇam? utānuvṛttapratyayapramāṇakam? athavānuvṛttatvam? āhosvinnityatve satyanuvṛttatvam? athavā nityamekamanekasamavetam? TP, p. 319.
7. Ibid. Cf. KKK, p. 324.

definition is not satisfactory, since the universal, in the realist view, is not the cause of identical cognition alone, but also of differential cognition. The universal 'cowness', for instance, is the basis not only of the co-ordination of all the cows but also of their differentiation from other things. Hence the definition of the universal as the cause of general cognition is not precise.[8] The realist, however, would not care to defend this definition, since it is not, according to him also, a precise definition of the universal. The defect from which this definition suffers is that it applies also to general characteristics (*upādhis*) which are not admitted by him as universals (*jāti*).

(ii) The definition of the universal as 'that which is proved by general cognition' is also too wide, since what is proved by general cognition is not merely the universal, but also the other causal factors involved in its production.[9] The realist might explain that the universal is proved solely on the basis of general cognition, while other causal factors are proved by other evidences; for example, the organ of vision is proved by inference from the cognition of colour, the light is proved by perception, and so on. Śrīharṣa points out that even if the above explanation be admitted, the present definition suffers in another way. It is too narrow, since it applies only to the universals discovered through perception and not to those dicovered through reason. The realist admits universals proved solely by inference, for example, the universal determinants of specific causalities required by the identical causal functions of different things. The above definition would not apply to the universals discovered in this manner.[10]

The realist might try to make the above definition more satisfactory by a slight modification. He might define the universal as 'that of which general cognition is the only right cognition'. This definition would exclude the causal apparatus, as general cognition cannot be called the right cognition of them. Śrīharṣa points out that this definition is too wide, since it applies also to the particular qualified by the universal. Although general cognition is not the right cognition of a particular as particular, nevertheless when it is cognised in its universal character, the general cognition is the right cognition of it. If the above definition is said to mean that the universal is that of

8. KKK, p. 324.
9. TP, p. 319.
10. Loc. cit.

which right cognition (i.e. general cognition) pertains only to the generic character, then it would be circular. The generic character being what is sought to be defined, it cannot itself be an element in the definition. The realist might again try to define the universal as 'that without which no general notion is possible'. But this definition also is too wide, since there are many other things beside the universal without which general notion is impossible, for example, the contact of soul and mind. This would also be included within the scope of the definition of the universal.[11]

(iii) The definition of the universal as 'that which is common', is also too wide, since it would apply to conjunction (*saṁyoga*) and the composite whole (*avayavī*) which are common, but are not recognised by the realist as universals.

(iv) This definition which adds the qualification of eternality to the previous one is also too wide, though it succeeds in excluding conjunction and the composite whole from its scope. It applies to atoms which, in the realist's view, are both eternal and common to all composite objects from dyad onwards, but are not universals.[12]

(v) This definition of the universal as 'the eternal unity inherent in many' is considered by the Nyāya as the most satisfactory one. Citsukha subjects it to a subtle dialectical scrutiny and rejects it as untenable. He first raises the question as to what is meant by the qualification 'inherent in many'? It might possibly mean any one of the three things: (a) that which is inherent in what is qualified by the number 'manyness', or (b) that which is inherent in what is different from some substratum, or (c) that which is inherent in what is different from its own substratum.[13] In the first alternative the definition of the universal would be too narrow, as it would exclude from its scope the universals subsisting in qualities and actions. Number, according to the Nyāya, being a quality, it does not subsist in any category other than substance. In the second alternative, the definition would be too wide, since it would apply also to the ultimate particularity (*antyaviśeṣa*) and the colour of atoms which are not

11. See KKK, p. 325.
12. TP, p. 319; cf. KKK, p. 325. The third and the fourth definitions would be rejected also by the realist precisely for the same reason.
13. tathāhi kimanekatvasaṁkhyāviśiṣṭeṣu samavetatvamanekasamavetatvam? utāśrayapratiyogikānyo'nyābhāvavatsamavetatvam? āhosvitsvāśrayapratiyogikānyo'nyābhāvavatsamavetatvam? TP, p. 319.

universals. The third alternative involves circularity (*ātmāśraya*), as the universal itself enters in its own definition.[14]

Having thus disposed of the qualification 'inherent in many', Citsukha turns to the other qualification of 'eternality' which enters into the Nyāya definition of the universal. What, he asks, is meant by the 'eternality' of the universal? Does it mean (i) having an indestructible existence? or (ii) not being the counter correlative (*pratiyogī*) of destruction?, or (iii) not being the counter correlative of its own destruction?[15] The first alternative is ruled out since existence, according to the Nyāya, being itself a universal (*jāti*), cannot subsist in other universals. In the second alternative it must be explained what is meant by the 'counter correlativity' of destruction the absence of which makes the universal eternal. Does it mean being the determinant (*nirūpaka*) of destruction ? or not being co-existent with destruction? In either case, Citsukha maintains, the universal cannot escape from being the counter correlative of destruction. In the first case, in such propositions as 'destruction is other than the universal' (*jāterdhvaṁso 'nyaḥ*) the 'otherness' of destruction being defined by the universal, the destruction is determined by it, just as, in the expression 'the destruction of pot', the destruction is determined or defined by pot. Similarly, in the second case, universals, such as 'existence', 'substancehood', 'earthhood', etc., as subsisting in threads are not co-existent with the destruction of pot subsisting in the two halves of it. Thus in both the cases, the universal becomes the counter correlative of destruction.[16] The absence of such correlativity, which is said to constitute the eternality of the universal in the second alternative above, is therefore impossible. The third alternative also is not possible since the destruction of the universal itself being unknown (*aprasiddha*), the counter correlativity of that destruction also cannot be known. Hence the absence of such correlativity would be unthinkable.[17] Citsukha thus shows that the eternality of the universal asserted by the realist cannot be explained in any of the three possible ways considered above.

---

14. Ibid., pp. 319-20.
15. nityatvaṁ ca svapracyutyanupalakṣitasattāyogitvam? pradhvaṁsapratiyogitvānadhikaraṇatvaṁ vā? svapradhvaṁsapratiyogitvānadhikaraṇatvaṁ vā? Op. cit., p. 320.
16. Ibid.
17. jātipradhvaṁsasyaivāprasiddhatayā tatpratiyogitvasyāprasiddheḥ. Ibid., p. 321.

It may be asked, why does the Advaitist deny eternality in the case of universal when he himself asserts it in the case of Brahman? Citsukha explains that eternality is not asserted by the Advaitist as an attribute of Brahman, since the latter is attributeless. Brahman is called eternal because its destruction is not definable.[18] The opponent might argue that if indefinability of one's destruction is the criterion of one's eternality, then things like pot, etc., may also be regarded as eternal, since their destruction also is not definable. Citsukha answers that only that which is ultimately real and of which destruction is not definable, is called eternal. Things like pot, etc., are not ultimately real; hence they cannot be called eternal, even though their destruction is not definable.[19] There is, therefore, only one thing which can be called eternal and that is Brahman. The realist cannot claim such an eternality for the universal because, in his view, eternality is an attribute (*dharma*) common to the categories of universal, particularity and inherence.[20] The conception of eternality as an attribute being completely indefensible, as shown above, the realist view of universals as eternal entities is not acceptable at all.

The essence of the whole criticism of Citsukhācārya is that no logically precise and self-consistent definition of the universal (*jāti*) can be formulated by the realist. All the possible ways in which he might try to define the universal end in failure.[21] Having dealt with

---

18. brahmaṇo nirdharmakatayā nityatvadharmānadhikaraṇatvāt. kathaṁ tarhi tadvyapadeśa iti cet, vināśasya durnirūpatvāditi brūmaḥ. Ibid.
19. svarūpeṇa paramārthasya tadanirūpaṇe nityatvavyapadeśāt, ghaṭādeścātathātvāt. Ibid.
20. Reference here is to the following passage in *Praśastapādabhāṣya* on the *Vaiśeṣikasūtras*, p. 6, also quoted in TP and its commentary on p. 321. 'sāmānyādīnāṁ trayāṇāṁ svātmasattvaṁ buddhilakṣaṇatvam akāryatvama-kāraṇatvam asāmānyaviśeṣavattvaṁ nityatvam arthaśabdānabhidheyatvaṁ ca.'
21. The Nyāya would, however, maintain that the objections urged by Citsukha against his definition of the universal are not at all effective. 'Manyness' is nothing but 'being different from one' (*anekatvam ekabhinnatvam*—See Dink., p. 56), and in this sense qualities and actions are also many. So, his definition of the universal would apply also to the universals inhering in qualities and actions. Again, when the universal is said to be eternal, the Nyāya would urge, what is meant is that it has an eternal 'self-being' (*svātmasattva*) and not eternal 'existence' (*sattā*). So, no harm is done to the definition if existence does not inhere in universals. (See, for the distinction of 'being' and 'existence', Chapter II). Moreover, the universal according to the Nyāya, cannot be denied 'eternality', since it cannot be conceived as produced. Whatever is produced must have an inherent cause (*samavāyikāraṇa*) but the universal cannot have an inherent cause, since the particulars in which it inheres are never without it. Thus, the

the realist's definition of the universal, Citsukha proceeds to examine his contention that the existence of universals is undeniable, since it is a fact of experience. He argues that the realist's claim concerning the existence of universals is not supported by any evidence. It is proved neither by perception nor by inference. Class-notions are explainable on the basis of general characteristics of things revealing community of nature; there is no necessity of assuming the existence of universals at all. Besides, if the existence of universals is assumed, their subsistence in particulars becomes inexplicable.[22]

Citsukha attacks the realist contention that in our perceptual experience of particulars, e.g., of cows, we apprehend an identical form (*abhinnākāra*) which is a universal. He holds that this contention of the realist does not stand to logical scrutiny. What, he asks, is meant by the apprehension of an 'identical form'? Does it mean (i) the apprehension of different particulars as 'cow'? or (ii) the apprehension of the identical 'cow-nature' (*gosvabhāva*) of particulars? or (iii) the apprehension of particulars as substrates of the identical attribute 'cowness'? None of these alternatives, Citsukha argues, can be availed of by the realist to prove his point.[23]

The first alternative does not prove the existence of the universal 'cowness', since the apprehension of different particulars as 'cow' is explainable even otherwise. Different particulars, according to Citsukha, are cognised as 'cow' because each one of them has the same 'cow-nature' (*gosvabhāva*). In support of his contention he gives the analogy of the reflections of moon in different pots of water, each one of which is cognised as 'moon'.[24] The realist might ask here, do we cognise all particulars as 'cow', or only those which are cows? The Advaitist cannot take the first alternative, as it would amount to maintaining the absurd view that anything might be the object of any cognition. Nor can he take the second alternative, since it would amount to the recognition of the universal 'cowness' Citsukha

definition of the universal as 'eternal unity inherent in many', the Nyāya would claim, is absolutely faultless. It is clear that the Nyāya and the Advaita represent two opposite stand-points, and in their arguments regarding universals they are merely explicating their basic metaphysical intuitions.

22. pratyakṣādanumānādvā na jātih seddhumarhati,
vyañjakairanyathā siddhes tadvrtteścānirūpanāt. TP, p. 484.

23. Loc. cit.

24. ekavyaktergosvabhāvavadvyaktyantarasyāpi gosvabhāvatvādevāntareṇāpi sāmānyamanekodakabhājanesvayaṁ candro' yaṁ candra itivadavabhāsopapatteh. Loc cit.

answers that the cognition of different particulars as 'cow' can be explained on the basis of general characteristics, such as possession of dew-lap, etc., without assuming the existence of the universal 'cowness'.[25] Even the realist has to admit these general characteristics, otherwise it would be impossible for him to answer the question whether all particulars are capable of manifesting 'cowness', or only those possessing 'cowness'.[26]

The second alternative also, Citsukha maintains, is not possible for the realist, since he cannot admit all cows to have identical nature. Such an admission would go against his view of absolute difference between particulars. And if the said identity of nature is admitted, then the assumption of the universal (*jāti*) would become gratuitous. The identity of nature itself would be sufficient to explain general conceptions.[27] In the same way, the third alternative, which is actually the position held by the Nyāya, also is not possible. Citsukha maintains that we never apprehend a cow as the substrate of the universal 'cowness', just as we do in the case of 'a man with a stick'.[28] The form of our apprehension is 'this is cow' and not 'this has cowness'. This shows that 'cowness' as such is never apprehended as the common character qualifying all cows. Moreover, when the realist admits identical characteristics, such as having dew-lap, etc., revealing community of nature possessed by all cows, what is the necessity of assuming the universal 'cowness' at all? The said identical characteristics, Citsukha argues, would be quite sufficient to explain the general conception of 'cow'.[29]

---

25. sāsnādimadvyaktestanmatigocaratvāt. Op. cit. p. 485.
26. Ibid.
27. sarvatra gosvabhāvasyaikasyānirūpaṇāt, nirūpaṇe vā jātisvīkāravaiyarthyāt. Ibid.
28. daṇḍī daṇḍavānitivadgotvī gotvavāniti pratyayābhāvāt. Ibid.
29. sāsnādimattvadharmasyaikasya sarvatra pratibhāso' stīti cet, kṛtantarhi jātyā, tata evānuvṛttavyavahāropapatteḥ. Ibid.

    The author of *Vedāntaparibhāṣā* maintains that the perceptual cognition of the form 'this is pot' is evidence for the existence of 'potness', but not also for its being a generic essence (*jāti*). That is, 'potness', as an eternal essence inherent in all pots is never perceived. For this reason, the universal (*jāti*) cannot be proved even by inference, since what is not already established in perception, cannot also be validly inferred. Inference can prove of a subject only a predicate which is already established in perceptual experience. But that which is wholly unknown cannot be proved also by reason. (ghaṭo 'yam ityādipratyakṣṁ hi ghatatvādisadbhāve, mānaṁ na tu tasya jātitve 'pi jātitvarūpasādhyāprasiddhau tatsādhakānumānasyāpyanavakāśāt.) Ved. Par., p, 193.

Thus the universal (*jāti*), according to Citsukha, is neither a perceptual fact, nor is its assumption necessitated by the existence of general conceptions. The realist view of universals, therefore, has no leg to stand on. Further, the realist's conception of universals, Citsukha argues, is fraught with unsurmountable difficulties. He has to explain why the universal, which is by hypothesis ubiquitous, has a limited manifestation. If it is said to be due to the dependence of the universal on a manifester (*vyañjaka*), then the location of the latter will have to be explained. If the manifester is said to be located where the universal is, there would be mutual dependence (*anyo 'nyāśrayatā*). If in order to explain the location of both, the universal and its manifester, a second manifester is assumed, there would be infinite regress. And if the second manifester is not assumed, the universal and its manifester would be everywhere without any limitation, resulting in the confusion of all universals (*jātisāṅkarya*).[30] Citsukha thus shows that the realist theory of ubiquitous universals manifested by specific characteristics belonging to particulars is not logically defensible, since the possession of those characteristics itself requires explanation.

The realist, however, might appeal to experience and say that the universal is located where it is apprehended. If so, Citsukha points out, the assumption of the manifester becomes quite unnecessary. Besides, the evidence of experience in itself cannot be regarded as infallible, since otherwise we would have to admit the perceived blue colour of the sky, which we know to be unreal, to be real.[31] Therefore, experience must be supported by reason in order to be accepted as valid. It is not sufficient that a valid experience must not be contradicted by another experience, but it must also not be contradicted by reason. Only such an experience can be accepted as a proof of reality. The said apprehension of the universal cannot be accepted as the proof of its reality, since, as has already been shown, it is contradicted by reason.[32] Moreover, Citsukha argues, even the realist admits a general characteristic (*upādhi*) in order to explain the general conception of universals themselves. Such characteristics may be

30. TP, p. 485. Cf. TMK, V, 117 and SS on it, p. 313.
31. pratītimātrācca tathātvāṅgīkāre, nabhonīlimāderapi tathātvāpātaḥ. TP, p. 486.
32. abādhitapratītervyavasthāpakatvāṅgīkāre vehāpi yuktibādhasya suvacatvena na tādrśapratīterapi vyavasthāpakatā. Ibid., p. 486.

admitted to explain general conceptions in all cases. What is the necessity of assuming universals (*jāti*) at all?[33]

The realist has to explain further the subsistence of universals in particulars, which involves formidable difficulties. The question is, whether universals subsist everywhere (*sarvasarvagata*) or only in their own particulars (*vyaktisarvagata*). On either alternative the subsistence of universals defies explanation. If universals are said to subsist everywhere, whether by identity (*tādātmya*) or by inherence (*samavāya*),[34] all things would belong to all classes, eliminating all class-distinctions. The realist may urge that the universal, e.g., 'cowness', though present everywhere, is perceived only in particular cows, since they alone have the power to manifest it. This argument, according to Citsukha, is not sound, because, if 'cowness' subsists everywhere, then the power to manifest it cannot legitimately be confined to the particular cows only.[35] The realist may argue that the ultimate nature of things is unquestionable. Certain particulars manifest 'cowness' and others do not because they have peculiar natures. Citsukha considers this appeal to the peculiarity of natures as unwarranted. If the subsistence of the universal 'cowness' everywhere was proved independently by some valid means of knowledge, then the peculiarity of natures could be assumed to explain its non-appearance in particulars other than cows. But the peculiarity of nature by itself cannot be admitted as a proof of the subsistence of the universal everywhere, i. e., even where it does not appear. Otherwise, how shall we prove the falsity of one's statement if he asserts that air also has colour, but it does not manifest it because

33. kiñca jātisvīkāravādināpīyaṁ jātiriyaṁ jātirityanuvṛttapratyayasiddhaye kaścidupādhireṣṭavyaḥ, tathā ca sārvatrikaḥ sa evānuvṛttapratyayakāraṇamastu tadalaṁ jātikalpanādurvyasanena. Ibid., p. 486.

According to the author of *Vedāntaparibhāṣā*, the distinction of the universal (*jāti*) and general characteristic (*upādhi*) is inadmissible, since it is not established by any valid means of cognition. Besides, he argues, the relation of inherence (*samavāya*) itself being unproved and nothing except Brahman being admissible as eternal the eternal and inherent universal (*jāti*) of the realist is not established. In the same way the general characteristic (*upādhi*) is also to be rejected (jātitvopādhitvaparibhāṣāyāḥ sakalapramāṇāgocaratayāprām-āṇikatvāt......samavāyāsiddhyā brahmabhinnasakalaprapañcasyānityatayā ca nityatvasamavetatvaghaṭitajātītvasya ghaṭatvādāvasiddheśca. evamevopādhitvaṁ nirasanīyam. Ved. Par., p. 19.

34. The reference here is to the views of both the Nyāya-Vaiśeṣika and the Mīmāṁsā.

35. TP, p. 487.

of its peculiar nature?[36] The essence of Citsukha's argument is that if the universal, e.g., 'cowness', subsists everywhere, it must be manifest in every place, i.e., even in non-cows. But since this is not so, it cannot be accepted as ubiquitous. He rejects the realist argument that 'cowness', though present everywhere, is manifest in some particulars and non-manifest in others due to their peculiar natures as unsound, since the subsistence of 'cowness' everywhere is itself unproved.

The other alternative, viz., that the universal subsists in its particulars only (*vyaktisarvagata*), also does not stand to logical scrutiny. It fails to explain, as has already been shown by the Buddhist, how a new-born thing becomes related to its universal (*jāti*) which is, by hypothesis, immovable, impartite and confined to its own substrates. The realist has explained that a particular coming into being becomes immediately related to its appropriate class-essence (*jāti*) due to its own causal factors. Citsukha contends that this relation is impossible, since the universal, by assumption, being absent from the locality where a thing is produced, the two cannot become related.[37] Moreover, he points out, universals subsisting in composite objects, on this view, must perish when all their substrates are destroyed at the time of deluge, since they will have no substratum to subsist in. And if they are said to subsist by themselves (*svarūpenāvasthānam*) when there are no composite objects, then qualities also might claim to be eternal inspite of the destruction of their substrates. Hence, Citsukha concludes, the realist conception of universals as eternal class-essences (*jāti*) is absolutely indefensible.[38]

3. *The Advaitic explanation of general cognition*

Citsukha in his criticism of the realist theory of universals has maintained that class-notions are explainable even without admitting the universal (*jāti*). They are, according to him, based on observed general characteristics (*upādhi*) possessed by particular things. The concept of cow, for instance, is based on the characteristics of having dew-lap, etc., common to all the particular cows. Similarly, all

---

36. siddhe pramāṇataḥ sarvatra sambandhe svabhāvabhedālambanam, na tu svabhāvavādapadaprasārikayaiva vastusiddhiḥ, anyathāstyeva pavanādāvapi rūpasaṁbhedaḥ svabhāvabhedādevāpratītirityanargalagarjanasya kah pratikārah syāt? Ibid., p. 488.
37. Ibid.
38. Ibid., p. 489.

concepts are explainable without admitting eternal and ubiquitous universals advocated by the realist. Citsukha has also argued that there is no evidence for the existence of such universals. They are neither facts of experience nor are they necessarily implied by our general cognitions. Besides, the assumption of universals as real entities involves serious difficulties which the realist fails to answer in a satisfactory manner.

According to Madhusūdana Sarasvatī, only one universal is admissible to the Advaita and that is the universal *Being* (*sattā*). All general conceptions are explainable on the basis of this one universal.[39] His main argument is that even if the universals of the realist's conception, such as 'cowness', etc., are admitted, it has to be explained what determines their limited manifestation. The manifestation of a universal by certain particulars alone cannot be said to be determined by another universal, since such a process would involve infinite regress. Ultimately, therefore, particulars, with or without common features, have to be admitted as manifesters of universals by their own nature. This being so, Madhusūdana argues, there is no justification for postulating a plurality of universals. What the realist seeks to explain by means of diverse universals, viz., the diversity of class-notions, can be explained on the basis of one universal *Existence.* One and the same universal Existence, according to Madhusūdana, as qualified or determined by specific particulars, may very well be admitted to serve as the basis of diverse class-conceptions. The concept of 'cow', for example, is based on the universal Existence determined by any one (*anyatama*) of the particulars which, in the realist view, are regarded as the substrates of the universal 'cowness'. All class-concepts, according to the Advaitist, are explainable in the same manner.[40]

Brahmānanda anticipates some objections against the Advaitic theory as set out above. The realist may argue that if universals are not admitted, words would not have identity of meaning. If the meaning of the word 'cow' is, as the Advaitist maintains, 'the Existence

39. satsāmānyātiriktagotvādisāmānyānabhyupagamāt gotvādyabhyupagame 'pi gotvādivyañjakatāvacchedakasāmānyānabhyupagamāt vyaktiviśeṣāṇāmevānanugatānāṁ sāsnādimattvādyupādhyanugatānāṁ vā tadvyañjakatvavad vyaktiviśeṣaviśiṣṭatvena satsāmānyasyaiva tattadvyavahārajanakatvopapatteḥ. Ad. Sid., p. 316.

40. gotvajātimattvena parābhimatāḥ yāvatyo vyaktayaḥ tāvadanyatamoparaktasadrūpaṁ gaurityākāravyavahāre kāraṇam, evaṁ ghata ityākāravyavahāre 'pi bodhyam. *Laghucandrikā*, p. 316.

determined by the particular cow' (*tadvyaktiviśiṣṭasadrūpa*), or 'the particular cow determined by existence' (*sadrūpaviśiṣṭatadvyakti*), then the word would have diversity of meaning, since there is no common determinant subsisting in all the cows. Similarly, in the absence of the universal determinant, viz., 'cowness', the causal functions of the particular cows would also be diverse. Consequently, the identical cognition of them as 'cow' would be impossible. To avoid these difficulties, the realist would urge, the universal (*jāti*) has to be recognised.

Brahmānanda answers that the meaning of a word and also the causality of particulars may be identical without being determined by a universal. The meaning (*artha*) of the word 'cow', he maintains, would not be diverse as alleged, since the word 'cow' may have an identical potency (*śakti*) for denoting all the particular cows.[41] But how, it may be asked, in the absence of a common determinant, viz., 'cowness', can the diverse particular cows be regarded as the contents of an identical meaning? Brahmānanda answers that, in his view, the word 'cow' has, potency (*śakti*) to produce the cognition of all the particular cows inspite of their diversity. This potency is of the nature of undivided causality (*akhaṇḍakāraṇatārūpā*) and the effect produced by it, viz., the cognition of particulars, is also undivided. There is no evidence, according to him, for their being determined (*avacchinna*); hence, no attribute as their determinant (*avacchedaka*) is admissible.[42] The Advaitist may also point out here that, in the realist view, diverse particulars are held to be the substrates or manifesters of an identical universal without being determined by another universal. So, the realist can have no legitimate objection to the diverse particulars being the contents of an identical meaning without being determined by a universal (*jāti*).

41. sarvagovyaktiṣu ekasyā eva śakteḥ sambhavena nānārthakatvābhāvāt. Ibid., p. 317.

42. tāvadvyaktidhījananānukūlā śaktirgopade svīkriyate, sā cākhaṇḍakāraṇatārūpā, uktadhīniṣṭhā kāryatāpyakhaṇḍā, tayoścāvacchinnatve mānābhāvāt na ko' pi dharmaḥ tadīyākhaṇḍāvacchedakatāśrayaḥ. Ibid., p. 317.

The potency of a word to produce the cognition of its meaning is, according to the Advaitist, an independent category, since, in his view, whatever capacity belongs to causes favourable to the production of an effect is a category by itself. The potency of words is known by inference from the cognition of respective objects generated by them.

sā ca śaktiḥ padārthāntaram, siddhānte kāraneṣu kāryānukūlaśaktimātrasya padārthāntaratvāt. sā ca tattatpadajanyapadārthajñānarūpakāryānumeyā. Ved. Par., p. 70.

Brahmānanda further maintains that, like the potency (*śakti*) of the word, the causality belonging to the knowledge of this potency, which is indispensable for verbal cognition, is also identical.[43] It would be agreed by all that for verbal cognition to take place two conditions are essential: (1) the word must have meaning and (2) the meaning must be known to the listener. The meaning of the word has been held to be of the nature of undivided (*akhaṇḍa*) and undetermined (*niravacchinna*) causality. Likewise, the causality belonging to the knowledge of this meaning also, according to Brahmānanda, is undivided and undetermined. The apprehension of the meaning of the word 'cow', for instance, as 'that particular qualified by existence' (*sadrūpaviśiṣṭatadvyakti*) has an undivided and undetermined causality for producing the cognition of 'that particular' whenever the word 'cow' is heard. What is meant by the phrase 'that particular' (*tadvyakti*) is, Brahmānanda explains, not a specific particular cow, but 'one of the particulars' (*anyatama*) which the realist regards as the substrates of the universal 'cowness'.[44] Thus the meaning of the word 'cow', according to Brahmānanda, is apprehended indifferently as cow and not as 'this' or 'that' cow, and , therefore, this apprehension produces indifferently the cognition of cow when the word 'cow' is heard. That is to say, the meaning of a word and its apprehension are always general, and the cognition of objects produced by them is also general. Thus there is no possibility of diversity of meaning as alleged by the realist. Brahmānanda further claims that in his view there is also no possibility of any confusion in the cognition of the meaning of different words. The meaning of the word 'pot', for instance, having been apprehended as 'that particular' (*tadvyakti*) in the sense explained above, there is no possibility of any other thing, say cow, being cognised when the word 'pot' is heard. The apprehended meaning of the word 'pot' does not possess any other efficiency.[45] Every word, according to the Advaitist, has specific potency (*śakti*) which is undivided and undetermined, and it produces in the mind of one who has apprehended it the cognition of its appropriate object.

Thus the causality (*śakti*) of a word and that of the knowledge of its meaning, according to the Advaitist, are identical and

---

43. ata eva śaktigrahaniṣṭhakāranatvamapyekameva. *Laghucandrikā*, p. 317.
44. gotvajātyāśrayatvena parābhimatavyaktīnāmanyatamasyaiva tadvyaktiśabdena kāraṇakāryakoṭyorniveśāt. Ibid., p. 317.
45. Ibid.

undetermined. In the same way, the Advaitist contends, the causality of particular things may also be identical without being determined by a class-essence (*jāti*). Diverse particulars may have an identical causality by their very nature, just as they have, in the realist view, an identical class-essence. The realist may urge that even if the causality of diverse particulars be admitted to be identical, its knowledge cannot be explained without admitting universals. The causality of cows, for example, is known through the knowledge of positive and negative concomitance (*anvayavyatirekajñāna*) between cows and their functions. Such knowledge would not be possible unless the particular cows, with regard to which the said relation is apprehended, are known to be of the same class (*jāti*), i.e., to be the instances of the universal 'cowness'. Hence, if the universal is not admitted, the knowledge of the causality of particular things would be impossible.

Brahmānanda replies that the knowledge of the causality of things can be explained even without admitting universals. He gives the example of the causality of fire belonging to grass (*tṛṇa*), wood (*araṇi*) and jewel (*maṇi*). We come to know this causality by observing a few particulars invariably producing fire. This knowledge is first confined to those particulars which we have actually observed to produce fire repeatedly. Subsequently when some other particular is seen to produce fire, we infer the existence of the same causality in that particular also. It is not that we come to know the causality of fire only when we have known all the particulars actually possessing it.[46] Brahmānanda further points out that we cannot confine the said causality to the particulars of any definite kind (*jāti*). It is seen to belong to grass, wood and jewel, which are of different kinds, and also to other kinds of things, such as oil, ghee, flesh, etc. So the causality of fire cannot be said to be determined by the class-essence (*jāti*) of a thing, nor can the knowledge of this causality be said to depend on the knowledge of this class-essence.[47]

The essence of Brahmānanda's contention is that the universal is required neither for explaining the identical causality possessed by diverse things, nor is it required to explain the knowledge of this causality. Things possess identical causality by their own nature and

46. tṛṇāraṇimaṇyādisthala ivopasthitānāṁ tricaturādivyaktīnāṁ pratyekānvayavyatirekajñānena kāraṇatā tāsveva prathamato gṛhyate, paścād vyaktyantarādapi kāryotpattidarśanāttatrāpi tasyāḥ sambandho' stīti kalpyate, na tu sarvakāraṇavyaktīnāmanvayavyatirekadhīstadgrāhikā. Ibid., p. 317.
47. Ibid. For the discussion of the Nyāya view on this point see the second chapter.

it is inferred from the identical effects which they are observed to produce. It is not necessary that a specific causality be possessed by a specific kind of things; different kinds of things might possess identical causality. Also it is not necessary that things be known as the instances of a universal in order to know the causality belonging to them. We come to know specific causalities in particular cases and on the strength of that we generalise. Such generalisations, therefore, do not presuppose universals.

Brahmānanda repudiates the realist contention that causality is always apprehended as determined by a universal. He points out that Raghunātha Śiromaṇi, the author of *Dīdhiti*, has admitted that in the apprehension 'smoke is pervaded by fire' (*dhūmo vahnivyāpya*) no 'smokeness' is felt as the determinant of pervadedness (*vyāpyatāvacchedaka*). In the same way, Brahmānanda argues, in the apprehension, e.g., 'the stick is the cause of pot', no 'stickness' is felt as the determinant of causality.[48] It may be urged that causality cannot be undetermined, otherwise anything might be the cause of anything. The universals determining the causality of things, therefore, have to be recognised. Brahmānanda replies that the determination of causality is explainable even without admitting universals. The universal Existence itself in specific determinations may be regarded as the determinant of specific causalities. For example, the determinant of the causality belonging to particular cows is the universal Existence as related to any one of (*anyatama*) the particular cows.[49] The relation of 'being any one of' (*anyatamatva*), by which Existence is said to serve as the determinant of specific causalities is indeed of the nature of differentiation or exclusion. Thus, to be a 'cow' is to be 'any one of' those existents which are differentiated from other existents. Existence thus determined or related in various ways which are general and exclusive can perfectly serve as the determinant of various causalities. There is, therefore, no necessity of admitting a plurality of class-essences (*jāti*) in order to explain the determinate causality belonging to particular things.[50]

48. 'daṇḍo ghaṭakāraṇam' ityādyanubhave daṇḍatvādeḥ kāraṇatāvacchedakatvābhānāt. Ibid., p. 317.

49. tāvadvyaktīnāṁ yāvanti sadrūpeṇa saha tādātmyāni tāvadanyatamatvaviśiṣṭasambandhena sadrūpaviśiṣṭaṁ gauriti vyavahāraviṣayaḥ tena sambandhena sadrūpaṁ tattatkāraṇatāderavacchedakam. Ibid., p. 317.

50. Brahmānanda quotes Bhartṛhari in support of his own view. Bhartṛhari maintains that Existence itself due to diversity of relations is called the class-essence (*jāti*) of things such as cow, horse, etc. It is to this that all words refer. It is the

Brahmānanda thus denies that there is any justification for admitting the universals of the realist conception. The reasons for which universals are admitted by the realist, viz., for explaining class-distinctions, the identity of the meaning of words and the determinate causality of particulars, are, according to him, without force, since these are explainable, as has been shown above, even without admitting universals. As a matter of fact, what the Advaitist rejects is the plurality of eternal and ubiquitous class-essences advocated by the realist. He is indeed not averse to admitting universals as the bases of class-notions in a different form. As Brahmānanda says, universals are acceptable to the Advaitist in two forms, either as *specific forms of Existence,* or as *determinate potencies of nescience.*[51] In the first case, as we have seen, universals are nothing but Existence in specific determinations or relations. 'Potness', 'cowness', etc., are Existence determined by the particular pots, cows and so on. In the second case, they are the diverse *potencies* (*śaktiviśeṣa*) in the form of which the *primal nescience* projects itself. The various capacities which the particular things are found to possess are, according to the Advaitist, determinate forms of the *cosmic nescience.* They are universals, since they are identically manifested by diverse particulars. Universals in these two forms, the Advaitist holds, are sufficient to explain general cognition and general designation of particular things. There is no necessity whatever of admitting a plurality of eternal and ubiquitous class-essences as the realist does.

It has been said above that universals are determinate forms of *cosmic ignorance* (*mūlāvidyā*). One might ask, what are their objects? This question arises because an ignorance cannot, presumably, be mere ignorance; it must be the ignorance or concealment of something. If, therefore, universals are specific forms of ignorance, what do they conceal? If the universal is said to be the ignorance concealing particulars, then it must be dispelled as soon as the particulars are known. And if it is said to be the ignorance concealing Brahman, then the diversity of universals would be impossible, since

universal Existence which constitutes the 'ness' (*tva*) of everything:
sambandhibhedāt sattaiva bhidyamānā gavādisu,
jātirityucyate tasyāṁ sarve śabdā vyavasthitāḥ.
sā jātiḥ sā mahāsattā tāmāhustvatalādayaḥ. Quoted in *Laghucandrikā*, p. 317. Cp. VP, III, 33-34.

51. jātīnāṁ sadrūpatvam avidyāśaktiviśeṣarūpatvaṁ veti pakṣadvayam asmadīyaiḥ kaiyyaṭādibhiścācāryairuktam. *Laghucandrikā*, p. 317.

the ignorance concealing one and the same object cannot be regarded as diverse. Brahmānanda explains that, in the Advaitic view, ignorance (*avidyā*) has dual aspects; the aspect of concealing (*āvaraṇa*) and the aspect of projection (*vikṣepa*). In the former aspect, ignorance is indeed concealment of something, i.e., it has object. But in the latter aspect it has no object, since it is ignorance in a positive role. It is not the concealment of something, but projection of itself in variety of forms. There are, therefore, infinite number of causally efficient projected potencies of the original nescience which are objectless.[52] These potencies, according to the Advaitist, are universals. 'Potness', for example, is nothing but a specific potency of the original nescience determined by the particular pots and favourable to the purpose of carrying water, etc. In the same way all universals are to be understood.[53]

4. *Concluding remarks*

It is plain from the foregoing discussion that the Advaitist approaches the question of universals from the stand-point of absolute identity. This is the main reason why he rejects the plurality of ultimate and eternal universals advocated by the realist. Such a plurality would not evidently be compatible with his fundamental stand-point. The Advaitist admits two levels of existence; the ultimate (*paramārtha*) and the phenomenal or the empirical (*vyavahāra*). The ultimately real is the undifferentiated universal Being, or Brahman, which is invariably given in all experience. And the phenomenally real are the diverse particulars constituting the objects of our empirical knowledge. The universal of the realist conception, according to the Advaitic view, finds place in neither of these two levels.

The Advaitist rejects the realist theory of universals not merely on the ground of its incompatibility with his own view of reality, but also for certain independent reasons. The universals of the realist, the Advaitist holds, have no evidence for their existence. They are neither perceptual entities like particulars, nor are they necessarily implied by our knowledge of things. Besides, the assumption of unversals as real entities on par with particulars leads to a host of difficulties which prove, for the realist, to be unsurmountable.

---

52. anantā hi mūlājñānīyāḥ kāryajananānukūlāḥ vikṣepanāmakaśaktayo nirviṣayikāḥ, āvaraṇaśaktereva saviṣayakatvāt. Ibid., p. 317.

53. tathā ca ghaṭavyaktibhiravacchinnā jalāharaṇādikāryānukūlā tādrśaśaktih ghaṭatvam, evaṁ paṭatvādikamapīti na ko 'pi doṣaḥ. Ibid., p. 317.

Having rejected the realist's conception of universals, the Advaitist is required to explain how general conceptions and classifications of things become possible. Citsukha tries to answer this question on the basis of general characteristics possessed by the particular things. He maintains that all general conceptions and classifications are explainable on the basis of observed general characteristics (*upādhis*) without assuming universals (*jāti*). Unfortunately Citsukha does not elaborate upon this point, for he is primarily interested in the refutation of the realist's view. The question is, how are we to understand the general characteristics which are said to be the bases of general conceptions and classifications of things? Are they identical qualities, such as shapes, etc., or similarities ? The example given by Citsukha is that of the concept of 'cow'. He says that this concept is based on the observation of a specific shape (dew-lap, etc.) possessed by the particular cows. But he does not explain how he conceives this shape, etc. Are the shapes possessed by the particular cows identical ? This would be controverted by the realist. He would maintain that the shape of each particular cow is as particular as the cow itself. If, on the other hand, the shapes are said to be similar, then it must be explained how the similarity of shapes is to be understood. Is it to be understood as a partial identity or as an independent relation by itself? The latter position would not be acceptable to the Advaitist, since identity for him is fundamental. In the former position he has to specify what is identical in the shapes of diverse particular cows. Unfortunately Citsukha does not consider these questions at all and consequently his position on the question of general conception of things is not very clear. This much seems to be certain that he does not regard general conceptions as pure fabrications of thought as the Buddhist does. For him they have basis in the empirical experience of particulars. But what is the nature of this basis (whether it is identity or similarity) is not clear from his discussion of this problem. However, since he rejects the reality of universals, his position may be characterised as conceptualistic.

A clearer account of the Advaitic position on the question of universals is given by Madhusūdana Sarasvatī and his commentator Brahmānanda. Madhusūdana maintains that there is no necessity of admitting a plurality of ultimate and eternal universals in order to explain general conceptions of particulars. One Universal *Being* (*mahāsāmānya*) determined or related in various manners may serve as the basis of diverse conceptions. In other words, the plurality of class-concepts and class-names, according to the Advaitist, does not imply an ultimate plurality of unversals (*jāti*). It implies only that there must be some basis for it in empirical experience. This basis is provided by the universal *Being* variously determined by the particular appearances.

The Advaitist evidently agrees with the realist's contention that class-concepts are rooted in the apprehension of identity. But this identity, for him, is nothing other than the identity of Existence. That is, the identity corresponding to class-concepts is the universal Existence itself. How, then, it may be asked, does the diversity of concepts arise? The Advaitist explains that the diversity of class-concepts is due to the diverse ways in which Existence is revealed by the particulars in empirical experience. The universal Existence which is the identical substratum of all particular appearances is apprehended as divided or diversified in so many ways due to the force of primordial nescience. The extreme division is in the form of empirical particulars. The other divisions are in the form of classes or categories having different degrees of comprehensiveness. These categories of Existence, according to the Advaitist, are the universals corresponding to concepts and words.

The main contention of the Advaitist is that when one universal Existence variously determined by particulars can explain diverse class-conceptions, there is no necessity of assuming a plurality of universals. Even the realist, the Advaitist points out, has to appeal to the nature of particulars for explaining the manifestation of universals. In the same way, it can be maintained that particulars by their own nature reveal the universal Existence in diverse forms. These forms are the universals (*jāti*) corresponding to our class-notions; they are phenomenally real, but ultimately they are non-different from Existence.

A question naturally arises as to whether, like the universals of the realist, the universal Existence of the Advaitist also may not be dispensed with? When particulars by their very nature, or by virtue of their properties, fall into distinct classes, what is the necessity of assuming the universal Existence? These distinctions may themselves serve as the basis of class-concepts. The Advaitist answers that this position may be held by the Buddhist who does not accept the identity of Existence at all. But, in his view, Existence, which is identically and invariably felt in the apprehensions of particulars, cannot be dispensed with. It is given as the universal substratum of all particular appearances.

Moreover, the Advaitist would maintain with the realist that class-concepts refer to identities and not merely to differences. He would, however, reject that there is any real plurality of such identities, just as he would reject that there are any real differences. But the identity of particulars felt in their general conceptions must be accounted for This identity, according to him, is the identity of Existence which, due to determination by particular appearances, is apprehended in diverse *names and forms* (*nāma-rūpa*).

It would be worth contrasting the Advaitic view of universals with that of the Buddhist. The Advaitist and the Buddhist approach the problem of universals from two opposite directions. While, for the former, identity is ultimate and diversity, whether of universals or particulars, is merely apparent, for the latter, diversity is ultimate and all identities, including the identity of existence, are conceptual constructions. Both would however agree that universals (*jāti*) are categories rooted in transcendental illusion (*avidyā*). But they would differ radically in their conceptions of this category. For the Advaitist, universals are false determinations (*nāma-rūpa*) of the ultimate identity of Existence, while, for the Buddhist, they are false determinations of the ultimate diversity of particular existents. For the former, they are diversifications of the identical, while, for the latter, they are identifications of the diverse. For the former, the universal is real as Existence, but, for the latter, it is merely a concept or a name. For the Advaitist, universals, as forms of Existence, are apprehended in perception, but, for the Buddhist, they are non-perceptual or purely conceptual fictions. The difference between the Advaitist and the Buddhist view arises from their diametrically opposed standpoints. The problem for the Advaitist is to explain the experience of diversity while identity is given, whereas that for the Buddhist is to explain the experience of identity while diversity is given. It is due to this fundamental difference that their views on universals are divergent.

The Advaitist view of universals is thus different from both the Nyāya-Mīmāṁsā realism and the Buddhist nominalism. Universals, for him, are neither eternal entities qualifying particulars, nor are they mere names. They are categories of Existence, generated by primordial nescience, lending unity to our knowledge of particulars. They are not mere concepts or fabrications of the individual mind. They are forms of Existence apprehended in empirical experience. Universals thus conceived are, for the Advaitist, empirically real, though ultimately illusory. It is noteworthy that universals as forms of Existence are regarded by the Advaitist not as predicates of particulars, but as subjects of which particulars are predicates. Just as Existence is the ultimate universal (*sādhāraṇa*) substratum of all particular appearances, so universals, as categories of Existence, are their limited (*asādhāraṇa*) substrata.[54] Particulars, therefore, are related to universals as appearance to reality. This means that universals, for the Advaitist, are on a higher level of existence than the particulars. What is called empirical (*vyavahāra*) level of existence would thus include objects belonging to two different orders: the universal and the particular. Universals, though empirical like particulars, are not the same kind of objects as particulars are. They are not spatio-temporal entities, but forms of Existence of which particulars are instances. Universals in themselves are never perceived; they are always perceived as embodied in the particulars. Similarly, particulars are never perceived as bare particulars, but always as instances of some universal. Our empirical knowledge thus involves both the universal and the particular elements. Both of them are epistemologically real—universals as forms of Existence and particulars as their instances—though ultimately they are illusory appearances of the universal Existence. The Advaitic position on universals is, therefore, neither realistic nor nominalistic. It may be characterised as a kind of conceptualism, or even as moderate realism, since some kind of objective basis for general concepts is recognised.

54. See *Laghucandrikā*, p. 317.

CHAPTER VIII

IMPORT OF WORDS

The problem of universals in Indian philosophy is intimately connected with the problem of the import of words. Just as the controversy over universals arises from the attempt to explain the generality of our cognitions, so does a similar controversy arise from the attempt to explain the generality of words and their meanings. It is a strange and significant fact that almost all words in our language, with the exception of proper names, are general. The primary function of these words is to provide means for communicating our thoughts to one another. It is due to the presence of general words in our language that extension of thought beyond the immediately here and now becomes possible. It is, therefore, of primary importance to ask: what do these general words stand for? what, indeed, is the part of language in our cognitions? Are words adequate expressions of reality? The answers given to these questions in Indian philosophy are varied and conflicting. The realist holds words to be adequate expressions of reality, while the Buddhist maintains that they are expressions of illusory constructions of thought. Even amongst the realists there is controversy over the question whether words stand for the individual, or the universal, or both. All the systems of Indian philosophy make significant contributions on this question. We shall discuss some important views on this subject in the present and the following chapters.

There are four distinct kinds of theories advocated by the realists: (i) the Individualist theory, for which the individual is the import of words; (ii) the Configuration (*ākṛti*) theory, according to which a specific conjunction of parts is the denotation of words; (iii) the Universalist theory, for which the universal alone is the denoted meaning of words; and (iv) the theory of Composite denotation, according to which all the three, namely, the individual, the configuration and the universal, are the contents of the meaning of words.

1. *The Individualist theory*

The protagonists of this view argue that there are many expressions in our language which can be said to refer neither to the universal (*jāti*) nor to the configuration (*ākṛti*), but to the individual (*vyakti*) alone. The Nyāya Sūtras enumerate some such expressions.[1] For example, all usages involving (a) the term 'that which', (b) grouping, (c) giving, (d) possession, (e) number, (f) enlargement, (g) contraction, (h) colour, (i) compounding and (j) procreation are such that they cannot pertain to anything except the individual. These expressions involve qualifications and it is the individual alone which can be qualified.[2] The universal which is identical and uniform in all the individuals cannot be the subject of these qualifications. We definitely mean the individual when we say 'that cow which is sitting' or 'that cow which is grazing'. Again the harmony between action and command can be achieved only with reference to the individual; the command 'bring a cow' calls for an action with reference to an individual and not to a universal or configuration. Similarly, the application of number, increase or decrease, or the notion of ownership can be possible only with reference to the individual. We will surely indulge in non-sense if we speak of a universal as moving or staying, or of owning a configuration having a certain colour. Further, the content of perceptual cognition, the Individualist argues, being the individual and not the universal, the former alone can legitimately be regarded as the import of words.[3]

Explaining his point further, the Individualist says that a word can denote only that which is capable of being connected with qualifications, since the adjective (*viśeṣaṇa*) and the substantive (*viśeṣya*) terms must both refer to one and the same thing.[4] That is, if the word denoted something which was incapable of any qualifications, then our expressions involving qualifications would become meaningless, as the thing signified and the thing qualified would fall asunder. For example, in the expression 'the cow is standing', if the word 'cow' did not denote the individual which is

---

1. yāśabdasamūhatyāgaparigrahasaṁkhyāvṛddhyapacayavarṇasamāsānubandhānāṁ vyaktāvupacārād vyaktiḥ. NS, II, ii, 61.
2. By the individual is meant that composite material body which is the substrate of distinctive qualities: vyaktirguṇaviśeṣāśrayo mūrtiḥ. Ibid., II, ii, 68.
3. See NM, I, p. 319.
4. viśeṣaṇaviśeṣyabhāvasyaikaviṣayatvāt. NV, p. 312.

referred to as 'standing', then the above expression would be nonsensical. The expression would be meaningful only if the word 'cow' denotes the same thing which is the subject of qualification 'is standing'. Only in such a condition can the word 'cow' serve its purpose of excluding other things and the qualification 'is standing' perform its function of excluding other actions. Under no other circumstance the coordination between the substantive term (cow) and the adjective term 'is standing' is possible.[5]

The principal objection raised against this theory is that it asserts the individual, pure and simple, without any reference to the universal, as the import of words. If the word 'cow', for instance, denoted the 'bare individual', then it might denote any individual, not necessarily the one belonging to the class 'cow'. Therefore, the word 'cow' appearing in such expressions as 'that cow which is standing' cannot be said to denote the bare individual without any reference to the class to which the latter belongs; it can denote the individual only as qualified by the universal. Again, the conception of all the individuals belonging to a class being absolutely impossible, the full relationship of a word with its meaning can never be apprehended, and, consequently, the communication of thought by means of words would be impossible. Besides, if the import of a word, say 'jar', is apprehended in respect of a particular jar, then it will be illegitimate to use the same term for denoting another jar, since the relation of that term with the latter has not been established. For these reasons the individualist theory of the import of words is considered to be unsatisfactory.[6]

2. *The Configuration theory*

This theory holds that it is the configuration (*ākṛti*) which is denoted by a word, because the determination of the exact nature of a thing is dependent on it.[7] *Ākṛti* is defined in the Nyāya Sūtras as 'that which signifies the universal'.[8] It is nothing apart from the particular arrangement of the parts of an object and the components of those parts. The apprehension of these parts arranged in a specific manner leads to the apprehension of the universal. The universal 'cowness',

5. Ibid., p. 313.
6. See NM, I, p. 320.
7. ākṛtistadapekṣatvāt sattvavyavasthānasiddheḥ. NS, II, ii, 64.
8. ākṛtirjātiliṅgākhyā. NS, II, ii, 69.

for example, is apprehended either by the perception of the similarity of shape, head, feet, etc., or by the perception of a composite substance of which these head, feet, etc. are parts.[9] According to the Mīmāṁsaka, however, *ākṛti* and *jāti* are synonymous terms; *ākṛti* means the universal and not the configuration, or the shape of a thing. The sense in which the universal is called *ākṛti* is that it is what serves to define the individual.[10] But the sense in which the word *ākṛti* is used in the theory under consideration is that of configuration as distinct from the universal and the individual which possesses it.

The main contention of this theory is that a thing is ascertained to be a cow, or a horse, or anything else only through its *configuration* and, therefore, that alone should be regarded as the denotation of a word. Besides, general words, such as 'cow', 'pot', etc. are used to refer to percepts only. The object of perception is always some form or shape, since the formless is never perceived. The distinction between the forms of things is perceived by the senses and that serves as the basis of all class-distinctions. Hence, configuration alone should legitimately be regarded as the denotation of words.[11]

The theory of configuration is severely criticised by the Naiyāyika. It is argued that configuration is never common, but always particular. The configuration of a thing is as particular as the thing itself. Therefore, all the objections raised against the individualist theory could be raised against this theory also. The denotation of a word, the Naiyāyika maintains, can only be that which is related to a universal, since it is the universal alone which is identically the same in all the individuals of a class. What is related to the universal is the composite substance in which the disposition of parts is of a definite kind.[12] Besides, a person desiring to possess a cow will not be satisfied if he is brought a clay-cow or the picture of a cow. But if configuration is what is meant by the word 'cow', then there is no reason why he should not be satisfied. Further, if the word 'cow' denotes the configuration of a cow, then we cannot use such expressions as 'the cow is white', for it is absurd to call a shape as having a colour.

---

9. See NV, p. 333.
10. jātimevākṛtiṁ prāha vyaktirākriyate yayā,
 sāmānyaṁ tacca piṇḍānām ekabuddhinibandhanam. ŚV, *ākṛti*, 3.
11. ataḥ pratyakṣaviṣaye padaṁ pravartamānam ākṛtāv eva vartitum arhati. NM, I, p. 318.
12. See NV, p. 314.

According to the Naiyāyika, configuration, which is nothing but conjunction of parts, is a quality and, therefore, colour, which is another quality, cannot be predicated of it.[13] Similarly, our commands, such as 'bring a cow', etc., do not refer to configuration, but to the composite substance possessing the universal 'cowness'. The universal 'cowness', according to the Naiyāyika, subsists only in the real individual cows and not in the clay-models or pictures of cow. These latter are called 'cows' only metaphorically owing to the similarity of forms (*ākṛtisāmānyāt*).[14] Moreover, as Vātsyāyana points out, it is absurd to call configuration as the meaning of words in the case of objects, such as clay, gold, silver, etc., which do not possess any definite shape.[15] Hence, the view holding configuration as the meaning of words cannot be admitted to be satisfactory.

3. *The Universalist theory*

The next theory, which holds the universal to be the meaning of words, is advocated by the Mīmāṁsakas. It is accepted also by the Advaitists and a section of the Grammarians. The main arguments advanced in favour of this theory are: (i) that the universal is apprehended before the individual in verbal cognition, (ii) that a word is not found to give rise to a mixed conception, and (iii) that when the order, e.g., 'bring a cow' is given, the person receiving the order brings any cow he chooses.[16]

When the word 'cow' is heard, the Mīmāṁsaka argues, it is the universal which is first comprehended before there is any idea of the individual. The cognition of the individual follows that of the universal. The Mīmāṁsaka attacks the Nyāya-Vaiśeṣika view according to which the word denotes the individual qualified by the universal. He argues that if qualification by the universal is an indispensable condition, then let the universal alone be the denotation of words. The universal 'cowness', for example, must be the first thing cognised when the word 'cow' is heard, otherwise the word 'cow' may denote any individual. The Naiyāyika also accepts that the cognition of the qualified individual is impossible without the cognition of its

13. See NM, p. 319.
14. NV, p. 315.
15. See NBH on NS, II, ii, 68.
16. See *Pūrva Mīmāṁsā* by Ganganath Jha, p. 146.

qualifications.[17] Thus, the universal must be apprehended before the cognition of the qualified individual arises. Therefore, the universal being the first thing apprehended in verbal cognition, it can alone be admitted as the denotation of words.

Further, the Mīmāṁsaka argues, the word 'cow' gives rise to a single uniform conception of 'cowness' irrespective of the individual differences amongst cows. The individual cows are found to possess divergent features in respect of colour, horns, etc., but these never figure in the comprehension of the meaning of the word 'cow'. Similarly, when a person is commanded to bring a cow, he, in the absence of specific instructions, brings any cow he happens to choose. What determines his choice is nothing but the universal 'cowness'. These considerations, according to the Mīmāṁsaka, compel us to admit the universal alone as the denotation of words.[18]

The Mīmāṁsaka advances some more arguments against the Nyāya-Vaiśeṣika theory of composite denotation. He argues that this theory involves prolixity (*gaurava*), since it must hold that the word denotes first the universal and then the individual. It is logically economical to hold that the word denotes the universal alone. One might ask, how then is the individual apprehended in verbal cognition at all? The Mīmāṁsaka answers that he does not deny the apprehension of the individual in verbal cognition; what he denies is the dual denotation of the word, that is, the denotation of both the universal and the individual, for such a function would put too much burden on the word. As for the cognition of the individual, it follows as an implication (*ākṣepa*) from the cognition of the universal which is denoted by the word. We can maintain neither that the word denotes the universal and the individual simultaneously, as it will be too much effort on its part, nor that it denotes them successively, since no such succession is ever felt.[19]

The Naiyāyika would object that verbal expressions referring to motion, such as 'bring a cow', etc., cannot be said to refer to the universal, since the universal, being incorporeal (*amūrta*) by hypothesis, is incapable of motion. The Mīmāṁsaka replies that this objection is not effective against his position, since, in his view, the

17. na agṛhītaviśeṣaṇe viśiṣṭe buddhiriti nyāyāt. NM, I, p. 320.
18. See NM, I, pp. 320-21.
19. śabdasya dvayābhidhāne yatnagauravād viramyavyāpārasya ca asamvedanāt. Ibid., p. 321.

universal acquires instrumentality for motion through the individual which it implies. Just as the self, though incorporeal, is said to be the doer of all deeds because it functions through the organs of the body, in the same way, the universal, though incorporeal, may be said to have motion through the individual in which it subsists. So, the expressions referring to motion may quite rightly be said to refer to the universal. Similarly, the expressions involving number may also be explained. The Mīmāṁsaka argues further that it is easier to establish the relation of a word to the universal; the individuals belonging to a class being innumerable, it is impossible to establish the relation of a word to each one of them. The Naiyāyika might urge that in perceptual cognition the universal is always apprehended along with the individual, that is, both the co-ordinating and the differentiating features of a thing are invariably perceived together. Therefore, the word also must be held to denote both the universal and the individual simultaneously. The Mīmāṁsaka replies that no single word is capable of denoting all the features of a composite object. There are different words for denoting different features. The general word denotes the universal alone, and there are other words to denote features other than the universal.[20]

4. *The Theory of Composite denotation*

The Nyāya subjects the Mīmāṁsā doctrine to a severe criticism. The Nyāya Sūtras declare that the universal alone cannot be the import of words, because its manifestation depends on the configuration and the individual.[21] No word ever produces the cognition purely of the universal without the apprehension of the latter.[22] Jayanta refutes the Mīmāṁsā arguments for the universalist theory one by one. He contends that the analogy drawn by the Mīmāṁsaka between the universal and the self is completely misconceived. The self possesses the attributes of cognition, effort, etc., whereas the universal possesses nothing of the sort. So, the universal cannot be said to have motion in the sense in which the self is said to be the doer of all deeds.

20. na ca tattādṛśaṁ kiñcicchabdaḥ śaknoti bhāṣitum,
sāmānyāṁśānapodhṛtya padaṁ sarvaṁ pravartate. ŚV, *ākṛti*, 62, also see NM, I, p. 322.

21. na ākṛtivyaktyapekṣatvājjātyabhivyakteḥ. NS, II, ii, 66.

22. na ca agṛhyamāṇāyām ākṛtau vyaktau ca jātimātraṁ śuddhaṁ śabdād gamyate tasmān na jātireva padārthaḥ. NV, p. 319.

Similarly, number also has meaning only with reference to the individual. Further, the contention of the Mīmāṁsaka that the cognition of the individual is mediated by the cognition of universal is not supported by experience. What is cognised when a word is uttered is, according to Jayanta, the individual qualified by the universal. The command 'give a cow' for example, refers to the individual cow qualified by the universal 'cowness' and not to the latter alone, since the act of giving can be related only to the individual. Similarly, the statement 'the lotus is blue' can be significant only with reference to an individual lotus. If the words 'lotus' and 'blue' in the statement are said to denote universals 'lotusness' and 'blueness' respectively, then the predication of the latter of the former would be impossible.[23]

The Mīmāṁsaka might ask, if the individual qualified by the universal is the import of words, which individual is to be understood when the word 'cow' is heard? Again, if the individual is held to be the meaning of words, would not all the objections raised against the individualist theory be applicable to the Nyāya view also? Jayanta answers that when the word is said to denote the individual qualified by the universal, what is meant is not a specific individual, but any individual which is the substrate of the universal. Thus, the word 'cow' denotes anything that is the substrate of the universal 'cowness' (*sāmānyāśraya*). Hence, the Mīmāṁsā objections are not effective against the Nyāya theory.[24]

Jayanta argues further that what is given in perception is not the universal pure and simple, but the individual qualified by the universal. Therefore, the word, which conforms to the object of perception, cannot be said to denote only one part of the object and leave out the other part. That is, the word must be held to denote both the universal and the individual.[25] The Mīmāṁsaka might contend here that the perceptions of the qualification and the qualified do not arise simultaneously; the perception of the qualification arises first and is the cause of the perception of the qualified object. The same holds true in the case of verbal cognition also. The word produces the cognition of the qualification (the universal) which, in turn, produces the cognition of the object (the individual) by

23. See NM, I, p. 323.
24. Op. cit., p. 324.
25. Loc. cit.

implication. Jayanta replies that the analogy drawn by the Mīmāṁsaka between perceptual cognition and verbal cognition is misleading. In perceptual cognition both the qualification and the qualified are perceived, though successively; it is not the case that one is perceived and the other is inferred. But what the Mīmāṁsaka asserts concerning verbal cognition is that the word produces the cognition of the universal alone and not that of the individual, not even successively; the individual is subsequently implied by the cognition of the universal. So, there can be no analogy between the two cases, and the argument of the Mīmāṁsaka stands self-refuted. In fact, Jayanta asserts, just as perception delivers both the universal and the individual, so does the word too denote both of them, that is, it denotes the individual qualified by the universal.[26]

Udayanācārya also subjects the Mīmāṁsā doctrine to a trenchant criticism. He specifically attacks the Mīmāṁsaka's contention that the universal implies the individual while the word denotes only the former. The universal, the Mīmāmsaka holds, being always found dependent on the individual for its manifestation, the latter is necessarily implied when the former is cognised through the word.

Udayana asks, what does the Mīmāṁsaka mean by the *implication* (*ākṣepa*) of the individual by the universal? He may mean either inference (*anumāna*) or presumption (*arthāpatti*). The former, that is, the inference from the universal to the individuals, Udayana argues, is logically impossible. For a valid inference, the knowledge of the invariable concomitance (*vyāpti*) between the sign (*hetu*) and the signifed (*sādhya*) is indispensable. The Mīmāṁsā inference from the 'universality' of the universal to its 'dependence' on the individual is invalid, since it is impossible to establish a universal concomitance between the two. For such a relation, the universals inhering in them must be apprehended, but both the 'universality' and the said 'dependence' being *upādhis*, no universal can be admitted to inhere in them.[27] The Mīmāṁsaka may argue that a concomitance can be said to exist between the universal and the 'individuality' (*vyaktitva*), so the individual can be inferred from the universal. Udayana maintains that this too is not possible, since 'individuality' is not a universal.[28] Individuality belongs to the universals also; therefore, it

26. Loc. cit.
27. Kus., I, p. 275.
28. vyaktitvasya sāmānyasyābhāvāt. Loc. cit.

cannot be regarded as a universal on pain of infinite regress. And even if a concomitance between the universal and the individuality be admitted, one can infer only the latter from the former and not the individual.[29]

The Mīmāṁsaka, Udayana argues further, cannot also take recourse to presumption (*arthāpatti*) to establish his point. When some general knowledge comes into conflict with a specific one, the assumption of the element which resolves the conflict is called presumption. In the present case, the Mīmāṁsaka would argue, we have the valid knowledge that the universal always subsists in the individual, because the latter is its manifester. On the other hand, we have verbal knowledge which has the universal alone as its content. Owing to the conflict of these two valid cognitions, the cognition of the individual arises by presumption. The presumption of the individual resolves the conflict and makes everything intelligible. Udayana asks : what is unintelligible without the individual? It cannot be the universal, because, being eternal, it exists even prior to and after the individual. The Mīmāṁsaka cannot say without self-contradiction that the cognition of the universal is unintelligible without the cognition of the individual, because, in his view, the universal alone is said to be cognised through a word. Thus, the Mīmāṁsaka fails to give any cogent reason for the presumption of the individual. The root of all the trouble is that the Mīmāṁsaka tries to keep the cognitions of the universal and the individual apart in verbal knowledge: the word is said to produce thc cognition of the universal, which in turn produces the cognition of the individual by implication. Udayana maintains that there is no justification for such a view. Moreover, there is no contradiction and there is economy, too, in maintaining that both the universal and the individual are the contents of one and the same cognition.[30]

The Mīmāṁsaka might rejoin that the necessity of presuming the individual arises in the case of such statements as 'the cow is white', where the relation (*anvaya*) between the two universals 'cowness' and 'whiteness' cannot be intelligible wihout the individual. Udayana points out that this argument involves the fallacy of mutual dependence (*parasparāśraya*). The intelligibility of the relation between 'cowness'

29. Loc. cit.
30. Op. cit., pp. 275-76.

and 'whiteness' is said to depend on the cognition of the individual, and the cognition of the individual itself is said to depend on the cognition of the Universal.[31] Besides this reciprocal dependence Udayana points out another drawback in the Mīmāṁsā position. When the Mīmāṁsaka says that the individual is implied by the universal in verbal cognition, what does he mean by the term 'individual'? Does he mean the *bare* individual, or individual *qualified* by the universal? The former alternative is impossible, since the bare individual cannot be the object of a determinate knowledge. And if the latter alternative is taken, that is, if the universal is said to imply the individual qualified by the universal, then the Mīmāṁsā position would involve prolixity (*gaurava*). The Nyāya position, Udayana argues, has the merit of being economical, because it admits the cognition of the individual qualified by the universal straight away from the word without the mediation of the cognition of the universal as is done by the Mīmāṁsaka.[32]

The Mīmāṁsaka may however adopt another line of defence. He may argue that although the word directly denotes the universal, yet, on account of a *special power* (*śaktiviśeṣa*) inherent in it, the individual also becomes cognised through it. Udayana attacks the assumption of this special power. He asks: are the cognitions of the universal and the individual, produced by the word, simultaneous or successive? The latter alternative is not acceptable, since there is no logical justification for it.[33] When the word has produced the cognition of the universal, its mission is over. It has no other function to serve, in the Mīmāṁsā view, so far as the denotation of its meaning is concerned. So the cognition of the individual which is said to follow that of the universal by a special power of the word is not logically justifiable. And if the former alternative is adopted, that is, if the cognitions of the universal and the individual are said to be simultaneous, then there remains no justification for assuming two separate potencies (*śaktidvaya*) of the word, one producing the cognition of the universal and the other that of the individual. A single potency of the word would be sufficient to account for the apprehensions of both the universal and the individual in verbal cognition.[34]

31. Loc. cit.
32. Loc. cit.
33. apekṣaṇīyābhāvena viramyavyāpārābhāvāt. Op. cit., p. 277.
34. Op. cit., p. 278.

Thus, the Nyāya maintains that the import of words cannot exclusively be confined either to the individual, or to the configuration, or to the universal. The Nyāya Sūtras therefore declare that all the three—the individual, the configuration and the universal—are included in the meaning of words.[35] There is no hard and fast rule concerning the predominance and subordination of these elements of meaning. In our statements one may be emphasised more than the other two. When difference is emphasised and the cognition pertains to the distinctive features, e.g., in the case of such expressions as 'that cow which is standing', it is the individual which is predominant in the meaning and the other two elements are subordinate. When, on the other hand, our cognitions pertain to general features, e.g., in the case of such expressions as 'the cow must not be touched by foot', it is the universal which is predominantly signified. Similarly, the predominance of configuration in the denoted meaning is exemplified by such expressions as 'make a cow out of clay'. The clay-cow is called 'cow' only because of configuration, for 'cowness' actually resides only in the real individual cows.[36] Thus, according to the Nyāya, the word denotes the determinate individual, that is, the individual qualified by the universal and the configuration. Any attempt to confine the import of words to one or the other of the three elements leads to insoluble difficulties.

5. *The Advaitic criticism of the realist theory of meaning*

The Advaita view concerning the import of words is the same as that of the Mīmāṁsā so far as empirical usage is concerned. Nevertheless, according to it, the meaning of words is ultimately indefinable. Citsukha examines the three main realist theories of meaning, viz., the universalist theory, the individualist theory and the theory of composite denotation and rejects all of them as logically untenable.[37] (i) According to the first theory, which is held by the Mīmāṁsaka, the meaning of a general word is universal (*jāti*). But, since the universal is intimately related to the particular and is dependent on it for its own apprehension, the particular also becomes apprehended along with it in verbal cognition. Citsukha subjects this view to a trenchant criticism. He asks: are the cognitions of the universal and the

35. vyaktyākṛtijātayastu padārthaḥ. NS, II, ii, 67.
36. See NV, p. 319; also see NM, I, p. 324.
37. See TP, pp. 425f.

particular, produced by the word, successive or simultaneous? He rejects the former alternative as untenable, since words and cognitions do not reveal their objects in a successive manner. The latter alternative, on the other hand, suffers from self-contradiction, as it goes against the Mīmāṁsā thesis that the universal alone is the meaning of words.[38]

The Mīmāṁsaka may rejoin that although the direct meaning of words is universal (*jāti*), yet it being inseparably related to the particular (*avinābhāva*) the latter also becomes cognised indirectly by implication. Citsukha considers this explanation as unsatisfactory, since the said inseparable relation itself is not established. What particulars, he asks, is the universal 'cowness', for example, inseparably related to? Is it so related to all the particulars, or to the particular cows only? In the former case, 'cowness' being inseparably related to all things, anything should be implied by the word 'cow'. And, in the latter case, there would be circularity (*ātmāśrayatva*), since it amounts to asserting that 'cowness' is inseparably related to particulars having 'cowness'. Besides, if the word 'cow' is said to mean, by implication, the particular qualified by 'cowness', then the qualifying attribute 'cowness' would also be implied along with it.[39] This would mean that 'cowness' is both the direct and the implied meaning of the word 'cow', which is absurd. To remove the defect of circularity it may be said that 'cowness' is inseparably related to the particulars having dew-lap, etc. Thus the direct meaning of the word 'cow' is the universal 'cowness' and the indirect meaning is the particular having the said characteristics. Even this explanation, Citsukha argues, does not succeed in avoiding the other defect pointed out above. 'Cowness' being inseparably related to the particulars having dew-lap, etc., it will necessarily be included in the indirect meaning of the word 'cow'. Thus, 'cowness' on this view, will be both the direct and the indirect meaning of the word 'cow', which is an absurd position.[40]

Further, Citsukha points out, words could refer to particulars indirectly only if the relation of the word to the particulars was previously known (*adhigata*). In the absence of such knowledge there would be no implication (*lakṣaṇā*) of particulars from the word. He

38. nādyaḥ padabudhyorviramyavyāpārābhāvāt. dvitīye 'pi......jātireva śabdārtha ityabhyupagamabhaṅgaprasaṅgaḥ. Ibid., p. 425.
39. viśiṣṭasya lakṣyatve viśeṣaṇabhūtāyā jāterlakṣyatvaprasaṅgāt. Ibid., p. 426.
40. Ibid.

maintains that the knowledge of the relation of the word to the particulars is impossible for two reasons. Firstly, it is impossible to know the relation of a word to all the particulars supposed to be implied by it, since they are infinite in number. And secondly, one and the same word cannot logically be related to different particulars without involving discrepancy.[41] Thus, the theory of indirect reference of particulars by the word, according to Citsukha, has no legs to stand on. It might be urged, to save the universalist theory, that the particular is not the meaning of words at all, either direct or indirect. Nonetheless, it becomes known in verbal cognition because it is inseparably related to the universal which is the sole meaning of words. This, Citsukha points out, is a self-contradictory assertion, since it amounts to asserting that though the particular is not the meaning of words yet it is known through them.[42]

Further, the theory which holds universals alone as the meaning of words is inadequate to explain the meaningfulness of all words. The words, such as 'space' (*dik*) and 'time' (*kāla*), which are not admitted to correspond to universals would cease to be meaningful. In the same way, words corresponding to general characteristics (*upādhi*), such as 'cook', 'universal', etc., would also have no meaning. In order to cover all these cases it might be held that the meaning of words is not the universal alone but any one of the three, viz., the universal, the particular and the general characteristics (*upādhi*). But even this modified theory, according to Citsukha, is not satisfactory, since the objections raised against the universalist theory still stand and they are equally applicable in the case of general characteristics (*upādhi*) also.[43] Thus Citsukha finds the universalist theory of the meaning of words logically untenable.

(ii) The second theory which holds particulars to be the meaning of words has already been shown by Citsukha to be inadmissible. Particulars being innumerable, it is impossible to apprehend the relation of a word to all the particulars supposed to be denoted by it. Besides, a word of which meaning has been apprehended in relation to a certain particular, cannot legitimately be used to refer to others, since such a use would be discrepant.[44]

---

41. na ca sā śakyā, viśeṣāṇāmānantyād vyabhicārācca. Ibid., p. 426.
42. Ibid.
43. jātiśabdārthatvadoṣāṇām upādhiṣvapi tulyatvāt. Ibid., p. 427.
44. Ibid.

(iii) According to the third view, which is held by the Nyāya-Vaiśeṣika, the meaning of a word is neither the universal nor the particular exclusively, but the particular qualified by the universal. This view, too, according to Citsukha, suffers from the same defects as have been shown in the case of the second view above, since, like particulars, particulars qualified by universals are also innumerable and mutually exclusive.[45] The Nyāya may explain that what is meant by the phrase 'the particular qualified by the universal' is not the mutually exclusive particular, but the common character of being qualified by the universal, and it is this common character which is the meaning of words. Citsukha maintains that even this explication would not save the Nyāya theory, since now it becomes subject to all the objections raised against the first theory.[46] If it is the common character of 'being qualified by the universal' which is denoted by a word, then the cognition of particulars by means of words would be impossible to explain. Thus, the Nyāya theory, like that of the Mīmāṁsaka, is also logically untenable.

Citsukha thus rejects all the three realistic theories of meaning. He maintains that the relation of the word to the object is impossible to explain. A word is said to be 'denotative' (*vācaka*) and the object 'denoted' (*vācya*). The characteristics of 'denotativeness' and 'denotedness' belong to the word and the object respectively. None of these characteristics is common to both. If there is a relation between the two, there must be something common to them. But, since there is nothing common to the denotative word and the denoted object, no relation between them is conceivable.[47] It might be held that the relation between the word and the object is conventional (*sāṅketika*). It is established by convention that a certain word would stand for a certain kind of objects. This relation serves as the common bond between the word and the object and produces appropriate verbal cognition. Citsukha, however, maintains that even this relation is not intelligible, since it is impossible to explain,

45. viśiṣṭasyāpi vyāvṛttatvāviśeṣādvyakteriva tasyāpi śabdārthatā nirasanīyā. Ibid., p. 427.

46. atha jātivaiśiṣṭyaṁ sarvatrānugatameva śabdārthaḥ, tadāpi jāteḥ śabdārthatāyāmuktaṁ dūṣaṇaṁ na pratyuddhriyeta. Ibid., p. 427.

47. kiñca vācyatvamarthasya dharmaḥ, vācakatvaṁ ca padasya tathā ca prativastuniyate vācyatve vācakatve ca sambandhavācoyuktiḥ kutastyā ? Ibid., p. 427.

as shown above, what the word is conventionally related to, that is, whether it is related to the universal, or the particular, or the particular qualified by the universal. Hence, the said conventional relation of the word to the object also is impossible to grasp.[48]

Citsukha's criticism of the realistic theories of meaning clearly brings out the inherent difficulties of defining the import of words. The crux of the problem is whether the import of words is to be determined as general, or as particular, or as both. It is evident that language would have failed to serve its purpose if the significance of words were confined exclusively either to the general or to the particular. Words seem to have an unmistakable reference to both of them. Hence, whether the realist theory of universals is accepted or not, an adequate theory of meaning cannot fail to take note of both the general as well as the particular aspects of the significance of words. Citsukha confines himself to the criticism of the various theories of meaning without putting forward the Advaitic view on this subject. Other Advaitic authors have, however, done it which we proceed to consider presently.

6. *The Advaitic theory of import of words*

A brief but clear statement of the Advaitic theory of meaning is found in *Vedāntaparibhāṣā* of Dharmarāja Adhvarīndra. The meaning of words, according to Dharmarāja is two-fold: direct (*śakya*) and implied (*lakṣya*). The direct meaning of words is their *primary* denotation (*mukhyā vṛttiḥ*), as, for example, the word 'pot' primarily denotes a particular object having a certain shape with a large-bottomed cavity, etc.[49] The potency (*śakti*) of the word to express its meaning is, according to the Advaitist, an independent category since it is of the nature of causality by virtue of which the word produces the cognition of its object.[50] Hence, to be the primary denotation of the word is to be the object of this potency (*śakti*) of the word. This object, according to Dharmarāja, is universal (*jāti*) and not the particular, since particulars being infinite in number, there will be prolixity

48. etena sāṅketikaḥ śabdārthayoḥ sambandha ityapi parāstam; saṅketasyāpi jātau vyaktau viśiṣṭe vābhihitanyāyena durgrahatvāt. Ibid., p. 427.
49. tatra, śaktirnāmapadānāmartheṣu mukhyā vṛttiḥ. yathā ghaṭapadasya pṛthubudhnodarādyākṛtiviśiṣṭe vastuviśeṣe vṛttiḥ. Ved. Par., p. 69.
50. Ibid., p. 70.

(*gaurava*).[51] This prolixity will occur in two ways: firstly, the relation of the word to an infinite number of particulars will have to be established, which is evidently impossible, and, secondly, the word would have diversity of meaning in the form of diverse particulars. Hence, the direct meaning of words, according to the Advaitist, has to be admitted to be universal (*jāti*). It must be noted here that the universal which is admitted to be the direct meaning of words by the Advaitist is not that of the Nyāya-Mīmāṁsā conception. It is the universal conceived as a determinate form of Existence, or as a determinate potency of the original nescience (*mūlāvidyā*).[52]

Now, if the direct meaning of words is universal, then how is the particular apprehended by the word at all ? It cannot be denied that a person commanded to bring a 'pot' undoubtedly understands that he is required to bring 'a particular pot', though not 'this' or 'that' pot. How does this become possible? Dharmarāja gives three alternative explanations of the apprehension of particulars in verbal cognition. The first explanation is that the particular becomes apprehended in verbal cognition because the universal, which is denoted by the word, is the content of the *same* cognition as the particular.[53] That is to say, the universal being *never* apprehended without the particular, the cognition of the former by the word invariably leads to the cognition of the latter. The second explanation given by Dharmarāja is that the word has a *self-existent* (*svarūpasatī*) capacity to denote particulars, which functions by itself *without being known*.[54] That is, the word produces the cognition of particulars not because its relation with them has been previously apprehended, but because it has an *intrinsic* capacity to do so. This capacity of the word is known by inference from the cognition of particulars produced by it. In the case of the cognition of the universal, however, the capacity of the word functions not by itself but by *being known*. The universal cannot be cognised by the word unless its relation to the latter has been previously apprehended. In other words, the knowledge of the potency of a word pertaining to a generic character is a *necessary* condition for the

51. tādṛśaśaktiviṣayatvaṁ śakyatvaṁ tacca jātereva, na vyakteḥ, vyaktīnāmānantyena gurutvāt. Ibid., p. 70.
52. See Ch. VII.
53. jātervyaktisamānasaṁvitsaṁvedyatayā iti brūmaḥ. Ibid.
54. yadvā gavādipadānāṁ vyaktau śaktiḥ svarūpasatī, na tu jñātā. jātau tu sā jñātā hetuḥ. Ibid., pp. 70-71.

knowledge of that character in verbal cognition. But such a condition is not necessary for the apprehension of a particular by the word, since, if it were necessary, there could be no cognition of the particular in verbal cognition at all. Particulars being innumerable, the relation of a word to all the particulars included in its meaning is immpossible to apprehend. Besides, such a knowledge is not necessary, since even in the absence of it, if the potency pertaining to the generic character is known, there is no delay in the cognition of the particular after the universal is known through the word.[55] One might ask, if the word has an intrinsic capacity to produce the cognition of the particular also, why then is the universal alone said to be the denotation of a word ? Dharmarāja answers that to be denoted is, by definition, to be the object of the *known* potency of the word, and not of its unknown, self-existent potency (*śakti*). Hence, universal alone can be admitted to be the denotation (*vācya*) of the word.[56]

The third explanation given by Dharmarāja is that the particular is apprehended by the word because of *secondary* implication. Just as in the proposition 'pot is blue' , the word 'blue' secondarily implies the object having the quality blue, so in the case of words signifying universals, there is secondary implication of particulars qualified by them.[57] That is, although particulars are not directly signified by words, they become indirectly signified by virtue of being substrata of universals.

The Advaitic theory of meaning discussed above is in essence, the same as that of the Mīmāṁsaka. The direct meaning of words is, for both of them, general in character, although they differ radically in their conceptions of this general character. It is quite reasonable to hold that the meaning of general words as apprehended by us is general and not any specific particular. It is because of this that we are able to understand and apply the words in completely new situations. Also, as the Advaitist points out, it is physically impossible to know the relation of a word to all the particulars included in its meaning.

---

55. na tu vyaktyaṁśe śaktijñānamapi kāraṇaṁ gauravāt; jātiśaktimattvajñāne sati vyaktiśaktijñānaṁ vinā vyaktidhīvilambābhāvācca. Ibid.
Dharmarāja points out that even the Nyāya admits self-existent capacity belonging to the relation of word-senses (in a sentence) for generating verbal cognition. Ibid.
56. jñāyamānaśaktiviṣayatvameva vācyatvamiti jātireva vācyā. Ibid.
57. yathā 'nīlo ghaṭaḥ' ityatra nīlaśabdasya nīlaguṇaviśiṣṭe lakṣaṇā, tathā jātivācakasya tadviśiṣṭe lakṣaṇā. Ibid.

Nevertheless, it is also true that particulars are *invariably* apprehended by us in verbal cognition, otherwise the practical activity following it, which pertains *always* to particular things or acts, would be impossible to explain. A satisfactory theory of meaning, therefore, has to account for both these aspects of verbal cognition. The Advaitist, who holds that the direct meaning of words is universal, explains the apprehension of particulars in verbal cognition in three different ways. It is said to be due either to the fact that both the universal and the particular are the contents of a *unitary* cognition, or to the *intrinsic* capacity of the word which is not known, or to the *secondary* implication. The Advaitist emphasises that the content of the known meaning of the word can only be universal, since particulars being innumerable, the relation of the word to all of them is impossible to grasp. At the same time he recognises also that the particular is invariably apprehended in verbal cognition along with the universal. Thus, he admits that the word has capacity (*śakti*) to produce the cognition of both the universal and the particular. In the case of the universal this capacity functions directly, while in the case of the particular it functions in anyone of the three ways indicated above.

We have discussed so far the Nyāya, the Mīmāṁsā and the Advaita theories of the import of words. But no discussion can be complete without considering the Grammarian's view on this subject. The Grammarian throws significant light on the nature of the word, its meaning and their mutual relation. A section of the Grammarians upholds the individualist theory of the import of words, while the other section advocates the universalist view similar to that of the Mīmāṁsā. Bhartṛhari, in particular, puts forth a very strong defence of the universalist theory of meaning. He throws considerable light also on the question of the ontological status of the universal. The whole discussion deserves to be treated in a separate chapter.

CHAPTER IX

THE GRAMMARIAN'S VIEW OF WORD AND MEANING

1. *The word as the Ultimate Reality*

The Grammarian has made significant contribution to the study of word and meaning. Our discussion of the Grammarian's view would be based mainly on Bhartṛhari's *Vākyapadīya* and the commentaries thereon by the author himself, Puṇyarāja and Helārāja. It is necessary to state at the very outset that the philosophical standpoint of the Grammarian is absolutistic. The ultimate reality (Brahman), as Bhartṛhari describes it, is of the nature of the word; it is without beginning or end, it is the cause of the manifested phonemes, it is what appears as the objects, and it is from which the creation of the world proceeds.[1] The Word-Absolute is said to have dual aspects of *unity* (*vidyā*) and *diversity* (*avidyā*), but, of these, the former alone is real, while the latter is merely apparent.[2] In itself the Word-Absolute is undifferentiated, but due to the power of *nescience* it appears as diverse. Thus, the world of objects, according to the Grammarian, is nothing but the appearance of the Absolute Word.

Bhartṛhari advances a host of arguments in support of his theory. Things are said to be ultimately of the nature of the word because they are apprehended as identical with it in all our cognitions. That is, all our cognitions of things are *always* intertwined with words. All divisions pertaining to things, such as beginning, sustenance and

1. anādinidhanaṁ brahma śabdatattvaṁ yadakṣaram,
   vivartate 'rthabhāvena prakriyā jagato yataḥ. VP, I, 1.
   Bhartṛhari adduces scriptural basis for his view. The knowers of tradition, he says, have declared that all things are transformations of the word. It is from the Chandas that the universe has evolved.
   śabdasya pariṇāmo' yamityāmnāyavido viduḥ,
   chandobhya eva prathamam etadviśvaṁ vyavartata. Op. cit., I, 120; see also VPV, p. 201.
2. VPV, p. 1.

end, are determinable only through words.[3] Bhartṛhari maintains that the power that creates and regulates this universe rests on words. It is through the eye of the word that all the diversity of understanding is perceived.[4] It is the word which sees the object; it is the word which speaks it; it is the word which reveals the object which was lying hidden.[5] Even an existent is no better than non-existent as long as it does not come within the range of verbal usage. And even a totally non-existent thing like 'hare's horn', when brought to the mind by words in various usages, appears as if endowed with primary reality.[6]

There is no cognition, according to Bhartṛhari, in which the word does not figure. All knowledge is, as it were, intertwined with words.[7] Even the indeterminate knowledge of objects is not free from words. The word-seed is present in it in unmanifested form, and it is for this reason that no verbal expression takes place.[8] The stage of determinate knowledge is reached (only sometimes) when the word-seed is awakened and its powers are manifested in the form of expressive words restricted to specific meanings. Only at this stage the object acquires a determinate shape and comes within the range of clear cognition. It becomes capable of being designated as such and such, and can really be said to be known.[9] Thus, all experience and thought being possible only through words, the word, Bhartṛhari declares, is the ultimate reality.

2. *The sentence as universal*

Although the Word-Absolute (*śabdabrahman*) is ultimately one and undivided, yet in our empirical experience it appears as divided into sentences, words and phonemes. Even from the empirical point of view, the Grammarian holds the sentence to be an indivisible unit (*sphoṭa*). The division of sentence (*vākya*) into terms (*pada*), according

3. Ibid., pp. 2-3.
4. śabdeṣvevāśritā śaktir viśvasyāsya nibandhinī,
   yannetraḥ, pratibhātmāyaṁ bhedarūpaḥ pratīyate. VP, I, 118.
5. VPV, p. 198.
6. Ibid., pp. 205-6.
7. na so 'sti pratyayo loke yaḥ śabdānugamādṛte,
   anuviddhamiva jñānaṁ sarvaṁ śabdena bhāsate. VP, I, 123.
8. yathāsya saṁhṛtarūpā śabdabhāvanā tathā jñeyeṣvartheṣūtpannenāpy-avikalpakena jñānena kāryaṁ na kriyate. VPV, p. 208.
9. Ibid., p. 209.

to him, is an unreal abstraction. Such a division may be necessary in order to make the unintelligent understand the nature of a sentence, but considered in themselves the terms are nothing but fictions, pure and simple.[10] The Grammarian is thus opposed to the Mīmāṁsā view according to which terms are real and sentence is nothing but a particular combination of them. Bhartṛhari says that just as for the *Padavādin* (one who holds terms to be real) the division of terms into roots, affixes, suffixes, etc., are artifices for understanding the term, so, for the *Vākyavādin* (one who holds a sentence to be an indivisible unit), the division of a sentence into terms is fictitious, though useful in understanding the sentence.[11] Sentences being innumerable and each being a unity different from all others, an understanding of them in their uniqueness is an impossible task. It is through similar terms appearing in different sentences that their understanding becomes possible.[12] It is for this reason that the Grammarian, for whom terms are imaginary abstractions, undertakes the study of the nature and the meaning of words.

The main argument of the Grammarian for his theory of the indivisibility of sentence (*sphoṭa*) is that the opposite theory is logically untenable. The theory of the divisibility of sentence, it is contended, would lead either to *regress ad infinitum*, or to atomism. If a sentence is divisible into terms, and terms into phonemes, there is no reason why the process should stop at that stage. The phonemes may also be divisible into parts and those parts into further parts and so on *ad infinitum*. This would reduce the divisibility theory to an absurdity. If, on the other hand, the process of division is said to come to a halt with the phonemes or with subtler parts of them, then atomism would become inevitable. The ultimate parts of speech would have to be regarded as indivisible atoms. Thus the proponent of the divisibility theory has to accept indivisibility at some stage. Why not, then, admit the sentence itself to be indivisible? Further, Bhartrhari points out, the atomic theory has its own notorious

10. tasmānmanyāmahe padānyasatyāni ekam abhinnasvabhāvaṁ vākyam. tadabudhabodhanāya padavibhāgaḥ kalpita iti.
PR, P. 91. Also see VP, II, 7-9.
11. yathā pade vibhajyante prakṛtipratyayādayaḥ,
apoddhārastathā vākye padānāmupavarṇyate.
VP, II, 10. Also see VP, III, i,1.
12. ānantyāddhi vākyānāṁ svālakṣaṇyenāśakyā vyutpattiḥ kartumiti, sadṛśapadadvārā tadupapattirityarthaḥ. HR, p.2.

difficulties. The atomic parts of a phoneme being impartite by hypothesis, their mutual cohesion is utterly unitelligible. An atomic part can unite with another atomic part either wholly or partially. If the union is total, then the parts will coalesce and no gross magnitude can come into being, and if, on the other hand, it is partial, then it would imply parts, which would contradict the hypothesis of impartiteness of the atomic parts. Thus, there will either be no phonemes and, for that matter, no terms, or there will be infinite division. The atomic parts in themselves, being indeterminate, cannot serve the purpose of speech. Also there is nothing besides them that can serve this purpose. Hence, the theory of the indivisibility of sentence, or *sphoṭa*, is, according to Bhartrhari, logically inescapable.[13]

Bhartrhari contends further that a sentence as an indivisible unit, or *sphoṭa*, is not only an individual, but also a universal.[14] Being the unity revealed by the terms and the phonemes it is akin to the universal. It might be objected that if sentence is a universal revealed by the terms and the phonemes, then it should be revealed wholly by each one of them, just as the universal 'potness' is revealed by each one of the pots. But since this is not true, the sentence cannot be regarded as a universal. Bhartṛhari replies that although a sentence is not completely revealed by any one of its individual manifesters it is nevertheless revealed by them in a progressive manner. Each term and phoneme in a sentence contributes to the gradual revelation of the latter as a universal. Bhartṛhari is advocating here a *new* concept of universal. The universal is not only that which is *completely* revealed by each individual in which it is inherent, but also that which is *progressively* revealed by different individuals composing it. Bhartṛhari

13. padāni vākye tānyeva varṇāste ca pade yadi,
varṇeṣu varṇabhāgānāṁ bhedaḥ syāt paramāṇuvat.
bhāgānāmanupaślesānna varno na padaṁ bhavet,
teṣāmavyapadeśyatvāt kimanyadapadiśyatām. VP, II, 28-9.
14. sphoṭaśca dvividho bāhya ābhyantaraśca bāhyo 'pi jātivyaktibhedena dvividhaḥ. PR, p. 64.
According to the Grammarian, *sphoṭa* is an internal as well as an external entity. As an external entity it is both an individual and a universal. But as an internal entity it is purely a spiritual principle assuming externality only when it is revealed by sounds. See VP, II, 30. For a detailed discussion on this point see Gaurinath Sastri : *Philosophy of Word and Meaning*, Ch. V.

gives the analogy of walking. The universal of walking is revealed by the repetition of the movements of feet. Although each movement of feet is different from the other, yet what is apprehended is not their diversity, but the unity of walking progressively revealed by them. Similarly, in the case of a sentence also, there is progressive revelation of it as a universal by the terms and the phonemes, the mutual differences of which are not apprehended. It might be urged that the terms and the phonemes being absolutely different from one another, how can they be said to reveal an identical universal—*sphoṭa*? Bhartṛhari replies that they do so because there is an affinity amongst them.[15] Even though each phoneme and word is different from others, being the effect of a different effort at articulation, they also resemble each other in respect of being articulated in a similar manner. It is because of this affinity that different terms and phonemes contribute to the manifestation of a sentence, or *sphoṭa*, as a universal. In fact this problem has to be faced also by the realist who maintains that different particulars manifest an identical universal. The only explanation he is able to give is that particulars do so by their own nature which is unquestionable.

Although the Grammarian holds the sentence to be indivisible, he admits that its cognition arises through the cognition of its parts. That is, epistemologically, the cognition of parts, viz., phonemes and words, precedes the cognition of the *simple* sentence.[16] The manifesters, it is argued, must necessarily be apprehended before *that* which is manifested by them. Bhartṛhari maintains that just as there is a definite sequence in the transformation from cause to effect (e.g., from milk to curd, or from seed to sprout), so also there is a definite sequence in the attainment of the cognition of a sentence by the cogniser.[17] Phonemes and words appear first in a sequence before the cognition of the sentence finally arises.

---

15. yathā kṣepaviśeṣe' pi karmabhedo na gṛhyate,
 āvṛttau vyajyate jātiḥ karmabhirbhramaṇādibhiḥ.
 varṇavākyapadeṣvevaṁ tulyopavyañjanā śrutiḥ,
 atyantabhede tattvasya sarūpeva pratīyate. VP, II, 20-21.
16. vyajyamāne tathā vākye vākyābhivyaktihetubhiḥ,
 bhāgāvagraharūpeṇa pūrvaṁ buddhiḥ pravartate. Ibid., I, 90.
17. Ibid., I, 91.

3. *The word as universal*

Just like the sentence, the word also, according to the Grammarian, is a simple indivisible unit revealed by the phonemes. In each significant word there are two elements: one is the element of sound which reveals the word and the other is the real word itself (*sphoṭa*) which is used to convey the meaning.[18] The cognition of the word also, like that of the sentence, is preceded by the appearance of parts (sounds) in a sequence. Even if the word is regarded as divisible, Bhartṛhari says, sequence of sounds has to be admitted. If the word is regarded as divisible, the sequence of sounds serves as the ground of the distinction of its parts, and if it is regarded as indivisible, the sequence of sounds serves as the means of the cognition of the word.[19]

The simple word (*sphoṭa*) manifested by the sequence of sounds may be regarded as both an individual and a universal. Some Grammarians regard the *sphota* as universal and the sounds (*dhvani*) as the individuals manifesting it.[20] The conception of word as universal, Bhartṛhari points out, is essential to the science of Grammar. The authors of the *Sūtras, Vārtikas* and the *Bhāṣya* have declared words, meanings and their mutual relations to be eternal.[21] This would be justified only if words were universals, since it is only as universals that the words could be eternal.[22] Thus, all that is taught by the science of Grammar about the word is essentially about the word-universal (*śabdākṛti*).

Bhartṛhari distinguishes the word-universal (*śabdākṛti*) from the universal 'wordness' (*śabdatva*).[23] He distinguishes the former also from the individual words. 'Wordness' subsists in all words irrespective of their mutual differences, but word-universals, such as 'tree-wordness', etc., subsist only in their respective instances. The word-universals which subsist in the individual words are also called words,

18. dvāvupādānaśabdeṣu śabdau śabdavido vidūḥ,
eko nimittaṁ śabdānāmaparo 'rthe prayujyate. Ibid., I, 44.
19. Ibid., I, 92.
20. anekavyaktyabhivyaṅgyā jātiḥ sphoṭa iti smṛtā,
kaiścid vyaktaya evāsyā dhvanitvena prakalpitāḥ. Ibid., I, 93.
21. Ibid., I, 23.
22. nityaḥ śabdo nityo 'rtho nityaḥ sambandha ityeṣā śāstravyavasthā. tatra hi śabda ityanena śabdākṛtirabhidhīyate. evaṁ hyāha— 'ākṛtinityatvānnityaḥ śabdaḥ' iti. VPV, p. 45.
23. sā ceyamākṛtiḥ śabdatvasāmānyaviśeṣād anyā. Ibid., p. 46.

because, due to vagueness, they are identified with the individual words manifesting them.[24] Logically they should be distinguished from the individual words in which they subsist. Thus, according to Bhartṛhari, several universals co-inhere in words without any opposition, just as they do in things. In a pot, for example, universals of substance, earth and pot co-inhere; in the same way, in the word 'tree' also the universals of being an attribute, a word and a tree-word co-inhere without mutual opposition.[25]

A serious objection may be raised against the above theory. It may be argued that in the case of objects, such as pots, etc., of which parts exist at the same time, one can see that the whole (*avayavī*) is the cause of the manifestation of the specific universal 'potness'. But in the case of words, of which parts (sounds) do not exist simultaneously, for they appear in a sequence, there can be no word as a whole (*avayavī*) which may be said to manifest the word-universal. In other words, the word as a whole being non-existent, there is no substratum for the word-universal to inhere in. If, on the other hand, the word-universal, e.g. 'tree-wordness', like the universal 'wordness' or 'soundness', is said to inhere in each part (sound), then the cognition of the word 'tree' should arise as soon as the first part is uttered, that is, there should be no need of uttering the other parts at all. The fact that no such thing happens proves the falsity of the Grammarian's view.

Bhartṛhari anticipates this objection and maintains that it is not valid against his view.[26] He explains and justifies his position by taking examples of particular actions, such as lifting, revolving, pouring, etc. In the case of these actions it is evident that their parts (the particular movements) do not produce another action corresponding to the whole (*avayavī*). Nevertheless, the manifestation of the universal of 'lifting', etc. by the particular parts, as distinct from the universal of action, is not denied. Also the cognition of 'lifting', etc. does not arise when only a part is seen, since all the actions necessary for generating that cognition have not yet come into being.[27] The cognition of a particular universal of action (lifting, etc.) and the corresponding verbal usage become possible only when the parts,

24. Ibid., p. 46.
25. Ibid.
26. Ibid., p. 47.
27. Ibid., pp. 47-48.

involving contacts and separations determined by specific directions are perceived in succession.[28] In the same way, in the case of words like '*vṛkṣa*' (tree), although the particular parts (*v*,*ṛ*, etc.), of which distinction is difficult to grasp, when uttered, suggest the specific universal of the word 'tree', yet the full cognition of the universal and the corresponding verbal usage do not arise until all the elements required to manifest the universal have come into being. When all the parts are gradually perceived in succession, verbal usage based on the specific universal becomes possible.[29]

The Grammarian thus rejects the view of the Vaiśeṣika regarding the mode of manifestation of universals. According to the Vaiśeṣika, the universal inheres in the particular which reveals it. That is, the particular reveals only *that* universal (*jāti*) which *inheres* in it. Therefore, in his view, the word-universal (e.g. the universal of the word 'tree') which does not inhere in the parts (phonemes) cannot be said to be revealed by them at all. Nor can the word-universal be said to inhere in the word and be revealed by it, since its parts (phonemes) being non-simultaneous, the word as a 'whole' (*avayavī*) has no existence. The Grammarian, on the other hand, maintains that manifesters do not necessarily manifest what inheres in them.[30] For example, light and the senses reveal objects which do not inhere in them but are external to them. Similarly, even though the word-universal may not inhere in the word, its distinctive cognition is progressively attained through the successive impressions left on the mind by the cognition of the phonemes of the word. So, the existence of the word-universals is undeniable, since it is evidenced by verbal perception. Also their existence is necessarily implied by our recognition of the words uttered by different persons at different times and places as 'the same'.[31]

The Grammarian thus upholds the eternality of words on the ground that they are universals. Bhartṛhari, however, maintains that

28. yadā tu digviśeṣāvadhiparicchinnasaṁyogavibhāgakāryāṇāṁ karmaṇām prabandhaḥ krameṇopalabdho bhavati, atha jātiviśeṣopādhiyuktā vyavahārāḥ prakalpante. Ibid., p. 49.
29. yadā tvavayavaprabandhaḥ krameṇopalabdho bhavati, atha jātiviśeṣopādhiyuktā vyavahārā avatiṣṭhante. Ibid.
30. na hy abhivyaktimatām abhivyañjakair āśritānāmevābhivyaktir niyamena kriyate. Ibid., p. 50.
31. Ibid.

whether words are admitted to be eternal or not, their beginning has to be admitted as unknown. There exists a continuity in the case of words as is found in the case of living beings.[32] There was no first stage when verbal usage did not exist, nor will there be a future stage when it will not exist.

It has been said above that, for the Grammarians, meanings, just like words, are also eternal. Some Grammarians establish it on the ground that meanings are universals which are, by hypothesis, eternal. Others who do not accept universals as the meaning of words establish it on different grounds. Nevertheless, all the Grammarians, whatever theory of meaning they might hold, admit the meaning of words to be eternal.[33] Similarly, the relation of word and meaning is also held to be eternal. When the two (word and meaning) are regarded as appertaining to one another, their relation expressed in the form 'it is that' cannot but be eternal and self-existing, because meaning is not assigned to the word; it is not something not known before and made for the first time by some speaker for the benefit of some listener. Thus the relation between word and meaning is beginningless and unbroken.[34] Bhartṛhari, however, mentions other alternative views. The relation between word and meaning may be held to be that of the illuminator and the illumined (*prakāśyaprakāśakabhāva*) based upon convention (*samayopādhiḥ*)—a kind of fitness like that between senses and their objects. Or, the relation may be said to be that of causality based upon unbroken tradition, since the word when uttered, causes the cognition of its meaning.[35]

Words, Bhartṛhari points out, have two distinct powers. Just like light, they have the power of revealing (*grāhakatva*) and that of being revealed (*grāhyatva*).[36] Things, e.g., pot, etc., are always revealed or

---

32. nityatve kṛtakatve vā teṣāmādirna vidyate,
prāṇināmiva sā caiṣā vyavasthānityatocyate. VP, I, 29. See VPV, p. 77.
33. See VPV, p.52.
34. nityaḥ sambandha ityasyedaṁbhāve sati śabdārthayoḥ so 'yam iti yaḥ sambandhaḥ so 'rthādeśanasya kartumaśakyatvād autpattikaḥ svabhāvasiddho na kenacitkartrā kañcit pratipattāraṁ pratyajñātapūrvaḥ tatprathamaṁ kṛta iti. tasmādanādirnityaṁ prāptāvicchedaḥ śabdārthayoḥ sambandhaḥ. Ibid., p. 53.
35. Ibid., pp. 54-55.
36. VP, I, 55.

cognised without in the slightest way helping their own cognition. Senses, on the other hand, function as the cause of the cognition of objects without themselves being cognised. But the word produces the cognition of objects and, at the same time, reveals its own form which excludes the form of other things and other words. The two powers of the word, Bhartṛhari holds, are not really different; they are distinguishable only in thought.[37] Also words reveal their meaning only when they are themselves cognised. The mere existence of words, of which significance is not known, does not reveal anything at all.[38]

4. *Import of words*

The Grammarians are divided over the question of the import of words. Bhartṛhari mentions three different views advocated by the Grammarians.[39] According to the first, all words, without exception, signify universals. The individual does not figure in the meaning of words at all. According to the second, it is the substance, or the individual, which is signified by words and not the universal. While, according to the third, both the universal and the substance, or the substance qualified by the universal, are the meanings of words. All the Grammarians, however, agree that the meaning of a word, in whatever manner it might be conceived, is eternal.[40] We have already discussed these views in detail in the previous Chapter. We shall, therefore, confine ourselves, as far as possible, to the essential features of the Grammarian's view in this Chapter.

The theory of universals as the meaning of words was propounded by Vājapyāyanācārya, while the opposite theory, viz., the theory of substance as the meaning of words was advocated by Vyāḍi. Patañjali discusses both these views in his *Mahābhāṣya* in great detail.[41] The

37. VPV, pp. 115-16; also see VP, I, 58, and VPV, pp. 118-19.
38. viṣayatvamanāpannaiḥ śabdairnārthaḥ prakāśyate,
na sattayaiva te 'rthānāmagṛhītāḥ prakāśakāḥ. VP, I, 56.
39. padārthānāmapoddhāre jātirvā dravyameva vā,
padārthau sarvaśabdānāṁ nityāvevopavarṇitau. VP, III, i, 2.
In another place Bhartṛhari records as many as twelve different theories of meaning current in his time. It is neither necessary nor within our scope to discuss these theories here. Basically most of these theories could be reduced to one or the other of the theories we have already considered. For an account of these theories see VP, Ch. II, 121-35. For a detailed discussion, see G. N. Sastri : *The Philosophy of Word and Meaning*, Ch. 7.
40. See HR, p. 8.
41. See MB, Vol. II, pp. 90 ff.

main contention of the universalist is that the meaning of words (such as cow, pot, etc.) being always apprehended as general and not as this or that particular, it must be admitted to be universal.[42] The fact that one and the same word is used to refer to different individuals proves the existence of a common essence in all of them which the word denotes.[43] Moreover, the individual cannot be said to be the denotation of a word, because, firstly, individuals being infinite in number, it is impossible for a word to denote all of them, and secondly, if a word denotes one individual it cannot denote others, and thus, an infinite number of words would be required to denote all of them. To avoid these difficulties, it is argued, the universal must be admitted as the meaning of words.[44] The universalist points out also that the scriptural passages could not be rightly understood if the universal is not accepted as the meaning of words. In the injunctions, e.g., 'the Brāhmin must not be killed' or 'the wine must not be drunk', the word 'Brāhmin' or 'wine' does not mean a particular Brāhmin or a particular wine, but the Brāhmin as such or the wine as such. Otherwise, the killer of a Brāhmin or a drunkard may also claim that he has not violated the injunction because he has not killed a particular Brāhmin or drunk a particular wine.[45]

As opposed to the universalist another Grammarian, named, Vyāḍi, propounds the view of substance, or the individual, as the meaning of words. The main arguments advanced in favour of this theory are: (1) The ideas of gender and number agree only with the individual.[46] We can speak of an individual as being male or female; we can talk of individuals as being two, or three, or more; but to make such statements with reference to universals would be absurd. (2) Actions referred to by injunctions or commands can be related only to an individual.[47] And (3) No entity is ever perceived to be present in different substrates at the same time.[48] For these reasons, the individualist argues, the individual, or the substance, alone can be regarded as the meaning of words.

---

42. ekā ākṛtiḥ, sā cābhidhīyate. MB, Vol. II, p. 90.
43. gaurityetena śabdenokte pratyāyite sāmānyalakṣaṇe 'rthe viśeṣānavadhāraṇādaikyaṁ sāmānyasyāvasīyate. MBP, Vol. II, pp. 90-91.
44. Ibid., p. 93.
45. MB, Vol. II, p. 92.
46. evaṁ ca kṛtvā liṅgavacanāni siddhāni bhavanti. Ibid., pp. 94-95.
47. codanāsu ca tasyārambhān manyāmahe dravyam abhidhīyata iti. Ibid.
48. na khalvapyekam anekādhikaraṇasthaṁ yugapad upalabhyate. Ibid.

The universalist has his own explanation of the points raised by the individualist against his theory. He maintains that although gender, number, etc., are the attributes of the individual, yet they become predicated of the universal by virtue of its inherence with them in the same substratum.[49] As Helārāja explains, a general name, e.g., 'cow', denotes the universal 'cowness' as if endowed with specific number, because both 'cowness' and the number co-inhere in the same substratum (individual) possessing a specific causal efficiency. A universal without substratum is utterly unthinkable. Thus the substance (though not directly signified) becomes invariably comprehended by the power of the word.[50] As regards the individualist's objection against the existence of the universal, namely, that no entity is perceived to inhere simultaneously in several places, the universalist answers that this contention may be true with regard to an individual, but not with regard to a universal. The universal has no spatial and temporal limitations and, therefore, it is ubiquitous and eternal. The existence of the universal attested by the experience of identity is undeniable.[51]

It is clear from the above explanation of the universalist that though, for him, the direct meaning of the word is universal, yet the individual, which is its substratum, is not entirely left out of cognizance, since it is through the individual that the universal becomes related to gender, number, action, etc. Similarly, the individualist also would have to take cognizance of the universal, otherwise the usage of identical words for different individuals would go unexplained. As Helārāja observes, the individualist denies the universal as the direct meaning of words and not as a character of substances. The universal, for him, is the mark (*upalakṣaṇa*) of the substance denoted by the word, just as crow, etc., may be the mark of a certain house.[52] Thus the word 'cow' denotes those individuals which are marked by the presence of 'cowness' in them. Patañjali, therefore, very aptly remarks that there is no fundamental difference between the universalist and

49. guṇāścātra dvitvastrītvādayo vivakṣitāḥ. taiscākṛteṛekārthasamavāyalakṣaṇaḥ sambandha ityākṛtāvapi padārthe liṅgasaṁkhyādisiddhirityarthaḥ. MBP, Vol. II, p. 96.
50. See HR, p. 8.
51. asti caikam anekādhikaraṇaṁ yugapat. tadyathā eka ādityo 'nekādhikaraṇastho yugapadupalabhyate.........evamākṛtir yugapat sarvatra bhaviṣyati MB, Vol. II, p. 92. Cp. MBP, Vol. II, p. 96.
52. anabhidhīyamānāpi jātirupalakṣaṇīkriyate, śabdārthe yathā gṛhādau kākādi. HR, p. 9.

the individualist so far as the two elements (the universal and the substance) as the constituents of meaning are concerned. For both, both the elements are signified by words. The difference is only with regard to emphasis. For the universalist, the universal is the primary denotation of words, while substance is a qualitative adjunct. For the individualist, on the other hand, substance is the primary meaning of words, while the universal is a qualitative adjunct.[53] Both, however, have to recognise that the meaning of words is complex and not simple. If either the universal or the individual is excluded from the meaning of words, the resulting view would be exposed to the objections from the opposite side.

The third view mentioned by Bhartṛhari strikes a balance between the two rival views discussed above. It recognises both substance and universal as the denotation of words, since both of them are comprehended as their meaning.[54] This view is similar to that of the Nyāya discussed in the previous chapter. It has the merit of being free from the difficulties inherent in the two extreme views of the universalist and the individualist, and it also succeeds in accounting for our verbal usage in a more satisfactory manner.

An explanation is necessary with regard to the individualist's view for which substance is the meaning of words. It has been stated in the previous section that for all Grammarians, without exception, the meaning of words is eternal. So far as the universalist is concerned there is no problem, since, for him, the universal, which is the meaning of words, is by hypothesis eternal. But how would the individualist explain his position in consonance with the general principle? Helārāja explains that for the individualist substance is eternal. It is said to be eternal not in the sense of a particular mode, but as a *continuous stream* which has neither beginning nor end.[55] By substance is meant the essence of the successive modes, which is indestructible. The Grammarian, as we have already remarked, is an absolutist, whether he holds the universalist or the substance view of meaning. For the universalist, as we shall see, the universal *Existence*

---

53. na hy ākrtipadārthakasya dravyaṁ na padārthaḥ, dravyapadārthakasya vā 'kṛtir na padārthaḥ. ubhayor ubhayaṁ padārthah kasyacit tu kiñcit pradhānabhūtaṁ kiñcit guṇabhūtam. MB, Vol II, pp. 98-99.
54. See HR, p. 8.
55. nityatvopavarṇanaṁ ca 'siddhe śabdārthasambandhe' ityatra bhāṣye 'yasminstattvaṁ na vihanyate' iti dravyasyāpi nityatvam, pravāhanityatayā śabdāt sadaiva pratīteḥ. HR, p. 10.

is the ultimate meaning of all words and the particular universals are merely empirical determinations of it.[56] For the individualist, on the other hand, *Brahman* is the ultimate meaning of all words. The particular substances—souls, bodies, objects, elements, etc.—which, from the empirical point of view, constitute the meaning of words are nothing but modes (appearances) of the ultimate substance (*Brahman*).[57] Thus the meaning of words, according to the individualist, being identical with *Brahman* which is the immanent reality of all particular substances, is eternal. Even the difference of words from *Brahman* is not ultimate. Just as particular substances are ultimately non-different from *Brahman*, so are words also. The empirical diversity of words and meanings as well as the difference between the two, though practically necessary and useful, are ultimately illusory.[58]

5. *Bhartṛhari's view*

Bhartṛhari strongly supports the universalist's theory of meaning. He maintains that the universal alone can legitimately be regarded as the meaning of words. The question as to what is denoted by a word can be decided only on the ground of what is apprehended when the word is uttered. On this criterion the universal alone can claim to be the denotation of words. It is true that the universal cannot be comprehended without the individual which is its substratum, but there is absolutely no justification for maintaining that the individual with all its characteristics which differentiate it from other individuals is denoted by a word.[59] The word 'pot', for example, does not denote the specific characteristics which make a pot an individual distinguished from other pots. It denotes only the universal, or the general feature, which makes it a 'pot'. But, since in actual experience the universal is always found to co-inhere with the individualising characteristics, the latter become associated with it in our mind and

56. See VP, III, i, 33-34.

57. ātmā vastù svabhāvaśca śarīraṁ tattvamityapi,
dravyamityasya paryāyāstacca nityamiti smṛtam. VP, III, ii, 1.

58. vikārāpagame satyaṁ suvarṇaṁ kūṇḍale yathā,
vikārāpagame satyaṁ tathāhuḥ prakṛtiṁ parām.
vācyā sā sarvaśabdānāṁ śabdāśca na pṛthak tataḥ,
apṛthaktve ca sambandhastayornānātmanoriva. Ibid., III, ii, 15-16.

Helārāja explains—tasya cidrūpasya cicchaktirapariṇāminīti vikārābhāvānnedaṁ sāṁkhyanayavat pariṇāmadarśanam, apitu vivartapakṣaḥ. HR, p. 119.

59. jātipratyāyake śabde yā vyaktiranuṣaṅgiṇī,
na tān vyaktigatān bhedān jātiśabdo 'valambate. VP, II, 124.

are uncritically supposed to be the meaning of words.[60] There is, therefore, no logical justification for maintaining that the individual with all its differentiating features is the denoted sense of the word, for it does not figure in the felt content of the meaning at all. It may, however, be admitted that the universal as the meaning of words needs to be supplemented by the individual in order to complete the syntactical relation. But this is only consequential to the denoted meaning and does not therefore justify the inclusion of the individual in the meaning of words.[61]

6. *The theory of superimposition*

We have already mentioned that Bhartrhari distinguishes the universal of the word (*śabdajāti*) from the universal of the thing (*arthajāti*) which constitutes its meaning. For brevity's sake we shall call the former as the *'word-universal'* and the latter as the *'thing-universal'*. Bhartṛhari maintains that all words signify their own universal first before signifying their meaning—the thing-universal.[62] This is quite logical, as the word itself has to be recognised before its meaning is comprehended. No word can convey its meaning without first conveying itself. But it might happen the other way round; a word might signify its own universal without signifying its meaning, as when a person ignorant of the meaning of a word recognises it to be 'the same' even without the comprehension of its meaning.[63] Bhartṛhari further maintains that in verbal cognition the word-universal is superimposed (*adhyāropita*) on the thing-universal. Although the word-universal is different from the thing-universal and the cognition of the former precedes the cognition of the latter, yet no distinction between them is felt in verbal cognition. This, he maintains, is due to the superimposition of the word-universal on the thing-universal. This superimposition is, again, according to him, only a hypothesis (*kalpanā*) made to explain empirical cognition. It is not real, since, as Helārāja explains, the distinction of word and meaning for the Grammarian is not ultimate but only empirical. There is no real

60. ghaṭādīnāṁ na cākārān pratyāyayati vācakaḥ,
vastumātraniveśitvāt tadgatirnāntarīyakī. VP, II, 125.
61. See PR, p. 133.
62. svā jātiḥ prathamaṁ śabdaiḥ sarvairevābhidhīyate,
tato 'rthajātirūpeṣu tadadhyāropakalpanā. VP, III, i, 6.
63. See HR, p. 17.

distinction between the two, as meaning is only the appearance (*vivarta*) of the word.[64]

Thus, the hypothesis of superimposition of the word-universal on the thing-universal, according to Bhartṛhari, is necessary in order to explain the felt identity of the two in verbal cognition inspite of their empirical difference. Helārāja points out that the relation of the word to its meaning itself cannot be grasped without such superimposition. The relation of the word 'cow' to its meaning, for example, is grasped as 'this is cow'. Both the terms 'this' and 'cow' in this expression have identical reference. Now, the word-universal being different from the thing-universal such identical reference (*sāmānādhikaraṇya*) cannot be explained without the hypothesis of superimposition. In the absence of superimposition no verbal convention (*saṅketa*), too, can come into being.[65] Further, just as the relation of word and meaning (*vācya-vācakabhāva*), as explained earlier, is beginningless and not generated by human agency, so also is the superimposition of the word-universal on the thing-universal. Without such superimposition the relation of word and meaning itself would not be possible.[66] The position of the Grammarian is analogous to that of the Buddhist. Just as, for the latter, the identification of the perceived (*dṛśya*) and the conceived (*vikalpa*) in a judgment, arising out of the non-apprehension of difference between the two, is beginningless and independent of individual's will, so also, for the Grammarian, the identification of the word-universal with the thing-universal by superimposition is beginningless and independent of human agency.[67]

The essence of Bhartṛhari's contention is that it is the word-universal which is significant, and it signifies its meaning, the thing-universal, as identical with itself. But how, it may be asked, can the word-universal inhering in a substratum (the word) different from

---

64. arthasya jhaṭityeva śabdasvarūpābhedenāvabodhe 'pi yathā pratipādita-kramāśrayeṇa tataḥ svajātipratyāyanād anantaram arthajātīnāṁ gotvādīnām atmasu tasyāḥ śabdajāteḥ samāropasya kalpanā na paramārthaḥ, śabdavivarta-tvenārthasya śabdāttattvato bhedābhāvāt. Loc. cit.
65. yadvā sambandhavyutpattikāle gaurayam artha ity arthajātyā śabdajāter atyantabhedāt sāmānādhikaraṇyānyathānupapattyā abhedādhyāropaḥ kalpyate.........anyathā saṅketasyaiva kartum aśakyatvāt. Loc. cit.
66. yathā cāyam anādir apauruṣeyo vācyavācakabhāvaḥ tathādhyāropo'pi anyathā vācyavācakabhāva eva na ghaṭeta. Loc. cit.
67. Loc. cit.

that of the thing-universal (the thing) signify the latter as identical with itself? Bhartṛhari explains this by an analogy. The word 'red', for example, signifies 'redness' inherent in the red quality. It is by virtue of this inherence that the quality is called red. The colour-substance supporting red quality is also called 'red' because the quality in which 'redness' inheres is inherent in it. Similarly, the cloth is also called 'red' because it is conjoined with the colour-substance which has inherent in it the quality in which 'redness' inheres. Thus, the designation of 'red' is not confined only to the quality in which 'redness' inheres; it is also extended to other things in which it does not directly inhere but is related to them in an indirect manner. In the same way, in verbal cognition, the universal inherent in the word designates the universal inherent in the thing as identical with itself. The relation in this case can only be that of superimposition of the former on the latter, since the two being inherent in different substrata, no other relation between them is conceivable.[68]

It should be clear from the above account that, for Bhartṛhari, the word-universal subsists in the *word* and not in the *phonemes* (*varṇa*). The phonemes being non-simultaneous, they can have neither denotative function, nor the inherence of word-universal in them.[69] It is only the word (*sphoṭa*) which is distinctly cognised as the particular and the universal. It is in the word as particular (*vyaktisphota*) that the universal inheres.[70] The word-universal has to be recognised as the ground of the notion of identity with regard to words which, as used for referring to different objects on different occasions, are different from one another. The word as universal alone functions as denotative (*vācaka*).[71]

The relation of a denotative word with meaning, according to the Grammarian, is natural (*yogyatālakṣaṇa*). Thus, all words used as denotative names are naturally related to all meanings.[72] The convention-maker does not give meaning to words; he only restricts their

68. yathā rakte guṇe tattvaṁ kaṣāye vyapadiśyate, saṅyogisannikarsācca vastrādiṣvapi gṛhyate. tathā śabdārthasambandhācchabde jātiravasthitā, vyapadeśe' rthajātīnāṁ jātikāryāya kalpate. Op. cit.,7-8. Also see HR, p. 19.
69. See HR, p. 20.
70. kevalaṁ sphoṭasya jātivyaktibhedena darśanadvayam iti vyaktisphoṭe jātiḥ samavetā. Ibid., p. 20.
71. ata eva jātyācchuritāyā vyaktereva vācakatvam. Ibid., p. 20.
72. śabdārtha-sambandhascātra yogyatālakṣaṇo'bhipretaḥ. sarvo hi śabdaḥ saṁjñātvena niyujyamānaḥ sarvatrārthe yogyatālakṣaṇena saṁbandhena saṁbaddhaḥ. Ibid., p. 20.

application to certain class of objects. The relation of word and meaning, for the Grammarian, is *apauruṣeya*, that is, it is not produced by human convention.[73] What is produced by human convention is the specific usage of words with reference to specific objects. There is, therefore, no contingency of all meanings being apprehended by all words, since the known meaning of a word can alone be apprehended. A word is known, by convention, to mean certain class of objects. Hence only that meaning is apprehended when the word is uttered.[74]

It has been said above that, according to Bhartṛhari, a denotative word denotes first its own universal, which is identical with it, and then the universal inherent in the object. This is the actual order of denotation. In verbal cognition, however, this order is not felt. The meaning is always apprehended as identical with the word. But this must not lead us to suppose that, for Bhartṛhari, the meaning, i.e. the thing-universal, has no existence apart from the word. Although the meaning is invariably apprehended as 'covered' (*ācchurita*) with the word, its own nature is not jeopardised.[75] Just as the pot, which is always perceived in the 'cover' of light, is not *in itself* a non-entity, so also the meanings of words which are always apprehended in the 'cover' of words are not non-entities.[76] Words, like light, says Helārāja, manifest their objects by imposing their own form. It is for this reason that the meaning is always apprehended as identical with the word. This apprehension, according to the Grammarian, is *natural*; it is independent of individual's will.[77] In the beginningless world, the relation of word and meaning has always been apprehended in this manner. There is no deliberate superimposition of one on the other.[78] Hence the thing-universal, which is always apprehended as identical with the word-universal in verbal cognition, must not be thought of as a non-entity. It must be admitted to have an independent existence and not be regarded merely as an objective projection (*adhyāropa*) of the word. Moreover, there is undeniable evidence for

73. kevalaṁ śaktyavacchedamātre saṁjñākarturvyāpāro na tvapūrvasaṅketakaraṇe, arthasambandhasyāpauruṣeyatvāt. Ibid., p. 20.
74. Ibid.
75. śabdācchuritatve pi cārthasya na svarūpavyapagamaḥ. Ibid., p. 20.
76. Ibid.
77. svābhāvikascāyamarthapratyāyane śabdānām abhedasambandho 'bhyupāya iti pratipādyo 'pi tathaiva pratipadyate. na hi puruṣādhīnam etat. Ibid., p. 21.
78. Ibid.

the existence of the universal independent of the word, since identical cognitions of things arise even in the absence of the knowledge of the conventional name.[79] Thus the difference of the word and the universal denoted by it is, for Bhartṛhari, as much a fact of experience as their identity, since the universal is definitely apprehended even prior to the knowledge of the conventional name. Hence, when Bhartṛhari says that, in verbal cognition, the thing-universal is always apprehended as superimposed by the word-universal, he does not mean that the former has no being at all. On the contrary, it is on the thing-universal apprehended independently of the word-universal that the latter is superimposed in verbal cognition and apprehended as identical with it.[80]

7. *All words denote universals*

Bhartṛhari advocates the view that all words without exception signify universals. He makes use of the theory of superimposition not only to account for the felt identity of word and meaning in verbal cognition, but also to explain the use of identical word in the case of objects in which no universal is admitted to inhere. For example, a universal is not admitted (by the Vaiśeṣikas) to subsist in universals on pain of infinite regress. Yet there exists the usage of identical word 'universal' relating to them. Now if the usage of identical word is said to be determined by the objective universal in every case, then the use of indentical word 'universal', which is not admitted to be determined by any objective universal, demands an explanation. Bhartṛhari maintains that in such cases the function of the thing-universal is performed by the word-universal itself.[81] The universal inherent in the word 'universal' itself determines the identical use of it in respect of universals. But how can the universal of the word perform the function of the universal of the thing? Helārāja explains that the word-universal superimposed on the objects functions as the thing-universal.[82] There is no rule that the function of the universal (of making the use of identical word possible) can be performed only by the universals inherent in things and not by those inherent in

79. avyutpannasaṅketasyāpi cābhinnapratyayotpatter arthajātirapyastīti na śabda-jātirevādhyāropitāstviti vācyam. Ibid., p. 21.
80. Ibid.
81. See VP, III, i, 8 already quoted. Cf. jātyādiśabde jātiṣu vācakatvena pravartamānā sthitā jātir na kevalaṁ vyapadeśāya kalpate yāvajjātikāryāya ca. HR, p. 19.
82. See HR, p. 20.

words.[83] In the case of objects in which the thing-universal is not admitted to inhere, the word-universal serves its function, that is, it determines the identical usage of words. Similarly, such identical (*ekaśeṣa*) usage as 'these are universals' (*jātaya imāḥ*) also becomes possible due to the superimposition of the universal inherent in the word 'universal' on universals in which no universal is admitted to subsist.[84] Thus, according to Bhartṛhari, all words signify universals. In the case of objects in which the inherence of an objective universal is denied, the universal of the word itself, superimposed objectively, becomes signified by the word.

Now, this is true not only in the case of 'thing-universals' but also in the case of 'word-universals'. The identical designation in the case of the latter (as 'word-universals') becomes possible due to the universal inherent in the word 'word-universal'. When different word-universals (cow-wordness, pot-wordness, etc.) are called 'word-universals' (*śabdajātaya imāḥ*), the identical usage is determined by the universal inherent in the word 'word-universal'.[85] One might object that if the universal inherent in the word 'word-universal' is different from word-universals (cow-wordness, pot-wordness, etc.), then the universal determining the identical designation of both will be still another, and thus there will be no end to this process. Bhartṛhari answers that no such contingency would arise, since the universal inherent in the word 'word-universal' belongs to the same class of word-universals to which other word-universals (cow-wordness, etc.) belong. Hence, the same word, namely, the word 'word-universal' would serve to designate all word-universals including the one inherent in the word 'word-universal'.[86]

Bhartṛhari thus tries to establish with the help of the theory of superimposition the thesis that all words without exception signify universals. In the case of things in which no universal is admitted to subsist, the universal of their name itself, as superimposed on them, is signified by the word. A serious objection may be raised against this view. It may be urged that the superimposition of the word-universal

83. Ibid., p. 22.
84. jātiśabdaikaśeṣe sā jātīnāṁ jātiriṣyate. VP, III, i, 9. Cf. tathā jātaya imā ityayamapi jātyāśrayāparajātyabhāvād vācakajātyadhyāsāśraya upapadyate. HR, p. 22.
85. śabdajātaya ityatra tajjātiḥ śabdajātiṣu. VP, III, i, 9. Also see HR, p. 22.
86. yā śabdajātiḥ śabdeṣu śabdebhyo bhinnalakṣaṇā,
jātissā śabdajātitvam apyatikramya vartate. Op. cit., 10. Also see HR, p. 23.

is conceivable in the case of things with which the relation of the word has been established. But in the case of things (e.g. universals) which are manifold and devoid of a common universal no word-relation being possible on the universalist's view, the superimposition theory breaks down. Hence the meaning of words in such cases cannot be shown to be universal with the help of this theory. Further more, if all meaningful words are said to signify universals, then all those words which have no objective universals corresponding to them would have to be regarded as meaningless. The universalist, therefore, would have to hold either that there is a large number of words in our language which are meaningless, since they have no universals corresponding to them, or that there are objective universals corresponding to all words.

Instead of defending his theory that the word-universal as projected objectively is signified by the word (at least in some cases), Bhartṛhari adopts the second alternative stated above for establishing his thesis that all words signify universals. He was perhaps aware that a defence of the above theory would logically lead him to a nominalism of the Buddhist type and to the acceptance of the corresponding particularistic metaphysics which was diametrically opposed to his fundamental universalistic standpoint. He, therefore, maintains that all words signify universals, even if obje-tive universals alone are held to be signified by them.[87] Thus, even the words, such as 'universal', etc., signify objective universals. But how, in the face of the established view of the Vaiśeṣika that no universal inheres in universals, can the word 'universal' be said to signify a universal? Bhartṛhari holds that there is no reason why the meaning of the word 'universal' may not be regarded as the universal inherent in universals, when there is identical usage of word in their case also. The Vaiśeṣikas may not admit the inherence of a universal in universals for reasons of their own. But, for the Grammarian, things are nothing but the meanings of words. There being an identical verbal cognition in the case of universals also, the universal in universals corresponding to the word 'universal' must be admitted. If identical cognition of particulars is admitted as the ground of the recognition of the universal in them, then there is no reason for denying the same in the case of universals.[88]

87. arthajātyabhidhāne 'pi sarve jātyabhidhāyinaḥ,
vyāpāralakṣaṇā yasmātpadārthāḥ samavasthitāḥ. Op. çit., 11.

88. vaiyākaraṇānāṁ śabdārtho' rtha ity abhyupeyatām anvayirūpāvacchedena śābdasya pratyayasyotpatter jātiṣvapi jātir aviruddhābhyupagamyā. etadeva hi vyaktiṣu api jātyabhyupagame nimittam ityatrāpi tathābhyupagame kaḥ pradveṣah? HR, p. 24.

For the Grammarian, who regards the authority of words as supreme, whatever is conveyed by the word is real.[89] The meaning of words being always apprehended as universal, the universal corresponding to every word must be recognised.[90] The universal may or may not be admitted to inhere in universals, but it is certainly required as the meaning of the word 'universal'. Words, the Grammarian insists, never touch the particulars in their uniqueness. A significant word is always apprehended as related to a general form. Even universals in their uniqueness are not signified by the word. They are identically designated as 'universal', because they are conceived as identical. And identity being nothing but universal, the universal as the meaning of the word 'universal' subsisting in all universals must be recognised.[91]

Bhartṛhari maintains that even the individual signified by a proper name is akin to the universal.[92] The unique particular can never be signified by the word at all. The proper name Devadatta, for example, does not stand for any particular state of the individual's existence. The particular states, viz., childhood, youth, etc., are not meant by the name at all. What is meant by it is something identical to all these states. Such an identity has to be admitted since otherwise recognition will be unexplainable.[93] This identity being something common to the particular states of the individual's existence, is akin to the universal. It is this identity which is signified by proper names. The point of the Grammarian is that some kind of generality being necessarily required by all significant words, all words, including proper names, signify universals.[94]

---

89. śabdapramāṇakānāṁ hi yacchabda āha tatparamārtharūpam. Ibid. p. 24.
90. Ibid., p. 25.
91. jātau padārthe jātirvā viśeṣo vāpi jātivat,
    śabdairapekṣyate yasmādataste jātivācinaḥ. VP, III, i, 12. See also HR, p. 25.
92. Op. cit., 12 already quoted above.
93. See HR, pp. 25-26.
94. itthaṁ ca saṁjñāśabdānāmapi jātivādimate jātiśabdatvam ity ekaiva śabdānāṁ pravṛttiḥ. Ibid., p. 26.
    Just as the universalist on the basis of the usage of words argues that all words signify universals, so does the individualist, on the same basis argue that all words signify substance (*dravya*). It is maintained that all objects signified by words have the properties of substance. Some words signify primary substances (*mukhyadravya*), while others only secondary substances (*upacaritadravya*). Even in the universalists' view, as Helārāja points out, some words signify primary universals, and others (such as proper names) only secondary universals. The criteria of substance,

Having argued on the basis of the usage of words that even the word 'universal' signifies a universal, Bhartṛhari proceeds to show that his view can be supported also from the Vaiśeṣika point of view. That is, the word 'universal' can be shown to stand for properties possessed by universals. All universals possess the property of being common to their substrata. This property, though different in each universal, is yet considered to be identical in all of them due to similarity. It may, therefore, be admitted as the universal common to all universals.[95] It is due to this property that they are identically designated as 'universal'. Helārāja mentions some more properties common to universals. Each universal generates the cognition of particulars in accordance with its own form. It also causes the designation of particulars appropriate to its own form. Similarly, each universal subsists in each of its substrata wholly. These properties are common to universals just as 'cowness', etc. are common to their respective individuals. Being thus similar to universals, they also function like them; they serve as the basis of identical conception and designation of universals as 'universal'.[96] In the same way, Bhartṛhari maintains, the universal may be admitted to inhere even in the Vaiśeṣika category of particularity (*viśeṣa*). All particularities exclude each other. If they did not, they will be universals and not particularities. The property of 'exclusion' common to all particularities may, therefore, be regarded as the universal determining their identical notion and designation.[97]

One might ask, if common (or similar) properties can be supposed to perform the function of universals, as is contended above in the

---

according to the individualist, are : (i) fitness for being judged as 'this is that' (*idaṁ tat*), (ii) existence (*pariniṣpannatā*), (iii) independence (*svātantrya*) and (iv) fitness for being related to number, gender, etc. (*liṅgasaṁkhyāyoga*). These properties primarily belong to substances, but they are superimposed, according to the individualist, on qualities, action, etc. when they are signified by words. The individualist thus maintains that since all objects denoted by words have the properties of substance, all words must be admitted to signify substances. dravyadharmā padārthe tu dravye sarvo 'rtha ucyate,
dravyadharmāśrayād dravyamataḥ sarvo 'rtha iṣyate. VP, III, i, 13. Also see HR, pp. 26-27.

95. anupravṛttidharmo vā jātiḥ syāt sarvajātiṣu. Op. cit., 14. See HR, p. 27.
96. yathā ca gotvādijātissarvā vyaktīrvyāpnoti tathaite dharmāḥ sarvajātīrvyāpnuvantīti jātyā tulyarūpatvājjātikāryāya kalpante. Op. cit., pp. 27-28.
97. vyāvṛttidharmasāmānyaṁ viśeṣe jātiriṣyate. Op. cit., 14. See HR, p. 28.

cases of universals and the particularities, then why not admit the same also in the case of particular things, such as cows, pots, etc.? The properties of having dew-lap, horns, hooves, tail and so on, which are common to all cows, may serve as the bases of identical notion and designation of them as 'cow'. What is the necessity of admitting the universal 'cowness' over and above them ? Helārāja answers that the properties of having dew-lap, etc. would generate the cognition of the object as possessing those properties and not as 'cow'. The cause, he argues, must be capable of explaining the effect. The cognition of 'cow' can be explained only by admitting the universal 'cowness' common to all the individual cows.[98] This answer is obviously unsatisfactory, for it may be urged again that if similar properties possessed by cows cannot produce their identical cognition as 'cow', then how can similar properties possessed by universals and particularities produce their identical cognition as 'universal' and 'particularity' respectively? Helārāja answers that in the case of universals and particularities similar properties are admitted to function as universals because there is no other alternative, the inherence of the universal in them (according to the Vaiśeṣika view) being logically inadmissible.[99] But in the case of particular things, such as cows, pots etc., there being no such logical bar against the inherence of universals, nothing other than the universal can be admitted as the cause of their identical conceptions. Similar (or common) properties are to be admitted to serve the function of universals where there is valid reason against the inherence of the latter, not everywhere.[100] Thus in the case of non-beings (*abhāva*) also, the inherence of the universal being logically inadmissible, the common property of 'non-beingness' may be admitted to serve as the universal, i.e., as the cause of identical cognition and designation of them as 'non-being'.[101]

Evidently Bhartṛhari is primarily interested in showing that the meaning of all words is general. Whether this generality is regarded as universal (*jāti*) or as common property (*upādhi*) is immaterial for

98. sāsnādimattvena sāsnādimān ityādipratyayo jāyate na tu gaur gaur iti. anurūpaṁ hi kāryaṁ kāraṇaṁ kalpayati. Op. cit., p. 28.
99. gatyantarābhāvād atra sadṛśā eva dharmā jātiḥ kalpate, mukhye jatimattve bādhakopapatteḥ. Loc. cit.
100. tadevaṁ yatra jātyabhyupagame pramāṇabādhāsti tatra sadṛśadharmarūpā jātiḥ. Loc. cit.
101. Loc. cit.

him. In his own view, all generality is universal (*jāti*), and all verbal usage is based on the apprehension of generality. Even the usage of words 'space' (*ākāśa*) and 'time' (*kāla*), according to him, is based on universals inherent in space and time respectively. The Vaiśeṣika does not admit the inherence of universals in them, because each of them, in his view, is a unitary all-pervading substance and inherence of the universal, by definition, requires a plurality of substrates. Bhartṛhari maintains that though space is one, it might be differentiated on the basis of the properties of objects with which it is conjoined. All perceptual objects are found to possess the property of 'limitedness' (*parimitatva*). It is because of this property that things in common parlance are said to be 'in limited space'. Thus, due to limitedness of objects the space which is conjoined with them is also regarded as limited. The place to which the conjunction of an object is confined is differentiated from places conjoined with other objects, and in this manner a plurality of spaces comes into being. This plurality of spaces, indeed, is not an intrinsic one; it is due to external adjuncts (*upādhikṛta*), namely, the limitedness of the conjoined objects. But, since in common parlance space is diversified, the universal 'spaceness' determining their identical conception and designation as 'space' must be admitted.[102]

Similarly, time, which is regarded by the Vaiśeṣika as one, is also differentiated into past, present, etc. on the basis of its relation with different persons. So the universal 'timeness' (*kālasāmānya*) as common to all times and as the meaning of the word 'time' must be admitted.[103] In the same way, direction (*dik*) is also differentiated by the observer into east, west, etc., on the basis of the conjunction of the sun with different points in space. Hence the universal 'directionness' (*diksāmānya*) as the meaning of the word 'direction' common to all the directions has to be postulated.[104] The Vaiśeṣikas regard inherence (*samavāya*) as one. Helārāja maintains that it may also be differentiated on the basis of its relata, and the universal of 'inherence' (*samavāyatva*) as the cause of the identical notion of constitutive locus may be admitted.[105] In this way, Bhartṛhari tries to show that all words signify universals even if the Vaiśeṣika scheme of categories is

102. saṁyogidharmabhedena deśe ca parikalpite,
teṣu deśeṣu sāmānyam ākāśasyāpi vidyate. Op. cit., 15; also see HR, pp. 29-30.
103. See HR, p. 30.
104. Ibid.
105. Loc. cit.

admitted. For him, unlike the Vaiśeṣika, a real plurality of particulars is not necessary for the inherence of the universal. Even an imagined plurality, as is shown in the case of space, time, inherence, etc., is sufficient for the postulation of the inherence of the universal which is necessarily required for the relation of the word.

Bhartṛhari further shows that his view is supported also by the Buddhist and the Advaitist. According to the Buddhist, the universal is the general form apprehended in identical cognitions of things and wrongly judged as external reality due to the confusion of the perceived (*dṛśya*) and the conceived (*vikalpa*). The Buddhist thus admits the identical cognition of things and the universal form apprehended in it, but he denies that it is anything outside cognition. This universal form, according to him, is the meaning of words, since this alone is apprehended in verbal cognition. The Buddhist denial of reality to universals does not affect the Grammarian's position, since the status of the universal as the meaning of words is not denied.[106]

Similarly, the Advaitist also holds the meaning of words to be universal. He, however, identifies universals with the identical causal potencies (*śakti*) possessed by things. These potencies (or universals) being ultimately non-different from Brahman their diversity is said to be nescience-generated, or conceived from the practical point of view, and not real (*svarūpabheda*). Just as the diversity of universals is conceptual (*kalpita*), so is the difference of the universal and the particular. The universal, according to the Advaitist, is not different from the particular as is held by the Vaiśeṣika. It is only the power of Brahman immanent in things.[107] Bhartṛhari thus tries to show that every system of thought, whether it admits the reality of universals or not, whether it regards the universal as identical with or as different from the particular, supports his view that all words signify universals.

It has already been mentioned that, for the Grammarian, meanings of words are eternal because universals, which are their meanings, are eternal. But why should the universal be admitted to be eternal? Bhartṛhari answers that the universal has to be admitted as eternal in order to explain its manifestation in a new-born effect. It is a matter of common experience that no effect comes into being without its

106. Op. cit., 19. Cp. sa hy ākāro bāhyo ' stu, ná vā, śabdavācyatvasya na kācit kṣatiḥ. HR. p. 33.

107. Op. cit., 22. yathā hi vaiśeṣikāṇāṁ vyatiriktaṁ sāmānyam, naivamiha, kevalaṁ viśvamūrteḥ padārthasya śaktimātram. HR, p. 34.

universal (*jāti*). All effects manifest their class essences in the very moment of their birth. This, according to Bhartṛhari, is accountable only on the hypothesis that the universal serves as an auxiliary to the causes determining the production of an effect. This implies that the universal exists prior to the effect manifesting it and is instrumental, as an accessory to the causes, to the manifestation of itself in the effect.[108] But, it might again be asked, how can the universal be said to be connected with the causes of an effect when it is not present in them? Bhartṛhari replies that the universal, in his view, being ubiquitous (*sarvasarvagata*), it subsists even in the causes in an unmanifest form and serves as an accessory to the production of the effect which subsequently manifests it.[109] The effect, according to Bhartṛhari, is pre-existent in its causes in the form of the universal and is thus pre-determined into that form. Hence it manifests its specific universal as soon as it is brought into being by its causes.[110]

Bhartṛhari maintains further that the theory of eternal universals as the denoted meaning of words serves to explain many of our linguistic expressions which would otherwise be unexplainable. In the expression, e.g., 'he is making a pot' (*ghaṭaṁ karoti*) the term 'pot' signifies its object as the instrument (*sādhana*) of the act of 'making'. But if the term 'pot' denoted a particular, then the particular pot which is yet to be produced being non-existent, it could not be denoted as the instrument of the said activity. Hence, it must be admitted that the term 'pot' denotes its object as the instrument of the activity of 'making' in the form of the universal which, as held above, functions as an accessory to the production of the effect manifesting it.[111] Thus, the pot is both the instrument as well as the object of the act of production; it is instrument (*sādhana*) as the universal (potness) and an object (*karma*) as the particular pot.[112] The universal and the particular, for the Grammarian of the universalist school, are not absolutely different from one another like a cow and a horse. They are as it were congealed into one another. There is, therefore, no contradiction if a linguistic expression

---

108. na tad utpadyate kiñcid yasya jātir na vidyate,
ātmābhivyaktaye jātiḥ kāraṇānāṁ prayojikā. Op. cit., 25.
109. Op. cit., 26; HR, p. 36.
110. See HR, p. 36.
111. nirvartyamānaṁ yatkarma jātistatrāpi sādhanam,
svāśrayasyābhiniṣpattau sā kriyāṇāṁ prayojikā. Op. cit., 27.
112. jātirūpāśrayeṇa ca sādhanatā, vyaktirūpāśrayeṇa ca karmatā. HR, p. 37.

is based on both of them.[113] The individualist, on the other hand, for whom the meaning of words is a particular, explains the problem in a different way. He maintains that the instrumentality of the particular pot (which is yet to be produced) signified by the term 'pot' in the expression 'he is making a pot' is only metaphorical or ideal.[114]

The contention of Bhartṛhari that the universal alone is the denoted meaning of words might be challenged in another way. It might be asked, how can the universal alone be signified by words when it is never found apart from the particular? Bhartrhari answers the question by an analogy. The reflection of one's face in water or mirror is called 'face'. Although such a designation is incorrect, yet what is signified by the term 'face' is the reflected face alone and not the reflecting medium, viz., water or mirror. In the same way, the word designates the universal alone without any reference to the particular manifesting it.[115] The essence of Bhartṛhari's contention is that even though the universal is inseparably related to the particular, yet in order to explain the identity of meaning the universal alone is to be admitted as the denotation of a word. On the authority of verbal cognition, says Helārāja, nothing other than the universal is admissible as the meaning of words.[116] In sense-cognition, however, both the universal and the particular may be admitted to be always apprehended as congealed into one another, since they are never found separately.

Now, this raises another important question. If the particulars are never apprehended by the word, how are verbal cognitions of universals differentiated? Universals which are admitted to be the denoted meanings of words, are, by hypothesis, ubiquitous. How, then, is the cognition of the universal conveyed by a word differentiated from the cognition of the universal conveyed by another? In order to meet this difficulty Bhartṛhari admits the function of particulars in verbal cognition, but he maintains that they function without being themselves apprehended by the word. He gives the example of sense-organs. Sense-organs cause the difference of sense-cognitions

113. na hi jātivyaktī atyantabhinne gavāśvavat, sammūrchitasvabhāvatvād ityubhaya-rūpāśrayo vyapadeśo 'viruddhaḥ. Ibid., p. 37.

114. vyaktipadārthapakṣe tu upacārasattāśrayaṁ sādhanatvaṁ vakṣyati. Ibid. p. 37. Also see VP, III, vii, 7.

115. yathā jalādibhirvyaktaṁ mukhamevābhidhīyate,
tathā dravyairabhivyaktā jātirevābhidhīyate. Op. cit., 29.

116. āśrayasamavāyāviyoge' pi sarvatrābhedātsaṅketopapattau jātiḥ śabdābhidheyā śuddhā, śābde jñāne tathā pratīteḥ. HR, p. 39.

without being themselves apprehended. In the same way, he argues, particulars cause the difference of verbal cognitions of universals without being themselves apprehended.[117] Just as the existence of different sense-organs is inferred to account for the difference of sense-cognitions, in the same way particulars, though not apprehended by the word, may be admitted to account for the difference of verbal cognitions of universals.[118] Helārāja explains that the universals apprehended as the meanings of words in verbal cognition being actually inherent in particulars, the latter also enter in that cognition and, therefore, there is no confusion in the apprehension of the meaning of words.[119] Thus the universalist has to admit finally that particulars are not entirely left out from verbal cognition though, according to his theory, they are not directly signified by words. He differentiates between the denoted meaning of a word and the cognition arising from it. The denoted meaning of a word is the universal alone, but the cognition arising from it includes the particular also, because in perceptual experience the universal is invariably found to inhere in the particulars.[120]

8. *Justification from the Advaitic stand-point*

The universalist theory as expounded above makes a distinction between the universal and the particular. How can this distinction be justified from the non-dualistic (*Advaita*) stand-point? For the Advaitist, all the categories of reality (*padārthas*), being rooted in ignorance (*avidyā*) and being declared as false by the scriptures (*āgama*), are particulars (*vyakti*). How then is the distinction of the universal and the particular to be explained in this view? Bhartṛhari replies that, from the Advaitic stand-point, whatever is identical and remains uncontradicted in the cognition of difference is real and is called the universal, and whatever is different is unreal and is called the particular.[121] Ornaments made of gold, for example, become the

---

117. yathendriyagato bheda indriyagrahaṇādṛte,
indriyārtheṣvadṛṣto ' pi jñānabhedāya kalpate.
tathātmarūpagrahaṇāt keṣāñcid vyaktayo vinā,
sāmānyajñānabhedānāmupayānti nimittatām. Op. cit., 30-31.

118. HR, p. 39.

119. śābde pratyaye śabdārthabhūtānāṁ sāmānyānāṁ vastutaḥ samavāyaniyamāt viśeṣamāvedayantīti na sāṅkaryaṁ śabdārtha ityarthah. Op. cit., pp. 39-40.

120. See HR, p. 40.

121. satyāsatyau tu yau bhāvau pratibhāvaṁ vyavasthitau,
satyaṁ yattatra sā jātirasatyā vyaktayaḥ smṛtāḥ. Op. cit., 32. Also see HR, p. 40.

objects of cognition by suppressing each other's form, that is, by excluding each other. Nevertheless, all of them are identically cognised as 'gold'. So, the reality of the particular ornaments, according to the Advaitic view, is the identity running through them, which is cognised as gold. This identity is the universal and the different ornaments are particulars. In the same way, gold is a particular mode of fire (*tejas*) which has several other modes. Hence, fire is the universal running through the particular modes of gold, light, etc., and constitutes their reality. Thus we arrive at the *primal cause* (*parā prakṛtiḥ*) which is the identity running through all the modes and constituting their reality. This primal cause, according to the Advaitist, is the foundational consciousness, Brahman, which is the ultimate Universal immanent in all the particular modes.[122]

Thus, from the non-dualistic stand-point, there is only one universal Brahman, the *Existence itself*, which is ultimately real. This universal appears in determinate forms as specific universals, such as 'substancehood', 'cowness', etc. One and the same universal Existence, due to the diversity of particulars through which it is manifested in our empirical consciousness, becomes (apparently) diversified into diverse universals. These universals are therefore ultimately non-different from *Existence*. 'Cowness' is nothing but the *Existence* of the cows, so is 'horseness' of the horses. No universal other than this, subsisting identically in different particulars, is ever apprehended. It is to this universal, viz., Existence appearing in the form of different universals that all the words ultimately refer.[123] But, since words refer to Existence as differentiated by the particulars into diverse universals, they convey their meaning without any confusion.[124] From the ultimate stand-point, however, all universals are identical with Existence and so are all the particular existents also. The diversity of universals and particulars, as also the distinction of the universal and the particular, is according to the Advaitist, true only from the empirical point of view. So, the contention of the universalist that all words denote universals is not affected since, even from the non-dualistic stand-point, all words refer to Existence which is the Universal par excellence.[125] Helārāja observes that ultimately the

122. See HR, p. 40.
123. sambandhibhedātsattaiva bhidyamānā gavādiṣu,
jātirityucyate tasyām sarve śabdā vyavasthitāḥ. VP, III, i, 33.
124. See HR, p. 41.
125. tataśca sarvaśabdānāṁ sattāvācakatvājjātipadārthavyāptiḥ. HR, p. 43.

positions of both the universalist and the individualist are identical. For the universalist, all words refer to Brahman as Existence under various determinations, and, for the individualist, all words denote Brahmaṇ as substance under various adjuncts. The two aspects might be distinguished on the basis of the difference of the imports of words 'existence' and 'substance'. But ultimately Brahman as Existence and Brahman as substance being non-different, the positions of both the universalist and the individualist are identical.[126]

9. *An account of the nature of universals*

Having argued that the universalist theory of meaning is justifiable from the stand-points of all the systems of thought, Bhartṛhari proceeds to give an account of the nature of universals from the empirical point of view. He begins by pointing out that universals, such as 'earthness', 'fireness', etc., do not depend on a definite shape or form for their manifestation, while universals, such as 'cowness', 'potness' etc., are manifested only in things having a definite shape. Again, universals do not perish with the particulars like qualities; their existence is not tied with the particulars, though their cognition is. This is evident from the fact that even after the destruction of a particular, the same cognition arises in respect of other particulars. As Bhartṛhari remarks, the universal is never without a substratum; there is always some particular to support it. Hence, the destruction of a particular does not imply the destruction of the universal also.[127]

One might ask, what happens to the universals at the time of deluge (*mahāpralaya*) when all the particulars are supposed to be destroyed? How could the universal be said to subsist in the absence of a substratum? These questions, as Bhartṛhari points out, are answered by different systems in different ways. The Mīmāṁsakas, who hold the universal to be eternal and never without a substratum, refuse to admit a state of deluge in which all the particulars are destroyed. A state of the universe in which there are no instances of universals, is denied by them. Just as there is no absolute beginning

126. yadyapi ca dravyapadārthe'pi brahmadravyasyābhidhānam upādhibheda-bhinnasya vakṣyati tathāpi tātparyabhedād avasthābhedaḥ ......ayameva ca pakṣadvaye 'pyekapakṣībhāvarūpah siddhāntaḥ paramārthadṛṣṭyā. Op. cit., p. 43.

127. Op. cit., 41; HR, p. 48.

of the universe, so also there is no absolute annihilation of all the particular existents.[128] Bhartṛhari seems to support this position.

The Sāṁkhya, the Vedānta and the Nyāya-Vaiśeṣika, on the other hand, admit the state of deluge and explain the problem in different ways. According to the Sāṁkhya and the Vedānta, who proclaim the unity of the universe in Prakṛti and Brahman respectively, there is no absolute annihilation of things. Deluge means only the merging of all things into the primordial cause—Prakṛti or Brahman. All things, in this state, are contained in the primordial cause in the form of potencies (*śaktirūpa*). These potencies may, without contradiction, be said to be related to their respective universals when there are no actual particulars. That is to say, universals, in the state of deluge, exist in the primordial substance itself. But, since there is nothing apart from the primordial substance in the state of deluge, the universal can be said to subsist in it only as identical with it.[129] In other words, universals exist in deluge in the form of the universal cause, whether regarded as Prakṛti or as Brahman. This is how the Sāṁkhya and the Advaita try to meet the problem of the existence of universals in the state of deluge. The Nyāya-Vaiśeṣika, on the other hand, holds that universals exist in deluge without any support.[130] The problem for him arises only with regard to unversals subsisting in composite objects alone. He maintains that the universal does not require the particular to support it, since it is not a physical object having weight. It can exist by itself without any support. It requires particulars only to manifest it. There is no contradiction, according to him, in maintaining that universals exist in deluge without being manifested.[131]

The problem where the universals reside in the state of deluge arises only if universals are regarded as confined to their particular instances (*vyaktisarvagata*). But if they are regarded as ubiquitous (*sarvasarvagata*), the problem would not arise at all. The Vaiśeṣika might hold that the universals reside in the eternal atoms in the state of deluge. One might object that if all universals reside in all things,

128. anucchedyāśrayāmeke sarvāṁ jātiṁ pracakṣate,
na yaugapadyaṁ pralaye sarvasyeti vyavasthitāḥ. Op. cit., 42.

129. prakṛtau pravilīneṣu bhedeṣvekatvadarśinām.
dravyasattvaṁ prapadyante svāśrayā eva jātayaḥ. Ibid., 43.

130. vaiśeṣikadarśane tu nirādhārā eva ghaṭatvādijātayo mahāpralaye āsate. HR, p. 49.

131. na hi gurutvād adhaḥpatanam āsāṁ mā bhūd ityādhāraḥ, abhivyaktimātre tasyopayogāt. tadānīṁ cānabhivyaktā eva āsatām, ko virodhaḥ? HR, pp. 49-50.

there will be confusion of classes (*jātisāṅkarya*). The answer is that there is no such danger, since all particulars do not manifest all universals. Particulars by their very nature manifest only specific universals. Hence, although universals are ubiquitous, there is no contingency of any confusion of classes.[132]

10. *A defence of the existence of universals*

Bhartṛhari strongly defends the existence of universals against the nominalist attack. The nominalist argues that universals are supposed to exist by the realist as the bases of identical conceptions. But such a supposition is unwarranted, since universals are never perceived apart from the particular. As regards the identical conceptions of particulars, they may be explained either on the basis of similarity (*sādṛśya*), or on the basis of a natural power (*sāmarthya*) possessed by the particulars. There is, therefore, no logical necessity of admitting universals. Against this nominalist objection Bhartṛhari argues that whether the cause of identical conceptions is regarded as similarity of particulars, or as a natural power possessed by them, it has to be regarded as a universal. The said 'similarity' and 'natural power' are essentially non-different from the universal.[133] The universal, by definition, is that feature of particulars which is the basis of their identical conceptions. There is no harm if someone prefers to call it 'similarity' or 'natural power'.[134]

Helārāja explains that the existence of universals is assumed because identical cognitions are not accountable on the basis of mutually exclusive particulars. If the said similarity and natural power are also non-different from particulars, i.e., if they are not common features, they cannot serve as the basis of identical cognitions. Hence, the universal, as something different from particulars and as their common feature, has necessarily to be admitted.[135] If, on the other hand, similarity and natural power are regarded as common features, they are, as has been said above, non-different from universals.

---

132. See VP, III, i, 44; HR, p. 50.
133. abhedarūpaṁ sādṛśyamātmabhūtāśca śaktayaḥ,
jātiparyāyavācitvaṁ eṣāmapyupavarṇyate. Op. cit., 92.
134. See HR, p. 93.
135. sādṛśyasāmarthye tu vyaktyavyatirikte tadvadanuyāyinī vyatiriktā jātir abhyupagantavyā. Op. cit., p. 94.

The opponent might adopt another line of attack. He may argue that, according to the universalist, the inherence of universals in particulars is determined by specific configurations (*viśiṣṭasaṁsthāna*), since otherwise there will be confusion of classes. It is due to the similarity of configurations that a specific universal is said to subsist in specific particulars.[136] Now, if the similarity of configurations, which are different in different particulars, can be said to determine the subsistence of an identical universal in them, then it can as well be said to determine their identical cognition. What is the necessity of admitting universals?

Bhartṛhari answers that the cause must be appropriate to the effect, that is, it must explain the effect. Again, every effect has a specific cause; everything is not the cause of everything. For example, the cause of the cognition of a man as 'the man with the stick' (*daṇḍī*) is the man actually holding the stick and not the one merely desiring to hold the stick. The desire to hold the stick may be the cause of holding the stick, but it cannot be said to be the cause of the cognition of the man as 'the man with the stick'. It may however be said to be the cause of the cognition of a person as 'one desiring to hold a stick'.[137] In the same way, the similarity of configuration, which is admitted to determine the inherence of universals in specific particulars, cannot legitimately be regarded as the cause of their identical cognition also.[138] Similarity of configuration may produce the cognition of particulars as 'similar'. In the same way, the said natural potency possessed by the particulars may produce the cognition of them as having that potency. But they cannot produce the cognition of particulars as 'the same'. The cognition of identity is different from the cognition of similarity, since the latter arises even in respect of things belonging to different species. Hence, the universal determining identical cognitions of things must necessarily be admitted.[139]

Helārāja puts forward a spirited defence of the reality of universals. The opponent might argue that from the identical cognition of particulars one might legitimately infer the existence of something as

136. See HR, p. 94.
137. Op. cit., 93-94.
138. evaṁ sādṛśyādeḥ sāmānyasya viṣayaniyamasāmarthye satyapi na tasmādeva sāmarthyād anugatākārajñānajanakatvaṁ yuktam. HR, p. 95.
139. See HR, p. 96.

its cause. But how can one assert that it is a universal, when no universal apart from the particulars is ever perceived? Helārāja answers that universals are definitely perceived as inherent in the particular things. They are not merely inferred entities. Inferential arguments for their existence are advanced only in order to convince the opponent.[140] The universal, which is admitted as the cause of identical cognitions, is not like sense organs (*adhipatipratyaya*) which are only inferable. It is the external basis (*ālambanapratyaya*) of identical cognitions and is perceivable.[141] Helārāja rejects the Buddhist contention that the universal is only the object of conception and not that of perception. If there were no universals, the conceptual cognition of universals could be said to be non-perceptual; but since there are universals, their cognition has to be admitted as perceptual.[142] Besides, the Buddhist argument that the universal is unreal because it is the object of conception, and it is the object of conception because it is unreal, involves circularity (*itaretarāśrayatā*).[143] Further, the Buddhist in his epistemology admits that the cognition having the form of 'blue' corresponds to the sensation of blue. What is wrong if the universalist in the same manner maintains that the cognition having an identical form corresponds to the sensation of the identical. What is the difference between the two? What is the ground for holding the 'blue' as perceptual and the universal, which has a similar claim, as non-perceptual?[144] As there is no ground for such discrimination, the universal must be admitted to be a perceptual entity. If there were no universals inherent in particulars, there could be no identical cognition of them at all. The cognitions of particulars are not different, because they are produced by an identical cause. The Buddhist contention that the identical cognition of particulars is illusory is rejected by Helārāja as illogical. There can be no illusion of identity unless there was a veridical experience of it. Hence, the reality of the universal as the basis of identical cognitions is undeniable.[145]

---

140. tatra rūpisamavāyāt cākṣuṣāṇyeva sāmānyānīti brūmaḥ. vipratipannaṁ tu prati kāryakalpyatvam ucyate. Op. cit., p. 96.
141. Loc. cit.
142. asati sāmānye vikalpo na pratyakṣam. na sati, satyaviṣayatvāt. Loc. cit.
143. Loc. cit.
144. yena nīlaṁ pratyakṣaṁ sāmānyam īdṛśamevāpratyakṣam iti. Loc. cit.
145. Loc. cit.

Bhartṛhari maintains that the reality of the universal can be admitted even from the Sāṁkhya and the Advaita point of view. According to these views, the experienced harmony in the universe proves that the universe is the effect of one self-identical cause, and since the non-existent cannot be produced, the universe and its cause are identical. Thus all things in the universe are related by identity-in-difference. One and the same identity being manifested in manifold forms, the element of identity is the universal and that of difference is the particular. The identity which is immanent in all the particulars is the highest universal (*mahāsāmānya*). The same identity in specific determinations is the plurality of minor universals.[146] All things are manifestations, or appearances, of one universal cause. The universal and the particular, according to this view, are neither absolutely identical nor absolutely different, since they are never so apprehended. Helārāja maintains that there is no contradiction in asserting the universal and the particular as both identical and different. There would be contradiction only if the terms 'identity' and 'difference' are used in the absolute sense. In the absence of a better word, the term identity-in-difference is used to indicate the specific relation apprehended between the universal and the particular.[147] The universal is not absolutely different from the particular. The particular itself, as Bhartṛhari says, is universal—the object of identical cognition—when the mind apprehends it as identical, rejecting its aspect of difference.[148] Although all things are ultimately identical with the primal cause, yet their empirical plurality, which is an experienced fact, has to be recognised. Thus, when the empirical differences are rejected, pure Existence shines forth as the object of identical cognitions. Similarly, when all predicates (*dharma*) are denied, the pure subject (*dharmī*) becomes apprehended as 'substance'. Things are cognised as 'earth', 'water', etc., by negating more determinate class-differences under them, and by recognising broader class affinities. In the same way, when individual differences are denied and mutual similarity of particulars alone is taken into

146. See HR, p. 97.

147. kevalaṁ svasaṁvijñānapadābhāvād agatyā bhedābhedaśabdābhyāṁ yadābhidhīyate tadā śabdasādṛśyamātrād avivakṣitabhedābhedarūpādhyāropeṇa parairvirodho nirviṣaya ivāpadyate. Loc. cit.

148. yadā bhedān parityajya budhyaika iva gṛhyate,
vyaktyātmaiva tadā tatra buddhirekā pravartate. Op. cit., 96.

account, classes such as 'cow', 'horse', 'pot', etc., come to be recognised.[149]

Bhartrhari draws some important distinctions between three types of cognitions, namely, the cognitions of identity (*abhedà*), similarity (*sādṛśya*) and group (*samūha*). The cognition of a group is not the cognition of the universal. The cognition of 'forest', for example, is not the cognition of identity like that of 'tree'. In the former cognition, numerous trees are cognised as though they were one due to superimposition of identity. Such cognitions arise only when there is a plurality of particulars and not, like the cognition of the universal, even when there is only one particular.[150] In other words, in the cognition of group, difference is fundamental and identity is imputed, while in the cognition of the universal, identity is fundamental and no difference is apprehended at all. Both these types of cognitions are, again, different from the cognition of similarity. The cognition of similarity presupposes the cognition of difference. Two things are cognised as 'similar' when they are first cognised as different and then are seen to share certain features in common. Thus, in the case of the cognition of similarity, the apprehension of identity (in certain respect) is preceded by the apprehension of difference. But in the case of the cognitions of identity and group, the situation is different. In the case of the cognition of identity (universal), no difference is felt at all. In the case of the cognition of group, on the other hand, the identity pervading difference is at once apprehended. While, in the case of the cognition of similarity, the apprehension of partial identity follows the apprehension of difference.[151] It is because of these differences of cognitions that similarity is not recognised as a universal (*jāti*).[152]

Bhartṛhari thus maintains that the identical cognitions of particulars necessarily imply the existence of the corresponding universals.

---

149. See HR, p. 97.
150. bhedarūpairanusyūtaṁ yadaikamiva manyate,
samūhāvagrahā buddhirbahubhyo jāyate tadā. Op. cit., 97. Also see HR, pp. 97-98.
151. sakṛtapravṛttāvekatvam āvṛttau sadṛśātmatām,
bhinnātmikānāṁ vyaktīnāṁ bhedāpohāt prapadyate. Op. cit., 98. See HR, p. 98.
152. evaṁ bhedābhedāvagraharūpatvānneyaṁ jātibuddhiḥ, tasyā ekāntenābhedāvasāyarūpatvāt. ..... evaṁ ca buddhibhedādeva na sādṛśyaṁ sāmānyam ityuktaṁ bhavati. HR, p. 98.

Now, this gives rise to an important question as to whether this principle is to be extended also to the case of cognitions. The realist might urge that in the case of particular cognitions also, as in the case of particular things, the identical cognition of them as 'cognition' must be admitted to imply the existence of the corresponding universal. Identity and difference of things, according to the realist, are determined by categories different from them. So, the identity of cognitions must be admitted to be determined by the universal subsisting in them. Again, it is on the basis of the universal inherent in cognitions that the universal inherent in things is ascertained. That is, identity of cognitions is the sole ground on which the existence of universals in particulars is admitted. Hence, the universal determining the identity of cognitions has to be recognised.[153]

Bhartṛhari maintains that cognitions cannot be equated to the objects of cognition. In the case of objects it may be true that they are known in the form of the universal which is different from them. But this is not true in the case of cognitions. It is the nature of the object to be known in the form of others, not that of cognition. A cognition is never known as an object at all. Hence, no universal subsisting in cognitions and determining their identity is admissible. Cognitions being rooted in objects, their identity is determined by the identical universal subsisting in the objects.[154] In the same way, no intrinsic difference in the cognitions is conceivable, since they are dependent on the external objects. Just as the identity of cognitions is determined by the identity of the universal inherent in things, so is the difference of cognitions determined by the difference of universals inhering in them.[155]

Why should cognition be not admitted as an object? Bhartṛhari answers that just as a light is not illumined by another light, so is a cognition not known by another cognition.[156] Objects, such as pot, etc., require to be illumined by light, but the light itself does not stand

153. jñāneṣvapi yathārtheṣu tathā sarveṣu jātayaḥ,
saṁsargadarśane santi tāścārthasya prasādhikāḥ Op. cit., 102. See HR, p. 101.

154. jñeyasthameva sāmānyaṁ jñānānāmupakārakam,
na jātu jneyavajjñānaṁ pararūpeṇa rūpyate. Op. cit., 103.

155. bāhyaparavaśatvenāsvādhīnatvāj jñānānāṁ svata eva vailakṣaṇyānupapatteḥ bahirabhinnena nimittena tatra bhāvyam. tadyathā ghaṭo ghaṭa iti ghaṭākāre bāhyaṁ nimittaṁ tathā bhede 'pi tadgataṁ sāmānyam iti yuktam. HR, p. 101.

156. yathā jyotiḥ prakāśena nānyenābhiprakāśyate,
jñānākārastathānyena na jñānenopagṛhyate. Op. cit., 104.

in need of another light to illumine it. In the same way, cognition which reveals the object does not require another cognition to reveal it, that is, it is self-luminous. Explaining further, Helārāja observes that to reveal is the nature of cognition as distinguished from the unconscious object (*jaḍa*) which is always revealed. If the former also required to be revealed, it would be indistinguishable from the latter.[157] Besides, if at the time of the revelation of the object the revealing cognition were itself unrevealed, there could be no consciousness of the object at all. A consciousness of the object without the consciousness of the light revealing it is an unproved assumption.[158] Hence, cognition must be admitted to be self-revealed, that is, not being the object of another cognition. It cannot, therefore, be cognised in the form of another like an object. The identity of cognitions is determined by the identical universal subsisting in the objects. It is due to this external determination that cognitions are apprehended as identical. Moreover, if the felt identity of cognitions were due to the universal inherent in them, there would be no logical ground for believing in the existence of universals external to mind.[159]

The Nyāya-Vaiśeṣika might urge that a cognition also, like the object of cognition, is apprehended as an object. Just as in the cognition 'this is pot' what is apprehended is 'pot', so also in the cognition 'this is the cognition of pot', what is apprehended is 'the cognition of pot'. What is the difference between the two cognitions? If the cognition of 'the cognition of pot' was not the cognition of an object, then it should not have been so expressed in the above judgment. A verbal expression is based on experience. It cannot be said that a cognition cognises itself, because such an assertion would be self-contradictory. As regards the distinction of cognition from the external object, it is explainable on another ground. Cognitions being of the nature of consciousness, they apprehend the object, though not themselves. This is sufficient to distinguish them from objects which apprehend nothing. However, when there is desire to know a cognition, another cognition is necessarily required. There

---

157. jaḍavailakṣaṇyam hi prakāśakatvam iti tasyāpi prakāśyatve jaḍatāpattiḥ. Op. cit., p. 102.
158. prakāśāsañcetane tallagnārthasañcetanāsiddheḥ. Loc. cit.
159. svasamavetasāmānyavaśena tvabhedapratibhāse bahiḥ sāmānyaparikalpo nirnibandhana eva syāt. Loc. cit.

is no contingency of infinite regress, as may be alleged, since in practice we never go about cognising each cognition.[160]

As opposed to the above contention of the Nyāya-Vaiśeṣika, Bhartṛhari maintains that there is an appreciable difference between the cognition of an object and the cognition of that cognition. The cognition 'this is the cognition of pot' is intrinsically different from the cognition 'this is pot'.[161] It is the cognition of a 'cognition', not that of an 'object'. The cognition of 'pot' is produced directly by a pot, but not the cognition of the cognition of pot. The cognition immediately following the given object can alone be regarded as caused by the object; that following the cognition of the object cannot be regarded as such, because there is breach of continuity (*vyavadhāna*).[162] Again, the cognition of 'pot' cannot be felt as an *object* in another cognition, because, the two cognitions being similar in nature as cognitions, there can be no subject-object-opposition between them.[163] That is, the congition of an object is never felt as an 'other' in another cognition. And even if it be granted, says Bhartṛhari, that the cognition of 'pot' is felt as an *object* in another cognition, it does not prove the opponent's point, because what is apprehended as an object is not its nature as cognition but its determination by the object, i.e., pot.[164] What is meant is that a cognition is never revealed by another cognition; it is always self-revealed, and what is revealed by another cognition is not a cognition at all. The nature of a cognition as cognition is never felt as an 'other' in another cognition.[165] Hence, cognition cannot be regarded as an 'object' similar to the external things.

Bhartṛhari thus rejects the Nyāya-Vaiśeṣika view of cognition and upholds the Advaitic view with regard to its nature. Consequently he maintains that no universal can be said to inhere in cognitions, since they are never felt as objects. The felt identity of cognitions is

---

160. See HR, p. 102.
161. ghaṭajñānamiti jñānaṁ ghaṭajñānavilakṣaṇam,
ghaṭa ityapi yajjñānaṁ viṣayopanipāti tat. Op. cit., 105.
162. anukāryapratyayā eva hi viṣayeṇa janyante nānye jñānālambanāḥ, vyavadhānāt. HR, p. 103.
163. sārūpyabalena ca grāhyagrāhakabhāvena vaidharmyeṇa na ca ghaṭajñānaṁ jñānāntare pratibhāsate. ato na tad gṛhyate. Ibid., p. 103.
164. See the verse 102 quoted above.
165. na tu sā tadīyā bodharūpatā tasya pratibhāsate parasaṁvedana iva. HR, p. 104.

explainable on the basis of the universal inhering in the objects. The identity of cognitions felt in introspection having been thus explained, there is also no logical necessity of admitting the inherence of the universal in them. Nevertheless, so far as the objects of cognition are concerned, Bhartṛhari maintains, the inherence of the universal in them as the basis of their identical conception and designation must necessarily be admitted.[166]

11. *Concluding remarks*

We discussed in the foregoing pages the Grammarian's view of word and meaning with special reference to Bhartṛhari. This discussion has contributed largely to the understanding of the nature of the word and that of the meaning conveyed by it. The distinction drawn by Bhartṛhari between the word as particular and the word as universal is highly significant. In his conception of the word as universal he comes very close to Russell's view according to which the word is not 'a single entity' but 'a class'.[167] It is indisputable that the word as universal alone is significant. Unless the word read or heard in the present moment is recognised to be 'the same' as known in the past, it cannot convey any meaning at all. To use a modern terminology, a word must be recognised to be a 'token' of a certain 'type', otherwise it will be nothing more than a meaningless mark or noise to us.[168]

As regards the question of the import of words, the Grammarians are divided into two camps: one holding the individual and the other the universal as the meaning of words. Both these views undoubtedly have some weighty arguments in their favour. The universalist view explains the generality of the meaning more satisfactorily, while the individualist view scores better in explaining the syntactical relation

166. See HR, pp. 104-5.
167. "The spoken word 'dog' is not a single entity : it is a class of similar movements of tongue, throat, and larynx. Just as jumping is one class of bodily movements, and walking another, so the uttered word 'dog' is a third class of bodily movements. The word 'dog' is a universal, just as *dog* is a universal." *An Enquiry into Meaning and Truth,* Pelican, p. 22.
168. Cf. "If I am to speak or listen understandingly, to write or to read, I have to recognise the sounds or black marks as being the words they are. I have to recognise this visible mark or noise as a sensible 'token' of a certain 'type'-word. Otherwise it will not function for me as a word at all; it will be just a curious sound or mark and nothing more". H. H. Price : *Thinking and Experience,* p. 38.

of words and their reference to action, number, gender, etc. However, an exclusive emphasis on one, either the universal or the individual, as the meaning of words leads, as we have seen, to insoluble difficulties. Ultimately both the views have to admit, though somewhat inconsistently, the rejected element through the back-door. The universalist admits the individual as the content of verbal cognition, though he denies that it is the content of the direct meaning of words. It is through the individual thus comprehended that the universal is said to become related to action, number, etc. Similarly, the individualist admits the role of the universal, which is not admitted as the content of meaning, in verbal cognition as the distinguishing mark (*upalakṣaṇa*) of the individual signified by the word. It is due to the universal thus comprehended that verbal cognition acquires a general character. This shows that verbal cognition cannot be explained satisfactorily if the import of words is confined exclusively either to the universal or to the individual. Patañjali, therefore, rightly remarks that both the individualist and the universalist have to admit both the individual and the universal as the content of the meaning of words. In our view, the Nyāya theory of composite denotation discussed in the previous chapter is far more satisfactory than the extreme views held by the universalists and the individualists.

Bhartṛhari, however, strongly defends the universalist theory of meaning. He tries to support his view from the stand-points of all the systems of thought. He maintains that all words, without exception, denote universals. Even the words standing for single entities, such as 'space', 'time', etc., and proper names signify universals. The principal reason behind this contention is that words always convey to us what is general; the particular, or the unique, is never touched by them. Even if the contention that words always signify some kind of generality be accepted, certain distinctions will have to be made. The generality signified by class-names, such as 'cow', 'pot', 'blue', etc., must be distinguished from the generality signified by proper names. The one is the identity of a class, while the other is the identity of a person. The notion of the former does not involve temporal continuity, while that of the latter does. Hence, the one cannot be equated to the other. Bhartṛhari seems to overlook this distinction when he says that all words denote universals. He may possibly have used the term *jāti* (universal) in a very broad sense; but, in any case, the distinction between the meanings of class-names and proper names cannot be ignored.

There is one more point which requires to be considered here. Bhartṛhari's contention that all words denote universals may with some reservations be accepted so far as the 'object-words' signifying substances, qualities, individuals, etc., are concerned. But how can words, such as 'if', 'either', 'otherwise', 'than', 'or', 'and', etc., which have meaning only in certain verbal contexts, be said to denote universals in any intelligible sense? These words are no doubt general and they serve important functions in language. But it would be absurd to maintain that they stand for objective features. It is possible that Bhartṛhari had in his mind only object-words and not those which have merely syntactical significance when he asserted that all words denote universals.

Further, the contention of Bhartṛhari that general words denote the universal alone is fraught with unsurmountable difficulties, The Nyāya criticism of this view discussed in the previous chapter reveals the inherent weakness of this theory. The main argument of Bhartṛhari in favour of his theory is that the individual with all its differentiating characteristics, which make it an individual, is never conveyed by a word. When the word 'cow', for example, is heard, what is understood is not a particular cow but any cow, or cow in general. This may be accepted without any serious dispute. Even the Naiyāyika, who holds the individual qualified by the universal as the import of words, does not assert that a specific individual is signified by the word. What is signified by the word 'cow' is any individual having the general feature called 'cowness'. Thus he maintains that the comprehension of the individual in verbal cognition is undeniable. Even Bhartṛhari, as we have noted, has to admit the function of the individual in verbal cognition in order to explain the difference of cognitions produced by different words. But he maintains at the same time that individuals serve only to differentiate verbal cognitions without being themselves apprehended by the word. In other words, the individual, according to Bhartṛhari, is the content of the cognition produced by a word, though not of its meaning. This is said to become possible because, in perceptual experience, the universal is always apprehended as inherent in particulars. It is because of the mental association of the universal and the particular generated by perceptual experience that the latter becomes the content of verbal cognition, though it is not conveyed by the word. Any way, Bhartṛhari has to admit the individual as the content of verbal cognition, though he denies that it is the content of the meaning of words. Is not the Nyāya view which accepts the individual qualified by the universal as the meaning of words more simple and straightforward?

Coming to the question of the ontological status of universals, it is clear that Bhartṛhari's view is the same as that of the Advaita. The Word for him is the Absolute which appears, on the one hand, as the plurality of words and, on the other, as the plurality of objects. Although everything is held to be ultimately identical with the word, the diversity of words and objects as also the plurality of universals manifested by particulars is recognised from the empirical point of view. Universals as well as particulars for Bhartṛhari are ultimately illusory (*kalpita*), though empirically real. He supports the Advaitic view that all universals are ultimately identical with the universal Existence. At the same time, he strongly upholds the empirical reality of universals. He argues like a realist that the identical cognitions of particulars necessarily imply objective universals. For him universals, as Helārāja explains, are not merely inferred entities, but perceptual facts. He rejects conceptualism when he maintains that identity alone, and not similarity, can serve as the basis of identical cognitions. Bhartṛhari's view of universals, therefore, may be characterised as epistemologically realistic; universals, like particulars, are, according to him, independent of our knowledge, though ultimately both of them are illusions of the mind. The ultimate illusoriness of universals, as also of particulars, is a necessary consequence of an absolutistic stand-point.

CHAPTER X

THE BUDDHIST NOMINALISM (APOHAVĀDA)—I

We have so far discussed the realistic and the conceptualistic theories of universals and the allied theories of the import of words in Indian Philosophy. But we have yet to discuss one of the most important theories of universals, namely, the nominalism of the Buddhist. Although a brief reference to the doctrine has already been made in Chapter four, yet the doctrine deserves a fuller discussion. As a matter of fact, the controversy between the realist and the Buddhist nominalist over the question of universals and the meaning of words forms the core of the discussion on this subject in Indian Philosophy. In the course of this controversy the whole range of questions concerning conceptual knowledge and its relation to reality are raised and discussed in great detail. We shall, therefore, devote two chapters, the present and the following one, for the discussion of the Buddhist doctrine.

I. *THE THEORY OF DIGNĀGA AND DHARMAKĪRTI*

The Buddhist, as we have already noted, rejects the reality of universals altogether. This rejection gives rise to some very important issues concerning the status of conceptual knowledge and the role of language as a source of the knowledge of reality. For the realist, conceptual knowledge is a direct apprehension of the real. Words and concepts stand for real universals, or particulars qualified by them. But, for the Buddhist, the real is the unique, causally efficient point-instant which is outside the reach of words and concepts. It is the non-empirical ultimate reality grasped in pure sense-apprehension. The universal, according to him, is an unreal fiction, as it is not given in sense-apprehension. It is the form constructed by the understanding in order to comprehend the flowing reality. Hence, it is necessary to ask what exactly is the status of conceptual knowledge in the Buddhist view? What is the relation, if any, between thought-constructions (universals) and the ultimately real particulars? The

Buddhist answers these questions by his theory of *apoha* (nominalism). This theory seeks to establish (i) that concepts and words have no direct relation to reality; the belief in their objective reference is a transcendental illusion; (ii) that the objects of conceptual cognitions are universals which are pure thought-constructions; and (iii) that conceptual knowledge, though ultimately false, is empirically valid, because it has an indirect causal relation to reality.

1. *Concepts or universals are thought-constructions*

Dignāga, the father of Buddhist nominalism, holds that concepts and words are intimately related to one another. All expressible knowledge is conceptual and, conversely, all conceptual knowledge is expressible.[1] Concepts and words originate in each other and cover the same field. All concepts are relative, because they are intelligible only in contrast with their opposites. So also all words express their meanings only in contrast with their opposite meanings.[2] This, according to Dignāga, proves that the import of words is negative. Words appear to assert a positive meaning, but actually they deny the contrary meaning. Pure affirmation is the function of sense-apprehension; judgments, which are the products of thought, only negate. There is nothing beside the negation of the contrary (*apoha*) that the words express. The word 'cow', for instance, does not convey the knowledge of all the individual cows, as they are innumerable, nor does it convey the knowledge of a real universal 'cowness', as it is non-existent. All that it communicates is 'the exclusion of non-cow'. Thus the meaning of both the words 'cow' and 'non-cow' consists in the negation of each other. There are, according to Dignāga, two kinds of knowledge: direct, or positive, and indirect, or negative. The former is pure sense-apprehension and the latter is judgment which, in Stcherbatsky's words, is "pure reason" and is "always dialectical."[3] The whole function of concepts, in Dignāga's view, is to represent as unity what involves spatial, temporal and qualitative differences. Words also perform the same function. Hence, concepts alone can legitimately be regarded as the meaning of words. These concepts are the universals constructed by thought owing to the

1. See BL, Vol. I, p. 459.
2. Ibid.
3. Ibid., p. 460.

innate conceptualising tendency of the human mind. They are, therefore, relative and negative.[4]

Dignāga rejects the realist theory that concepts are formed by abstracting identical or similar features observed in repeated perceptions. In the realist view, concepts are rooted in the experience of real objective universals. Dignāga and his followers, on the contrary, maintain that concepts are due not to experience, but to an innate constructive tendency of reason. This theory is obviously rooted in the Buddhist metaphysics which has no place for similarity or identity. The abstraction theory of concepts necessarily implies the objectivity of the character abstracted. If concepts are abstractions from experience, common characteristics and relations would be real. This being incompatible with the Buddhist conception of reality, Dignāga adopts the theory of construction. Concepts are the products of creative thought, having absolutely nothing corresponding to them in the real world.

2. *Words signify mere negations*

Dignāga's nominalism was systematically developed and defended by Dharmakīrti. He maintains that words stand for determinate concepts, and the determinateness of concepts consists in their difference from the contrary concepts. This difference is what is conventionally established as the meaning of words. Words, according to Dharmakīrti, do not have any positive meaning, since what is positive is inexpressible.[5] He rejects the theory of 'double meaning' of words according to which a word directly expresses a positive meaning and indirectly implies the negation of the contrary meaning. He maintains that what is essential for the comprehension of the meaning of words is the exclusion of the contrary meaning. Positive reference is not necessary at all. Moreover, the so called positive meaning of words cannot be comprehended without excluding the opposite meaning. Therefore, 'exclusion of the contrary' can alone be legitimately regarded as the meaning of words.[6] The Buddhist emphasis on the negative meaning of words is a logical consequence of his denial of the reality of universals in any form. If words had positive meaning, universals would be real, since, in the Buddhist

4. Ibid., p. 461.
5. For the Buddhist the words 'positive' and 'real' are synonymous.
6. PV, II, 172 and PVV on it.

view, 'being positive' and 'being real' are one and the same. Thus the imports of words, universals, being negative, they are non-entities. Words signify neither external entities nor internal ideas, for both of them are positive and momentary. They signify 'the difference from others' which is a thought-construction having its source in the innate constructive tendency of the mind.[7]

Dharmakīrti supports the above conclusion by another argument. If verbal cognition is a cognition of the real, then on hearing the word 'red' one should have the sensation of red. That is to say, verbal cognition should be as lively and vivid as sensory cognition. This being not the case, the former must be distinguished from the latter. According to Dharmakīrti, the difference between the two cognitions derives from the difference of their objects. He rejects the realist view that both conceptual and perceptual cognitions may have one and the same object. If objects are held to be common to different types of cognitions, there would be confusion of different sources of knowledge (*pramāṇasamplava*). Difference of sense-organs, for instance, is derived from the difference of objects apprehended by them. In the same way, the difference of conceptual and perceptual cognitions also must be derived from the difference of their objects.[8] Consequently, the object of conceptual cognition must be non-perceptual, and that of perceptual cognition must be non-conceptual. The realist would however urge that one and the same object may be revealed by the two cognitions in two different ways. What is vividly presented by perceptual cognition is presented in a hazy manner by conceptual cognition. The Buddhist rejects this explanation on the ground that the apprehension of the real cannot be both vivid and non-vivid. The vivid apprehension alone is the apprehension of the real. The non-vivid apprehension, by implication, is the apprehension of the illusory.[9] If this dichotomy is not admitted, argues Dharmakīrti, there would be no logical ground for distinguishing perception and conception as two different sources of

---

7. vikalpapratibimbeṣu tanniṣṭheṣu nibadhyate,
(tato 'nyāpohaniṣṭhatvāduktānyāpohakṛcchrutiḥ.)
vyatirekīva yajjñāne bhātyarthapratibimbakam,
śabdāt (tadapi nārthātmā bhrāntiḥ sā vāsanodbhavā). PV, II, 164-65.
8. PV, II, 11 and 24. Also cp. Ap. Sid., p. 6.
Cf. ekarūpaviṣayā ca bhinnapratibhāsā ceti viruddham. PVV, II, 24.
9. See TS, 879; TSP, pp. 280 f; AP. Sid., p. 7.

knowledge. If two sources of knowledge are said to produce the cognition of an identical object, then one of them would become superfluous. Perception presents the self-identical indivisible thing in its entirety leaving nothing to be ascertained by the other source of knowledge. If conceptual cognition is also said to present the same thing, then it is useless, since it adds nothing to our knowledge.[10]

3. *All distinctions are purely conceptual*

The difference between the objects of perceptual and conceptual cognitions for which arguments have been advanced above is, according to Dharmakīrti, not ultimate, but only logical. The 'difference from others' (*apoha*), or the universal, is not an entity apart from the thing itself. If 'the difference from non-cow', for instance, was different from the real cow, then the distinction of 'cow' and 'non-cow' would disappear. Consequently, there would be neither 'cow', nor 'non-cow' nor 'the difference from non-cow'. Hence, the difference (*vyāvṛtti*) and the different (*vyāvṛtta*) cannot be regarded as ultimately different.[11] The objects of conceptual and perceptual cognitions, as has already been shown, cannot also be ultimately identical. The object of the former is general, a thought-construction, while that of the latter is the unique particular, the real. The object of conceptual cognition (*apoha*) is, therefore, neither identical with nor different from the particular. It is a non-entity having no status in reality.[12]

Dharmakīrti extends the above conclusion also to the distinctions of substance and attribute and subject and predicate in a judgment. These are also purely conceptual distinctions. In the same way, the co-existence of different attributes in a single substance is also conceptual. If these distinctions and relations are regarded as real, they become unintelligible. They are however perfectly admissible in the realm of concepts and language which is solely meant for the guidance of practical life.[13] Even the difference between ultimate particulars, according to Dharmakīrti, is not ultimate. Ultimate things in themselves neither unite nor differ; they are only conceived

10. PV, III, 44-45; also PVV on them.
11. PV, III, 58.
12. PV, III, 125 and 128, and PVV on them.
13. PV, III, 60, 62; also PVV on PV, III, 78.

as identical or different.[14] The characterisation of the real as 'product' or 'momentary' is also conceptual. The real cannot legitimately be said to be a 'unique particular' (*svalakṣaṇa*), because such a characterisation involves thought-distinctions. All words, therefore, refer only to conceptual distinctions and relations which are necessary for practical life. In reality they signify nothing.[15]

The question naturally arises, if conceptual cognitions have no objective reference, how then do they succeed in inspiring pragmatic activity? Dharmakīrti answers that they do so because they are wrongly believed to have objective reference.[16] This belief is grounded in the fulfilment of pragmatic activity following conceptual cognitions. So, in an indirect sense, conceptual cognitions may be said to have reference to particular things. But the universal of the realist, Dharmakīrti contends, is not referred to even in this indirect manner, since it has no causal efficiency.[17] Not only conceptual cognitions have no direct reference to external things, they have no direct reference to ideas or images (*buddhyākāra*) either. The latter, in the Buddhist view, are as unique and momentary as the external particulars. There can be no verbal convention relating to them as in the case of external particulars. Besides, ideas being purely mental facts, they have no pragmatic value whatsoever.[18]

4. *Criticism of the realist theory of meaning*

The realist holds that words signify real universals or particulars qualified by them. Both these views are rejected by the Buddhist on the ground that universals are not facts of experience. Dharmakīrti draws attention to the absurdity resulting from the view holding individuals to be the meaning of words. If words, such as 'cow', 'horse', etc., signify individuals, they would be proper names and,

---

14. saṁsṛjyante na bhidyante svato'rthāḥ pāramārthikāḥ,
rūpamekamanekañ ca teṣu buddherupaplavaḥ. PV, III, 86.
15. PV, III, 89-91.
Dharmakīrti advocates the ultimate ideality of all distinctions and relations, and at the same time he propounds the Sautrāntika theory of *svalakṣaṇas*, the real unique point-instants, external to mind. His view is thus a combination of idealism and the Sautrāntika realism. His ultimate stand-point is idealistic, but he adopts the critical realism of the Sautrāntika for the purpose of logic. See CPB, p. 100.
16. Ibid., III, 167-68.
17. Ibid., III, 92-96, also PVV on them.
18. Ibid., III, 167 f. Also cp. TS, 884 f.

consequently, innumerable words will be required to refer to numerous individuals. This would make common discourse impossible. It might be rejoined that words should be taken to refer to individuals collectively and not to individuals as such. This view, Dharmakīrti points out, involves greater absurdity, since it eliminates the necessity of the plurality of words altogether. If in the absence of objective universals or resemblances, which are not recognised by the Buddhist, words are said to refer collectively to arbitrary selections of individuals, then we should need only a one-word language. A single word may be used to refer to anything and everything. Moreover, this view would result in the elimination of all individual differences, since there cannot be an identity of name without there being an identity of meaning.[19]

In fact particulars *qua* particulars cannot be regarded as the import of general words, since there can be no verbal convention with regard to them. Particulars, in the Buddhist view, being discrete and distinct, a verbal usage fixed in relation to one cannot be extended to others of which no such fixation has been made. If such an extension is considered legitimate, then the word 'cow' might also be used to refer to a horse. This would render all verbal convention meaningless. But a more important question is : can there be a verbal convention even with regard to one particular? In the Buddhist view it is impossible. The particulars being discrete and momentary, being destroyed in the very moment in which they are born, no verbal convention is possible with regard to them. Hence, all verbal usage, in the Buddhist view, pertains not to the real but to the illusory constructions of thought.[20]

It might be objected that if words have no positive reference, there can be no convention with regard to their significance. According to the Buddhist, the meaning of the word 'tree', for example, is 'the negation of non-trees'. But what is the meaning of the word 'non-tree'? Obviously, it is 'the negation of tree'. Thus the meanings of both the terms 'tree' and 'non-tree' are mutually dependent. Consequently the meaning of neither term can be independently established. Dharmakīrti retorts that the realist theory of meaning also suffers from the same defect. The meaning of the word 'tree' cannot

19. arthābhedena ca vinā śabdābhedo na yujyate. PV, III, 139; also PVV on it.
20. Cp. TSP, p. 279.

be made definite by the realist unless he differentiates it from the meaning of the word 'non-tree'. But such differentiation would be possible only after the meaning of the word 'tree' is fixed. So, the realist also has to face the difficulty of establishing a definite positive meaning of words.[21] Dharmakīrti however attempts to give an account of the psychological process by which the meaning of a word comes to be established. In the first place, certain things are noted to produce a series of images which other things do not produce. Next the two sets of things are mentally differentiated. These operations precede the act of verbal designation. Then, of the two sets thus differentiated, the first is designated by a name. This name does not refer to any positive attribute of things named, but to their difference from others. Dharmakīrti holds that this process by which the meaning of words comes to be established is free from the alleged defect of mutual dependence.[22]

To sum up, the theory of knowledge and meaning advocated by Dignāga and Dharmakīrti replaces the realist's universals by concepts. These concepts are not abstractions from experience, but mental constructions having their source in the creative nature of reason. They refer to nothing in the external world, for the latter consists of fleeting particulars which are non-conceptual and non-relative. Nor do they refer to mental facts, or ideas, because, in the Buddhist view, all ideas are particular and momentary. The position of these concepts is peculiar: they refer neither to the internal nor to the external facts. They are neither identical with nor different from the real things. They are therefore said to be illusory. Their illusoriness follows also from their negative character. All existence, according to the Buddhist, whether mental or non-mental, is positive (particular). Hence it follows that whatever is negative (universal) is non-existent or illusory.

The above theory is clearly nominalistic, because concepts are said to have no objective foundation. They are pure and simple fabrications of the mind. But the nominalism of the Buddhist is of a special type. He does not hold that concepts are mere names having

---

21. PV, III, 113-114.
22. PV, III, 115-123; and PVV on them. According to Ratnakīrti, the perception of a particular is followed by a conceptual image of it which appears to be something external and common to different individuals. If verbal usage is held to be established with reference to such a conceptual image, there would be no fallacy of mutual dependence. See Ap. Sid., p. 5.

no common basis whatsoever. Such a view would lead to complete arbitrariness in the use of words and would ultimately result in scepticism. Dignāga and Dharmakīrti admit that language is a source of common knowledge, and that it is the medium of communication of ideas and thought. They recognise also that such knowledge and communication presuppose a common basis which makes mutual understanding possible. What they deny is that the required common basis for language and concepts can be found in the immediate experience of the real world. This, according to them, must be sought outside experience, and they discover it in the creative reason which is transcendental and universal. Reason creates *a priori* general forms or concepts in order to express the data of immediate experience through them. Although these concepts fail in their mission, yet they succeed in supplying the basis for thought and communication. It is important to note that, inspite of being thought-constructions, these concepts are always accompanied with the belief in their objective reference. This explains the stimulation of pragmatic activity by conceptual knowledge. The said belief, according to Dharmakīrti, has an indirect basis in experience. The fulfilment of pragmatic activity following conceptual cognition naturally engenders the belief in the objective reference of the latter. This belief is the universal basis of practical life. If conceptual knowledge were believed to have no objective reference, there would have been no purposive activity at all.[23]

The creative reason, the source of conceptual knowledge, is transcendental and universal. It is described as 'beginningless ignorance' (*anādi-avidyā*). It is an independent source of knowledge like sense-apprehension. The two sources are distinguished on the ground of their respective objects. The object of pure reason is relational or logical, while that of sense-apprehension is non-relational or ontological. The former is useful but not ultimately real, the latter is ultimately real but not useful. Yet the two sources of knowledge are not absolutely unrelated. Reason works on the data supplied by

23. Conceptual, knowledge, according to Dharmakīrti, is neither a pure imagination nor ultimately true. It is the phenomenal knowledge of reality. The real may be known either directly or indirectly. The direct knowledge of reality is sense-apprehension. The indirect knowledge, or empirical knowledge (*saṁvṛti*), consists in the knowledge of the real through thought-forms. This knowledge though ultimately false is phenomenally true. Cf. BL, Vol. I, pp. 70 f.

experience. It represents the real in its own forms, though these forms have no objective basis. The relation of the logical with the real is proved also by the attainment of the real through conceptual knowledge. It is this pragmatic verification which distinguishes conceptual knowledge from pure imagination or dreams. However, the harmony between reason and reality exhibited by practical life is not a real harmony, for they are absolutely dissimilar. It is a negative harmony consisting in common contrast. This lends an indirect validity to our conceptual cognitions and also supplies the basis for practical life.

II. *CRITICISM BY KUMĀRILA AND UDDYOTAKARA*

The *Apoha* theory of Dignāga and Dharmakīrti, which denied objectivity to words and concepts, was vehemently attacked by the realist thinkers. The Mīmāṁsā and the Nyāya took leading part in the onslaught against the Buddhist nominalism. The word, according to the former, is an eternal entity having an eternal relationship with the universal which constitutes its meaning. For the latter, though the word is not eternal and its meaning is established either by Divine or by human convention, yet it denotes a positive real having a definite class character. The theory of Dignāga, which reduces words to mere conventional signs of negation, cuts at the very root of their realism. For them, the world consists of both positive and negative facts; there are both existences and non-existences in reality. Accordingly, there are positive and negative words in our language to signify these facts respectively. For the Buddhist, on the contrary, there are only positive facts and negations are mere non-entities. Words and concepts are concerned with the latter alone, since the former is beyond thought and language. These fundamental differences between the stand-points of the Buddhists and realists gave rise to a bitter and prolonged controversy over the objectivity of verbal or conceptual knowledge.

To begin with, Kumārila argues that the import of positive words is never felt as negative; it is always felt as positive. *Apoha,* which is a pure and simple negation, cannot be said to be the object of verbal cognition, since such a negation never figures in it. According to the Buddhist view, *apoha* is a non-entity, a pure nothing (*śūnya*). It is absolutely meaningless to assert it as the meaning of words. It could as well be asserted that words have no meaning at all. Even if the meaning of words is regarded as ideal, i.e., devoid of all externality its positive character is undeniable. Kumārila avers that words are invariably understood as referring to positive entities. The meaning of a word no doubt excludes the opposite meaning, but such an exclusion is never felt as the content of verbal cognition. The Buddhist theory of negative meaning, therefore, is contrary to all experience.[24] Uddyotakara points out that the exclusion of the contrary meaning can be understood only if the positive meaning of a word is first known. If words have no positive meaning at all, it is absurd to talk of the exclusion of the contrary meaning as their import. Further, he argues, the import of words can never be negative, since nothing negative can be the object of a command or comprehension thereof. What is not felt as the content of a cognition cannot legitimately be regarded as its object, for such a view would lead to absurd consequences.[25]

Further if words signify non-entities *(apohas)*, Kumārila argues, there can be no distinction between the meanings of words. Only an entity is distinguishable. Since *apoha* has no character, it cannot be distinguished from anything. The notions of unity, multiplicity and similarity cannot be applied to *apohas* which are devoid of all determinations.[26] This criticism of Kumārila is, indeed, directed against the Buddhist conception of non-being (*abhāva*). For the Buddhist, *abhāva*, being devoid of causal efficiency, is a non-entity. It is not a perceived fact, but an object of thought.[27] In the realist view, on the other hand, non-being has a positive correlative (*pratiyogī*) and a locus (*adhikaraṇa*). So, it is real and distinguishable on the basis of these latter. But, in the Buddhist view, there is no such basis for the distinction of non-beings. *Apohas* have no positive correlative. They are like the negation of 'hare's horn' which is purely imaginary. Nor can they be distinguished on the basis of locus, for they have no locus at all. The particular point-instants cannot be their locus, since they are non-conceptual. Besides, if particulars are regarded as the basis of the distinctions of *apohas*, the latter would lose their general character.[28]

---

24. ŚV, *apoha*, 37-39.
25. abhāvastu na yuktaḥ praiṣasampratipatyoraviṣayatvāt. NV, p. 328.
26. ŚV, *apoha*, 45; also cp. NM, p. 304.
27. For a detailed account of the Buddhist conception of negation, see BL. Vol. I, pp. 363 ff.
28. See SM, p. 201; NM, p. 304; NK, p. 320.

Another serious consequence of the *Apoha* theory will be that inference and verbal cognition would be impossible. Inference and verbal cognition, Kumārila argues, depend on the knowledge of positive relationship between the sign and the signified. This relationship being general in nature, it obtains between universals in the case of inference and between a word and a universal in the case of verbal cognition. These universals are independently established by perception prior to the knowledge of the said relations. Now, in the Buddhist view, universals being replaced by *apohas*, these latter must be independently established and their relations apprehended in order to make inference and verbal knowledge possible. But, how are the *apohas* established? Not by perception, because they are non-entities. Nor by inference or verbal cognition as that would involve circularity. Thus, *apohas* being themselves not established, their relations too cannot be apprehended. Consequently, inference and verbal cognition would be impossible. Besides, it is absurd to talk of relations between *apohas* which are non-entities. Again, the Buddhist cannot hold that the relation of sign and signified obtains between the ultimate particulars, since the latter, by hypothesis, are non-relational. Moreover, a relation obtaining between particulars cannot be said to have universal validity. The Buddhist theory of *apoha*, therefore, results in the elimination of inference and verbal knowledge.[29]

Kumārila argues further that the theory of *apoha* leads to certain absurd consequences. The meaning of a word is said to be 'the negation of the contrary'. Now, the contrary which is negated must be either positive or negative. If it is positive, it must be a universal, since particulars, in the Buddhist view, being indeterminate cannot be negated. And if it is negative, it cannot be negated, since the negation of mere negations (non-entities) is inconceivable. And if the Buddhist admits negation of negations, then it would be positive and a universal.[30] Kumārila poses a dilemma to the Buddhist: if 'the negation of the contrary' is different from the contrary, then it is a positive universal; and if it is not different, then the contrary and its negation would be identical. In the former case, the Buddhist has to

29. nacānvayavinirmuktā pravṛttiḥ śabdaliṅgayoḥ,
tābhyāṁ ca na vināpoho na cāsādhāraṇe 'nvayaḥ. ŚV, *apoha*, 73.

30. Ibid., 96.

admit the universals, in the latter case, the Buddhist theory of meaning will completely collapse, since a word might mean anything and everything.[31]

The Buddhist might reply that the 'negation of the contrary' is not the negation of negation, but that of positive things comprehended under the contrary. So the above objections are not valid against his theory. Kumārila points out that this explanation does not hold good in all the cases. In the case of the word 'being', for example, it will be absurd to maintain that its meaning is the negation of positive things comprehended under its contrary 'non-being'. This would make non-being positive, i.e., there will be no non-being. Consequently, there will be no being too, since, according to the Buddhist, being is the negation of non-being. This would make both the terms 'being' and 'non-being' meaningless. These absurd consequences, Kumārila argues, can be avoided only if positive meanings of words are recognised.[32]

Kumārila rejects the Buddhist theory that innate beginningless disposition (*vāsanā*) is the primal source of all conceptual activity. He denies the existence of innate dispositions. All dispositions owe their genesis to the experience of objects. The disposition to regard the meaning of words as positive is not natural, as the Buddhist contends. On the contrary, it arises out of the experience of positive universals. The Buddhist theory of an uncaused transcendental ignorance determining all conceptual knowledge is an unproved assumption.[33]

Kumārila raises an important question concerning the nature of the word itself. Is the word a particular or a universal? If it is a particular momentary sound, it cannot have the denotative function. The particular sound in relation to which a meaning has been grasped is never repeated. So the sound heard at a subsequent time will carry no meaning. A denotative word, therefore, must be a universal which is the same throughout its use at different times. If the Buddhist does not admit this, all words would be reduced to meaningless sounds. The Buddhist might reply that, in his view, words also, like their meanings, being *apohas*, they are general. So the above contingency would not arise at all. But this, Kumārila argues,

31. abhāvasya ca yo'bhāvaḥ sa cettasmādvilakṣaṇaḥ,
bhāva eva bhavenno cedgauragauste prasajyate. Ibid., 97.

32. Ibid., 99; cp. NK, p. 320.

33. ŚV, *apoha*, 100-101.

would make the diversity of words a fiction. In the Buddhist theory both words and their meanings being non-entities (*apohas*), there can be neither the diversity of words nor the diversity of meanings. Also there can be no real difference between a word and its meaning. Nor can there be any denotation, since the relation of denotation cannot be said to exist between non-entities.[34]

The Buddhist contention that the import of words, though negative, is apprehended as positive is rejected by Kumārila on two grounds. Firstly, there can be no negation without affirmation. Secondly, there can be no positive apprehension of what is negative, or a non-entity. We can have a negative conception of what is positive, but not vice versa. We can always say that the cow (a positive thing) is not something else, but we cannot have a positive conception of a non-entity.[35]

Further, Kumārila produces instances of words in the case of which the *Apoha* theory is not applicable. The words 'knowable' and 'nameable', according to Kumārila, being co-extensive with reality, they exclude nothing from their denotation. The meaning of the word 'knowable' cannot be said to be 'the negation of the unknowable', since such an assertion would be self-contradictory. What is unknown cannot be negated. Similarly, the meaning of the word 'nameable' also cannot be said to be the negation of the unnameable, since what is unnamed cannot be negated.[36] Uddyotakara gives the example of the word 'all'. The meaning of the word 'all' excludes nothing; so the *Apoha* theory is not applicable in this case. The Buddhist cannot say that the word 'all' excludes determinate numbers (one, two, etc.), since the latter are its constituents, not its contradictories. If a word is said to exclude its own constituents from its meaning, there remains nothing for it to denote.[37] The essence of the above objection is that, on the *Apoha* theory, words like 'knowable,' 'nameable' and 'all', which are all-inclusive, would be meaningless.

Kumārila rejects also the image theory of cognition advocated by the Buddhist. According to this theory, words produce mental images, differentiate them from others and signify them. Kumārila

34. Ibid., 102-105.
35. Ibid., 108, 110, 113 f.
36. Ibid., 144.
37. NV, p, 329.

denies that cognitions have any form. Form, according to him, is the property of external things, not of mental facts. The form apprehended in verbal cognition belongs to the external things, not to the cognition itself.[38] It may be noted that the Buddhist advocates the image theory of cognition because it is necessary for his epistemology. The external things, in his view, being indeterminate, cognitions cannot be distinguished from one another if they had no form. But there is no such necessity for the realist. Cognitions, in his view, can be distinguished on the basis of things themselves. If cognitions have no form, as Kumārila maintains, then the meanings of words in the *Apoha* theory would be indistinguishable from one another.

Dignāga held that all the characteristics of the positive universal of the realist's conception, such as oneness, eternality, complete subsistence in each individual and so on, may be said to belong to the *apoha* itself, since it is also identical and continuous like the realist's universal. Besides, it has additional excellence and superiority over the latter because it explains conceptual knowledge more satisfactorily. Hence, the *Apoha* theory of the import of words alone is right.[39] Kumārila remarks that Dignāga's attempt to characterise *apoha* is like trying to weave cloth without yarns. It is absurd to hold that *apoha*, a non-entity according to the Buddhist himself, possesses any of the characteristics mentioned above. These characteristics can be said to belong to positive things alone. However, Kumārila does not wholly deny the negation of others as part of the meaning of sentences. He admits its presence in the meaning of expressions in which such a negation is explicitly stated, e.g., in such injunctions as 'the domestic pig is not to be eaten'. In all other cases, he maintains, the positive meaning alone is expressed by words.[40]

To sum up, the criticism of the *Apoha* theory by Kumārila and Uddyotakara raises three important issues concerning verbal cognition. (1) Is 'the negation of the contrary' (*apoha*) a felt element in the apprehension of the import of words? (2) Can there be, logically, a negation without affirmation? And (3) Can there be real distinctions and relations among concepts if they are pure thought-constructions? Kumārila and Uddyotakara answer all the three questions in the negative and, hence, reject *Apohavāda* as an untenable theory.

38. ŚV, *apoha*, 145-46.
39. See the passage from Dignāga quoted by Kamalaśīla under TS, 1000.
40. ŚV, *apoha*, 163-64.

III. DEFENCE OF APOHAVĀDA BY ŚĀNTARAKṢITA

1. The meaning of apoha

Kumārila's objections, according to Śāntarakṣita, reveal a gross ignorance of the meaning of *apoha. Apoha* literally means 'the negation of the other'. But the meaning of this negation must be understood clearly. He distinguishes between two kinds of negations—*simple* (*niṣedha*) and *special* (*paryudāsa*). An example of the former is the judgment 'the cow is not non-cow'. In this 'the negation of the other' is very clearly apprehended. The latter is of two kinds—*conceptual* (*buddhyātmā*) and *ontological* (*arthātmā*). The former consists in the comprehension of different things under one class-concept by negating their mutual differences, and the latter consists in the all exclusive particularity of the real.[41]

Concepts, according to Śāntarakṣita, arise not from the apprehension of real universals, but from the experience of things themselves which, by their very nature, become the basis of class-notions.[42] Kamalaśīla in his commentary describes the psychological process by which concepts arise. Sense-apprehensions of momentary particulars are followed by their momentary images in the mind. These images are then, owing to an innate tendency, classed under one identical concept by neglecting their mutual differences. These concepts are pure mental constructions; nevertheless they are believed to have external reference. This belief, according to Kamalaśīla, is rooted in the said indirect connection between concepts and the external things. These concepts, which come under the first kind of special negation (*paryudāsa*), are called *apohas.* The reasons for which they are so called are, according to Kamalaśīla, four in number: (1) they are always understood *in contrast* with their contrary concepts; (2) they produce *distinctive* cognition of their objects; (3) they proceed on the strength of the *all-exclusive* thing; and (4) they are *wrongly judged* by ignorant people to have external reference.[43]

The name *apoha,* according to Śāntarakṣita, is primarily significant with reference to all-exclusive particular—the ontological negation. But it has also a derived significance with reference to concepts, since they are indirectly connected with ontological negations.[44] It is in this

41. TS, 1004.
42. Ibid., 1006.
43. See TSP, p. 274, also cp. Ap. Sid., p. 12.
44. TS, 1007-9.

second sense that *apohas* are said to be the import of words. The direct object of verbal cognition is thus neither the simple negation (*niṣedha*) nor the ontological negation (*svalakṣaṇa*). That is, the direct import of a word is neither the difference of its meaning from that of its contrary, nor the external thing itself. It is not even a subjective reality, since the content of verbal cognition is not a momentary idea originating directly from the external things and apprehended as such. In fact, the import of words is a constructed identity arising out of the non-apprehension of difference among particular images and wrongly cognised as external. *Apoha* is thus neither a subjective nor an objective reality. It belongs to a third category of mental constructions. It is said to be negative, because it has no positive nature; its essence consisting merely in differentiation. And yet it is not purely negative, since it is felt as positive and external.[45]

2. *Import of words explained*

The relation of denotation, according to Śāntarakṣita, is akin to the causal relation. A word directly produces the conceptual image (*apoha*) which is denoted by it. This is the primary denotation of a word. But a word also denotes secondarily the other kinds of negations described above. The word 'cow', for example, directly denotes the concept of 'cow', but it implies also that its meaning excludes the contrary meaning. The latter is simple negation apprehended in an indirect manner. Similarly, a word also denotes, by implication, the external thing (ontological negation), since there exists an indirect causal relation between the real and the concept denoted by the word. This denotation by implication, Śāntarakṣita cautions, must not be construed as a real relation. Words do not touch the external things at all, as the latter are, by nature, inexpressible. They denote only conceptual images which are wrongly believed to be external.[46]

The important point to be noted here is that, according to Śāntarakṣita and Kamalaśīla, the direct import of words is not negative. It is a constructed concept felt as positive. 'The negation of the contrary' is said to be comprehended only by implication, since every determinate concept logically excludes its contrary. The compre-

45. TSP, p. 318.
46. TS, 1012-18; TSP, p. 320.

hending of this negation, though indirect, is nevertheless essential for a distinctive cognition. Thus a word, in Śāṇtarakṣita's view, performs two functions—one of denoting directly the concept corresponding to it, and the other of implying the negation of the contrary concept. This double function of words—one affirmative and the other negative—is said to be supported by our common usage. For example, the assertion 'fat Devadatta does not eat during the day' directly negates Devadatta's eating during the day-time. But it also affirms, by implication, his eating during the night. Affirmation and negation, according to Śāntarakṣita, are two sides of the same coin; they imply one another. The positive meaning of a word necessarily implies the negation of the contrary meaning. In the absence of such implication, the positive meaning cannot be definitely understood. Kamalaśīla holds that the apprehension of the positive and the negative meanings is not simultaneous, but successive. In the case of general words, the positive meaning is apprehended directly, while the apprehension of negative meaning follows by implication.[47] It must be noted that the direct meaning of words is positive for the Buddhist only in the sense that it is felt as positive. It is not *really* positive, i.e., an existent, since it is not an object of sense-apprehension. The positivity, externality and identity attributed to the meanings of words are, according to Śāntarakṣita, illusory. This illusion springs from the innate constructive tendency of the human intellect.[48]

It may be urged that an illusion of identity is always preceded by the perception of similarity. But the particulars, or the ideas corresponding to them, being absolutely dissimilar, there is no possibility of such an illusion. Kamalaśīla replies that all illusions do not proceed from the perception of similarity.[49] They may arise from mental aberrations also, like the perception of two moons. The conceptual identity apprehended as a positive content in verbal cognition is pure and simple illusion, since the universality and externality attached to it are not derived from sense-experience.[50] However, the illusory character of verbal or conceptual cognition

47. See TS, 1012-1021 and TSP on them.
48. Ibid., 1023.
49. nahi sarvā bhrāntayaḥ sādharmyadarśanādeva bhavanti. kintarhi? antarupaplavādapīti. TSP, p. 322. Cf. The Advaita also holds that *sādṛśya* is not necessary for *adhyāsa*.
50. TS, 1024; TSP, p. 322.

does not affect its practical value. Being indirectly rooted in reality, as shown above, it leads to pragmatic activity and its fulfilment. Thus, conceptual knowledge, though illusory, is not useless. It has empirical value, being ultimately grounded in the experience of external things. Kamalaśīla explains how an erroneous cognition can lead to fruitful activity by the example of 'jewel illusion'. On perceiving the brightness of a gem emanating from the chink of a door, one is motivated towards it mistaking it to be a jewel. His activity, though springing from an illusion, is rewarded by the attainment of the jewel, because the brightness perceived by him was causally connected with the real jewel. Similarly, conceptual or verbal cognition, though illusory, leads to successful activity, because concepts are indirectly determined by reality.[51]

Clearly the *Apoha* theory propounded by Śāntarakṣita and Kamalaśīla is not essentially different from the one propounded by Dignāga and Dharmakīrti, but there are some important differences between them regarding the details. Although for both the parties verbal cognition is ultimately illusory, yet the former does not agree with the latter's exclusive emphasis on the negative import of words. For Dignāga and Dharmakīrti, the whole meaning of a word is exhausted in 'the negation of the contrary'. Śāntarakṣita, on the other hand, distinguishes between the direct and the indirect meanings of words. He clearly concedes to the theory of successive cognition of positive and negative meanings, which was rejected by Dharmakīrti. The apprehension of the negative meaning was direct for Dignāga and Dharmakīrti, while it is indirect for Śāntarakṣita. *Apoha*, for the former, is negative, while, for the latter, it has a felt positivity. Replying to Uddyotakara's question as to whether *apoha* is positive or negative,[52] Śāntarakṣita says, 'it is neither positive nor negative, neither diverse nor same. It is neither subsistent nor non-subsistent, neither one nor many. In reality, it does not exist in the form in which it is cognised; hence it is not positive. Nor is it negative since it is cognised as positive.'[53] Clearly this is a denial of all real

---

51. TS, 1026-27. yatra hi pāramparyādvastuni pratibandho'sti tasya bhrāntasyāpi sato vikalpasya maṇiprabhāyāṁ maṇibuddhivanna bāhyārthānapekṣatvamasti ato 'siddhaṁ bāhyārthānapekṣatvam. TSP, p. 323.
52. NV, p. 229.
53. na bhāvo nāpi cābhāvo 'pṛthagekatvalakṣaṇaḥ,
nāśritānāśrito 'poho naikānekaśca vastutaḥ.
tathā 'sau nāsti tattvena tathā 'sau vyavasīyate,
tanna bhāvo na cābhāvo vastutvenāvasāyataḥ. TS, 1189-90; cp. TSP, p. 361.

characterisations of *apoha* as positive, negative, one, many, etc. *Apoha* being an *a priori* concept, a mental construction, it cannot be said to have any character in the real sense of the term. However, from the stand-point of thought such characterisations are quite legitimate.[54] Śāntarakṣita's recognition of the felt positivity of the direct meaning of words and the relegation of the negative meaning to the status of indirect implication, is not to be construed as a surrender to realism. He accepts Kumārila's contention that the meaning of words has a felt positivity because such acceptance is quite compatible with the ultimate illusoriness of the import of words. But, at the same time, he avers that the felt positivity is not the only element in the meaning of words; there is also the element of negation cognised by implication. The apprehension of the negative meaning, though indirect, is an essential element in verbal cognition, since in the absence of it no definite cognition would be possible. Dignāga and Dharmakīrti also accepted the felt positivity of the import of words, but they considered differentiation as the essence of meaning and, therefore, emphasised 'the negation of the contrary' as the sole content of the meaning of words.

3. *Objections of Kumārila answered*

Śāntarakṣita agrees with Kumārila's criticism that there can be no real difference among *apohas*, since they are featureless. But, for the same reason, he points out, there can be no non-difference too amongst them. Kumārila's objection regarding the synonymity of all words would be valid only if their meanings were identical. But *apohas*, which are signified by words, being neither identical nor different,

54. Śāntarakṣita and Kamalaśīla represent a phase of the Buddhist thought which is a combination of both the Mādhyamika and the Sautrāntika—Vijñānavāda positions. With regard to the ultimate they accept the Mādhyamika position, while with regard to the empirical they adopt the position of Sautrāntika-Vijñānavāda. Like the Sautrāntika they propound the doctrine of *svalakṣaṇas*; and like the Vijñānavādin, they deny the existence of empirical objects. Dignāga and Dharmakīrti, on the other hand, were Vijñānavādins so far as their ultimate point of view was concerned. But they accepted the Sautrāntika position of critical realism for the sake of logic. On the question of the reality of the objects of empirical knowledge the positions of both Dharmakīrti and Śāntarakṣita are identical. Empirical objects, such as universals or things qualified by universals are, for both of them, non-entities. They are thought-constructions superimposed on the non-empirical reality (*svalakṣaṇas*). See in this connection CPB, pp. 100-2.

the objection has no foundation at all. Words, according to Śāntarakṣita, cannot legitimately be characterised either as synonymous or as non-synonymous, because their meanings are neither identical nor different.[55]

One might ask, how can there be, in this theory, any restriction with regard to the use of words? Śāntarakṣita explains that the said restriction becomes possible because the usage of words is based on the identity of causal functions of particular things. Things perform various functions by their very nature. These functions are classified by us under various concepts and names for our own convenience. But how can the causal functions of things, as also their apprehensions, be identical when they proceed, according to the Buddhist, from absolutely different particulars? Śāntarakṣita admits that the said identity is not real. Nevertheless, the causal functions are supposed to be identical because they produce an identical conceptual cognition.[56] Such supposed identities, he holds, are sufficient to guide our use of words in different contexts.

Śāntarakṣita thus tries to show that Kumārila's objections are not at all valid against his theory. The diversity of *apohas*, according to him, is based neither on the diversity of correlatives, nor on the diversity of loci. It is, in fact, merely conceptual, not real. This conceptual diversity of *apohas*, according to him, arises from three sources: (1) the constructive power of thought, (2) the unique nature of things, and (3) convention established by tradition.[57] Śāntarakṣita, like Dharmakīrti, holds that the unique and non-relational point-instants are neither identical nor different. Identity and diversity, similarity and dissimilarity are attributed to them by our thought. Thus the identity of cows, for example, as also the difference of them from horses, etc., are merely conceptual. Things generating the conceptual cognition of identity are regarded as similar, and those giving rise to the cognition of difference are regarded as dissimilar.[58]

Both Śāntarakṣita and Dharmakīrti recognise an indirect connection between thought and reality, because in the absence of such connection the distinction between valid and invalid knowledge

---

55. TS, 1031, 1033.
56. ekapratyavamarśasya hetutvādekamucyate. TS, 1037; also see 1036.
57. svabījānekaviśliṣṭavastusaṅketaśaktitaḥ,
vikalpāstu vibhidyante tadrūpādhyavasāyinaḥ. TS, 1048.
58. See TSP, p. 328.

would be impossible. Although the conceptual identity is not admitted to belong to the real, yet it is held to be indirectly based on the latter. Concepts, though constructions of thought, possess pragmatic value because of such indirect connection. As opposed to Kumārila, Śāntarakṣita maintains that language is based not on the real, but on the logical distinctions among concepts. Logical distinctions being the very nature of concepts, there is no contingency of the alleged confusion of the meaning of words. The logical distinctions of concepts, again, being indirectly rooted in the causal functions of things, they acquire pragmatic value.

Further, as opposed to the realist, Śāntarakṣita maintains that inference and verbal cognition can be explained without assuming real universals. The concomitant relation (*vyāpti*) between the middle and the major terms required for inference has its basis in the conceptions of things as different from unlike things. Kamalaśīla holds that the particulars themselves, with their peculiarity unapprehended, serve the function of the universal in inference.[59] As regards Kumārila's question as to how is *apoha* known, Śāntarakṣita answers that it is self-cognised like all other cognitions. It does not depend either on inference or on verbal knowledge for its own cognition. Hence, the charge of circularity levelled against *Apohavāda* by Kumārila is not valid.[60]

Kumārila, however, maintains that concepts are not pure fabrications of thought; they cannot be said to arise without real universals. Nor can they be said to be determined by particulars, either directly or indirectly, since they are general. The Buddhist theory of non-apprehension of difference, which is advanced to explain the genesis of concepts, makes all class-distinctions purely arbitrary.[61] In the absence of an objective determination of classes, no rules can be set up for the use of words. Kumārila further alleges that the Buddhist theory of meaning involves the fallacy of mutual-dependence. The meaning of the word 'cow', for example, is said to be 'the negation of non-cow'. But what is the meaning of 'non-cow' other than 'the negation of cow'? Thus the meanings of both the terms depend upon one another. Consequently, the meaning of neither terms can be

---

59. TS, 1057. Cp. tena sāhacaryamapi liṅgaśabdayoḥ svalakṣaṇenaiva kathyate. TSP, p. 329.
60. TS, 1061-62.
61. ŚV, *apoha*, 77.

established definitely.[62] This predicament can be avoided, according to Kumārila, only if the Buddhist accepts the positive meaning of words independently of 'the negation of the contrary'.[63]

Śāntarakṣita meets the above objections of Kumārila by raising counter-questions with regard to the realist theory. How does the realist explain class-distinctions? The reply would be that they are based on universals manifested by the individual things. But what determines the manifestation of specific universals by the individuals? The realist would answer that it is determined by *the nature of things* which is unquestionable. Śāntarakṣita retorts that the same reply would hold good in the case of the Buddhist theory also. Class-distinctions may be said to rest on the ultimate nature of things directly, without assuming the intermediary universals. A concept stands exclusively for certain things, not for others, because it is brought about by those things alone by their very nature.[64] As regards the fallacy of inter-dependence of meaning alleged by Kumārila, Śāntarakṣita holds that it constitutes no objection to his theory. Every concept, being relative, is comprehended only in contrast with its opposite. The direct apprehension of particulars alone is free from such inter-dependence. Conceptual knowledge being relational by nature, such inter-dependence is unavoidable. Thus, according to Śāntarakṣita, meanings of words are not absolute. They are born of arbitrary convention and depend for their understanding on their contraries. Concepts, in his view, are nothing but intellectual patterns devised to give articulation to what is exclusively an object of immediate consciousness.[65]

Regarding Kumārila's contention that negation cannot be negated, Śāntarakṣita says that this is admissible only in the sense that the negative character of negation cannot be negated, as that would be a self-contradiction. But one can legitimately assert that a positive entity is not negative. In this sense a negation may very well be negated.[66] Again, one thing is said to be the negation of another when the two are of different natures, but this does not make the thing negative. In the same way, when a positive thing is asserted to be not

62. gavyasiddhe tvagaurnāsti tadabhāve tu gauḥ kutaḥ. ŚV, *apoha*, 85.
63. Ibid., 83-84.
64. TS, 1058-61.
65. Ibid., 1064-65.
66. Ibid., 1081.

negative, the negation does not become positive. Thus, Śāntarakṣita rejects Kumārila's contention that negation of negation is positive.[67] He makes use of this theory of negation to meet the problem raised by Kumārila concerning the concept of 'being'. Since negation of negation is possible, as explained above, 'being' can be said to be the negation of 'non-being'. It is not denying the negative character of 'non-being' which is the negation of 'being' existing in its own right; it is only denying that 'being' is 'non-being' or negative. This denial, according to Śāntarakṣita, does not make the negation of 'non-being' positive. Kumārila has argued that if the negation of the contrary is different from the contrary, then it must be positive, otherwise cow and non-cow, for example, would be identical. Śāntarakṣita replies that if by 'the negation of non-cow' what is meant is the unique particular cow, then it is positive and different from non-cow. So the contingency of cow and non-cow becoming identical would not arise at all.[68] But if 'the negation of non-cow' means the concept of cow, as it does in the Buddhist view, then 'cow' is not qualitatively different from 'non-cow'. Obviously, the whole argument of Śāntarakṣita rests on the distinction of the conceptual and the real. The latter alone is really positive; the former is essentially negative or relative, although it is felt as positive. For the Buddhist, the concept of cow and that of non-cow are of the same order, i.e., both are negative and relative. It is significant to note that both the 'real cow' and the 'conceptual cow' are, according to the Buddhist, 'the negations of non-cow'. But, while the former is positive, the latter is negative. The positivity of the former is said to be based on the evidence of sense-apprehension. The latter, having no such evidence in its favour, is exhausted in the negation itself. This dichotomy of the conceptual and the real is not admitted by the realist, and , therefore, he does not consider the Buddhist explanation as satisfactory.

Śāntarakṣita repudiates Kumārila's contention that all dispositions originate from experience. The mind is inherently creative; it creates dispositions even for imaginary things. This creativity of the mind is the source of all dispositions. These are transferred from moment to moment in the history of one's mental life. The diversity of words and their meanings, as also their felt positive character, are

67. TS,1082-84.
68. Ibid., 1083-85.

all due to our predispositions, as is the case with regard to imaginary things.[69] Ultimately, for the Buddhist, there is no difference between the concepts of empirical things and those of pure fictions. Both are creations of the mind. The difference is only practical; while the former has pragmatic value, the latter does not.

Śāntarakṣita agrees with Kumārila's view that words are universals, but their universality, like that of their meanings, is, according to him, only conceptual. The question about the diversity of words is answered by him in the same manner as that concerning the diversity of their meanings. Words also, like their meanings, being conceptual, their mutual differences are self-cognised. In the same manner, the difference between words and their meanings also becomes apprehended. As regards Kumārila's criticism that there can be no relation of denotation between non-entities, Śāntarakṣita says that this is not an objection to his theory. All relations, in his view, are only conceptual, not real. In as much as the meanings of words are regarded as external things, they are not empirically non-entities. So, a word may well be said to denote its meaning. In reality, however, nothing can be said to denote or be denoted. All things being momentary, it is impossible to apprehend concomitance between words and things. Such relationship presupposes duration and stability which are possessed only by concepts.[70]

Kumārila's contention that negation always presupposes affirmation is accepted by Śāntarakṣita. Hence, he admits the felt positivity of the meanings of words, though he holds them to be ultimately illusory. As already discussed, the direct meaning of a word, according to him, is always positive; the negation of the contrary is apprehended only by implication. Kumārila's criticism on this point, says Kamalaśīla, is absolutely irrelevant.[71]

With reference to Kumārila's objection that, in the theory of *apoha*, words like 'knowable', 'nameable', etc., which are all-inclusive, would be meaningless, Śāntarakṣita replies that words are meaningful only in sentences, not independently. If they are consid-

69. TS, 1086-88.

70. Ibid., 1089-90.
The particulars are regarded as unspeakable by the Buddhist only from the ultimate point of view. Empirically, however, it is the particular which is believed to be expressed by words: yadvyaktīnāmavācyatvam asmābhirvarṇitam, tatparamārthacintāyām, na punaḥ saṁvṛtyāpi. TSP, p. 335.

71. TSP, p. 339.

ered independently of all connections with other words, they become meaningless. If Kumārila's objection asserts that the word 'knowable', on the Buddhist theory, cannot be meaningful by itself because it has no contrary to be differentiated from, then it is pointless. In common discourse words are significantly used for conveying information, removing doubts, etc. Obviously these functions can be performed only by sentences. Even in the cases where apparently a single word is used meaningfully, other words making up the sentence are implicitly conveyed.[72] The word 'knowable' is used meaningfully in such sentences as 'all knowable things are momentary', 'all knowable things are illusory', and so on. In these sentences what is negated is the contrary supposition. Similarly, the word 'all' is meaningfully used in such propositions as 'all things are soulless', 'all men are mortal', etc. What is negated by them is the contrary proposition.[73]

It may be urged that words do convey some meaning even independently of a sentence, though it is of a nebulous character. A single word, by itself, in the absence of the context in which it is used, may not produce a clear comprehension of its meaning, nevertheless a vague understanding of its meaning is definitely produced. Śāntarakṣita maintains that a vague understanding is not a genuine understanding of the meaning at all. Besides, even the vague understanding of the meaning of a word, according to him, becomes possible because it has been clearly grasped in some proposition on a previous occasion. The vagueness of the comprehension of the

72. TS, 1166-68.
73. Ibid., 1185-88.
According to Kumārila, words convey their meanings independently of the sentence in which they are used. In fact, the meaning of sentence itself depends upon the meaning of words. The meaning of a sentence is understood only when the meanings conveyed by different words are related with one another. This theory is known as *abhihitānvayavāda*. The Prābhākaras, on the other hand, propound just the opposite theory which is called *anvītābhidhānavāda*. According to this theory words convey their meanings only in relation with other words. That is, the meanings of words are conveyed along with the meaning of the sentence in which they are used. While, for Kumārila, the comprehension of the meaning of words and that of the sentence in which they occur are successive, for the Prābhākara, they are simultaneous. Śāntarakṣita's view is similar to that of the Prābhākara.
See in this connection *Tattvabindu* of Vācaspatimiśra Ed. by V. A. Ramaswami Sastri, Annamalai University Sanskrit Series, No. 3, Pub. 1936.

meaning of a solitary word itself proves that it is not a genuine understanding of the meaning. Śāntarakṣita agrees that words are always intended to refer to positive things and not to non-entities. So also what is understood as the meaning of a word is always an entity believed to be positive and external. But this understanding of the positive meaning also includes the comprehension of 'the negation of the contrary' by implication. This negation, though not intended consciously, is an essential part of the meaning of words. It gives the verbal cognition its definite character.[74]

Referring to Kumārila's rejection of 'form' of cognition Śāntarakṣita remarks that it is the denial of a self-evident fact.[75] We do become aware of appearances in dreams and illusions, which are pure mental forms devoid of all externality. Similarly, all determinate cognitions have forms pertaining to the specific objects apprehended by them. These forms, which are the very natures of cognitions, have been variously called by the Buddhist as *ākāra* (form), *pratibimba* (reflection or image), *tadābhatā* (appearance), and so on.[76] In the absence of these forms there would be no determinate cognition at all. There would be nothing to distinguish one cognition from another, since all cognitions *qua* cognitions are indistinguishable. These forms, though mental constructions, constitute the very peculiarity of cognitions.

Replying to Kumārila's criticism of Dignāga's view, Śāntarakṣita says that the attributes of oneness, eternality, etc., were not regarded by Dignāga as real attributes of *apoha*. On the contrary, they were regarded as purely imaginary and have been mentioned by him only in view of the common misconceived notions. So, Kumārila's criticism on this point is without any foundation. Also the other contention of Kumārila that negation is cognised only where it is explicitly stated by a negative term, is rejected by Śāntarakṣita. 'The negation of the other', he asserts, is cognised even in the absence of a negative term. For example, when it is said that 'the thing *itself* is the import of words', the emphasis on 'itself' means nothing but that 'others' are negated. Hence all propositions, whether they include the negative term or not, include 'the negation of others' as an element of their meaning.[77]

---

74. TS, 1179-89.
75. jñānākāraniṣedhastu svavedyatvānna śakyate. TS, 1181.
76. Ibid., 1182-83.
77. Ibid., 1200-1. Also see TSP on them.

The realist would ask, how, in the absence of objective universals, does a common understanding of meanings of words and communication of ideas become possible? The speaker and the listener may understand the meanings of words differently. Concepts or ideas are private; the concept in the mind of the speaker cannot, therefore, be communicated to the listener. How, then, could there be a common comprehension of meanings of words? Further, in a philosophy of flux, nothing can be the same for two moments, not even conceptual images (*apohas*). The conceptual image with reference to which a verbal convention has been established is dead and gone. How can the same convention hold good in the case of the present conceptual image which is absolutely different from the past one?

In reply to the above questions Śāntarakṣita says that even though each person knows his own ideas, yet there is something in the conceptual cognition of external things which is common to both of them (the speaker and the listetner).[78] Kamalaśīla explains that although the speaker and the listener actually apprehend their own ideas, yet the seed of all illusions, the creative reason, being common to them they understand an identical object.[79] Both of them believe, again due to the same reason, that they are understanding one and the same object. This transcendental illusion lies at the root of all empirical knowledge and activity. It is due to this that one believes in the identity of objects occurring at two different points of time—the time of making a convention and that of the subsequent use of a word. All verbal communication of ideas and common understanding of objects are, therefore, ultimately illusory.[80] This is the nature of all empirical knowledge. It is said to be valid only in so far as it serves to achieve our pragmatic ends.

To sum up, the theory of *apoha* propounded by Śāntarakṣita and Kamalaśīla is essentially a restatement of the view of Dignāga and Dharmakīrti in a more clear and precise terminology. The fundamental dichotomy of the conceptual and the real and ideality of all relations implying the ultimate illusoriness of all conceptual knowledge, are re-emphasised with greater vigour. Śāntarakṣita's answers to the issues raised by Kumārila and Uddyotakara succeed in clarify-

---

78. svasya svasyāvabhāsasya vedane 'pi sa vartate,
bāhyārthādhyavasāye yaddvayorapi samo yataḥ. TS, 1210.
79. taimirikadvayasyeva bhrāntibījasya tulyatvāt. TSP, p. 365.
80. Ibid.

ing the nominalistic stand on many important logical and epistemological questions. The explicit recognition of the felt positive element in the import of words, the distinction of the direct and the indirect meaning, the restatement of the relation between concepts and reality and the theory of non-apprehension of difference, serve to make the theory of *apoha* more clear and intelligible. The realist, however, does not consider these explanations and clarifications satisfactory. He regards the whole nominalistic stand as contrary to reason and experience.

IV. *VĀCASPATI MIŚRA'S CRITICISM OF APOHAVĀDA*

Vācaspati's criticism is directed against two main contentions of the Buddhist: (1) that the negative similarity (*sādṛśya*) between the concept (the universal) and the particular thing consisting in the common negation of the contrary, is the basis of co-ordination between the two; and (2) that the illusion of objectivity with regard to a subjective construction arises due to the non-apprehension of difference (*bhedāgraha*) between the conceptual and the real. The substance of Vācaspati's criticism is that all similarity being positive, there can be no similarity between the illusory and the real; hence, there can be no co-ordination between the two as asserted by the Buddhist. Also there can be no illusion of identity between the two. due to 'the non-apprehension of difference', since an illusion of identity always arises due to an 'apprehension of non-difference'. Vācaspati, therefore, concludes that our concepts and words must be regarded as referring to particulars qualified by universals. These positive objects of cognition are later distinguished from others which are dissimilar to them. All determinate activity follows upon the cognition of positive objects and not of the negation of the contrary alone.[81]

Vācaspati begins with the criticism of the Buddhist conception of similarity. The Buddhist holds that there is negative similarity between the universal (concept) and the particular, for both are negations of the same contrary. For example, the concept 'cow' and the real cow are similar because both are 'negations of non-cow' This is the only kind of similarity possible between the real and the illusory and this serves as the basis of co-ordination between the two.

81. TT, p. 487.

Vācaspati asks : is this 'negation of the contrary' real or ideal? If the former, is it identical with the real point-instant or different from it? It cannot be identical, because to assert the identity of negation with a positive entity would be a contradiction. If the contradiction is denied, then the negative universal and the positive thing would be one and the same. Both will either be positive or negative. In the former case, there would be no sense in denying the positive character of the universal. In the latter case, the particular would lose its positive character and become a non-entity like the universal. The Buddhist cannot say that 'the negation of the contrary' is different from the particular, for, in that case, it must be an attribute of the latter. The Buddhist would not admit that the real point-instant possesses a negative attribute.[82]

The Buddhist might take the other alternative, namely, that 'the negation of the contrary' is only an ideal principle supposed to serve as the basis of co-ordination between the concept and the real thing. Vācaspati remarks that if such a principle is made the basis of similarity, then a fly and an elephant may also be regarded as similar, for both of them are different from donkeys.[83]

The Buddhist might rejoin that nothing is held to be common between the efficient point-instant of external reality and the general image internally constructed by the mind. But the particular which is the content of conceptual cognition is not the ultimate particular; it is also a thought-construction like the universal. Therefore, there is no contradiction in holding such a particular to be both positive and negative. Contradictory attributes cannot belong to a real entity, but an imagined one can very well be said to possess both of them. It is such a particular which is said to be similar to the constructed universal.[84]

What is sought to be established, asks Vācaspati, by the similarity of the unreal imagined particular with the unreal imagined universal? There can be no pragmatic activity directed towards such a

82. Ibid., p. 488.
83. Ibid.
84. A judgment, in the Buddhist view, expresses an illicit synthesis of pure affirmation 'this' with the negative or relational 'that'. In other words, a judgment is an illicit synthesis of *svalakṣaṇa* and *sāmānyalakṣaṇa*. Therefore, both, 'this' and 'that' of conceptual cognition are relative, i.e., 'negations of the contrary', whereas the thing itself is non-relative. (yacca gṛhayate yaccādhyavasīyate te dve apyanyavyāvṛttī na vastuna iti.) Dignāga quoted in TT, p. 488.

particular The goal of our purposive activity is always the real thing, but that being absolutely dissimilar to the imagined universal, there can be no motivation towards it either. And if, to get out of this difficulty, some kind of similarity between the real thing and the imagined universal is recognised, the assumption of an imagined particular becomes quite gratuitous.[85]

The Buddhist might argue that the causal efficiency of the real thing is wrongly associated with the constructed image of it in our mind and thus the latter succeeds in inspiring purposive activity. For example, the burning and cooking efficiency, which is the test of the real fire, is falsely connected by us with the constructed image of it in our mind. The latter is not ultimately real, because the efficiency which we can name and extend to other things is not real. The real is unique, shorn of all extensions; it is unutterable and unimaginable. Thus the function of our concepts is to inspire activity, with its various aims, by imputing efficiency to an unefficient image which is general and relative. These concepts, constructions though they may be, are indirectly related to reality and, therefore, they lead to the causally efficient real. This ensures the efficacy of thought, and makes consistent human experience possible.

Vācaspati asks, what, according to the Buddhist, is the cause of the imputation of causal efficiency to a thought-construction? Is it due to former experience, or to the innate tendency of human mind? The former alternative would not be acceptable to the Buddhist, for conceptual activity, according to him, has no direct foundation in the experience of things. And if the latter alternative is adopted, then a man who sees fire for the first time in his life should *a priori* be cognizant of its powers of burning and cooking.[86]

The real issue, according to Vācaspati, is whether the real thing is the object of conceptual cognition or not. In the Buddhist doctrine, the real and the conceptual fall asunder. Sensation is confined to the bare thing; it does not introduce its object into our conceptual thinking. The two, sensation and thought, are complete strangers to each other. Thought can never seize the bare particulars, even if we assume with the Buddhist an indirect function of the immediately

85. Ibid., pp. 488-89.
86. Ibid., p. 489.

preceding sensation, because thought apprehends only determinate objects capable of being associated with names.[87]

The Buddhist might explain that the first moment in the cognition of an external object is pure sensation. The conceptual image follows immediately in its track. The particular momentary thing is not adequate to the image, but it appears as though it were its object, because the image is indirectly produced from it. Vācaspati maintains that this explanation would hold good only on the realistic hypothesis, i.e., if it is admitted that images arise from traces left in our consciousness by former experience (*anubhavavāsanābhāveṣu*). But this would imply that our images exactly correspond to reality, which would go against the Buddhist position. On the idealistic hypothesis, on the other hand, the Buddhist explanation would not hold good at all. If forms of our thought have nothing corresponding to them in the external world, and if they are pure and simple creations of the mind ceaselessly engaged in producing transcendental illusions, then our mental images cannot even be said to appear as external object. What has never been experienced as external cannot even appear as such.[88] The Buddhist explanation that our concepts are indirectly produced from sensory stimulus is not helpful, because, if the real is indeterminate and absolutely alien to thought, there can be no illusion of it in the image constructed by thought.[89]

Having criticised the Buddhist theory of similarity, Vācaspati passes on to the criticism of the Buddhist theory of non-apprehension of difference. He shows that the theory of 'non-apprehension of difference', which is advanced by the Buddhist to explain the apprehension of identity in every case, leads to certain consequences which are undesirable for the latter. If fire, for example, as an ultimate particular remains untouched by thought, and our image of fire is nevertheless wrongly identified with it because of the non-apprehension of difference between the two, then the image might as well be identified with the whole universe, since there is no reason for restriction. If fire as a thing-in-itself is not apprehended when we have its concept present to us, the whole universe is in the same position. Even if the limitation is said to be due to the fact that the

87. Ibid.
88. Ibid.
89. Ibid., p. 490. Cp. NM, p. 316.

concept has its origin from the sensation of real fire, the problem is not solved. There is no reason why the concepts of non-sensory entities like God, Master, etc., which are also conceptual constructions, should not be identified with real fire because of the non-apprehension of their difference. Hence, the Buddhist explanation of the correspondence between the conceptual image and the momentary particular on the principle of 'non-apprehension of difference' completely fails. The Buddhist contention that the constructed image is erroneously regarded as external due to the non-apprehension of difference between the real and the imaginary is, according to Vācaspati, nothing but an empty talk.[90]

The Buddhist propounds the theory of objectivised conceptual image in order to explain conceptual knowledge. Reality, in his view, being an incessant stream of point-instants, is incapable of being grasped and described by discursive thought. Conceptual knowledge comprehends objects having stability and duration. Vācaspati holds that even the so called objectivised image fails to serve as an object of conceptual cognition. It is also a momentary event like the idea (*jñānākāra*) and the thing (*svalakṣaṇa*) and, therefore, cannot be thought of or named. It depends, indeed, on the act of our productive imagination. It arises and vanishes with the momentary act of our mind and changes with every change in the activity of our discursive thought. Hence, it can never be regarded as a unity having relative stability.[91] The Buddhist might argue in defence that the unity of momentary conceptual images is imagined due to the non-apprehension of their mutual differences. Vācaspati points out that there is equal possibility of unity, which is their essential character, being not apprehended and difference being imagined, since non-apprehen-

---

90. tasmādalīkasya bāhyatvaṁ vikalpagocara iti riktaṁ vacaḥ. TT, p. 490.

Udayana holds that the non-apprehension of difference between the constructed concept and the real thing would be possible if the former were apprehended devoid of its negativity and the latter devoid of its positivity. But this is impossible, because both the concept and the real thing, in the Buddhist view, being partless (the former being a non-entity and the latter being a point-instant), there can be no partial apprehension of them. Hence, there can be no illusion of identity due to the non-apprehension of difference. ĀTV, p. 121.

91. api ca jñānākāravatsvalakṣaṇavaccālīkagrāhyatvạmapi na vikalpagocaro bhavitumarhati. etaddhi kalpanādhīnamutpannāyāṁ kalpanāyāmutpannamiva vinaṣṭāyāṁ naṣṭamiva vikalpanābhede bhinnamiva na śakyam ekatvena pratikartum. TT, p. 490.

sion exists in the case of both unity and difference.[92] The Buddhist might urge that the discontinuity of the objectivised conceptual images being not real like that of the particular point-instants, they are cognised as a unity. Vācaspati points out that even if the discontinuity of the conceptual images is held to be ultimately unreal, the Buddhist must admit that the conceptual image depends upon an act of imagination. It must change whenever there is change in the latter, or else it would not depend on it. If it did not so depend, it would not be imagined, and it would not be an image erroneously regarded as an external entity. So, the question of the reality of continuity or discontinuity of the images is irrelevant here. The real issue is, can the conceptual image, which depends upon the changing act of imagination, appear as a unity? Vācaspati denies it. He maintains that such an image must appear as being discontinuous—as split into discrete moments. Hence, the conceptual image cannot be the object of determinate cognition, because, being as momentary as fleeting pleasures or pains, it is indeterminate.[93] The Buddhist is thus driven to the position that whatever is conceived is indeterminate. This is just the opposite of what he sought to establish. If both concepts and things are indeterminate, there would be no determinate knowledge at all.

Vācaspati's criticism of the two theories, viz., the theory of 'negative similarity' (*sādṛśya*) and that of 'non-apprehension of difference' (*bhedāgraha*) caused a serious damage to the theory of *apoha* as propounded by Śāntarakṣita and Kamalaśīla. Vācaspati by his subtle dialectic drew out the necessary consequences of the doctrine of momentariness which is fundamental to the Buddhist theory. Śāntaraksita had explained the genesis of concepts and their external reference on the basis of the theory of 'non-apprehension of difference'. Similarly, the co-ordination between the conceptual knowledge and the successful culmination of pragmatic activity was explained on the basis of the theory of 'negative similarity'. Both these theories having been demolished by Vācaspati, the Buddhist nominalism required a reformulation. This task was performed by

92. Loc. cit. Jayanta asks, if the conceptual images are really different, then how can their mutual difference remain unapprehended? See NM, p. 315; also cp. NK, p. 319.
93. Op. cit., p. 490.

Jñānaśrī and Ratnakīrti. They do not adopt, as will be seen, the theories of 'negative similarity' and 'non-apprehension of difference' advocated by their predecessors. They discard also the theory of successive cognition of positive and negative meanings propounded by Śāntarakṣita. However, they admit that the meaning of words necessarily involves a negative element, and that the objects of conceptual and perceptual cognitions must be distinguished. They also emphasise, more than the other Buddhists, that it is the external thing which is empirically cognised, though this cognition is ultimately illusory.

CHAPTER XI

THE BUDDHIST NOMINALISM (APOHAVĀDA)—II

I. *DEFENCE OF APOHAVĀDA BY JÑĀNAŚRĪ AND RATNAKĪRTI*

1. *The import of words*

Jñānaśrī and Ratnakīrti maintain that import of words (*apoha*) is neither merely positive nor merely negative. It is a positive thing qualified by 'the negation of others'.[1] They reject the theory of successive cognitions of positive and negative meanings. Such a succession is not psychologically felt. The meaning of a word, on the contrary, is felt as both positive and negative at the same time. The object of verbal cognition is a determinate thing. Although it is felt as positive, its difference from others does not remain unapprehended, otherwise the cognition would not be that of a determinate thing. In the determinate cognition of a thing, argues Ratnakīrti, there is an implicit reference to its efficiency. The apprehension of this efficiency is what is called the apprehension of 'the negation of others'. If this negation were not apprehended simultaneously with the cognition of the positive thing, no determinate activity could be inspired by the cognition.[2]

The realist, on the other hand, maintains that the object of verbal cognition is the thing qualified by the universal. This cognition is purely positive. The exclusive nature of the thing, i.e., its difference from others, is cognised subsequently by implication.[3] The said determinate activity, it is claimed, is explainable without assuming the simultaneity of the two cognitions. Criticising this view Jñānaśrī argues that a momentary verbal sign cannot have two successive fruits. Nor can there be a definite cognition of the thing if its

1. nāsmābhir apohaśabdena vidhireva kevalo 'bhipretaḥ. nāpy anyavyāvṛttimātram, kintu anyāpohaviśiṣṭo vidhiḥ śabdānām arthaḥ. Ap. Sid., p. 3; also see JN, *apoha*, p. 203.
2. Ap. Sid., pp. 3-4; JN, p. 206.
3. TT, p. 487.

difference from others is not simultaneously apprehended. If the content of verbal cognition in the first moment is the undifferentiated thing, then it is not intelligible how the subsequent implication of its difference from others becomes possible. If the thing as apprehended in the first moment does not exclude others, then it is impossible for it to do so even in a subsequent moment. Hence the determinate cognition of a thing must be admitted to be the cognition of a positive thing different from others.[4] Ratnakīrti argues that if, in addition to the positive universal, the realist has to admit the exclusive nature of the thing which is said to be cognised by the subsequent implication, then the thing itself in that very nature may be regarded as the object of verbal cognition. What is the sense in denying 'exclusion of others' as a necessary element in the meaning of words?[5]

2. *The objects of perception and conception distinguished*

Jñānaśrī makes it clear that, when the positive thing qualified by 'the negation of others' is said to be the import of words, what is meant is not the real thing-in-itself, but a conceptual object.[6] The reason for this distinction is that the object of conception is not found to possess the same character as that of perception. While the conceptual content is hazy and is invariably comprehended in contrast with its opposite, the perceptual object is vivid (*parisphuṭa*) and is apprehended as a spatio-temporally determined datum.[7] The realist view that the difference of perceptual and conceptual cognitions is due not to the difference of objects but to the difference of natures of the instruments of cognition, is rejected by the Buddhist on the ground that one and the same indivisible thing cannot have the contradictory characters of being vivid (*spaṣṭa*) and non-vivid (*aspaṣṭa*). The

4. tasmād goḥ pratītirityago'poḍhapratipattirucyate. JN, *apoha*, p. 206.
   This criticism applies also to the doctrine of Śāntarakṣita and Kamalaśīla who advocate the theory of successive cognition of positive and negative meanings of words.
5. Ap. Sid., p. 4.
6. JN, p. 208; also Ap. Sid., p. 6.
7. Ibid. Also see PV, II, 235.
   śabdenāvyāpṛtākṣasya buddhāvapratibhāsnāt. arthasya dṛṣṭāviveti, —A passage probably from Dignāga quoted in JN, *apoha*, p. 208 and also in Ap. Sid., p. 6.

difference of things, says Jñānaśrī, is nothing but the difference of characters, and the latter is nothing but the difference of apprehensions. Hence, the difference of apprehensions implies the difference of objects, otherwise the whole universe would be one.[8] It might be urged that this view is contrary to experience; one and the same tree, for instance, may be perceived vividly by a person close to it, and non-vividly by a person remote from it. It would be absurd to hold that the two persons perceive two different trees. Ratnakīrti explains that difference of apprehensions is said to be due not always to the difference of things, but to the difference of *objects*.[9] It is said to be due to the difference of things only when it arises owing to the difference of causal efficiencies.[10] Thus the difference of cognitions always implies difference of objects, otherwise cognitions will be indistinguishable. Even the distinction of direct and indirect cognitions cannot be explained merely on the basis of their instruments as is done by the realist. Indirectness of a cognition consists in nothing but the apprehension of an object different from that of the direct cognition.[11]

Jñānaśrī advances another argument to prove his point. The object of conceptual cognition is subjected to both affirmative and negative judgments. If it is regarded as real, such judgments would be impossible. For example, in the judgments 'the tree is' and 'the tree is not', the object 'tree' is common to both affirmation and negation. If the 'tree' is said to be a real thing whose essence is existence, then affirmation would be a useless tautology and negation a contradiction. And, conversely, if the 'tree' is said to be unreal, affirmation would be a contradiction and negation a tautology. Hence, the object of conceptual cognition cannot be a real thing, as it is common to both affirmation and negation.[12]

Jñānaśrī must have borrowed this argument from some of his predecessors, since it is mentioned and criticised by Vācaspatimiśra

8. na hi svarūpabhedādaparo vastubhedaḥ, na ca pratibhāsabhedādaparaḥ svarūpabhedaḥ; anyathā trailokyam ekameva vastu syāt. JN, p. 209, Ap. Sid., p. 7.
9. na brūmaḥ pratibhāsabhedo bhinnavastuniyataḥ kintu ekaviṣayatvābhāvaniyata iti. Ap. Sid., p. 7.
10. arthakriyābhedopakṛta eva pratibhāsabhedo bhedakaḥ. JN, p. 209.
11. Ap. Sid., p. 7, JN, p. 210.
12. JN, p. 211, Ap. Sid., p. 8.

in his *Tātparyaṭīkā*. Vācaspati maintains that the conclusion, viz., 'whatever is common to both affirmation and negation is unreal', cannot be accepted as valid unless its contrapositive, viz., 'whatever is real cannot be common to both affirmation and negation', is first established. The latter proposition, according to him, is false, since it can be shown that alternate affirmation and negation is possible in the case of real things. The universal, in the realist view, is in itself an eternal entity, but as inhering in infinite number of particulars scattered in space and time, it can be alternately affirmed and denied. We can sometimes say that 'it is' and sometimes that 'it is not'. The existence of the universal expressed by the first judgment is nothing but its actual presence in some locus, and the non-existence of it expressed by the second judgment is its absence in a present locus, not its absolute non-existence. Thus a real thing may become the object of both positive and negative judgments; both being and non-being may be predicated of it in different contexts.[13]

Criticising the above contention of Vācaspati, Jñānaśrī argues that our affirmative and negative judgments refer to particulars, not to universals. The judgments, e.g., 'the tree is' and 'the tree is not', respectively affirm and deny the particular object denoted by the word 'tree'. The former is not equivalent to the assertion—'treeness is present in a locus', nor is the latter equivalent to the denial—'treeness is absent in the present locus'. Such stretching of meanings is warranted neither by logic nor by experience. Further, even if the universal is admitted to be the object of alternate affirmation and negation, it can be such only as related to some particular locus, present or absent. And if the locus of the universal is regarded as a real thing, the problem of affirmation and negation raised above remains. Jñānaśrī remarks that by shifting the reference of affirmation and negation to universals Vācaspati has implicitly admitted that concepts and words do not refer to real particulars.[14]

The realist might rejoin that a general word denotes only the universal character and tells nothing about the existence or non-existence of its locus—the particular. It affirms or denies the existence of particulars only when the term signifying existence or non-

13. TT, p. 487.
14. JN, p. 211; Ap. Sid., pp. 7-8.

existence is added to it. Things possess numerous attributes, all of which cannot be denoted by a single word. Hence, there are different words in our language to denote each one of them uniquely. The word 'tree' denotes only the universal 'treeness'; it tells nothing about 'existence' which is another attribute of the thing. When the term 'is' is added to it, the actual existence of a particular tree becomes signified. Jñānaśrī remarks that if 'treeness' and 'existence' are really different from one another, they cannot be asserted together in a judgment.[15] The real, in the Buddhist view, is an indivisible point-instant. It is cognised in its entirety in sense-apprehension. If a word does not denote it in its entirety, it must be held to be not referring to the real at all.[16] The Nyāya conception of substance as possessing various attributes related to it by inherence is rejected by the Buddhist as contrary to experience and reason. The difference of substance and attribute is neither a perceptual fact nor is it supported by reason. If two different things can be related as substance and attribute, then anything might be the attribute of anything. Besides, inherence being a separate category (*padārtha*) according to the realist, it fails to relate its terms. Thus the difference of substance and attribute itself being unproved, the argument asserting the need of different words to signify diverse attributes of a thing becomes *ipso facto* invalid. If the real thing is apprehended by the word at all, argues Ratnakīrti, it must be apprehended in its entirety by a single word without needing another.[17]

Ratnakīrti argues further that even if the difference of substance and attributes is granted, the situation is not altered. Inherence (*samavāya*) being inadmissible, the relation between the two must necessarily be that of the support and the supported (*upakāryopakārakabhāva*). This relation he holds, is analogous to the causal relation.[18] Thus, if the support (*upakāraka*) is known by a word, the totality of the supported attributes (*upakārya*) must also be known

15. tāttvikatve vṛkṣaḥ sanniti sāmānādhikaraṇyānupapattiḥ, ghaṭapaṭavat. JN, p. 213.
16. Ibid.
17. Ap. Sid., p. 10:
18. Ratnakīrti cautions that it is not to be regarded as a natural relation (*svabbāvataḥ*) like one between fire and smoke, but only as an assumption, because the difference of fire and smoke is real, while that of substance and attribute is not. See Ap. Sid., p. 11.

along with it. The causal efficiency of a real thing is indivisible and non-different from the thing itself. The apprehension of the thing, therefore, must include the simultaneous apprehension of all its characters.[19] Thus, if a word is said to signify a real thing, then a single word should suffice to convey all the attributes of the thing without needing other words. The realist must face this consequence, or admit that the conceptual cognition with all its distinctions expressed through different words, is not the cognition of the real at all.[20] Ratnakīrti holds that the real has no need for words. Neither does it permit affirmation and negation of attributes, nor does it stand in need of being substantiated by different means of knowledge. All this is, indeed, required in the case of the conceptual object. Therefore, that alone is to be regarded as the proper object of verbal cognition.[21]

3. *Judgments empirically refer to real external things*

The object of our judgments, according to Jñānaśrī and Ratnakīrti, is empirically (*saṁvṛtyā*) positive and external to mind. The mental images or ideas (*buddhyākāra*) are never the objects of affirmation or negation—neither ultimately (*tattvataḥ*) nor empirically (*saṁvṛtyā*). Ideas, which are fleeting mental states directly aware of themselves, are ultimately inexpressible. They are not affirmed or denied (*anadhyavasita*) even empirically, because our judgments are intent upon objects having practical value. So, the objects of our judgments must be acknowledged to be the external causally efficient things. But this is admissible only from the empirical point of view. Ultimately, however, the real is inexpressible. If the real were absolutely inexpressible, i.e., even empirically, then our practical life would have been impossible.[22]

19. Ap. sid., p. 11; JN, p. 215.
Cp. ekopakārake grāhye, dṛṣṭāḥ tasminna santi te,
sarvopakārakaṁ hyekaṁ tadgrahe sakalagrahaḥ. PV, III, 54. Also see PV, III, 51-57.
20. Ap. Sid., p. 11; JN, p. 215.
21. Ap. Sid., pp. 9-10. Cp. JN, p. 213.
22. ata eva sarvadharmāṇāṁ tattvato' nābhilāpyatvaṁ pratibhāsādhyavasāyābhāvāt. tasmāt bāhyasyaiva sāṁvṛtau vidhiniṣedhau. anyathā saṁvyavahārahāniprasaṅgāt. Ap. Sid., p. 16; JN, pp. 225 and 229.
Cp. nākārasya na bāhyasya tattvato vidhisādhanam,
bahireva hi saṁvṛtyā saṁvṛtyāpi tu nākṛteḥ.
This is a quotation appearing in both JN, p. 229 and Ap. Sid., p. 16 but its source is not traceable. It is probably a quotation from some work of Dharmakīrti. It is noteworthy that it denies even empirical reality to the realist's universal.

Jñānaśrī severely criticises Dharmottara's view[23] that objects of our empirical judgments have an illusory externality (*āropitabāhyatva*). He considers this view as contrary to common belief, tradition and logic.[24] There are only two kinds of truths—empirical (*saṁvṛti*) and ultimate (*paramārtha*). All explanations, therefore, must fall within the scheme of these 'two truths'. The object of Dharmottara's conception having an illusory externality is, according to Jñānaśrī, neither empirical nor ultimate. Empirical truth is nothing but what is commonly accepted to be true (*lokābhimāna*). Our judgments are commonly believed to refer to external things. This belief is based on repeated experience. The externality of empirical object is never believed to be illusory, as its cognition leads to the fulfilment of volitional activity. So the externality of the objects of our judgments is not a case of illusion. Nor is the so called illusory externality a character of the real, because the latter, by accredited tradition, is beyond affirmation and negation.[25] Further, Jñānaśrī points out, Dharmottara's theory is inconsistent with his own view expressed elsewhere. He has himself stated that what is not conceptual (*anadhyavasita*) cannot be affirmed or denied, and that our judgments refer to nothing other than the ultimate particular (*svalakṣaṇa*).[26] There is thus no basis for the view that the objects of affirmation and negation have illusory externality. Such objects are neither felt in our mental apprehensions (*pratibhāsa*), nor are they referred to by our empirical judgments (*adhyavasāya*).[27]

23. The reference here perhaps is to Dharmottara's commentary on some of Dharmakīrti's works. See JN, p. 229.
24. alaukikam—anāgamam—atārkikīyam. Ibid.
25. JN, p. 229; Ap. Sid., p. 17.
26. kiñca nānadhyavaseyasya vidhiniṣedhau, na ca śabdādadhyavasāyaḥ svalakṣaṇād anyatreti svayamapyudghuṣyate. JN, p. 229.
27. Ibid., p. 230.

According to Jñānaśrī, words refer to two kinds of things—the external particulars and the mental images (*buddhyākāra*). The former is referred to as an object of judgment (*adhyavasāya*) and the latter as an object of mental reflection (*pratibhāsa*). What is meant is that our use of words with reference to external things is determined by our ends and purposes, while that with regard to mental facts depends upon our reflective consciousness. Both these references however, though empirically true, are ultimately illusory.

adhyavasāyena bāhyasya budhyākārasya tu pratibhāsena śabdavācyatva-mucyate. Ibid., p. 230. pratibhāsādhyavasāyadvārā ca sarvavyavasthitistattvam aspṛśati. Ibid., p. 229.

The question naturally arises how can the real external particular be referred to by our judgments and be, at the same time, inexpressible? Ratnakīrti explains that our judgments are said to refer to external things because they are intent upon the latter. It is only in this sense that the latter are said to be the objects of our judgments. They are not seized by our judgments in the manner of sense-apprehension.[28] Thus the real, though in itself beyond affirmation and negation, is made the object of judgments for empirical purposes. Jñānaśrī maintains that empirical activity can be explained neither by sense-apprehension (*pratibhāsa*) nor by conception (*avasāya*) alone. The two have to be synthesised in a single consciousness in order to make empirical activity possible. The judgment (*adhyavasāya*) represents such a synthesis of the real and the conceptual. This synthesis, though ultimately illusory because the real is not seized in it in its own nature, is, nevertheless, empirically valid, for it leads to the fulfilment of pragmatic activity.[29]

It may be asked, if our concepts do not touch the real, how does determinate activity guided by them become possible? Ratnakīrti replies that our concepts, being born of specific factors (*niyatasāmagrī-prasūtatvena*), being endowed with specific form (*niyatākāratayā*) and specific capacity (*niyataśaktitvāt*), motivate us towards specific objects.[30] The function of concepts is analogous to that of inferential sign (*liṅga*) which produces the congnition of the signified object (*liṅgī*) and motivates us towards it, without the object itself being perceived. A judgment is nothing but the generation of motivation for a thing through a specific concept.[31] It is wrong to regard it as an apprehension of the real as the realist does. Now, since these judgments refer to the positive real as differentiated from other things, their object is called *apoha*. It is the cognition of this *apoha* which determines our empirical activity.[32]

The theory of Jñānaśrī and Ratnakīrti makes two important points against the realist theory: (1) that the meaning of words though empirically positive and external to mind necessarily contains within

28. apratibhāse 'pi pravṛttiviṣayīkṛtamiti yo 'rthaḥ. Ap. Sid., p. 17; cp. JN, p. 226.
29. adhyavasāyasahāpohipratibhāsaḥ sāṁvyāvahārikāpekṣayā tattvato jneyasya jñānaviṣayatāmupanayati pratyakṣavat. JN, p. 230.
30. Ap. Sid., p. 17; JN, p. 226.
31. tadadhyavasāyitvam ākāraviśeṣayogāt tatpravṛttijanakatvam. Ap. Sid., p. 17; JN, p. 226.
32. Ap. Sid., pp. 17-18; JN, p. 232.

it the negative element of 'difference from others', and (2) that the object of conceptual cognition is not ultimately real like that of perception. Their whole argument rests on the distinction of two 'truths' which is a necessary consequence of the Buddhist belief in the ultimate indeterminacy of the real. The realist does not accept this distinction, because for him the real, by definition, is determininately knowable. Udayana, the renowned Nyāya logician, launches a bitter attack against the Buddhist nominalism in general and Jñānaśrī's theory in particular. His defence of realism is classic and may be considered as the last word regarding the realist stand in Indian philosophical literature. We shall conclude our discussion of the conflict of Realism and Nominalism after considering Udayana's criticism of the Buddhist view as found in his *Ātmatattvaviveka.*

II. *UDAYANA'S CRITICISM OF APOHAVĀDA*

1. *Negation not a felt element in conceptual cognition*

Is 'the negation of the contrary' a necessarily felt element in the conceptual cognition of things? Udayana answers in the negative. He maintains that the negation of the contrary is not apprehended at all in the conceptual cognition of positive objects. What is apprehended is a positive thing without any reference to its difference from others.[33] But does not the cognition of a determinate thing (*vyāvṛtta*) necessarily include the cognition of its difference from other things (*vyāvṛtti*) which is its essential nature? Udayana replies that the apprehension of difference could be admitted if it were expressed in the judgment following the conceptual cognition of a thing. Our cognition of a cow, for example, is expressed as 'this is a cow' and not as 'this is not non-cow'. If the difference from non-cow were the content of cow-cognition, it would be expressed in the judgment following it.[34] The Buddhist argues that if the difference from others is not admitted to be the content of a determinate cognition, the definite, non-discrepant activity following it would be inexplicable.[35] Udayana maintains that a determinate activity follows the apprehension of a positive thing and not that of its difference from others. A person commanded to bring a cow successfully executes the

33. ĀTV, p. 112.
34. Ibid., p. 113.
35. See JN, p. 201.

order because he understands the command to refer to the positive object cow, and nothing else. The absence of discrepant activity is not due to the apprehension of 'the difference from non-cow' as the import of the command, but to the fact that the idea of anything other than cow does not arise at all when the command is heard.[36]

Udayana rejects the Buddhist theory of conceptual cognition as logically untenable. If 'the difference from others' is a necessary element in all conceptual cognitions, what about the cognition of this difference itself ? If this also involves the apprehension of another difference, there will be a *regress ad infinitum.* Consequently, there will be neither a definite cognition nor a determinate non-discrepant activity following it. If, to avoid these consequences, 'the difference from others' is regarded as self-differentiating, i.e., as not involving any reference to the 'other', then why not admit the same with regard to the positive object itself.[37] Further, a positive entity alone can be self-differentiating. 'The difference from others', in the Buddhist view, being an illusory construction of thought, it cannot be admitted as such. The real self-differentiating entity (*svalakṣaṇa*) being, *ex hypothesi,* indeterminate, the Buddhist has to face the consequence of the impossibility of determinate cognition.[38]

Jñānaśrī, as we have seen, acknowledges the positivity of the object of conceptual cognition, but he maintains also that the difference from others, which is its essential feature, becomes apprehended along with it. The determinate activity following the conceptual cognition is its evidence.[39] Udayana argues that the cognition of the

36. ĀTV, pp. 114 -15.
37. svarūpabhedenaiva niyame vidhimātrapratibhāse'pi tathā kinna syāt. Ibid., p. 115; also cp. NM, I, p. 304.
38. Ibid., p. 116.
39. See JN, p. 203.

For the realist, the determinateness of a cognition consists in the apprehension of the positive class-essence (universal) possessed by a thing. For the Buddhist also it consists in the apprehension of a universal, but this universal is not the positive class-character of the thing, but a subjective construction consisting in 'the difference from others'. For the realist, every word has a definite meaning and it conveys that meaning faithfully and never goes beyond it. The word 'cow' conveys a thing having certain class-character and nothing else. The difference of the cow from other things is the content of another cognition following the pervious one. In fact, according to the realist, the latter cognition is dependent on the former one. Negation pressupposes affirmation. For the Buddhist, there is no affirmation without negation. Both are one and the same, i.e., negative.

difference of a thing from 'other' things cannot be unconscious of the latter. For example, if the determinate cognition of 'cow' necessarily includes in its content the difference from 'non-cow', then it presupposes the cognition of 'non-cow'. But how can the cognition of 'non-cow', which is the negation of cow, be possible before the cognition of 'cow' itself? The result is a mutual dependence of cognitions. This can be avoided only if the conceptual cognitions of all kinds (perceptual, inferential, verbal, etc.) are admitted to be the apprehensions of positive things without any reference to 'other' things.[40] Udayana remarks that Jñānaśrī tries to befool the ignorant by relating the charge of mutual dependence of cognitions to the initial convention (*saṅketa*) by which the significance of a word is established.[41] As a matter of fact, this charge is not directed against the initial convention at all, but against the Buddhist theory of conceptual cognition. If the conceptual cognition of a thing necessarily includes reference to its difference from others, as the Buddhist maintains, then there is no escape from the charge of mutual dependence.[42]

2. *The object of conceptual cognition not unreal*

Udayana repudiates the Buddhist view that the object of conceptual cognition is a thought-construction (a non-entity), although it is apprehended as positive. He holds that there can be no positive apprehension of a non-entity. If the positive character of the conceptual object is said to be a superimposition, then it must be admitted to belong to some real entity. The positive character of the ultimate particular cannot be superimposed, as it is untouched by conceptual thought. The universal as a positive entity has no place in the Buddhist metaphysics. And if the superimposed positive character

40. ĀTV, p, 118.

41. Jñānaśrī maintains that the charge of mutual dependence would be valid if the meaning of the word 'cow' were initially established as 'difference from non-cow'. But if, on the contrary, it is established independently by referring to individuals with regard to whom a common form is apprehended in repeated cognitions, there is no mutual dependence. Once the meaning of the word 'cow' is thus established, it is recognised as different from things other than cows. Hence, it is also called as 'different from non-cows'. All this is subsequent elaboration and not the initial convention.

(tāvatā agovyāvṛtte gośabda iti siddhānuvāda eva na saṅketākāraḥ, abhimate gośabdavṛttāvagośabdena śeṣasyābhidhātuṁ śakyatvāt). JN, p. 204.

42. ĀTV, p. 119.

is itself said to be a non-entity, there would be self-contradiction.[43] Further, our conceptual cognitions apprehend a common positive form continuous in space and time. This form cannot be a non-entity, for a non-entity cannot have a spatio-temporal continuity. This continuity cannot be said to be ideal, because ideas, in the Buddhist view, are momentary or discontinuous. It cannot even be said to be a superimposition, for continuity, in the Buddhist theory, is unknown as a feature of reality.[44] Hence, the object of conceptual cognition, which is apprehended as positive and continuous, cannot be disposed of as a thought-construction.

Jñānaśrī had argued that the object of conceptual cognition, being common to both affirmation and negation, cannot be ultimately real.[45] Udayana holds that one and the same real can be affirmed and denied with reference to different place and time. Contradiction would arise only if 'being' and 'non-being' were predicated of the same real in an identical context. But it is perfectly logical to make positive and negative predications with regard to an object in two distinct contexts. A real thing, for instance, has the positive character of 'being itself and the negative character of 'not being the other'. The Buddhist must admit this even in the case of the ultimate particular (*svalakṣaṇa*). Thus, we say that 'the cow exists' when a particular locus of 'cowness' is living, and that 'the cow does not exist' when that locus of 'cowness' is destroyed. So, the fact that the objects of conceptual cognition are common to both affirmation and negation, does not make them unreal.[46]

Jñānaśrī had contended that if the object of conceptual cognition is held to be a positive real, its affirmation would be a tautology and negation a contradiction.[47] Udayana retorts that the same situation obtains in the Buddhist view also. If the content of conceptual cognition is held to be unreal or negative, as the Buddhist does, its affirmation would be a contradiction and negation a tautology. The Buddhist might reply that the conceptual content, in his view, being common to both being and non-being (*bhāvābhāvasādhāraṇa*), it can be both affirmed and denied. But this is not possible in the case of a

43. Ibid., pp. 119-20.
44. Ibid., p. 122.
45. JN, p. 211.
46. ĀTV, pp. 126-27.
47. JN, p. 211.

purely positive particular existent. Udayana denies that there can be anything which is both positive and negative, or both real and unreal. Nor can there be anything which is neither positive nor negative. Both these positions are self-contradictory.[48] Thus, in the Buddhist theory, affirmative and negative judgments pertaining to the conceptual object would be impossible. But these judgments can very well be explained from the realistic point of view. The term 'cow', for example, denotes an individual endowed with 'cowness'. It tells nothing about the presence or the absence of the cow, or about any of its other attributes. The affirmation or nagation of its existence signifies its presence or absence respectively in a particular space-time. The connotation of the word 'cow', though positive, does not include existence or non-existence. The Buddhist, Udayana charges, greatly confounds the issue by identifying positivity with existence. Existence means 'actual presence' which is not included in the connotation of a positive term like 'cow'. The word 'cow' does not have spatio-temporal reference. Hence, there is no tautology in asserting that 'the cow exists'. In the same way, there is no contradiction in asserting that 'the cow does not exist', as it means only that a particular locus of 'cowness' is no more alive.[49]

Udayana's explanation obviously rests on the ontological distinction of substance and attribute and the conception of substance as the locus of manifold attributes. The Buddhist is radically opposed to this ontology.[50] For him, not only the distinction of substance and attribute, but also the conception of substance itself is a fiction of imagination. His ontology consists of indivisible fleeting point-instants. They are either self-aware ideas or the external particulars apprehended in pure sensation. They are, by hypothesis, beyond the reach of thought. Hence arises the Buddhist distinction of the objects of sensation and conception. The two-level theory of reality advocated by him has its roots in the metaphysical intuition of ultimate reality as an incessant

---

48. For the Naiyāyika, the terms positive and negative, or real and unreal, are contradictories. Anything we might conceive of must belong to either of these two categories. The categories of 'both real and unreal' and 'neither real nor unreal' are inadmissible to him. The former is obviously self-contradictory. The latter is also said to be contradictory because it violates 'the law of excluded middle'.
49. ĀTV, p. 128.
50. We have already discussed the Buddhist criticism of these distinctions in a previous chapter. Refer in this connection to PV, III, 60 ff. and III, 51 ff; Ap. Sid., pp. 10 f, and JN, p. 215.

flow. The realist, on the other hand, takes his stand on common empirical experience. The real, for him, is what is determinately known. The distinction of substance and attribute, and the conception of substance as the locus of diverse attributes, have their foundation in the common determinate experience of reality. This experience is expressed by our judgments in subject-predicate form. The subject term denotes substance with its class-nature and nothing more. Hence, different predicate terms are required to signify the various attributes belonging to a substance.[51]

The Buddhist attacks the realist identification of the objects of sensation and conception. Sensation seizes its object vividly and entirely, while conception apprehends its object hazily and partially. These differences must be owing to the difference of objects and not merely to the difference of the efficiency of the instruments of knowledge as the realist holds. The point is that if both sensation and conception are caused by one and the same object, i.e., the particular existent, then their characters must not differ. The difference of characters implies the difference of causal efficiency. And this latter difference implies the difference of objects, for two opposed causal efficiencies cannot belong to an identical thing.[52]

In Udayana's view, however, substance and attributes being different, the cognition of a substance does not necessarily involve the cognition of all its attributes. Diverse factors are operative in the cognition of the various attributes of a thing. In the verbal knowledge of a thing different terms are required to produce a fuller knowledge of its diverse attributes. Similarly in perceptual knowledge also, different senses are required to produce the cognition of the diverse qualities of a thing.[53] The Buddhist insistence that the cognition of a

51. ĀTV, p. 129.
52. See JN, pp. 213-15; Ap. Sid., pp. 9-10.
53. ĀTV, pp. 134-136.

In the Buddhist view, the objects cognised by the different senses are different; they are not the qualities of one and the same thing. Not only this, even the object cognised by one sense is not the same in two different moments. It is this momentary object which is real. This object being devoid of spatial and temporal extension, is cognised clearly and entirely in a single sensation. The substance of the realist with its diverse attributes is, according to the Buddhist, a thought-construction. It is not given in sensation; it is a product of conceptual thought. Hence it is the proper object of conceptual cognition. The realist, however, is radically opposed to the Buddhist conception of reality and his doctrine of perception. He, therefore, refuses to admit the conclusion drawn by the Buddhist on his own premises.

real must be complete has no foundation in experience. Our cognition of a thing is partial when all the factors necessary for its complete cognition are not present. As the favourable conditions are gradually realised our cognition of it grows completer. The Buddhist argument that the cognition of a real must be complete since its causal efficiency is identical, is rejected by Udayana as inadmissible. The argument could be valid if the cognition of all the attributes of a thing depended solely on the thing itself, or its cognition, or the factors contributing to its cognition. But this being not so, the Buddhist argument is without any foundation.[54]

The Buddhist has argued that there will be no real difference between the various sources of cognition, if their objects are held to be identical.[55] Udayana, on the contrary, holds that the difference between the various sources of cognition is due not to the difference of objects, but to the peculiar efficiency possessed by them.[56] The efficiencies of the diverse sources of cognition are determined by specific conditions. Inference depends on the apprehension of concomitance between the middle and the major terms and the perception of the middle term in the subject. Verbal cognition depends on the apprehension of the significance of the conventional verbal symbols. Perceptual cognition depends on the sense-object contact. It is due to the difference of specific conditions determining their functions that the sources of cognitions differ. The contents of cognitions derived from these different sources are, according to Udayana, not qualitatively different as the Buddhist assumes. The difference is only quantitative. Thus, Udayana maintains against the Buddhist that the difference of the sources of cognitions does not necessarily imply a qualitative difference of their objects. One and the same thing may be cognised in different ways by the same person successively, or by two different persons simultaneously.[57] He admits that the content of perceptual cognition differs from that of conceptual cognition; the spatio-temporal determination, vividness, etc., present in the case of the former are absent in the case of the latter. But this

54. yattu śakterabhedādityādi, tattadā śobheta yadi dharmimātrādhīnas tadbodhamātrādhīno vā tāvanmātrabodhasāmagryadhīno vā yāvadupādhibhedabodhah syāt, na caivam. ĀTV, pp. 134-35.
55. See PV, III, 44-45; JN, p. 213.
56. vicitraśaktitvācca pramānānām. ĀTV, pp. 135-36.
57. Ibid., p. 138.

difference is only quantitative. It does not imply that the conceptual cognition is not a cognition of the real at all.[58] Cognitions are distinguished as vivid and hazy on the basis of the number of attributes apprehended. A thing perceived from a distance appears hazy, but as one draws nearer and more of its attributes are apprehended, the same thing appears more and more distinct. Hence, it is opposed to reason and experience to deny objectivity to the conceptual cognition merely because it is hazy.[59]

Udayana denies that there is any contradiction, as Jñānaśrī has alleged,[60] in maintaining that both direct and indirect cognitions refer to an identical object. Directness and indirectness are not features of things, but those of cognitions. Difference of cognitions, according to Udayana, may be determined in two ways: (1) by the difference of their objects, or (2) by the difference of their class-natures (*jāti*). In the former case, difference of cognitions implies difference of objects as, for example the cognitions of pot and cloth. But, in the latter case, the situation is different. The class-nature of a cognition is not determined by its object, but by the causal factors producing it. A cognition is said to be verbal if it arises purely due to the apprehension of the meaning of words. It is called perceptual if it owes its genesis solely to the sense-object contact. Similarly there are specific determining factors in the case of inferential and other forms of cognitions. The classification of cognitions as direct and indirect is also due to their causal factors and not to their objects.[61] If directness and indirectness were the properties of objects, they would be apprehended as such at the time of the cognition (*vyavasāya*) of objects. But, as a matter of fact, they are apprehended as the

58. Ibid., p. 140.
59. Ibid.
It may be observed here that the Buddhist insistence on the qualitative difference between the objects of perceptual and conceptual cognitions is a necessary consequence of his view of reality. If the real is an indivisible efficient point-instant, its cognitions cannot differ in character. The difference of cognitions, in that case, would necessarily imply the difference of objects. But the realist, who starts with a radically different view of reality, is not committed to this conclusion. He believes in the difference of substance and attributes and in the stability of things. He can very well explain the difference of characters of cognitions on the basis of the quantity of attributes apprehended.
60. JN, p. 210, also see Ap. Sid., p. 7.
61. ĀTV, p. 144.

properties of cognitions in a subsequent reflective cognition (*anuvyavasāya*). Following the latter we classify our cognitions under various heads as perceptual, inferential, recollective, etc. The usage of such expressions as 'mediate object' and 'immediate object', warns Udayana, must not mislead us into thinking that mediateness and immediateness are the properties of objects. These expressions like others, such as 'perceived', 'inferred', 'recollected', etc., merely indicate the particular mode of the cognitions of things and not their properties.[62]

3. *Volitional activity not explained*

Udayana tries to show that the *Apoha* theory fails to explain our pragmatic activity following conceptual cognition. If conceptual cognition has nothing to do with the real at all, how can it inspire volitional activity? The Buddhist has generally given two kinds of answers to this question : The said volitional activity becomes possible because (1) the conceptual content is regarded as real due to the non-apprehension of difference between the conceptual and the real, and (2) the conceptual content is regarded as real due to the force of innate disposition. Both these answers are examined by Udayana and rejected as unsatisfactory.[63]

Against the first Udayana argues that if the non-apprehension of difference between the conceptual and the real is said to inspire pragmatic activity, then the consistency of volitional activity becomes unintelligible. The non-apprehension of difference being present in respect of everything, there can be no bar to the discrepant activity.[64] For example, if the conceptual cognition of cow inspires activity towards the real cow because the difference between the *conceptual* cow and the *real* cow is not apprehended, then such non-apprehension being true with regard to other things also, viz., real horses, buffaloes, etc., the cognition of cow may produce activity towards them as well. The Buddhist might rejoin that in the conceptual cognition of cow the difference from non-cow being apprehended, there is no possibility of discrepant activity. Udayana points out that the cognition of difference from non-cow presupposes the cognition of non-cow.

62. ĀTV, pp. 144-45.
63. Ibid., pp. 147-48.
64. pravṛttisāmāndhikaraṇyaniyamānupapatteḥ, bhedāgrahasya sarvatra sulabhatvāt. ĀTV, p. 148.

But, in the Buddhist view, the cognition of non-cow is impossible, since particulars are untouched by concepts. Thus the possibility of discrepant activity still remains. The Buddhist cannot logically hold that the difference from unknown things is cognisable, for such a position would be self-stultifying. For, in that case, the difference between the conceptual cow and the real cow cannot remain unapprehended, and, consequently, there will be no volitional activity towards the real cow at all.[65]

Further, if the difference of the conceptual content (*apoha*) from the particular (*svalakṣaṇa*) is real, then the former cannot be a fiction of thought; and if it is unreal, then there is no point in saying that it is not apprehended. Again, if difference is the nature of the conceptual content (*svarūpalakṣaṇa*), then its difference from anything cannot remain unapprehended. Only the apprehension of identity can prevent the apprehension of such a difference. But there being no such apprehension, the difference between the conceptual and the real cannot remain unapprehended. And if the conceptual content, by virtue of being a thought-construction, is denied a self-differentiating nature, then its difference from nothing can be apprehended. Consequently, the possibility of discrepant activity remains.[66]

According to Jñānaśrī, conceptual cognition, though not apprehending the real, motivates us towards it because of its own causal factors consisting in the revival of subtle mental impressions left by past experience.[67] The Buddhist recognises an indirect causal relation between the conceptual and the real in order to explain motivation and fulfilment of pragmatic activity. Volitional activity, according to him, does not require direct presence of the real to our consciousness; it can arise even from mental dispositions generated by the past experience of things. The absence of a direct causal relation between the conceptual cognition and the real, according to the Buddhist, means that there is no real cognitive relation between the two. The Naiyāyika, however, is radically opposed to this identification of cognitive relation with causal relation. It is true that in the case of

65. Ibid., pp. 148-49.
66. Ibid., pp. 149-50.
67. svavāsanāparipākavaśādupajāyamānaiva sā buddhir apaśyantyapi bāhyaṁ bāhye pravṛttimātanoti. JN, p. 226.

perception the two coincide. But this coincidence cannot be made a universal rule. The absence of a direct causal relation between the conceptual cognition and the real cannot be made the ground for denying a real cognitive relation between them. Causal relation, according to Udayana, has nothing to do with the objective reference of cognitions.[68]

Udayana severely criticises Jñānaśrī's explanation of the objective reference of conceptual cognitions indirectly through the impressions born of direct experience. This could be accepted if it was proved that both cause and effect necessarily have the same objective reference. In the Buddhist view, Udayana points out, two successive ideas, e.g., of 'blue' and 'yellow', are related as cause and effect. If objective reference is said to consist in an indirect causal relation also, then the ideas of 'blue' and 'yellow' should have the same objective reference. The idea of 'yellow' following the idea of 'blue' has an indirect causal relation to the blue thing (*svalakṣaṇa*). So the perception of 'yellow' should refer to the latter. The Buddhist might explain that the above rule applies only to the conceptual and not to the perceptual cognition, for the main issue under consideration is the possibility of motivated activity. This cannot be explained by the perceptual experience directly, as it is non-conceptual. Conceptual cognition also cannot explain it by itself if it has absolutely no relation to reality. It cannot be said to have a direct relation to reality, as it is not directly born of the real thing. Its objective reference, therefore, can be explained only on the basis of an indirect causal relation to reality. Udayana rejects the above explanation as inadmissible because it rests on a host of unproved assumptions. The Buddhist first assumes that perceptual cognition is non-conceptual. Then he assumes that conceptual cognition is not the cognition of reality. And when he is faced with the problem of explaining volitional activity, he assumes an indirect causal relation between the conceptual cognition and reality. But he refuses to draw the full implication of his own assumptions. If indirect causal relation to reality is admitted as the ground of objective reference of conceptual cognitions, then no exception to this rule can be made in the case of perceptual cognition. The Buddhist attempt to exclude perception from this rule is absolutely arbitrary and illogical.[69]

68. ĀTV, pp. 151 f.
69. Ibid.

The Buddhist has contended that conceptual cognition inspires pragmatic activity because it is erroneously regarded as having the same objective reference as perception. Udayana denies the possibility of such an error, since it can neither be a case of superimposition, nor of non-apprehension of difference. All cognitions, in the Buddhist view, are self-aware and essentially non-conceptual and non-erroneous. Thus, there can be no superimposition of perceptual character on conceptual cognitions. Nor can there be such a superimposition on the object of conceptual cognition, as its conceptual character in the form of speakability is definitely apprehended.[70] Similarly, there is no possibility of confusion between conceptual and perceptual cognitions due to non-apprehension of their difference, since both of them, in the Buddhist view, are fully aware of their own character. Thus there is no reason why two cognitions having distinct objective references—one to the real and the other to a thought-construction—should at all be confounded.[71]

Another contention of the Buddhist is that the objects of perceptual and conceptual cognitions being similar, the latter inspires motivated activity. Udayana asks, what kind of similarity obtains between the real and the illusory? Similarity can be understood either as the identity of substance, or as the identity of one or more of the attributes. Neither of them can hold between the real and the unreal.[72] The Buddhist conception of negative similarity consisting in the common exclusion of the contrary is also not helpful. The said exclusion itself being featureless, it cannot serve as a link between the real and the unreal. The Buddhist might say that this does not harm his position, because the similarity in question is only a subjective belief (*ābhimānika*) and not an objective fact: But the question is, why is there such a belief ? Why is the illusory believed to be real? The Buddhist has not so far provided a satisfactory answer to this question.[73]

Jñānaśrī advances another explanation of motivated activity. He holds that concepts produce volitional activity because of their own nature. Every concept has a determinate form and it motivates us towards a definite particular, just as a seed by its own nature produces

70. Ibid., pp. 152-53.
71. Ibid., p. 154.
72. Ibid., p. 155.
73. Ibid., pp. 155-56.

a specific sprout.[74] Udayana rejects this explanation on the ground that a concept absolutely unrelated to the real cannot be thought of as motivating us towards it. The nature of concepts to which Jñānaśrī appeals cannot be anything other than a natural relation (*Svabhāvasambandha*) of the concept of the real. This, again, can be nothing but the cognitive relation, or the subject-object relation, which is ultimately unanalysable. But no such relation between the concepts and the real being acceptable to the Buddhist, he cannot make an appeal to the nature of concepts for explaining the generation of volitional activity.[75] Jñānaśrī has argued that even in the absence of a real cognitive relation concepts can be said to produce motivation, just as, in the Nyāya view, a cause, by its own nature, is said to produce a non-existent effect to which it is absolutely unrelated. Udayana replies that the causal function of a thing, in his view, is determined by its class-nature (*jāti*). The causal relation is not a relation between particulars as such, but that between particulars determined by universals, otherwise anything might be the cause of anything. Thus, a cause, though not actually related to its effect prior to its production, is capable of entering into such relation by virtue of its eternal class-nature, the universal. But no positive universal being admissible to the Buddhist, he cannot explain the production of specific volitional activity by appealing to the nature of concepts. In the absence of a universal determinant the concept of fire, for example, may generate activity towards water. There is no reason why the concept of fire should motivate us towards fire alone and not towards water, since, according to the Buddhist, there is neither an objective relation between them, nor a determination of the concept of fire by a positive universal.[76]

The Buddhist might rejoin that, although positive universal is not admitted by him, a determinant universal of the form of 'the exclusion of the other' having been recognised, the contingency stated above would not arise at all. The concept of fire would generate activity towards the real fire alone and not towards water, for both (the concept and the real fire) are commonly determined by 'the negation of non-fire'. If such is the case, Udayana argues, there should be no volitional activity in the case of erroneous

74. JN, p. 226.
75. ĀTV, p. 157.
76. Ibid., p. 158.

perception where the thing conceived is different from the thing actually present. But a volitional activity is seen to follow a mistaken cognition, even though the thing present is not the same as the thing conceived. The Buddhist might explain that in the case of perceptual error the generation of volitional activity is determined by the mistaken cognition of the thing itself. Udayana points out that the Buddhist cannot consistently regard the production of volitional activity as determined by the cognition of the thing itself, whether mistaken or true, for the thing, in his view, is untouched by concepts. And if the mistaken cognition of the thing is admitted as the determinant of volitional activity, there is no reason why the true cognition of the thing should be denied that function. As a matter of fact, all volitional activities are determined by the cognition of the thing, whether mistaken or true. If the Buddhist does not admit this, he cannot explain why the concept of fire should not inspire activity towards water.[77]

According to Jñānaśrī, conceptual cognition inspires activity towards real things, because the former has the same form as the latter.[78] Udayana points out that this is not true in the case of error in which the form of cognition is different from that of the thing actually present. Besides, there can be no similarity between the external thing and its cognition, because the two, as unconscious and conscious entities respectively, are diametrically opposed to one another. They are born of different sets of causal factors having no common element whatever. They cannot be said to be derived from one and the same cause, as the cognition of a thing does not depend upon the cause of the thing. Fire, for example, is the cause of smoke; the latter cannot exist without the former. But the cognition of smoke arises even without fire. This proves that the cause of smoke and that of its cognition are different. Consequently, smoke and its cognition are also different, having nothing in common between them. Thus, there being no similarity of form between the concept and the

---

77. svīkuru vā tasyāpi sphuraṇam, parihara vā vahnivikalpād avahnau pravṛttimiti. ĀTV, p. 169.

The whole tenor of Udayana's argument is that if the real is completely shut out from the conceptual ken, then the motivation for it becomes absolutely unintelligible. Pragmatic activity presupposes the judgment of the thing as desirable or undersirable. But if our judgments never touch the real at all, the volitional activity guided by them becomes an inexplicable mystery.

78. pratyāsattticintayā ca tāttvikasyāpi vahner jvaladbhāsurākāratvaṁ vikalpollekhasyā-pīti, tāvatā tatraiva pravartanaśaktir jvalanavikalpasya na jalādau. JN, p. 226.

external thing, Jñānaśrī's explanation of the generation of volitional activity does not hold good. There is no way out from this impasse, according to Udayana, unless the Buddhist concedes that the objects of conceptual cognition and volitional activity are one and the same.[79]

According to Dharmakīrti and Śāntarakṣita, the object of volition is the same as that of conceptual cognition; but it is a conceptual image and not the real thing. It inspires pragmatic activity because it is wrongly believed to be external. Also it leads to the attainment of the real, just as one motivated by the lustre of the jewel, succeeds in attaining the real jewel.[80] Udayana contends that volitional activity is never directed towards a conceptual content. We are motivated towards things that are capable of satisfying our needs. The Buddhist argument that the motivation towards the conceptual content becomes possible because it is erroneously supposed to be external has no force. The error in the case under discussion can arise only in two ways : either the conceptual form is superimposed on the external thing, or the externality of the thing is superimposed on the conceptual image. The former alternative is impossible because, in the Buddhist view, the external thing is untouched by thought. The latter alternative also is impossible, since the conceptual image being immediately aware of itself, there is no possibility of its being supposed as external. The analogy of the jewel also breaks down, as one is not motivated towards the lustre of the jewel as such, but towards the jewel itself. If one took the lustre merely as an appearance, there will be no motivated activity at all. Besides, such a mistake is impossible in the case of the conceptual content which, as a cognition, is immediately aware of its own nature.[81]

The most damaging consequence of the above view for the Buddhist is that it eliminates the logical necessity of postulating the existence of external things. If conceptual cognitions are confined to mental contents only, what is the evidence for the existence of external reality? The Buddhist has urged that the succession and variety of mental contents cannot be explained without assuming external determination.

79. ĀTV, pp. 160-61. Udayana's insistence on the absolute difference between the cognition and its object is consistent with his fundamental realism. The acceptance of any similarity between the cognition and the external thing would throw the door open to idealism.

80. PV, II, 167-68; TS, 1026-27; TSP, p. 323.

81. ĀTV, p. 162.

The difference of the contents of successive cognitions necessarily imply the existence of external causes. Udayana refuses to acknowledge any such necessity, since erroneous cognitions are seen to arise even in the absence of an external determination. Thus, there is nothing to prevent us from regarding all conceptual cognitions with all their variety of contents as mere illusions or dreams.[82] If concepts do not touch the real at all, there is nothing to distinguish between the true and the false cognitions. The Buddhist argument for the existence of external things based on the fulfilment of pragmatic activity also has no force. The said fulfilment itself being cognitional in nature, it proves merely the existence of mental contents and not that of external things. Thus the cognition of fulfilment may be said to have arisen out of innate dispositions just like erroneous cognitions. The Buddhist view in this way leads to the subjectivity of all knowledge. The assumption of the existence of external things by the Buddhist is absolutely unfounded. Udayana further points out that the image theory of cognitions (*Sākārajñānavāda*) becomes necessary for the view which denies the existence of external objects, since otherwise cognitions would be indistinguishable from one another. But, in a view admitting the existence of external objects, the difference of cognitions can be explained on the basis of their respective objects without assuming the forms of cognitions. The Sautrāntika insistence on retaining both—the form of cognition as well as the external thing—has, therefore, no logical justification.[83]

Udayana now proceeds to show that the problem remains insoluble for the Buddhist even if the particular things themselves are admitted to be the objects of conceptual cognition. Jñānaśrī has maintained that particulars, though in themselves indeterminate, become the objects of conceptual cognition under the form of 'the exclusion of the other'. The conceptual cognition of a particular as 'cow', for example, is nothing but the cognition of it, not in its own nature, but under the form of 'the exclusion of non-cow'.[84] Udayana holds that such an exclusion is impossible without admitting the reality of the universal. The concept of 'non-cow' cannot be the result of the

82. Ibid., pp. 163-64.
This is precisely the reason why the Sautrāntika position led to the Yogācāra denial of external objects supposed to account for the variety of perceptions.
83. Ibid., p. 164.
84. JN, pp. 203, 206; also see Ap. Sid., p. 3.

negation of individual cows, as they are infinite in number. The universal 'cowness' has to be admitted to explain its genesis. But, since the Buddhist denies the existence of positive universals, there can neither be the concept of 'non-cow' nor its exclusion. Consequently, the conceptual cognition of particulars under the form of 'the exclusion of the other' would be impossible.[85]

The Buddhist has held that the genesis of concepts can be explained even without assuming the existence of unversals. Particulars themselves by their own efficiency generate diverse concepts which become the bases of conceptual cognitions. The efficiency of the particulars is determined not by a universal subsisting in them, but by their own causal factors.[86] Even the realist, the Buddhist points out, recognises certain concepts, such as those of 'universal', 'negation', etc., which are not founded on objective universals. There is no reason why the same may not be held with regard to all concepts. Besides, the realist has no satisfactorv answer to the question, viz., why does a certain universal, say 'cowness', inhere in certain particulars only and not in others? There will be an infinite regress if another determinant universal is postulated to explain the limitation. And if an appeal is made to the nature of particulars, then the same nature may be regarded as the cause of concepts directly, without needing the mediation of fictitious universals.[87]

Udayana considers the Buddhist position as logically untenable. If an identical concept is said to be generated by the diverse particulars without any objective identity, then a single self-identical individual may be said to generate the idea of diversity without any objective difference. An appeal to the natural efficiency of particulars can equally be made in both the cases.[88] So the Buddhist cannot logically retain difference as real and deny the reality of identity. If difference is implied by the experience of diversity, identity is also implied by the experience of unity.[89] The Buddhist must also answer the question

85. ĀTV, pp. 165-66.
86. See TS, 1005-6; also cp. Ap. Sid., p. 12.
87. See TS, 1058-61.
88. yadyevaṁ nimittāntaram anapekṣyaikavyavahāro'tyantabinnaiḥ, evaṁ bhinnavyavahāra evābhinnenaikena kenacit kiṁ na sādhyate, śaktisvabhāvālambanasyobhayatrāpi tulyatvāt. ĀTV, p. 168.
89. This is the crux of the matter. For the realist both identity and difference are real, for they equally appear in our experience. For the Buddhist and the Advaitist, on the other hand, only one is real and the other is 'subjective' or false.

whether the natural efficiency of the individuals, appealed to by him, varies with the individuals or is identical? If the former, then it cannot generate an identical concept, and if the latter, then it is a universal. The Buddhist contention that the experience of unity is an illusion like the perception of 'two moons' is an unwarranted dogma. If the uncontradicted experience of unity is erroneous, then the experience of diversity also meets the same fate. Experience, Udayana avers, attests the reality of both. It is due to the objective identities that different individuals fall into classes. Diversity and unity are real features of things given in uncontradicted experience. The rejection of either as false is opposed to experience and reason.[90]

As regards the concept of 'universal' referred to by the Buddhist, the Nyāya position is that it is not without an objective foundation. Although an objective universal corresponding to it is denied due to logical reasons, nevertheless it is admitted to have a basis in the common character of 'subsisting exclusively in certain particulars' which belongs to all the universals. This character is not a universal (*jāti*), but a common property (*upādhi*). A concept must be based on either of them. The particulars *qua* particulars cannot explain the genesis of general concepts.[91]

4. *Concluding remarks*

It is clear from the above discussion that the whole controversy between the realist and the Buddhist nominalist is a clash between two radically opposed metaphysical standpoints. All their disputes over logical and epistemological issues are traceable to their respective metaphysical presuppositions. The metaphysical assumption underlying the realist's position is the conception of the real as determinately knowable and expressible. Thus universals are not fictions of thought but objective features existing in the extramental world. The realist, therefore, sees no need of distinguishing between the objects of direct and indirect knowledge. They are different ways of knowing one and the same kind of reality. The assumption underlying the Buddhist position, on the other hand, is the conception of the real as the unique point-instant of causal efficiency. Thus, in reality, there is neither recurrence nor similarity. The non-recurring,

90. Ibid., p. 169.
91. See Chapter II for a detailed discussion on this point.

absolutely dissimilar particulars are the objects given in pure sense-apprehension. The Buddhist accordingly defines perception as an apprehension free from thought determinations. This implies that universals and resemblances are not given facts but fictions of thought projected on the extramental reality. Hence arises the dichotomy of the objects of direct and indirect knowledge. The former is real and the latter a thought construction. Indirect knowledge, or conceptual cognition, is a wrong synthesis of the given and the constructed—the particular and the universal.

We have already shown that the extreme realism of the Nyāya and the Mīmāṁsā fails to be a satisfactory theory of conceptual cognition. We have now to see whether the Buddhist nominalism fares any better. Reality, according to the Buddhist, is constituted of unique point-instants which are absolutely discrete and dissimilar. All identities and similarities are, therefore, fictions of imagination. A direct disproof of the metaphysical assumption of the Buddhist is indeed impossible. Nevertheless, it can be shown that such an assumption fails to explain human knowledge adequately. At least an alternative theory of reality which explains our knowledge more satisfactorily is conceivable. We may quite legitimately hold that our knowledge is what it is because there are recurrences and resemblances in reality. This view is corroborated by common empirical experience also It seems undeniable that we observe recurring qualities and relations which form the basis of our generalisations and classifications. To deny the existence of these empirical facts is to sacrifice the data of valid experience at the altar of a metaphysical theory. If there were no recurrences or resemblances in reality, conceptual cognition would not have been possible at all. The world could neither be thought about nor spoken about, but only felt. We could never come to possess any concepts, and even if our mind fabricated them in some way, they could not be applied to anything in the external world. If the Buddhist view of conceptual cognition is granted, then all human knowledge, except immediate experience, would become indistinguishable from dreams and illusions.

The ontology of the Buddhist is reflected in his theory of the import of words as well. The general thesis is that words signify concepts, or thought-constructions, and not the real things. This theory is presented in three distinguishable forms. Dignāga and Dharmakīrti emphasise the negative aspect of the meaning of words. A word expresses its meaning only through the negation of the opposite meaning. The 'negation of the opposite' is the concept constructed by thought and exhausted in that negation. Śāntarakṣita, on the other hand, distinguishes between the direct and indirect meanings of words. The direct meaning is the vague general image produced by the word in the mind of the listener which is felt as positive, while the indirect meaning is the negation of the opposite meaning. The latter follows the former by implication. He maintains also that words may be said to signify the unique particulars in an indirect manner, since the concepts, which the words directly signify, are functionally dependent on external reality. Thus the import of words, according to Śāntarakṣita, cannot be exclusively regarded either as positive or as negative. It is not really positive, because the real external particulars are by hypothesis inexpressible. It is also not purely negative, because it is apprehended as positive. The meaning of words is, therefore, neither positive nor negative.

According to the third view, represented by Jñānaśrī and Ratnakīrti, a word signifies both the positive and the negative meanings simultaneously. They reject Śāntarakṣita's theory of direct and indirect meanings apprehended successively. Such a succession, they maintain, is not psychologically felt. A word, according to them, is intended to signify the external thing. Nevertheless, this signifying invariably involves the negation of the opposite meaning which is a thought-construction. Thus a word does not signify the real positive thing as it is in itself, but as concealed or covered by the constructed form of 'the negation of the opposite'. This is really tantamount to saying that words do not signify the real at all. They signify a synthesis of the real and the constructed which is the work of thought.

It is evident that the three forms in which the Buddhist theory of the import of words is presented differ only in their emphasis concerning the positive and negative significations of words. Essentially all of them maintain that words and concepts correspond to nothing in reality. The real issue between the realist and the Buddhist is whether the meaning of a word logically includes the negation of the opposite meaning, and whether such a negation is felt in the comprehension of the meaning of words. The Buddhist holds that unless the meaning of a word includes the negation of the opposite meaning, no definite comprehension of it is possible. The realist, on the contrary, maintains that the negation of the opposite meaning cannot logically be the part of the meaning of a word, since the former presupposes the latter. Unless the word had a meaning of its own, the negation of the opposite meaning would be logically impossible. The realist undoubtedly has a point here. In the absence of a positive meaning the negation of the opposite meaning is inconceivable. It seems quite legitimate to hold that the meaning of a positive word is positive, though it necessarily implies the negation of the opposite meaning. As regards the comprehension of the meaning of words, the Buddhist view is that it cannot be definite unless the negation of the opposite meaning is included in it. The realist, on the contrary, holds that verbal comprehension is definite because nothing other than the specific meaning of the word is apprehended in it. The truth seems to be that a definite comprehension of the meaning of words implicitly involves the exclusion of the opposite meaning, though this exclusion is not consciously felt. When the word 'cow', for instance, is heard we definitely understand an animal of a determinate kind excluding the other kinds, though this exclusion is not psychologically felt. Thus the word may be said to have both positive and negative meanings, the latter logically presupposing the former. In verbal cognition also both are necessarily comprehended; the positive meaning is apprehended directly and consciously and the negative one implicitly. The question whether the comprehension of the positive and the negative meanings is simultaneous or successive is difficult to answer. It is also irrelevant to our main problem. All that we feel justified in saying is that no succession is psychologically felt.

The question about the meaning of words assumes importance because it is closely linked with the problem of universals. If general words signify nothing, as the Buddhist maintains, then the universals which they are said to stand for become pure fictions of imagination. The ontological theory of the Buddhist is repeated in his theory of the import of words. We have already indicated that the Buddhist ontology does not satisfactorily explain human knowledge. Similarly we find that the Buddhist theory of concepts and of the import of words is also unsatisfactory. It is absurd to maintain that all words correspond to fictions of thought, or that all concepts are pure fabrications of the mind corresponding to nothing in reality. It is also equally absurd to maintain that all words and concepts correspond to real identities existing in their own right. The problem demands a proper analysis of our concepts and words which we make use of in our thinking and speaking.

It will be agreed by all that we have a number of concepts, such as those of 'unicorn', 'dragon', 'fairy', etc., which do not have their counterparts in the external world, at least not so far discovered. Similarly, we have general words in our language, such as 'if', 'but', 'either', 'or', 'perhaps', 'otherwise', etc., which do not correspond to anything in the outside reality, but have important functions in our language. We have another set of words and concepts, such as 'cow', 'man', blue', 'sweet', 'hot', etc., which, though not devoid of objective basis, are yet not based on real essences or identities common to particulars. There is no 'humanity' or 'sweetness' as such in the external world over and above the individual human beings and particular sweet things. Our concepts of 'man' and 'sweet' as identities have only a mental existence. But they come into being because there are similar individual human beings and similar tastes of sweet. There is a third group of words and concepts which correspond to identical qualities and relations observed to exist in the external world. This specific shade of white before us is a recurrent quality; similarly, the relation of 'being on top of', or 'being to the left of', identically recurs in so many instances. These identical qualities and relations are not mental fabrications; they are universals discovered by us in the external world. Thus all concepts cannot be said to be without any foundation in the extramental reality. Some of them correspond to identical qualities and relations and some to real similarities of things and qualities. Others are pure fabrications of the mind corresponding to nothing in the external world. No theory which fails to take into account the recurrences and resemblances discovered in the external world can satisfactorily explain human knowledge.

The criticism of the Buddhist nominalism by Vācaspati Miśra and Udayana clearly brings out the weak points of this theory. The Buddhist, in order to establish his nominalism on a secure foundation, propounds the theories of 'negative similarity' (*sādṛśya*), 'non-apprehension of difference' (*bhedāgraha*) and 'superimposition' (*āropa*). All these theories have been shown by the realist to be logically untenable. The Buddhist did realise that if thought and reality are held to be absolutely divorced from one another, consistent volitional activity inspired by conceptual knowledge could not be explained. Hence he advocates the theory of indirect causal relation between the real point-instants and the universal concept in the mind. Concepts, even though thought-constructions, are said to be indirectly stimulated by the external thing. It is maintained that particulars by their very nature generate universal concepts, though in themselves they are absolutely dissimilar. This doctrine, to say the least, is quite unintelligible to us. If particulars are absolutely discrete and dissimilar, it is not intelligible why they should generate one or the other universal concept. Why should certain particulars generate the concept of 'cow' and not that of an 'ass'? It has been argued that the ultimate nature of things is unquestionable. But how are we to understand this nature? If it is an identical capacity to produce an identical concept, then it is a universal. And if, as the Buddhist really maintains, the particulars have no identical or similar nature, or identical causal efficiency, then it is quite unintelligible how they generate identical concepts.

It must however be granted that the Buddhist is the most thorough-going nominalist in the history of thought. He does not allow real unity or similarity on any level. If things are called by the same name, it is not because of any identity or resemblance. Again, between two occurrences of the same name, there is no real identity or similarity. The conceptual identity to which a word corresponds is itself unreal. If this theory is accepted, then there is no reason why the thing present before us on the table should be called an 'ink-pot' rather than a 'horse'. If someone comes and calls it a 'horse' or an 'elephant', we should not be surprised. Our calling it an 'ink-pot' must itself be quite accidental. And even when we call it an 'ink-pot', we are not using the same word as we did before. Whether we understand a word as a sound or a mark, there is no real identity or similarity between our present and the past use of it. If this theory were true, there could be no common understanding or communication of thought by means of words. All grouping or classification would have been purely arbitrary. There could be no purposive activity, and if at all there was any, its fulfilment would have been purely accidental.

The Buddhist tried to meet the above difficulties by his theory of transcendental illusion (*anādi avidyā*, or *vāsanā*). It is said to be a natural malady from which all human beings suffer. It is the source of our belief in common understanding and communication of thought whereas, in reality, there is none. It is because of it that we regard things as similar and identical, group them under different classes and give them a common name. It is due to this natural illusion that we believe in recurrences and are inspired to act. The Buddhist maintains, however, that at the culmination of a successful act inspired by this illusion, we attain the real. We know that our act is successful, or that we have attained the real, by the resulting satisfaction. But, as Udayana points out, the consciousness of satisfaction being itself judgmental in nature, it may, by the same logic, be illusory. Thus the Buddhist nominalism would logically lead to scepticism. Moreover, the Buddhist theory of transcendental illusion is a metaphysical assumption necessitated by his view of reality as a flux of unique indeterminate point-instants. But there is no reason why one should accept this view at all. There seems to be no justification for reducing all experience of recurrence and similarity to the status of illusion. If these experiences are illusory then nothing prevents us from regarding the experience of difference also as illusory. Besides doing violence to our valid empirical experience, the Buddhist theory also fails to explain human knowledge and activity in a satisfactory manner. Our knowledge is what it is, and we speak and act in the manner we do, not because we are suffering from a natural malady, but because there are recurrences and resemblances discovered by us in the external world. If this is denied, the only alternative is scepticism.

We have thus come to the end of our discussion of the various theories of universals in Indian Philosophy. We have found all the important theories of universals known in the West, viz., extreme realism, moderate realism, conceptualism and nominalism, represented here. We have noted that every view of universals involves an underlying view of reality. Our attempt, therefore, has been to consider, in the first place, whether the view of universals advocated by a particular system is consistent with its general view of reality, and secondly, whether it explains human knowledge in a satisfactory manner. We have held that a theory of universals should be based on a proper analysis of concepts, and that such an analysis takes us beyond the traditional theories of universals.

It must finally be remarked that all the systems of Indian Philosophy, without exception, confine themselves to the consideration of class-essences (*jāti*) called genera and species in Western Philosophy. They never raise the question whether there are universals of other types, namely, identical qualities and relations. The assumption seems to be that qualities and relations are particulars, though they may be instances of universals. The universal, as the Nyāya clearly states, could not be a quality or a relation; it is an attribute forming a distinct category. This seems to be implicitly accepted by all the systems in their own way. So, the whole discussion centres round the question whether there are generic and specific universals, or real class-essences (*jāti*). But, as we have pointed out, what we actually discover in Nature are identical qualities, identical relations and resemblances; the generic and specific universals never appear in our experience. They are postulated by the realists to account for our general notions, such as 'cow', 'blue', etc. But such a postulation does not seem to be necessary, since recurrent qualities and resemblances supply the necessary and sufficient foundation for our generic concepts.

Our discussion of the problem of universals would not be complete unless we considered also the contributions of the Western thinkers on this problem and compared their views, wherever possible, with their Indian analogues. The problem of universals has been a fundamental problem in Western Philosophy also, and almost every philosopher has something to say about it. However, it is not within our scope to discuss the contribution of every Western philosopher on this problem. We shall have to confine ourselves to some important theories and their leading exponents. We shall endeavour to trace the development of the problem in Western Philosophy through its main stages, and conclude with the discussion of the modern controversy between the Philosophy of Universals and the Philosophy of Resemblances.

CHAPTER XII

UNIVERSALS IN GREEK AND MEDIEVAL THOUGHT

The concept of universals and the problems arising out of it have been perennial topics of discussion in Western Philosophy. The starting point of the discussion was provided by Plato's theory of Forms or Ideas, just as, in Indian Philosophy, it was provided by the Nyāya-Vaiśeṣika theory of *sāmānya* or *jāti*. Plato in his Dialogues argued for the existence of universals. Like the Nyāya-Vaiśeṣika, he thought that the existence of universals was required not only to explain the nature of the world, but also to explain our knowledge of it. That is, it is required both ontologically and epistemologically. He advanced his theory of Forms to meet these requirements. Ever since philosophers in the West have been discussing the nature and the status of universals.

Most of the philosophers would however agree that the reality of universals in some sense or the other is undeniable. But disagreement arises when they try to make the concept of universals precise. It is indisputable that generality is an essential feature of the objects of experience. Although every individual thing is numerically different from all others, its features are general, that is, it possesses characteristics which are recurrent. This generality is recognised in our experience, and it is by virtue of this recognition that the objects are classified into kinds and called by the same name. It is also reflected in our language, all the words of which, with the exception of proper names, are general. Philosophers have advanced various theories to explain the nature and experience of this generality. We shall discuss some leading theories of universals as propounded by their chief exponents, and compare them with their analogues in Indian Philosophy.

1. *The Extreme Realism of Plato*

Plato in his theory of Ideas advocates the existence of universal entities that are absolutely different from the particular objects of experience. Aristotle tells us that the initial step towards a theory of universals was taken by Socrates himself when he sought a precise definition of human virtues, such as beauty, courage, justice, etc.[1] What was required was not particular instances of these virtues, but the identical character common to the particular instances by virtue of which they were what they were. Taking the cue from Socrates, Plato maintained that the universal essence common to all things of a given kind must necessarily be admitted. Not only in the case of abstract virtues, but also in the case of natural objects and artifacts, the existence of universals, according to Plato, must necessarily be recognised. "We are in the habit of postulating one single Form for each class of particulars to which we give the same name."[2]

Plato emphasises absolute difference between universals and particulars. Universals, according to him, are "Forms" or "patterns" fixed in the nature of things, while things are made in their image and are "likenesses."[3] In the *Timaeus* Plato argues that if "intelligence" is to be distinguished from "true belief", then Forms which we cannot see but only think of must be admitted to exist "in themselves." Universals and particulars must be regarded as "different things," for they are "distinct in origin" and "unlike in nature." Universals are "unchanging," "ungenerate" and "indestructible," while the particulars are the opposite of all these. The Form "neither receives anything else into itself from elsewhere, nor itself enters into anything else elsewhere." That is, the Forms are absolutely independent and transcendent entities. The particulars, on the other hand, have their being in "something else," i.e., the Form, without which they will be non-entities. The Forms, which are the very principles on which the particulars have come into being, do not really belong to them; the particulars are merely "semblances" or appearances of the Forms.[4] Thus, for Plato, universals are absolutely different from sensible things; they are apprehended not by the senses but by the intellect. They are completely objective and exist separately from the particulars.

1. See *Metaphysics*, 1078b 18. Tr. by Richard Hope, Columbia University Press, New York, 1952.
2. *Republic* 596a. See *Dialogues of Plato* translated by B. Jowett, Oxford, Clarendon Press, Third Ed.
3. *Parmenides*, 132 pp. 1-3.
4. See *Timaeus*, 51b7 52d1

Plato held the Heraclitean doctrine of flux with regard to the objects of sense-experience.[5] He agreed fully with Protagoras that knowledge gained through sense-experience was always relative. Of the corporeal world and its changing states, he maintained, there was no science but only perceptions and opinions. But he disagreed with the Sophist's view that all knowledge was confined to sensible objects, since, in that case, there could be no science or universal knowledge.[6] Hence, if science or knowledge is to be possible, non-sensible realm of unchanging, incorporeal Forms must necessarily be admitted to exist side by side with the sensible realm of incessantly changing corporeal objects. These Forms, which are the proper objects of scientific knowledge, are apprehended purely through thought. Plato believed that his theory of Forms adequately explained the possibility of the knowledge of universal truths, which was the only kind of knowledge worth the name. This knowledge is not a generalisation based on sense-experience which might subsequently be proved false. It is a piece of *a priori* knowledge, like we have in mathematics, which no possible experience could falsify. It is the knowledge of Forms and their relations which are transcendent and immutable, and not of particular empirical facts which are unstable and imperfect.

The main consideration which led Plato to regard Forms as transcendent was the problem of the geometrical and the value concepts, such as those of 'straightness', 'circularity', 'goodness', 'beauty', etc. For a line to be straight or a figure to be circular, there must be Forms of 'straightness' and 'circularity'. But, however carefully we may try, even with the aid of special instruments, it is impossible to draw a line which is perfectly straight, or a figure which is perfectly circular. On the other hand, the objects which we study and discuss in geometry are not the imperfect diagrams drawn by us, but the perfect forms which diagrams represent. Thus we must accept both the imperfect diagrams and the perfect forms of which they are representations. Similarly, with regard to 'Goodness', Plato maintains that it is not only the pattern which the particular objects judged as

5. See *Metaphysics*, 987a.
6. See Windelband, W. : *A History of Philosophy*, Macmillan, New York, 1950, pp. 117-118.

'good' imperfectly represent, but it is itself a perfect good; it is the perfect essence which the particular objects only imperfectly reveal.[7]

Thus Plato was led to the conclusion that, since propositions of Mathematics, Aesthetics and Ethics must apply to something, and since they do not apply to objects perceived by the senses, the objects of these sciences must belong to a realm of non-sensible realities. These realities are only roughly or approximately manifested by the objects of the sensible world. In so far as objects in the sensible world approximate to them, they are capable of being thought intelligibly. But because it is only an approximation, the thinking is essentially different from scientific knowledge. It is never certain, and is always liable to confusion and contradiction.

Now the question arises : how are the Forms known if they are not given in sense-perception? Plato propounds the 'Doctrine of Reminiscence' in order to answer this question. He maintains that perceptions of objects give suggestions which remind the soul of the Forms which it has known, in a non-sensuous manner, in a previous existence.[8] Plato gives a mythical account of how the soul comes to possess the knowledge of Forms. Before its earthly life the soul is said to have beheld the pure Forms in the incorporeal world itself. In this "supra-celestial region," the Forms are apprehended as "the colourless, figureless, intangible, truly real reality, seen only by the steersman of the soul, reason."[9] It is due to this knowledge that the perception of similar things reminds us of the Forms forgotten in earthly life. This remembrance, according to Plato, awakens in us the philosophical impulse, the love of Forms, by which the soul becomes raised again to the knowledge of true reality.[10]

It is evident that Plato's doctrine of knowledge as recollection is closely connected with his conception of the relations of Forms to the world of phenomena. Between the higher world of Forms and the lower world of objects there is a relation of similarity as is found to exist between the archetypes and their copies, or images. It is due to this similarity that the perception of an object reminds the soul of the

7. See *Meno* 72a and 72c. Cf. Taylor, A. E. : *Plato, the Man and his Work*, Methuen, 1952, pp. 204-5. Also see A. D. Woozley's article on '*Universals*' in *Encyclopedia of Philosophy*, Macmillan, New York, 1967, Vol. 8, p. 196.
8. *Phaedo* 76d7—e7. Also see Ross, W. D., *Plato's Theory of Ideas*, Oxford 1951, p. 25.
9. *Phaedrus* 247c3—e2; see Ross, op. cit., p. 81.
10. See Windelband, op. cit., p. 119. Cp. Field, G. C. : *The Philosophy of Plato*, Oxford, 1951, p. 63.

corresponding Form. Plato regarded the world of phenomena as an imitation, or a copy, of the higher world of Forms, because he found that particular objects always correspond to their class-concepts only to a certain degree and never come up to the ideal represented by them.[11]

Plato held that there were archetypal Forms corresponding to every general name. The immaterial world was peopled with the archetypes of the entire world of experience. According to the Platonic doctrine, there are forms of everything possible; of things, qualities, relations, of the good and the beautiful as well as the bad and the ugly. Every class-concept whatever corresponds to the higher world of pure Forms.[12]

Plato believed also that Forms were related to one another as higher and lower in a hierarchy. In the *Republic* the Form of the Good is said to be the 'Supreme Form' giving being and intelligibility to the whole world of Forms.[13] Plato never attempted to give a precise formulation of his theory, but he did believe in a hierarchy of Ideas with the Idea of the Good as the supreme principle. It must be noted that, for Plato, the subordination of lower Ideas to higher Ideas and finally to the highest Idea is not the logical subordination of the particular under the general, but teleological subordination of the means to the end.[14]

The idea of teleological subordination fulfils a great demand in Plato's doctrine of Forms. It explains the relation between the two realms of Being (Forms) and Becoming (phenomena). Forms being eternal, incorporeal and changeless entities entirely separated from the world of phenomena, contained no principle which could explain the facts of change in the empirical world. But the conception of Forms as 'true being' ultimately demanded that they should be regarded as the cause of all occurrence and change in the world of phenomena. This demand could be met only in one way, that is, by regarding the Forms as causes in the sense of the end for which the occurrence takes place, since Forms being, by hypothesis, changeless, they could not be regarded as causes in any mechanical sense. Thus the relation between the world of Forms and the world of phenomena, according to Plato, is teleological; all change and occurrence is for

11. See *Parmenides*, 132a1—b2, 132c12—133a7.
12. See *Parmenides*, 130b1—10, cp. *Metaphysics*, 1070a.
13. See *Republic*, 505a2—4.
14. See Windelband, op. cit., 122.

the sake of the Form which is the final cause of all phenomena. The world of Forms as a whole and the highest Form, the Form of the Good, in particular, is the final cause of all occurrence.[15]

Plato's theory of universals as expounded above presents a number of difficulties when we try to think about it. Plato was himself aware of them as is evident from his penetrating criticism of his own theory in the *Parmenides.* The main difficulty arises in connection with his view of the relation of universals to particulars. In different places he expresses this relation in different ways. He speaks of Forms 'being in' their particulars, of particulars 'participating' or 'sharing' in their Forms, and of particulars 'copying' or 'imitating' their Forms. If these expressions are taken literally, they give rise to logical difficulties, and if they are taken metaphorically, they fail to give a precise idea of the relation of the universal to the particular.

It is pertinent to ask what is exactly meant by saying that particulars 'participate' or 'share' in the corresponding Idea or universal? Plato himself raises this question in the *Parmenides.*[16] Does the particular share in the whole Idea, or in a part of it? If the particular shares in the whole Idea, i.e., if the whole Idea is present in each particular, then it would be separate from itself, which is a contradiction. And if a particular shares only in a part of the Idea, then no particular can be regarded as a complete instance of it. We cannot say, for example, that each particular large thing is large by virtue of having a part of largeness less than 'Largeness itself.' The absurdity, Parmenides points out, becomes more apparent in the case of the Idea of smallness. If each small thing has only a part of smallness, the 'Smallness itself' will be larger than that part; and if a small thing acquires that part of smallness which at first it lacked, it will become smaller instead of being larger by the addition.[17] Parmenides further points out that the theory of Forms involves an infinite regress. If particular things are called large by virtue of their sharing in the 'Large itself', then we must postulate another Form of 'Large' in which particular large things and the 'Large itself' share, and yet another Form of 'Large' in which all the three share, and so on *ad infinitum.* This difficulty persists even if particulars are said to

15. See *Republic,* 509b2—8; also see Ross, op. cit., p. 41; Windelband, op. cit., p. 128.
16. See *Parmenides,* 130e4—131e7.
17. See Ross, op. cit., pp. 85-86. Cp. Dharmakīrti's arguments against the Nyāya-Vaiśeṣika theory of Universals, Ch. IV.

'participate' in the Forms, not in the sense that the Forms are immanent in them, but in the sense that they are imperfect 'copies' or 'imitations' of the Forms which are transcendent patterns established in nature. If a particular is a copy of a Form, it must be in virtue of both of them sharing in a common nature which will be a real Form, and so there will be Form above Form *ad infinitum.*[18]

Plato nowhere answers the difficulties which he anticipates in the *Parmenides.* He, presumably, thought that the difficulties were not fatal to his theory. But they are, in fact, fatal, not to the theory of Forms as such, but to the way in which Plato formulates it. Plato treats of Forms as if they were things which particulars shared or imitated, instead of being characteristics of things. To speak of a Form as 'the large itself' is certainly objectionable, since it treats of the Form of largeness as just another large thing, something more perfectly large than particular large things. It is only if Forms are conceived in this manner that Parmenides' question, viz., whether Forms are shared wholly or partially by the particulars, presents a difficulty. The only answer to this difficulty is to realise that the Form is not another thing, but a characteristic of things to which the distinction of whole and part does not apply. In Plato's theory of Forms, Forms being not immanent characteristics but transcendent entities, the problem of their relation to particulars is in principle insoluble.[19]

Apart from the question of the relation of Forms to particular objects, there are other questions which arise in Plato's doctrine. Do we necessarily postulate the existence of a perfect Form in every case

---

18. See Ross, op. cit., p. 88.
19. Crombie maintains that Plato never thought Forms to be things like particulars. Although he sometimes uses of a Form such phrases as "the thing itself which is", Crombie says. 'I am not prepared to concede that Plato ever thought that "the very thing which is beautiful" was in fact a concrete though non-physical thing (p. 263). Such a charge, according to him, is 'slanderous' and 'absurd' (p. 262). The primary purpose of the language which Plato uses with regard to Forms, he maintains, 'is to insist that the Forms are definite properties with no blurring of the lines between them.' 'We ought not to interpret "the very thing which is beautiful" as "the very thing which has the property beauty," but as "the very thing which is the property beauty" (p. 264). (See *An examination of Plato's doctrine* by Crombie, I. M., Routledge and Kegan Paul, London, 1963, pp. 261-65). If this contention is granted, it is very difficult to explain why Aristotle attributed to Plato the theory of Forms as self-subsistent substantial entities. It is hard to believe that Aristotle should have so thoroughly misinterpreted his teacher with whom he was constantly associated for years. Cf. Ross, W. D., *Aristotle*, Methuen, London, 1949, p. 158.

of classification? In a passage in the *Republic* Plato maintains that whenever a number of things is called by the same name we postulate a Form. But this is not true, since we do make quite arbitrary classifications, or classifications based on certain adventitious features that have no necessary connection with the essential nature of the objects classified. The Indian realists were alive to this point, for they distinguished between the essential nature of a thing (*jāti*) and the adventitious character (*upādhi*), both of which equally served as the basis of classification.

Another point which is of greatest obscurity in Plato's doctrine is of the relation of Forms to each other. Obviously there must be some sort of relation between Forms, and between certain Forms the relation must be quite close. And again some Forms seem as if they must be regarded as sub-species of others. In the *Republic*, as we have shown above, Plato speaks of different levels of Forms related as higher and lower in a hierarchy. But it is a very difficult conception to grasp. In the case of the imperfect objects of sense-perception it is not difficult to see that there might be different degrees of remoteness from the perfect Form, but it is very difficult to see how there can be different degrees of perfection among the perfect Forms themselves. Again Plato's references to the highest Form, the Form of the Good, are extremely obscure, and it is very difficult for us to form any clear idea of how he conceived it. Plato conceived the process of knowledge as going from the first simple Forms dealt with in the particular sciences to those on a higher level which lay behind them, until eventually we arrive at the first principle of all, the Form of Forms, the Form of the Good which was the ultimate object of knowledge. And then in the light of that we should understand the particular Forms we began with, no longer as isolated entities, but as members of a hierarchical system.[20] The supreme position assigned by Plato to the Form of the Good is not difficult to understand when we are considering the Forms of moral qualities and ideals. But how it can be regarded as the ultimate first principle of the mathematical and the scientific Forms is hardly intelligible.

Plato's doctrine of universals resembles in some respects the Nyāya-Vaiśeṣika and the Mīmāṁsā doctrine of *jāti*. For both, universals are changeless, eternal and incorporeal entities different from the

20. See Field, op. cit., p. 56; also see Ross, op. cit., pp. 41-42.

particular objects of experience. The Indian realist would agree with Plato that the intelligibility of the particular objects and the knowledge of universal truths depend on the existence and the apprehension of unversals. But there are also some important differences between the two. While, for Plato, universals are absolutely transcendent and are non-sensible, for the Indian realist they are immanent in particulars and are apprehended in sense-perception. For the former, the knowledge of universals is *a priori;* the perception of objects only evokes their memory by virtue of the resemblance which they have to them. For the latter, on the contrary, the knowledge of universals is empirical; it is obtained from the observation of particulars manifesting them. Again, for Plato, universals alone are truly real, and particulars are real only to the degree to which they resemble their universals. For the Indian realist, on the other hand, both the universals and particulars are equally real and have independent being of their own. While, for the former, universals are only imperfectly manifested by the particulars, for the latter, they are fully manifested in each of their instances.

Further, as already pointed out, the Indian realist would not agree with Plato's contention that we must postulate universals corresponding to every general name. The universal (*jāti*), for him, is the essential character belonging to the particulars and is inseparable from them throughout their life-history. Thus, the adventitious characters corresponding to general names, such as 'cook', 'teacher', etc., are not recognised by him as universals, though they serve as the bases of many of our classifications. All general notions and classifications, according to the Indian realist, are not based on real universals, though some of them are. The reasons for which he maintains this view have already been discussed in Chapter II.

The Indian realist, like Plato, holds that universals are related as higher and lower in a hierarchy. But his conception of the hierarchy is radically different from that of Plato. Firstly, the highest universal for Plato is Goodness, while that for the Indian realist is Existence. And secondly, the relation of higher and lower between any two universals means, for Plato, that one is more perfect than the other (which, as we have pointed out, is intelligible in the case of perfect universals), while, for the Indian realist, it means that one has greater extension than the other. The highest universal for Plato is one having the highest perfection, while that for the Indian realist is that having greatest extension. The conception of the hierarchy of universals as held by the Indian realist is quite intelligible, for we can understand how one universal has greater extension than the other. But the Platonic conception of the hierarchy passes comprehension, because Plato, so far as we know, nowhere explains how a perfect Form can also be imperfect in relation to another Form. Thus there are important differences between the Platonic and the Nyāya-Mīmāṁsā doctrines of universals. In fact, in certain respects, the view of Indian realists is closer to the Aristotelian doctrine rather than to the Platonic one.

2. *The Moderate Realism of Aristotle*

Aristotle's theory of universals grows out of the criticism of Plato's theory of Ideas. His objections to the Platonic theory are numerous, but some of them are the same as those already anticipated by Plato himself. He, presumably, repeats those objections not because he overlooks the fact that Plato had foreseen them, but because he is convinced that Plato had never found a satisfactory way of answering them.

The main objections of Aristotle (apart from those anticipated by Plato in the *Parmenides*, including the infinite regress argument) against the Platonic theory are five. Firstly, Plato, by conceiving forms as perfect entities, introduced an unnecessary and unhelpful duplication of things met with in ordinary experience. The attempt to explain our knowledge of particular things by postulating "equal number of other things" is like supposing that "it was easier to count many than few."[21] Such a postulation does not solve the problem, but merely repeats it on a different level. All the questions arising in the case of particulars will arise again in the case of Forms. Thus, mere multiplication of entities is no solution to any problem.

Secondly, the existence of Ideas is not really demonstrated by the arguments advanced by Plato. 'From some, the conclusion does not necessarily follow; from others it would follow that there are Ideas even of matters of which we believe there are none.' For example, they would prove that we must assume the existence of the Ideas of negations, of things that have perished and of artificial things, which is precisely what many Platonists deny.[22]

21. *Metaphysics*, 990b1—8.
22. Ibid., 990b10—18, 991b6—7.

Thirdly, Plato's doctrine of Ideas does not provide us with any explanation of the sensible world, "for the Ideas do not explain any movement or change in perceptible objects."[23] The Ideas cannot function as efficient causes, since, being changeless patterns, they contain no principle of motion. Plato's recognition of Ideas as final causes does not solve the problem, since it does not explain efficient causality.[24]

Fourthly, if Ideas are the essences of things, they must be inherent in them. "How could the Ideas, if they are the primary being of concrete things, be in isolation?"[25] To say that Ideas are transcendent patterns in which particular things participate in varying degrees is, according to Aristotle, "to use empty words and poetic metaphors."[26]

And lastly, Plato commits the logical mistake of treating a Form both as an individual substance and a property, both as the perfect exemplar of a quality common to similar things, and the quality which is common. Since Forms are separate beings, they have to be regarded as individual substances, and since they are universals, they have to be regarded as properties. But how can one and the same thing be both an individual substance and a property? It is impossible, according to Aristotle, that anything 'general' should be an individual substance or a 'primary being', since "what constitutes the primary being peculiar to an individual object is that it does not belong to another, whereas anything general is common to a class; for we mean by 'general' what naturally belongs to more than one object."[27] A substance, for Aristotle, is really the same as subject in the logical sense; it is always that to which predicates are assigned, and not that which is in turn a predicate of something else. Thus, if Forms are regarded as individual substances, they cannot be universals, since substances *have* properties, they cannot *be* properties; and if they are

23. Op. cit., 991a9—10.
24. Allan remarks that "this is an ineffective criticism when Plato's system is viewed as a whole, for he makes more than one attempt to provide this missing element (the efficient cause); but the charge might have some force against those who retained the doctrine of Ideas, while discarding the theology of Plato whereby the foundation of the visible world was explained." Allan, D. J. : *The Philosophy of Aristotle*, Oxford University Press, 1952, p. 19.
25. Op. cit., 991b1—3.
26. Op. cit., 991a21—22.
27. Op. cit., 1038b9—12.

regarded as universals, they cannot be individual substances, since no common predicate indicates a "this-something" but a "this-such."[28] The defect of Plato's theory is that it regards a Form both as an individual substance and a universal, which is logically impossible.

Although Aristotle denies that universals are individual substances, he maintains that they must be regarded as having some sort of substantiality. He distinguishes between two senses of the term substance, viz., primary and secondary. Universals, for him, are not substances in the primary sense, but they are substances in a secondary or derivative sense.[29] He saw that both in mathematical and physical sciences the subjects, of which properties are demonstrated, are species and not particular things. Therefore, secondary substances which are the subjects of the propositions in sciences must be recognised. These substances exist only as embodied in the particular things, and, for that reason, are not substances in the primary sense; but, for the purposes of science, they must be treated as if they were separate from the particular things, discarding all that is accidental and does not belong to the whole class.[30] Thus, the universal which is a common predicate may also be a subject, since something may be said of it; but what it cannot be is to be a unique individual thing.

It follows from this that we can never state fully what an individual is in terms of universals. The unique is not analysable into universals; and since we think in terms of universals, the true individual or the primary substance eludes our thought. But it is also true that we manage to speak and think about such substances, so that the word substance must have a secondary sense, namely, substance as objects of thought.[31]

---

28. Op. cit., 1039a1—2.
29. "What is most properly, primarily, and most strictly spoken of as substance is what is neither asserted of a subject nor present in a subject—a particular man, for instance, or a particular horse. But people speak, too, of secondary substances, to which, as species, belong what are spoken of as the primary substances, and to which, as genera the species themselves belong. For instance, a particular man belongs to the species 'man', and the genus to which the species belongs is 'animal', that are spoken of as secondary substances." See *The Categories* translated by A. E. Wardman and J. L. Creed in *The Philosophy of Aristotle*, Mentor Classic, 1963, pp. 137-38.
30. See Windelband, op. cit., p. 143.
31. See *Metaphysics*, Book z, ch. 15.

The characterisation of universals as secondary substance should not be taken to mean that, for Aristotle, what we think (the universal) is absolutely different from what is. On the contrary, he holds that the universals (genera and species) which we think are as real, as objective, as the individuals themselves which elude our thought. They are not in any sense the work of the mind, any more than are Forms to Plato. In fact, Aristotle's doctrine of universals is based upon the apprehension of attributes shared in common by the individuals which we group and classify and speak of as members of species and genera. Thus, Aristotle does not deny the reality of universals as common properties of individual objects; what he denies is the existence of universals as individual substances[32] Universals are not substances existing independently of particulars; they exist only as common elements in particulars. It is on the basis of these common elements that individual objects are classified by natural science into the real kinds to which by nature they belong.[33]

Aristotle thus eliminates Plato's realm of universals existing separately from the realm of individual objects. The universal has not any second or higher reality beside and apart from the concrete individual things given in our experience. It exists only as its particular instances by means of which it realises itself. The universal is actual only in the particular; the particular is actual only because in it the universal realises itself. For Aristotle, unlike Plato, the individual man, for example, is not an imperfect copy of the universal Man, but he is actually a man. The properties constituting the nature of an object, i.e., its being an object of a certain kind, are really immanent in the object. If objects do not possess the properties which they are observed to possess in actual experience, then scientific knowledge would become either impossible or wholly unrelated to the material world.

Aristotle's view differs from that of Plato also with regard to the knowledge of universals. Both would, however, agree that awareness of universals is implicit in ordinary sense-experience, and that we become aware of universals not by sense itself but by the intellect.[34]

---

32. See Ibid, 1071a 19 ff.
33. Cf. Ross, W. D., *Aristotle*, Methuen, London, 1949, pp. 157 f. Also cf. Woozley, op. cit., p. 197.
34. Intellect, or thought, according to Aristotle, is the faculty by which we grasp essence, while sense is that by which we grasp essence embodied-in-matter. See *De Anima*, III, 4; Ross, op. cit., p. 146.

For Plato, as already shown in the previous section, the awareness of universals is of the nature of "recollection"; the knowledge of universals and their mutual relations acquired by human soul in its pre-natal existence is revived in its post-natal experience of sensible objects. Plato could not accept that the knowledge of universals is acquired by abstraction, since universals for him have a separate being and they are only imperfectly manifested by particular instances. Aristotle, on the other hand, maintains that the apprehension of the universal arises from actual experience aided by the memory of past experiences. The universal is apprehended not in a single experience, but in a gradual process. The perception of an object gives rise to memory, and memory conditions subsequent perceptions, so that they are not mere perceptions but recognitions of what is more or less familiar. By this process the first indeterminate awareness of a universal becomes stabilised in the mind leading ultimately to a determinate concept of it.[35] Thus, for Aristotle, as for Plato, the knowledge of the universal is by the intellect; but while for Plato it is *a priori*, for Aristotle it is derived from sense-experience by abstraction.

It is clear from the above account that Aristotle's theory of universals is realistic, though it considerably modifies the extreme realism of Plato. There are no *universalia ante rem*, but still there are *universalia in rebus*. There is an identical 'humanity' in all the individual human beings, an identical 'treeness' in all the trees. These, of course, are not sensible entities like particulars, but abstract characters, or essences, apprehended by intelligence. There may be innumberable layers of these universals in any given thing. A man, for example, obviously embodies 'being' which is the highest of universals, but in descending order he embodies also the universals of 'material-being', 'animate-being', 'sentient-being' and 'rational-being'. All these universals, according to the Aristotelian theory, exist in him, and when we make generalisations about him, it is these universals, selected from certain level, that we assert to be connected with others.

The main objection urged against this theory is that it is hard to verify the existence of these universals. We are sure to meet with failure if we try to discover an identical 'colourness' appearing in all the colours, but which is not any determinate colour; or an identical 'animality' present in all the animals without modification. We do think somehow of colour in general and we do succeed in making

35. See Ross, op. cit., pp. 143f and p. 148. Also see Woozley, op. cit., p. 198.

generalisations about animals; but we fail to discover a colourless universal of colour, or a bodiless, featureless animality. Not only is it impossible to form a mental image of these universals, it is also impossible to isolate, even conceptually, an identical character where the instances vary widely. There is difficulty not only in the case of genera but also in the case of species from which the former are supposed to be extracted. The theory asserts that 'blueness', for example, is a universal appearing identically in all the different hues of blue. But where does blue end as it passes through violet and purple towards red on the one side, and through peacock-blue towards green on the other? If the concept of blue is definite, there should be no doubt where 'blueness' is present and where not, but there is doubt on both sides. Thus universals of quality, if they exist at all, will be so blurred as to melt away into each other. Similarly, in the case of species of living things it is difficult to regard them as marked off by a definite essence peculiar to each of them. The theory of biological evolution has shown that to find the essence of a certain organism is not only practically difficult but theoretically impossible. The precise boundary, separating it from forms above and below it, could only be arbitrary. If indistinctness lay in our knowledge, it could be removed, but, as a matter of fact, it lies in nature itself. The sharp boundaries required by the Aristotelian theory are not there.[36]

What would be Aristotle's answer to these criticisms is not clear. He, however, holds that there are universals common to individual objects corresponding to our concepts of genera and species. As a matter of fact, his doctrine of universals is based upon the apprehension of common properties possessed by the individual objects. It is because of this apprehension that sciences which deal with the universals become possible. The question, however, arises how do the individuals in fact share these common properties? Is the property one and the same in all the individuals? Or do the properties in different individuals resemble one another? Aristotle does not raise these questions, presumably, because all common properties, for him, are identical properties, and even similarity involves partial identity. If this is true, then the problem of the verification of the existence of such properties does arise. Allied with this is the problem

36. Cf. B. Blanshard: *Reason and Analysis*, George Allen and Unwin, 1962, pp. 405-6; Woozley: *Theory of Knowledge*, Hutchinson, London, 1949, p. 82, and Allan, op. cit., p. 112.

whether resemblance does or does not involve identity. We shall be deeply concerned with these problems in the forthcoming discussions.

Aristotle's doctrine of universals resembles in some respects the realistic theories of universals in Indian Philosophy. The Nyāya-Vaiśeṣika would agree with Aristotle that universals do not exist apart from the individual things in a realm of their own. They exist in the individual things as their predicates constituting the foundation of their classification and generalisation. But there is a major difference between the Aristotelian and the Nyāya conceptions of the universal. While, for the former, universals are not entities having an existence different from and independent of the individual, for the latter, they have a being of their own. Unlike Aristotle, and like Plato, the Nyāya regards the universals as existentially independent of the particular, although it depends on the particular for its knowledge. In this respect, Aristotle's theory is closer to the Jaina theory of universals. For the Jaina, as for Aristotle, the real is the concrete individual, i.e., the unity of the universal and the particular. Neither the universal nor the particular exists in abstraction; they have no reality apart from one another. For both, Aristotle and the Jaina, generality and particularity are not realities, but aspects of one and the same concrete reality—the individual. Even as aspects they are not mutually independent, but related to one another. They may be viewed by the mind in abstraction from one another, but in reality they exist in a concrete unity.

3. *The Controversy over Universals in the Middle Ages*

In the Middle Ages there arose a great controversy over the question regarding the logical and metaphysical significance of genera and species. Medieval philosophers were not primarily interested in questions about the nature of human knowledge, but their concern with metaphysics, especially in those aspects which carried theological implications, led to a continuation of the dispute between the two versions of realism (the Platonic and the Aristotelian) and later to a conceptualistic rejection of both.

(i) *Porphyry's Problem*

The starting-point for the discussion on the problem of universals was supplied by Porphyry's Introduction (the *Isagoge*) to Aristotle's *Categories,* which was introduced to the medieval philosophers by Boethius who translated and commented upon it. In the very opening passage of the *Isagoge* Porphyry sets out the problem in three stages: (a) do genera and species exist really in nature, or are they purely mental constructions? (b) are they corporeal or incorporeal? and (c) do they exist apart from the sensible things, or are they realised in them? Of these the first question alone attracted attention, inasmuch as the other two had no meaning unless the reality of universals in some sense was recognised. Porphyry himself only enunciates the three-fold problem in the *Isagoge* and refuses to answer it. He, however, answers the problem in his other works from the Platonic stand-point.[37]

Some critics hold that Porphyry posed the problem of universals wrongly in consequence of which the medieval philosophers were led astray. He speaks only of genera and species and keeps silent about universals of quality and relations, which are quite as important as the former.[38] Without the universals of quality any classification would be impossible, and without the universals of relation we can never understand spatial positions of things. The reason why Porphyry speaks of genera and species alone and avoids making reference to accidents seems to be that he tended to think of universals as things. He was a neo-Platonist, and so the problem of universals for him was the problem of Forms which were more substantival than adjectival. This bias of Porphyry accounts for the tendency amongst the early scholastics to discuss universals as if they were discussing things.

Another and more damaging criticism brought against Porphyry is that he completely failed to understand Aristotle and so failed to transmit the problem of universals as Aristotle had left it. He missed the most essential point in Aristotle's teaching about universals, namely, that universals were not to be regarded as individual substances. If Porphyry had reflected on this point, he would not have talked of 'thing-universals', whether corporeal or incorporeal. For Aristotle, the universal could never exist as an individual thing; it could not exist as Platonic Form too. The individual, that which is, is unique and cannot be common to many; the universal which is common to many cannot *be* in the sense in which the individual is. If Porphyry had understood this it would have made a great difference

---

37. See Maurice De Wulf: *History of Medieval Philosophy,* Vol. I, Thomas Nelson and Sons Ltd., 1935, pp. 140-41. Also see Aaron, R. I.: *The Theory of Universals,* Oxford, 1952, p. 1.
38. See Wulf, op. cit., pp. 142-43.

for the medieval thought. Up to the end of twelfth century philosophers were engaged in discussing the question whether the universal was a thing, which Aristotle had already answered in the negative. Porphyry had posed the problem of universals as if Aristotle had never existed.[39]

Boethius in his commentary on the *Isagoge* sets out the problem in the same way as Porphyry. He also asks the question only in connection with genera and species, and the questions about the objectivity of other types of universals (qualities and relations) apparently do not interest him. He distinguishes between two ways in which an idea may be so formed that its content does not exist in the extramental reality precisely as it exists in the idea. We may form an idea by composition as, for example, the idea of 'Centaur' by joining together arbitrarily man and horse which are not joined together by nature. Such arbitrarily constructed ideas are false. On the other hand, we may form an idea by abstraction as, for example, the idea of a line as considered by a geometer. Although it is true that no mere line exists by itself in extramental reality, the idea is not false, since bodies involve lines and all that we do is to isolate the line and consider it in abstraction. Thus, composition produces a false idea, whereas abstraction produces an idea which is true even though the thing conceived does not exist extramentally in the state of abstraction or separation. The ideas of genera and species, according to Boethius, belong to the latter type, i.e., they are formed by abstraction. Consequently, "genera and species are in individuals, but, as thought, are universals." "They subsist in sensible things but are understood without bodies."[40] Thus genera and species are at one and the same time '*subsistentia*' and '*intellecta*'. The resemblance between things is the basis both for their individuality in nature and for their universality in thought. Genera and species are incorporeal, not indeed by nature, but by abstraction; they exist both as empirical things and apart from them.[41] Boethius thus offered the material for an Aristotelian solution of the problem of universals on the lines of moderate

---

39. Cf. Aaron, op. cit., p. 10.
40. See F. Copleston, S. J. : *A History of Philosophy*, London, Burns, Oates and Washbourne Ltd., 1950, Vol. II, pp. 137-38.
41. See Meyrick H. Carre : *Realists and Nominalists*, Oxford University Press, 1946, pp. 38-39. Also cf. Wulf, op. cit., p. 141.

realism. But the first solution of the medievals, owing to the influence of Augustinian thought, was on the lines of extreme realism, and not on the lines suggested by Boethius.

(ii) *Extreme Realism*

St. Augustine, who considerably influenced the early solutions of the problem of universals, championed Platonic realism with suitable modifications to make it consort with Christian faith. His profound interest in discovering the conditions upon which the possession of truth and certitude depended attracted him to the Platonic doctrine in which he found a satisfactory answer to his problem. He saw that sense-knowledge never attains immutable truth, while rational knowledge, or thought, succeeds in attaining it. This is so because the former is dependent upon a corporeal organ and has for its object the transient things of the sensible world; while the latter is independent of a corporeal organ and has for its object the intelligible world, the sum total of eternal, necessary and immutable truths.[42] Our intellect does not only attain the knowledge of these eternal truths but also makes use of them as incorporeal standards in judging about the material objects of sense-knowledge. In judging a physical object to be beautiful, we imply the objective existence of 'beauty' both as a universal and as a standard. These eternal truths which constitute the intelligible structure of the temporal world, and which the reason of man can alone grasp, are themselves non-temporal as, for example, the concepts and truths of mathematics which, although empirically applicable are timeless necessities.[43]

Thus, the general features of experience and thought, the universals, in virtue of which recognition and thought become possible, are, according to Augustine, entities subsisting beyond the sensible world, though the objects of sense provide information of them. The universal forms constitute the nature of things, and they are the true objects of scientific understanding. Although Augustine advocated Platonic realism, he did not profess the Platonic doctrine of 'reminiscence'. He replaced it by his doctrine of 'divine illumination'. By the help of divine light we discover within our soul the ideas or the concepts of empirical things. We attribute these ideas

42. See Carre, op. cit., p. 12. Also see Wulf, op. cit., p. 84.
43. Ibid., pp. 24-25.

to things because we perceive in them the material realisation of the former.[44] Divine illumination, for Augustine, performs much the same function as Plato's Form of the Good rendering intelligible by its light the necessity of eternal truth which the human intellect could grasp.

Augustine radically transformed Plato's theory of Ideas by his doctrine of 'exemplarism'. The world, according to him, existed in God as 'exemplars' before it was created, just as the plan of a building exists in the mind of a builder before it is erected. These exemplars, or divine ideas, are the ultimate bases of all contingent reality, since all beings are created in conformity with them. They are the supreme foundations of the intelligibility of essences, and upon them rests the certitude of our knowledge. The norm of the certitude of rational knowledge, as we have seen, is its conformity with the divine ideas, the prototypes of beings known in sense-experience. Thus, the ideas as objective essences which, for Plato, exist independently of God, are, for Augustine, exemplars contained in the divine intelligence. Ontologically they are not different from God, but identical with Him considered in the infinite perfection of His knowledge.[45] Plato's theory of Forms thus enters theology. The question, therefore, arises whether Augustine in his theory of ideas supposed that men were in direct contact with the mind of God when they come to know ideas by the help of divine light. It is fairly clear that he did not, but much less clear how he could avoid it.

The extreme realism of Augustine was the key-note of the earliest answer given by the medievals to the problem of universals raised by Porphyry. It was maintained that our generic and specific concepts correspond to a reality existing extramentally in objects, a subsistent reality in which individuals share. This realism differed from the Platonic realism in an important respect. While for Plato the concept 'man' represents the ideal of human nature existing apart from and outside individual men, an ideal which individual men 'imitate' or 'copy' to a greater or lesser extent, for the medieval realist the concept represents a unitary substance existing extramentally, in which men participate, or of which they are accidental modifications.[46]

44. See Wulf,op. cit., pp. 85-86.
45. Ibid., pp. 88-89.
46. See Windelband, op. cit., p. 294; cf. Copleston, op. cit., Vol. II, p. 140; Wulf, op. cit:, p. 145, Carre, op. cit., p. 36.

This view assumes like the Nyāya that unless the object reflected by the concept exists extramentally in exactly the same way as it exists in the mind, the concept is purely subjective. In other words, it assumes that the only way of saving the objectivity of our knowledge is to maintain a naive and exact correspondence between thought and things.

Now, if species man is regarded as the substantial unity of all human beings, it would mean that all individual men have a common substance which is numerically one. That is, individual men differ from one another only accidentally and not in substance. Odo of Tournai maintains this position. According to him, when a child comes into being, God produces a new property of an already existing substance, not a new substance.[47] Evidently this view assumes that the logical and the real orders are exactly parallel. Since the meaning of the term 'man' in the statements 'Socrates is a man' and 'Plato is a man' is identical, there must be a substantial identity in the real order between Socrates and Plato. But it would be a mistake to suppose that the extreme realists were influenced simply by logical considerations; they were influenced also by theological considerations. Odo of Tournai clearly makes use of extreme realism in order to explain the Christian dogma of the transmission of the original sin. He was faced with the problem of explaining how all human beings suffer from the consequences of the 'original sin' committed by Adam and Eve, their first ancestors. He found the answer in extreme realism : the substance of Adam and Eve, which was infected by the original sin, is handed on at each generation of human beings and thus every human being, by virtue of sharing in the same vitiated substance, suffers from the consequences of the original infection. God does not create a new substance every time a new human being is born; what he creates is simply a new property of an already existing substance.[48]

Logically, this extreme realism should result in sheer monism. We have the concepts of substance and being, and on the principles of extreme realism it would follow that all substances are modifications of one substance and, more comprehensively, that all beings are modifications of one Being. This line of thought seems to have weighed heavily with John Scotus Erigina in so far as he can justly be called a monist. He frankly drew the consequences of Platonic-

47. See Copleston, op. cit. p. 141, and Wulf, op. cit., p. 146.
48. Ibid.

Augustinian realism. If truth and being is to be sought in the universal, then the universal must be accepted as the essential and original reality—which produces from itself and contains within itself the particular. Universals are, therefore, not only substances, but, as contrasted with the particular things, they are more real and more primitive substances. They are more real in proportion as they are more universal. In this conception the logical relation of concepts becomes metaphysical; logical subordination becomes changed into a production and inclusion of the particular by the universal. This view logically culminates in the concept of the highest universal which, according to John Scotus Erigina, is the Deity. All things are manifestations of the most universal and, therefore, the most real Being; they are in it and exist only as its modes of appearance. The world is God developed into the particular. God and the world are one. The same "nature" is, as creative unity God, and as created plurality the world.[49]

Thus, according to John Scotus Erigina, the order from being through genera and species was first a real order, and only secondly one in thought. The universals existed first and the particulars were derived from them. Out of God comes at first the realm of universals—"the nature which is created and itself creates". These universals form the working forces in the world of phenomena. It is only the universal which is efficient in the phenomenal world : the corporeal things as a whole form "the nature which is created and does not create." In this world, the particular is not as such active; it is rather active according to the degree in which the universal attains manifestation in it.[50] Finally, all things return into God; all individual forms resolve into eternal primitive Being. God as the final goal of all generation and change, as the extinction of all that is particular, is distinguished as "the nature which neither is created nor creates." It is the return of all particular things into the distinctionless unity of

49. See Windelband, op. cit., p. 290, also Copleston, op. cit., p. 120; cp. Carre, op. cit., p. 40. Note the similarity of this view with that of the Advaita and the Sāṁkhya. In the Sāṁkhya view Prakṛti takes the place of God as the most universal Being. In the Advaita, Being, or Brahman, is regarded as the universal substratum of all particular appearances.

50. Compare this view with the Advaita view of universals as specific forms of the primordial force of nescience (*avidyāśaktiviśeṣarūpa*) manifested by the particulars. The universal, in this view, is nothing but the specific causal efficiency of the particulars.

Being at the end of the world process. Thus even in the final destiny of things, the superior reality of the universal, in which is merged, without residue, all that is particular, preserves itself.[51]

(iii) *Adversaries of Extreme Realism*

The extreme realists soon encountered numerous opponents, all of whom agree in maintaining that universals are not things realised in the universal state in nature, for what exists is individual. If the implied principle of the extreme realists was the exact correspondence of thought and extramental reality, the principle of the adversaries of extreme realism was that only individuals exist. The 'species' does not exist as such, but is merely a way in which mind groups individuals; similarly, genus is nothing but a way in which we gather together species or lower genera under one name.

Roscelin initiated the attack on extreme realism. He maintained that the individuals alone exist in nature. Genera and species are nothing but collective names, common designations, for different things. They are sounds (*flatus vocis)* composed of letters and syllables, which serve as signs for a multiplicity of substances or their accidents.[52] The statement that the universal is a mere '*flatus vocis*' is clearly a denial not only of realism but even of conceptualism and the presence of universal concepts in the mind. It is an assertion of extreme form of nominalism which ignores even a real occasion for the collective names. But some critics maintain that it is difficult to decide whether Roscelin was a nominalist or a conceptualist, for we have not sufficient evidence to say what Roscelin held about the concept as such. He might have simply meant that only individuals exist and that the universal does not, as such, exist extramentally, but without meaning to say anything about 'the universal in the mind' which he might have taken for granted or never have thought about.[53] According to Abelard, the identification of genera and species with words by Roscelin should be understood as an affirmation of its subjectivity rather than as a denial of the existence of general

51. See Windelband, op. cit., p. 291. In this respect also, as in others, the view of John Scotus Erigina comes very close to the view of the Advaita and the Sāṁkhya.
52. See Wulf, op. cit., p. 149; Copleston, op. cit., p. 144. Cp. Carre, op. cit., pp. 40-41; Windelband, op. cit., p. 296.
53. See Copleston, op. cit., pp. 144-45. Cp. Wulf, op. cit., p. 149.

ideas. John of Salisbury, on the other hand, understands Roscelin as a pure and simple nominalist.[54] However, on the basis of what Roscelin has asserted, ignoring what he might have thought about concepts, it seems legitimate to regard him as a nominalist. Even Abelard, as we shall see, treats him as a nominalist when criticising his view.

At the basis of this nominalism of Roscelin lies the empiricist theory of knowledge. For his metaphysics, knowledge consists only in the experience of the senses, and what is given in the world of sensibility is only individual. Universals, therefore, are mere names invented by the human mind to designate arbitrary collections of individuals. Roscelin's view naturally came in conflict with the theological orthodoxy, as he consistently extended his nominalism to the realm of faith. On the ground that individuals alone exist he maintained that the Persons of the Blessed Trinity are three Gods, not one. This 'tritheism' of Roscelin evoked a vehement opposition from St. Anselm who stoutly defended the essential unity of the Godhead.[55] Against Roscelin he argued that he who does not understand how a multitude of men are specifically one man, cannot understand how several Persons, each of whom is perfect God, are one God. St. Anselm evidently belonged to the school of extreme realists, for he maintained that just as there is but one substance in the Godhead, so there is but one substance or nature in all men.[56]

Although Roscelin initiated the attack on extreme realism, it was, indeed, Abelard who dealt a death blow to it. Abelard vehemently attacked the view of the extreme realists that the same essential nature is wholly present at the same time in each of the individual members of a species, and that the individual members of a species differ from one another, not substantially, but only accidentally. This realism, he argues, leads to absurd consequences. If the human species, for example, is substantially, and therefore wholly, present in both Socrates and Plato at the same time, then Socrates must be

54. Ibid.
55. St. Anselm says, "In the minds of these philosopheres reason which ought to be the guide and judge of all that exists in man is so wrapped up in material imagination, that it cannot extricate itself from them, nor distinguish from them those things which ought to be contemplated in their intrinsic purity." See Carre, op. cit., p. 41.
56. See Copleston, op. cit., p. 142; Wulf, op. cit., p. 165, cp. Carre, op. cit., pp. 37 and 41.

Plato, and he must be present in two places at once; on the other hand, if it is only partially present in both, then neither, on this theory, is a whole man.[57] Again, if the essence is the same, for instance, in all members of the genus 'living being', then essentially Socrates and ass are the same. Furthermore, such a doctrine leads to pantheism which is opposed to Christian faith, since God is substance and all substances will be identical with the divine substance.[58] The essence of Abelard's criticism is that by making individual differences adjectival or superficial, everything becomes everything else and clear thinking becomes impossible.

Having rejected extreme realism, Abelard turns to the nominalistic theory of universals advocated by Roscelin. He agrees with Roscelin that every existing substance is individual; the universal as such does not exist. He reasserts the Aristotelian definition of the universal: a universal is that which can be predicated of many individuals taken one by one. Hence, it follows that the universal cannot be a thing, an existent, since a thing is not predicable of many.[59] But this does not mean that universals are mere words, as Roscelin maintains. If it is false to think of the universal as a thing, it is equally false to think of it as a mere word or sound. A name, Abelard argues, is more than a sound, it is a significant sound. The general word is a word in a sentence, a term, usually a predicate term of a proposition. On the one hand, this word covers an abstract and general notion and hence it is a '*nomen*' or '*sermo*', i.e., a discourse related to a content which is signified, a reality that is thought of. On the other hand, this '*nomen*' has a logical function, it is capable of being predicated of several subjects in a judgment. The unity of the logical order which belongs to the name 'man' when we say 'Peter is a man, and Paul is also', effects only the predicate of a judgment. Hence, the universal is not a '*res*', for a '*res*' being an individual substance can only be predicated of one subject. Nor is it a mere word; it is indeed the logical content signified by a general word.[60]

The logical content, or the universal, expressed by a general word,

57. Compare this with the Buddhist argument against the Nyāya-Vaiśeṣika realism. See Ch. IV.
58. See Copleston, op. cit., p. 146. Aaron, op. cit., p. 14., cp. Windelband, op. cit., p. 298, and Carre, op cit., pp. 46-47.
59. See Carre, op. cit., p. 45.
60. See Wulf, op. cit., pp. 196-97, cp. Copleston, op. cit., p. 150, and Carre, op. cit., p. 54.

according to Abelard, is a concept formed by abstraction. Through these concepts we conceive what is *in* the object, though we do not conceive it *as* it is in the object.[61] Each human individual, for instance, is a substance distinct from every other, yet we grasp something which is similar in all men. This content of thought leaves aside the individualising envelope which clothes every element of reality, and it is this characteristic stripping off by the mind which constitutes the abstractive process. The universal, therefore, exists in nature, not as a numerical or substantial identity, but as a multiplicity with like qualities. It becomes a unitary concept, which makes predication possible, only when it has been apprehended and conceived by human thought. The concepts obtained by the abstractive process of the mind are, therefore, faithful, though inadequate. There is nothing in the concept of man which does not as a matter of fact belong to every man, although we do not and cannot grasp the complete reality of which each man is constituted. If we deny the existence in the individual state (*status*) of the universal which we conceive, then our concepts would be false. But this, according to Abelard, is not the case. Our mind abstracts universal concepts from the apprehension of similarity of the essential characteristics of the individual substances, and does not construct them.[62]

Universals, then, are neither '*voces*' nor '*res*'; neither words nor things. They are, according to Abelard, concepts abstracted by the mind. This suggests that Abelard's position is conceptualistic. Conceptualism like nominalism denies the reality of universals, but admits general notions, or concepts, as the content of thinking. These concepts, however, are constructions of our mind; they are abstractions from particular impressions. On this view, universals are derived entirely from the mind. Abelard's position, in so far as he lays stress on the process of abstraction instead of the metaphysical problem, has a decided conceptualist note. But his doctrine may also be characterised as moderate realism. For he insists against Roscelin that the process of abstraction does not necessarily falsify our knowledge of the object. Universals are the actual features of things;

61. See Copleston, op. cit., p. 151 and Carre, op cit., p. 57.
62. See Wulf, op. cit., p. 198; Windelband, op. cit., p. 299; Carre, op. cit., p. 60. Ibid. Abelard's view closely resembles the view of the Jaina conceptualists for whom also the universal concepts correspond to the universal existing in the individual state as similarity (*sadṛśapariṇāma*) of individuals. See Ch. VI.

they are corporeal in relation to the nature of things, and incorporeal in relation to their meaning, for they refer to general qualities artificially isolated from individual things. Universals are faithful representatives of reality, but they are partial aspects, never reaching the concreteness of perception. This is not conceptualism. It is an early expression of moderate realism which was later developed by St. Thomas Aquinas.[63]

(iv) *Moderate Realism*

Abelard's treatment of the problem of universals gave a death-blow to extreme realism, and considerably influenced the subsequent thinking on universals. Discussing the problem of universals, John of Salisbury says that anyone who looks for genera and species outside the things of sense is wasting his time. Genera and species are not things but are rather the forms of things which the mind, comparing the likeness of things, abstracts and unifies in the universal concepts. Abstractly considered, they are mental constructions, since they do not exist as universals in extra-mental reality. But the construction in question is one of comparison of things and abstraction from things, so that universal concepts are not void of objective foundation and reference.[64]

St. Thomas Aquinas follows Abelard and John of Salisbury when he declares that universals are not subsistent things. He reasserts Aristotle's realism and accepts the contrast made by him between essence and existence. The essence, according to St. Thomas, is what an object is. It is the source of all its properties. It is the universal. The essence or the nature of an object includes only those elements which fall under the definition of the species, just as 'humanity' includes those features which fall under the definition of man. In virtue of these features man is man; 'humanity' means that by which man is man. But we can conceive such essences without assuming that they

63. See Copleston, op. cit., p. 151; Carre op. cit., pp. 62-63.

Even Abelard explains likeness of character in a multiplicity of individuals upon the hypothesis that God created the world according to the archetypes which he carried in his mind. Thus, according to his view, the universal exists firstly, before the things, as concepts in the mind of God; secondly, in things, as likeness of the essential characteristics of individuals; thirdly, after things, in the human understanding as its concepts and predicates acquired by abstractive process. Abelard thus clearly foreshadows the doctrine of St. Thomas Aquinas. See, Windelband, op. cit., p. 299.

64. See Copleston, p. 153.

actually exist. Actual existence implies a further principle. To the unity of man or dog, for example, is added the contingent multiple shapes by which these natures are actually manifested. Thus essences have no being apart from existence, but they are intelligible without the supposition of existence.[65] The existence of things does not follow from their essence, otherwise existence could not be, as it clearly is, contingent. Universals are apprehended directly by the mind, but only in the material things the nature of which they comprise; they are not to be found in themselves, although by the process of abstraction and comparison the mind can approximate to thinking of them in themselves.

Thus, universals, according to St. Thomas, have being only in the individual things. Humanity has existence only in this or that man, and the universality which attaches to humanity in the concept is a result of abstraction. But this does not involve the falsity of the universal concept. If we thought that the specific form of a thing abstracted by our mind exists in the state of abstraction, our idea would indeed be false, for a false judgment concerning the thing itself would be involved. But, though in the universal concept mind conceives something in a manner different from its mode of concrete existence, our judgment about the thing itself is not erroneous. It is simply that the form which exists in the thing in an individualised state, is abstracted, i.e., is made the object of exclusive attention of the mind by an activity of the intellect.[66] The abstraction itself, according to St. Thomas, is more than a mere selection, it is also the illumination of the form, and that is why the active intellect, as opposed to the passive, alone can abstract the forms. It follows that the unviersal, in the case of human knowledge, is a product of human intelligence, but at the same time it is grounded on objective facts.[67] The objective foundation of the universal specific concept is the individual essence of the thing, which is, by the activity of the mind, set free from the individualising factors (that is, according to St. Thomas, matter) and considered in abstraction. For example, the mind abstracts from the individual man the essence of humanity which is alike, but not numerically the same in the members of the human species. Similarly,

65. See Carre, op. cit., pp. 73-74.
66. See Copleston, op. cit., p. 154; Carre, op. cit., p. 88.
67. See Aaron, op. cit., p. 15; Carre, op. cit., p. 86.

the foundation of the universal generic concept is an essential determination which several species have in common, as the species of dog, man, horse, etc. have animality in common.

St. Thomas recognises both the universal and the particular ingredients of experience. It is a cardinal error, according to him, to separate the two modes of knowledge—perception and thought. St. Augustine, as we have seen, had maintained that intellect and sense are distinct and have different spheres. Understanding cannot know bodies, nor sense essences or forms. St. Thomas points out that if sense is divided from thought, knowledge would become impossible. If we suppose with Heraclitus that there is nothing in experience but what is apprehended by the senses, experience becomes a perpetual flux. And what is in a state of perpetual flux cannot be an object of knowledge, for this state ceases to be and is replaced by another before the mind can say what it is. If, on the other hand, we hold with Plato that genuine knowledge consists in the knowledge of eternal Ideas which exist apart from material things in a realm of their own and from which particular existences derive their being, other difficulties arise. In the first place, if genuine knowledge were confined to immaterial entities, we should possess no understanding of bodies in motion. There could be no science of matter in change. In the second place, in order to understand objects, we are asked to refer to entities which have no connection with them.[68]

It is indeed an error to believe that the understanding is constituted so as not to know the individual things. Universality is no doubt the characteristic of thought, but the object of thought need not exist also as universals. The form of the known need not be in the known in the same way. The sensible form exists in the real world outside the mind in one way; it appears in another way in the mental apprehension of it. The understanding grasps in its own way the species of individual things. What is material and in motion becomes in the understanding immaterial and motionless. Yet, it is the knowledge of the species of things and not of another order of being. Thus, the mind in apprehending the universal is always apprehending the truth. It is in conformity with reality. The concept arbitrarily abstracted from experience has a counterpart immanent in particular things, and so it is founded on experience.

St. Thomas thus stands midway between extreme realism and

68. See Carre, op. cit., p. 85.

nominalism. He denied both forms of extreme realism, that of Plato and that of early medievals, and reasserted Aristotelian realism. But he did not reject Platonism lock stock and barrel, since he accepted the Augustinian doctrine of exemplarism. Universals, as exemplar ideas, exist in the divine mind, though not ontologically distinct from God, nor really a plurality. As far as this truth is concerned, the Platonic theory is justified. St. Thomas thus admits (i) the *universale ante rem* while insisting that it is not a subsistent thing, either apart from things (Plato) or in things (early medievals), for it is God considered as perceiving. His essence as imitable *ad extra* in a certain type of creatures; (ii) the *universale in re* which is the concrete individual essence alike in the members of a species or a genus; and (iii) the *universale post rem* which is the abstract universal concept.[69]

The chief follower in the Thomist tradition was Duns Scotus, who introduced certain modifications in the Thomist doctrine. He advocated the doctrine of 'formal distinction'. In brief the doctrine is that there is a distinction which is less than a real distinction and more objective than a purely mental distinction. A real distinction obtains between two things which are physically separable. A purely mental distinction is that which has no corresponding distinction in the thing itself. A formal distinction according to Duns Scotus obtains when the mind distinguishes in an object two or more qualities "*formalitates*" which are objectively distinct, but which are inseparable from one another, even by divine power. For instance, Scotus asserted a formal distinction between the divine attributes. Mercy and justice are formally distinct, though the divine justice and the divine mercy are inseparable, since, in spite of the formal distinction between them, each is really identical with the divine essence.[70]

Duns Scotus thought that the recognition of formal distinction was demanded by the nature of knowledge and the nature of the object of knowledge. Knowledge is the apprehension of being, and if the mind is compelled, so to say, to recognise a distinction, then the distinction cannot be purely mental. So it is necessary to admit formal distinction which is less than a real distinction, but which at the same time is founded on an objective distinction in the object, a distinction which can be only between different but not separable features of

69. See Copleston, op. cit., p. 154.
70. See Copleston, op. cit., pp. 508-9.

one and the same object. Such a distinction, according to Scotus, will maintain the objectivity of knowledge without, however, impairing the unity of the object.[71]

Scotus applies the principle of formal distinction to the contrast between essence and existence in the creatures. He refuses to admit a real distinction between essence and existence. He argues that the doctrine of real distinction between essence and existence advocated by St. Thomas, goes against the Christian idea of creation. Creation is production out of nothing; a thing has no existence whatsoever before its creation. But if a real distinction between essence and existence is admitted, a thing will have real being before its creation in the form of its essence. Thus when a thing is produced by its efficient cause, it will not be produced from nothing. Hence no real distinction between essence and existence can be admitted, since essence cannot be said to have any real being before its actual existence. The existence of an essence in the divine mind before its actual production is simply ideal "*esse cognitum*". Scotus and St. Thomas are agreed on the point that creation means the production of the whole object out of nothing, and that the essence before its creation did not possess any being of its own. But Scotus differed from St. Thomas in his view of the relationship between essence and existence in the created object, since he rejected a real distinction between the two and substituted a formal distinction in its place.[72]

The doctrine of formal objective distinction was applied by Scotus also in his discussion of universals. The universal in fact, according to Scotus, does not exist except in the intellect. There is no actually existing universal which is predicable of more than one object. The common nature is not numerically the same in the individual members of a species. It cannot be compared to the divine essence which is the same in the three divine persons Nevertheless, there is a unity which is less than numerical. There is no real distinction, according to Scotus, between the nature of an individual object and its individuality (*haecceitas*), yet there is a formal distinction between them. The nature of an individual object (which distinguishes it from the objects of other kinds) is formally distinct from the 'thisness' of it (which distinguishes it from other objects of the same kind). So the nature

71. Ibid.
72. Ibid., pp. 510-11.

of an object can be considered simply as such, without reference to its individuality. It is necessary, Scotus argues, to recognise this formal distinction between the nature of an object and its individuality, since otherwise there would be no objective foundation for our universal judgments. The abstraction of a unviersal concept presupposes a distinction in the object between the nature and the "*haecceitas.*"[73]

It is clear that Scotus is neither an extreme realist nor a nominalist. By denying that the distinction between the common nature of a thing and its individuality is a real distinction, that is, the distinction between two separable entities, Scotus is denying extreme realism, for he is denying that the common nature is numerically the same in all the individual members of a species. But by recognising a formal objective distinction between the common nature and the individuality of a thing, he is accepting an identity which is less than numerical, and thus admitting a moderate form of realism. Scotus is evidently concerned, not only to deny extreme realism, but also nominalism, since the latter cannot satisfactorily account for the objective reference of our universal judgments.

(v) *Conceptualism*

The controversy over universals in the middle ages finally came to an end with the rejection of all forms of realism by William Ockham. The universal, Ockham holds, cannot be a real thing. The individual alone exists, and the universal is essentially not an individual. The main objection of Ockham against extreme realism is that there is no single, identical and simple entity which is present in each of a number of particular things at the same time. The assertion of such an entity is a contradiction in terms.[74] Against moderate realism Ockham argues that there is no universal essence or nature common to different members of a species. One man can be annihilated by God without any other man being annihilated or destroyed. But if there were any nature common to both, it would be annihilated and, consequently, no other man would retain his essential nature. St. Thomas maintained that the universal is not actually different from the individual; it is present in each individual in a specific way, i.e., in an individualised state. Ockham points out that this doctrine

73. Ibid., pp. 511-12.
74. See Carre, op. cit., p. 108.

would imply as many universals as there are individuals. And this would mean the denial of universals, since there would be no common nature. Ockham criticises also the doctrine of formal distinction advocated by Duns Scotus. If the formal distinction between the common nature and the individuality of an object is objective and not a purely mental distinction, it must be real. The doctrine of Scotus is thus subject to all the difficulties which were encountered by extreme realism.[75]

Knowledge, Ockham maintains, can be explained without assuming universals. Intuition, according to him, is the basis of all knowledge. Intuition reveals to us individual things, the same as the objects of sense-perception. It does not reveal to us any essences or universals. However, intuition does not grasp only individual objects in the sensible world; it also apprehends immediately the relations between objects. Thus intuition for Ockham is not mere sensation. Within it a sensory and an intellectual factor are distinguished. Sensation by itself is not sufficient to produce the knowledge of an object; an intellectual intuition is further required. The function of this factor is to classify the object of our intuition, to pronounce what it is. The sensory factor tells us that the thing exists, the intellectual factor allows us to recognise it. Any genuine perception requires both the elements.[76]

The doctrine that intellect knows sensible things intuitively is directly against the Scholastic teaching that intellect, or understanding, could not know particular sensible things. Even for St. Thomas our knowledge is confined to the abstract nature of things, the universals. But, for Ockham, there are no universals immanent in things. It is the individual itself which is apprehended as a recognisable object by the combined activities of intellect and senses in intuition. Thus the world, according to Ockham, is directly perceived. All theories of representative knowledge are repudiated. Ideas which are asserted to resemble the reality of which they are copies assume acquaintance with that reality. Therefore, ideas, or '*intelligible species*', which convey a similitude of the real world are logically impossible, and the introduction of them offends against the principle of economy.[77]

75. See Copleston, op. cit., Vol. III, p. 56.
76. See Carre, op. cit., p. 110.
77. See Windelband, op. cit., pp. 325-26; and Carre, op. cit., pp. 110-11.

Ockham thus rejects all forms of realism and grounds knowledge on the direct apprehension of individual objects. What then is a universal according to him? To find an answer to this question we must turn to Ockham's logic. In his logic Ockham distinguishes between a 'conventional sign' and a 'natural sign'. The word 'man', for instance, is a conventional sign; it signifies something or has a meaning. But that this particular word has that particular meaning is a matter of convention. This is clear from the fact that in other languages other words are used to express the same meaning. A natural sign, on the other hand, is a concept which is the real material of all reasoning. A conventional sign is significant only to an intelligence possessing a concept by which the significance of the word is established. Thus the universal, according to Ockham, is the concept which is the content of all intellectual activity. It is not to be understood as a psychological reality, since as a psychological fact it is not a universal. The concept as a universal, in Ockham's view, has no being apart from the act of conceiving.[78]

Ockham called the concept a 'natural sign' because he thought that the direct apprehension of anything causes naturally in the human mind a concept of that thing. This concept may be expressed by different words in different languages. The fact that Ockham did not ascribe universality to words, or conventional signs, but to natural signs, or concepts, proves that he rejected the nominalism of Roscelin.

Ockham distinguishes further between two kinds of terms. The term man, for instance, signifies things, that is, men which are not themselves signs. It is, therefore, a 'term of first intention'. But there are also terms, such as 'species' and 'genera', which do not stand immediately for things which are not themselves signs, but for class terms like 'man', 'horse', 'animal', etc., which are themselves signs. These terms, therefore, are 'the terms of second intention.'[79] In other words, the terms of second intention stand for the terms of first intention and are predicated of them, as when it is said that 'man' and 'horse' are species. The terms of the natural science, according to Ockham, are terms of first intention, and those of logic are terms of second intention.[80] Universal, in his view, is a term of second intention.

78. See Aaron, op. cit., p. 16; Copleston, op. cit., p. 54.
79. See Carre, op. cit., p. 114; Copleston, op. cit., p. 55, cp. Windelband, op. cit., p. 343.
80. See Copleston, op. cit., pp. 59-60.

A fruitful source of error is to regard it as a term of first intention, and so confound sign and the thing signified.

So universals, according to Ockham, are terms (concepts or natural signs) which signify individual things and which stand for them in propositions. The term 'universal', however, does not signify things; it signifies terms which stand for things. Thus only individuals exist; there are not and cannot be existent universals. Everything which is predicable of many things is by nature in the mind. There is no universal reality corresponding to the universal concept. The existence of the universal consists in the act of understanding and it exists only as such. It is not, however, a fiction in the sense that it does not stand for anything real; it stands for individual real things, though it does not stand for any universal thing. It is, in short, a way of conceiving or knowing individual things.

The main point which Ockham emphasises is that there is no need to postulate any factor other than the mind and the individual things in order to explain the universal concepts. Now, does he mean that universal concepts are purely arbitrary fabrications of the mind? Does he assert the absurdity that universal concepts are absolutely devoid of objective basis? Ockham certainly did not subscribe to such a position. He accepts that there are varying degrees of similarity between individual things, and that our universal concepts are based on them.[81] Socrates and Plato are more similar to one another than either is to an ass, and this fact of experience is reflected in the formation of the specific concept of man. This does not mean that there is a nature common to Socrates and Plato in which they share or agree, but that the nature which is Socrates and the nature which is Plato are similar. The foundation of generic concepts can also be explained in a similar manner.

It is clear from the above account of Ockham's view that he was not a nominalist. He was, indeed, a conceptualist.[82] It is important to note

81. See Copleston, op. cit., p. 57.

82. In the later medieval period the term 'nominalist' was frequently used to describe a position which was in effect conceptualist. All those who denied the reality of universals were dubbed as 'nominalist'. Yet most of them were in fact conceptualists. The distinction between conceptualist and nominalist lies in this that the former asserts the existence of a concept along with a name, whereas the latter denies the need for a concept and holds that the universal is merely the name. Ockham and his school were certainly described in the fifteenth and the sixteenth centuries as nominalists in spite of the fact that the assertion of the concept, as

that Ockham did not reject only '*universale in re*' but also '*universale ante rem.*' He rejected the Augustinian doctrine of exemplar ideas in the divine mind. There is no necessity, according to him, to assume the existence of such ideas. Moreover, even if exemplar ideas existed in the divine mind, their existence is entirely irrelevant in our attempt to understand human knowledge. St. Thomas held that the similarity of natures possessed by things could be explained only on the ground of exemplar ideas in the divine mind. The metaphysical ground of the similarity of natures is that God creates things belonging to the same species, that is, things with similar natures, in accordance with the ideas in His mind. Ockham, however, discarded this theory. For him the similarities which give rise to universal concept are simply similarities of facts. There is no metaphysical reason for these similarities, except the divine choice, which is not dependent on any divine ideas. The theory of divine ideas, according to Ockham, implies a limitation of divine freedom and omnipotence. The metaphysics of essences is a non-Christian invention which had no place in Christian Theology and philosophy.[83]

Ockham's conception of knowledge thus breaks with the main tradition of Scholastic thought. Since there are no common natures in things, existence is composed of individual items in various relations. Everything that is, is an individual thing. For St. Thomas, as we have seen, essence is what the object really is. It is its universal nature expressed in its definition. An essence can be known without anything being known of its existence. Existence is a function of matter, by which the essences of composite things multiplied in numerous individuals. But, for Ockham, there are no universal essences which require to be expressed in matter in order to become individuals. The singular thing requires no metaphysical 'principle of individuation'. He rejects the notion of pure potentiality, possessing no actuality or form.[84] Primary matter is always actual, that is, it always has some embodiment, and these embodiments are all uniquely different. The positivist and the phenomenalist tendency of Ockham's position is quite apparent.

---

we have seen, was the heart of Ockham's theory of universals. Much confusion was caused by the failure to distinguish between conceptualists and nominalists. Roscelin certainly was a nominalist, if Anselm's description of his theory is correct.

83. See Copleston, op. cit., pp. 50-51. Also cp. Carre, op. cit., p. 116.
84. See Carre, op. cit., p. 119.

The moderate realist would agree with Ockham's criticism of extreme realism, but he would not accept the latter's explanation of the universal concept. He would insist that the objectivity of universal characters in some sense must be recognised. He would, of course, admit that such characters are in each instance as particular as the particular things which manifest them. But this, according to him, does not falsify their universality. If the conceptualist or the nominalist position is accepted we must believe that the common principles sought for in particular things are fictions. But to abolish the objectivity of universals, in every sense, is to abolish, as St. Thomas would say, the possibility of exploring the nature of anything. He insisted that universals have their foundation in objects and so far are indisputably real. All thinking, he maintained, presupposes certain irreducible modes of unity, and these are not concepts constructed by the mind, but essential features of objects. However, the acceptance of universal features does not imply the existence of universal entities, man in general, or animal as such, upon which the conceptualists and the nominalists poured their scorn. What are sought are essential features which are intrinsic to the nature of things.

CHAPTER XIII

CONTRIBUTION OF MODERN THINKERS

The transition from the medieval to the modern period was marked by a revolt against the over-academic formalism and intellectualism of the Scholastic thought. The new stress was on the observation of the particular and avoidance of abstract speculation. It was felt that the Schools were out of touch with the real; concentration on abstractions and endless arguments about them led nowhere. The scientific spirit of the age emphasised the observation of nature in the concrete. Advance of knowledge was said to consist in gaining particular ideas; the universal belonged to the realm of the abstract and the empty.

It is, therefore, not surprising that the denial of the reality of the universal was common amongst the leading thinkers of this period. The spirit of the age favoured conceptualism. In the *Principles of Philosophy* Descartes says, 'number when we consider it abstractly or generally and not in created things is but a mode of thinking; and the same is true of all that which is named universal.'[1] That is, according to Descartes, the universal is not *in re,* it is only a concept. The conceptualist character of Descartes' view becomes more evident from his explanation of the origin of the universal. 'Universals', he says, 'arise solely from the fact that we avail ourselves of one and the same idea in order to think of all individual things which have a certain similitude; and when we comprehend under the same name all the objects represented by this idea, the name is universal.[2] A general name, that is to say, stands for a group of similar objects represented in the mind by one and the same idea. It does not stand for a real universal which the intellect apprehends.

1. '*The Philosophical Works of Descartes*', tr. by E. S. Haldane and C. R. T. Ross, Dover, 1931, Vol. I, Pt. I, 58, p. 242.
2. Ibid., 59, pp. 242-43.

1. *Hobbes' Nominalism*

Although the dominant trend of thought in the modern period was conceptualistic, yet the nominalistic trend was not completely absent. It is found in its most explicit form in the thought of Thomas Hobbes. According to Hobbes, 'the word universal is never the name of anything existent in nature, nor of any idea or phantasm formed in the mind, but always the name of some word or name.'[3] Again, in the *Leviathan* he remarks, 'there being nothing in the world universal but names; for the things named are every one of them individual or singular.'[4] This is clearly a denial not only of realism but also of conceptualism. The universal is merely the 'name' and we should not look for any other universal beyond the name.

The position of Hobbes obviously involves serious difficulties. The question is why do we call different things by the same name? Does classification consist merely in calling certain things by the same name? Again, how can Hobbes consistently talk of the name being the universal, when everything in the world is singular? We have already brought out the difficulties involved in such a position while discussing the Buddhist nominalism. Hobbes seems to have recognised the difficulties of the extreme nominalistic position; hence he accepted resemblance between individual things as the basis of their being called by the same name. 'One universal name is imposed on many things for their similitude in some quality or the other accident.[5] Again, 'a man', he says, 'denotes anyone of the multitude of men, and a philosopher anyone of many philosophers, by reason of their similitude.'[6] This considerably modifies the extreme nominalistic position attributed to Hobbes. Classification, for him, is not merely naming, it is founded on the similitude of things. His theory, therefore, stands or falls with the theory of resemblance.

It is clear that Hobbes' nominalism falls short of the extreme nominalism of the Buddhist. The latter does not recognise any positive similarity amongst particulars. Again, by recognising names as universals Hobbes inconsistently assumes that some things, at least

---

3. A passage from Hobbes, '*Elements of Philosophy*' quoted by Aaron, op. cit., p. 20.
4. *Leviathan*, Pt. I, IV quoted by Woozley in '*Theory of Knowledge*' p. 90.
5. Loc. cit.
6. *Logic*, pt. I, Ch. II, quoted by Woozley, op. cit., p. 90.

names, may be identical in various uses. The Buddhist would deny even this claim. For him there is no similarity or identity anywhere except in our imagination. Neither are things similar, nor are words the same. All 'sameness' and 'similarity' is a make-belief. The Buddhist is the most consistent nominalist. He knows that the acceptance of identity or similarity on any plane would open the door for realism. It must also be noted that the Buddhist and Hobbes differ in their conceptions of particulars. For the Buddhist the particular is the unique point-instant transcending thought and language. But for Hobbes, the particular is the concrete individual determinately known in empirical experience. In the Buddhist view, the particular of Hobbes, just like the universal of the realist, is also a thought-construction having no real existence. Thus the two, the Buddhist and Hobbes, differ not only in their theories of universals, but also in their ontology.

Conceptualism is primarily associated with the three classical British thinkers, Locke, Berkeley and Hume, all of whom propounded views about what, in the terminology of the time, were called general ideas. They were all empiricists in that they agreed that all ideas come from, and can come only from experience. There is no access to the external world except through the senses. The mind can work on what is given to it by sense-experience but can neither have ideas prior to any experience, nor create ideas *de novo.*

2. *The Conceptualism of Locke*

Before discussing Locke's positive theory of universals we should consider his reasons for rejecting both the forms of realism: the Platonic and the Aristotelian. He rules out the Platonic theory on the ground that 'all things that exist are only particulars.'[7] He does not discuss this principle but introduces it as something which must be granted generally. He is convinced that in sense-perception we know the existence of particular things—tables and chairs. He was so sure of this that he took it as a fundamental principle that what existed in the external world was invariably a particular of this kind. Hence he concluded that a universal could not possibly exist separated as the Platonic Form is supposed to exist.[8]

7. '*An Essay Concerning Human Understanding*', Ed. Raymond Wilburn, Everyman's Library, 1947, Book III, Ch. iii, Sec. 6.
8. See Ibid., III, iii, 17.

Locke rejected the Aristotelian theory also on the ground that we do not know any 'real essence' which is alleged to be common to all the members of a species.[9] He brings forward two main arguments to prove his contention. First, if we know the real essence of a thing, we should, prior to experiencing it, have certain knowledge of what it is and how it will behave; that is, we should know before examining it that it must have such and such qualities, and that it must behave in such and such manner. As a matter of fact, we have to depend on experience for such a knowledge. We possess, of course, a great deal of probable knowledge inductively established which enables us to say what the behaviour of the object is likely to be. But the very fact that this knowledge is probable is itself proof that we do not know the real essence.[10]

In the second place, Locke argues, if we know the real essences, we should know the precise boundaries of each species. That is to say, we should have no difficulty with borderline cases. In such cases we frequently classify things by arbitrary decision into one species rather than another. This shows that in their case we do not discover any real essence allegedly common to all the members. This is our predicament frequently in attempting to classify natural objects, and this shows that classifying does not consist merely in discovering those individual things which share one and the same real essence.[11]

Locke thus rejects both the Platonic and Aristotelian theories of universals. Universals, he holds, are not discovered and are not in the world of particular existences. 'Universality belongs not to things in themselves which are all of them particular in existence.'[12] Now, what is Locke's own view of universals? Locke holds that they are 'the inventions and creatures of the understanding made by it for its own use, and concern only signs whether words or ideas.'[13] That is, they do not belong to the realm of being, but to the realm of discourse. They 'concern' the signs of thinking, our language and our ideas. Locke is clearly reasserting the Ockhamist view of universals.

A clear statement of Locke's conception of universals is to be found in his doctrine of 'nominal essence', or general ideas, in which he finds his solution of the problem of universals. The universal,

9. III, vi, 9.
10. III, vi, 8.
11. III, vi, 12.
12. III, iii, 11.
13. Ibid.

Locke holds, is the nominal essence, i.e., a general idea or a concept. It differs fundamentally from the real essence, for it is not discovered by the mind but made by it. It is not an essence in the real world but an essence in the world of discourse, something belonging to our ways of talking and thinking. At the same time, it is not to be identified with the word. It is the concept for which the word stands. Locke thus rejects also nominalism; for him the general word always stands for a general idea. The nominal essence must be distinguished not only from the real essence, but also from the word.[14]

Now, how does the nominal essence or the general idea come into being? According to Locke, general ideas are formed by us by a process of abstraction from particular ideas. He gives what appears to be two different accounts of abstraction. In the first account he says that what is actually before the mind when we are generalising is a particular, but a particular used in a representative capacity. The general idea is not an idea different from the particular idea; it is the particular idea regarded in a special way, that is, as 'representing more individuals than one, each of which having in it a conformity to that abstract idea, is of that sort.'[15]

An important question arises with regard to the account of generalising given above, namely, how is the representative character of a particular idea to be explained? Why does the particular idea of a triangle, for instance, represent the ideas of other triangles and not those of squares and circles? A particular idea is said to represent all the particulars of the same 'sort'. But how can a particular represent a sort? Again, what does Locke mean by a sort? We do not have Locke's answer to any of these questions except the last. He, presumably, realised the difficulties involved in his first account of abstraction and hence proceeded to give another account of it. Nevertheless, this strand is present in his thought (which Berkeley later took up), and he is always anxious to emphasise the point that the general idea as occurring in thinking is a particular.

As regards the last question raised above as to what Locke means by a 'sort', Locke explains that he used this term in place of 'species' and 'genus' of the School.[16] A sort he thinks is suggested by experience but not discovered in it, and the difference is important, for it

---

14. III, iii, 15-17.
15. III, iii, 6.
16. III, iii, 12.

means that the sort must be a fabrication of our thought suggested by experience. But how does the mind fabricate it? The answer to this question is to be found in his second account of abstraction. Generalising in the sense of fabricating sorts is the process of abstracting a core of qualities which we find to be common to many particulars and ignoring those which differ. A general idea, for example, of man is formed by leaving out of the particular ideas of various individual men all features that are 'peculiar to each' and retaining only 'what is common to them all'.[17] The general idea of animal is arrived at by still further leaving out and "retaining only a body, with life, sense and spontaneous motion comprehended under the name 'animal'." In the same way, mind proceeds to form more comprehensive general ideas of 'body', 'substance' and at last of 'being' and 'thing'.[18] The general idea thus obtained is new in the sense that it did not exist before, but there is nothing new in its content, for it consists of common features which were already contained in the particular ideas.

Thus the content of the general idea is derived from experience, but the fabrication is ours. It is we and not nature, who set up the final Boundaries. "The boundaries of the species whereby men sort them, are made by men."[19] It is we also who decide what content each general idea is to possess. Thus the general idea is subjective in so far as it depends on the mind creating it. It can be objective only in the sense that the same word conveys the same general idea to more than one person. But it is never objective in the sense of existing objectively so that all may discover it. Even in the narrow sense described above, it is rarely that the general idea is fully objective. Indeed, it is always possible that the term 'T', signifying a general idea, signifies for one a b c d e and for another a b c f g. We cannot assume that the same general term signifies precisely the same general idea to any two persons.[20]

Two consequences follow from this position. Firstly, concepts are not permanently fixed, as on a simple realist theory they would be; a concept is liable to development and change as fresh experience or changes of view show the need or utility of it. Secondly, the

---

17. III, iii, 7.
18. III, iii, 9.
19. III, vi, 37.
20. III, vi, 29, 30 and 36.

meaning of the word, i.e., the concept, as understood by different persons, need not necessarily be exactly the same.

The general character of Locke's theory of universals is now plain. It is clearly conceptualistic. Both realism and nominalism are rejected. He, of course, does not deny that classifications are suggested in the first instance by nature. They have their foundation in the similitude of things.[21] Nevertheless, they remain 'the workmanship of the understanding'. It is one thing to observe resemblance in objects and to classify accordingly, and quite another to discover a real essence common to all these objects and thus recognise them as instances of one and the same species. In the latter case the species could not be regarded as the 'workmanship' of the mind, but rather as the mind's discovery. Yet this is a discovery, Locke holds which never in fact occurs.[22]

There are, however, some serious difficulties in Locke's theory of universals. The theory as it is stated, is inconsistent with itself. It says first that all that exists is particular, and then that general ideas are formed by abstracting common qualities. But if all that exists is particular, how could we abstract common qualities? Locke cannot say that common qualities are also particulars, as it would be contradiction in terms. Moreover, the denial of the reality of universals loses much of its force if the reality of common qualities is accepted. It would mean the denial of only one type of universals, namely, real essences, such as 'humanity', 'animality', etc., but, at the same time, it would mean the acceptance, though inconsistently, of the other kind of universal, namely, the common qualities.

---

21. III, iii, 13.
22. Locke appears to talk like the Buddhist when he says that universals are 'workmanship of the understanding'. But there are fundamental differences between the two. For Locke, universal concepts are formed by abstracting common qualities from the experience of particulars, but, for the Buddhist, they are *a priori* constructions rooted in the creative reason. For Locke the universal concept has objective basis in the real resemblance of particulars, but for the Buddhist, there is no such basis, as there is no identity or similarity in reality. Both would, however, agree in the denial of the existence of real essences in the external world. Similarly, Locke's position differs also from that of Hobbes. For the former, the word signifies particulars through their general idea. But, for the latter, there are no general ideas; words signify particulars having certain resemblances directly.

But can Locke consistently accept real qualities common to different individuals of a species? We know that secondary qualities, in his view, are not '*in re*', i.e., in the physical object. So the common quality, say red, which appears to be identical in two different objects is, on Locke's view, not '*in re*' but '*in the mind.*' Thus there cannot be real common qualities in Locke's view. This renders his account of the formation of general ideas through abstracting common qualities quite unintelligible.

Lastly, it must be remarked that Locke, like the Scholastic thinkers, concentrates on the problem of species and genera to the exclusion of other kinds of universals. He neglects the two kinds of universals which are of great importance, namely, qualities and relations. Now, it may prove to be true that what is true of genera and species is not true of the universals of quality and relation. That is to say, we might deny that we know real essences in the case of species and genera and yet affirm that we know universals, in the realist sense, in the case of the universals of quality and relations. But Locke never considered this point.[23]

3· *Berkeley's Criticism*

Berkeley's view of general ideas and universals grows out of his criticism of Locke's view. In his *Introduction to the Principles of Human Knowledge*[24] he severely attacks Locke's doctrine of abstract general ideas. He repudiates Locke's contention that the mind has a power of framing abstract general ideas or notions of things. He confesses that he does not find within himself the ability to imagine, for instance, a hand which lacks determinate shape and colour. Nor can he frame an idea of a man who is coloured and has a height, and yet has no particular colour and particular height. He further remarks: "It is equally impossible for me to form abstract idea of motion distinct from the body moving, and which is neither swift nor slow, curvilinear nor rectilinear, and the like may be said of all other abstract general ideas whatsoever."[25] That is, we cannot single out a

23. For a detailed criticism of Locke's conceptualism, see Aaron, *The Theory of Universals*, pp. 36 ff.
24. See *Treatise concerning The Principles of Human Knowledge in British Empirical Philosophers*', Ed. A. J. Ayer and Raymond Winch, Routledge and Kegan Paul, London, 1952.
25. Sec. 10.

general quality common to many objects, such as 'motion' or 'being coloured'. If we think of 'motion', it is always the motion of a particular body moving quickly or slowly as the case may be. Similarly, if we think of objects as 'being coloured', it is always of a particular colour, whatever colour it might be. Berkeley, however, admits abstraction to be possible 'in one sense'. We can think of "some particular parts or qualities separated from others, with which though they are united in some object, yet it is possible they may really exist without them." But he denies that we can "abstract one from another, or conceive separately, those qualities which it is impossible should exist so separated."[26]

This is evidently a psychological criticism. It may be true to say that one cannot imagine a man who has height but has no particular height, or again that one cannot imagine a hand that has shape and colour without having some particular shape or colour. But does this justify the view that to 'think' of a man is always to 'imagine' a man of a particular height and to 'think' of a hand is always to 'imagine' a hand of a particular shape or colour? This does not seem to be so. Berkeley is propounding an 'imagist theory of thinking' and identifying 'imagining' with 'conceiving'.[27] But it seems that the two must be distinguished. Berkeley's criticism would appear to be appropriate to 'imagining' only and not to 'conceiving'. The fact that we cannot imagine a man who has no particular height does not at all prove that we cannot think and speak of 'man' meaning men of all heights at one and the same time. Thus, if by 'abstract general idea' what is understood is a 'concept' and not an 'image', then Berkeley's argument against it does not hold.

It is to be noted that although Berkeley denies abstract general ideas, he does not deny general ideas altogether. "I do not deny absolutely that there are general ideas, but only that there are any 'abstract general ideas' ....I believe we shall acknowledge, that an idea, which considered in itself is particular, becomes general, by being made to represent or stand for all other particular ideas of the same sort."[28] Thus generalisation, according to Berkeley, consists in taking a particular and letting it stand for many particulars.

---

26. Loc. cit.
27. See for a detailed discussion of the Imagist and other theories of thinking. H. H. Price : *Thinking and Experience,* Chapter VIII and X.
28. Sec. 12. This is the same as the first account of abstraction given by Locke discussed in the preceding section.

But there is an important question: what particulars is this particular to stand for? What makes them out for grouping? Why do we choose a particular to represent just these? Berkeley says that a particular idea, say of a triangle, represents "all other particular ideas of the same sort." Berkeley has to introduce the notion of 'sort', in order to make sense of his theory. But unfortunately he does not tell us what he means by 'the same sort'. As a matter of fact, it is the 'sort' which is in question, and Berkeley while advancing his theory of general ideas begs the question.

Although Berkeley discards Locke's theory of abstract general ideas, he agrees that 'all knowledge and demonstration are about universal notions'. He, however, denies that "these notions are formed by 'abstraction' in the manner premised." Universality, according to him, consists not in "the absolute 'positive' nature or conception of anything, but in the 'relation' it bears to the particulars signified or represented by it, by virtue whereof it is that things, names and notions, being in their own nature 'particular', are rendered 'universal' "[29] It is clear that, for Berkeley, the universal is neither objective in the realist sense, nor is it a conception framed by the mind. Universality consists in the 'relation' a particular bears 'to the particulars signified or represented by it'. What he seems to mean is that when, for example, we prove something of a triangle we have a universal idea of a triangle before our mind, though not an abstract general idea; we have immediately before us a particular triangle which signifies or represents all triangles. The universality of this particular idea lies in its capacity for representing all other triangles.

It may be objected that a demonstration made of any particular triangle may hold of that triangle, but why should it hold of any other? Berkeley anticipates this objection and answers that while making demonstration, the idea he has 'in view' is tnat of a particular triangle, nevertheless, the differentiating features of this triangle are not 'at all concerned in the demonstration.'[30] Hence, what is demonstrated of this triangle is true of all triangles.

Now this amounts to affirming that our real object of demonstration is not that particular triangle which we have 'in view', but that which is common to all triangles. In other words, our demonstration

29. Sec. 15.
30. Sec. 16.

is concerned not with a triangle in particular but the triangle in general. But what is this triangle in general according to Berkeley? Berkeley explains that "It must be acknowledged, that a man may consider a figure merely as triangular, without attending to the particular qualities of the angles, or relations of the sides. So far he may abstract : but this will never prove that he can frame an abstract general inconsistent idea of a triangle."[31] We may grant Berkeley's point against Locke's conception of abstract general ideas.[32] What is important to note here is that Berkeley now agrees that we can abstract triangularity neglecting particular features of the triangles. This is the abstract idea of triangularity. And triangles are particulars which make up one sort because they all share triangularity.

Thus, Berkeley's polemic against abstract ideas ends with the admission of abstract ideas with the acknowledgement of the universal abstract idea of triangularity. But Berkeley merely acknowledges the existence of such ideas; he does not give a satisfactory account of these ideas in his *Introduction.*[33]

In the closing sections of the *Introduction* Berkeley makes some valuable observations concerning language, which may briefly be noted here. He finds the source of the erroneous theory of abstraction in the false notion about language. He points out that Locke's assumption, namely, that a general word invariably stands for a general idea, is false, because it ignores ends and functions of language. Firstly, communication of ideas is not "the chief and only end of language, as is commonly supposed;" it has other functions also. It may be used for "the raising of some passion, the exciting to, or deterring from an action, the putting the mind in some particular disposition"[34]—to which we may add still others, such as asking questions, praying, vowing, swearing, making promises, declaring intentions, and expressing wishes or fears. Secondly, even when it is

31. Loc. cit.
32. Locke in IV, vii, 9 of his *Essay* describes the general idea of triangle as 'neither oblique nor rectangle neither equilateral, nor equicrural, nor scalenon; but all and none of these at once. In effect, it is something, imperfect, that cannot exist; an idea wherein some parts of several different and inconsistent ideas are put together'. This means, says Berkeley, that to think the abstract general idea is to think that which involves a self-contradiction within itself, an impossibility. (see *Introduction*, Sec. 13 and 14).
33. For a detailed discussion of Berkeley's view refer to Aaron: *The Theory of Universals*, Ch. III.
34. Sec. 20.

used descriptively for communicating ideas the account which Locke gives of it is still erroneous. Locke assumes that whenever a general word is used, there is a precise, determinate idea in the mind. Berkeley denies this. Men use words for communicating their thoughts without having such precise, determinate ideas annexed to them. "There is no such thing as one precise and definite signification annexed to any general name, they all signify indifferently a great number of particular ideas."[35] It may be objected that every name that has a definition, is thereby restricted to one definite signification. For instance, a 'triangle' is defined as 'a plain figure bounded by three straight lines' by which that name is limited to denote a definite idea and no other. Berkeley answers that "there is 'no one settled idea' which limits the signification of the word 'triangle.' It is one thing to keep a name constantly to the same definition, and another to make it stand everywhere for the same idea; the one is necessary, the other useless and impracticable."[36]

Coming to the final assessment of Berkeley's view, we must say that he is mainly concerned with the refutation of Locke's theory of abstract general ideas. But, as we have shown, he himself ends with acknowledging abstraction in a sense when he says that one can single out 'triangularity.' The most serious lacuna in Berkeley is that he completely ignores the main problem, namely, the problem of status and nature of what he called the 'sorts.' His arguments are incomplete without a discussion of this matter and lack a solid foundation. Thus, in spite of valuable points in Berkeley's discussion, the *Introduction* as a whole, viewed as a positive contribution to the question of universals, is disappointing. His observations on language in the concluding sections are, however, very valuable. They suggest that the conceptualist view of universals, as advanced by Locke, needs correction. It is not true that a general word invariably signifies a general idea. There are occasions when it does not signify any idea whatsoever, and occasions when we use words merely to arouse emotions or incite to action. Locke's theory of language was, therefore, too narrow. It must, however, be pointed out that the meaning conveyed by words, whether it be an idea or anything else, is always general. The unique particular, whether it be a thing, a quality, an action, an idea, an emotion, or any

35. Sec. 18.
36. Loc. cit.

other thing, can neither be thought nor expressed by words. So long as we make use of words, it is impossible to get out of the realm of generalities and abstractions.

4. *Hume's Theory of Disposition and Resemblance*

Hume accepts Berkeley's principle that all general ideas are nothing but particular ideas used in a representative capacity. "Abstract ideas are, therefore, in themselves individual, however they may become general in their representation. The image in the mind is only that of a particular object, though the application of it in our reasoning be the same as if it were universal."[37] Hume emphasises the role of words more strongly than Berkeley had done. Whereas Berkeley had supposed that a word became general by its relation to a particular but representative idea, Hume puts it the other way round. He holds that "A particular idea becomes general by being annexed to a general term; that is, to a term which from a customary conjunction, has a relation to many other particular ideas, and readily recalls them in the imagination."[38]

Whereas Berkeley had contented himself with maintaining that an idea became general by representing all ideas of 'the same sort', Hume offered an account of how a particular idea could represent others. It did this through custom or habit, by the association of ideas and the association of words. At any given moment a man has only one individual idea before his mind, but because of the resemblance which he has found in his experience, the one individual idea is associated with others of the same kind, which are not actually present to the mind at that time but which would be called up by the stimulus of suitable experience or suitable word. As he says, "When we have found a resemblance among several objects, that often occur to us, we apply the same name to all of them,... After we have acquired a custom of this kind, the hearing of the name revives the idea of one of these objects....."[39] Thus the possession of a general idea or concept becomes a mental disposition, the readiness engendered by custom, to have some idea belonging to a given kind, when the appropriate stimulus occurs.

37. '*A Treatise concerning Human Nature*' Book I, Part I, Section vii, in '*British Empirical Philosophers*', Ed. A. J. Ayer and Raymond Winch, p. 313.
38. Op. cit., p. 315.
39. Op. cit., p. 313.

The important point emphasised by Hume is that a concept must be thought of in terms of disposition; having a concept is having an expectation on hearing a name, a readiness to recognise an instance and to reject what is not an instance. In other words, to have a concept actually in the mind at any given time is to have in mind an individual idea plus the appropriate associative disposition. Universal concepts, therefore, cannot be adequately described in terms of bare ideas or images, we must also think of them in terms of tendencies and mental dispositions produced by habit.

Hume assigns words a key-role in his doctrine of association of ideas, supposing that particular ideas which resemble one another, however inexactly, tend to be associated with one another because each is associated with a general word. Hume's theory may be regarded as a protest against the view that prior to the use of general words there is always, or even usually, a conscious selection of common characteristics followed by the framing of a universal. This, it holds, is too sophisticated an account of the process in question. We cannot suppose that children set out to isolate common characteristics, and abstract them to frame a universal. In their case, as in the case of adults, for most of the time, custom is king; familiarity with a world in which certain resemblances recur, creates within the mind, almost without our knowing, a customary grouping whose links are strengthened by the learning of a common name.[40]

Hume missed an important point here. He failed to see that the attempt to account for the generality of an idea in terms of the generality of the word will not do, for the sense in which he insisted that every idea is particular, so is every word. Whatever reasons there are for denying the existence of general ideas will also be reasons for denying the existence of general words as distinct from particular words. Consideration of this point would have required Hume to explain how words become general. He could explain it only on the basis of resemblance between particular occurrences of the word, as he did in the case of general ideas.[41] Thus Hume's conceptualism,

40. Ibid., pp. 314-15.

41. Conceptualism of Hume and nominalism, such as Hobbes', here converge, difference being in approach and emphasis rather than in substance. Both require a resemblance theory to account for the generality of words since they have rejected universals. The sameness of the word cannot consistently be explained by them except in terms of resemblance between its different

like that of Locke and Berkeley comes down on the side of resemblance as being the ontological basis of general ideas and general words. All that exists is individual; generalisation or concept formation is possible only to the extent that individual objects and occurrences, their features and their mutual relations display perceptible resemblances to a greater or lesser extent.

Now what is Hume's conception of resemblance? Hume accepted first the traditional theory of resemblance (propounded also by Locke), according to which two objects would resemble each other if they possess certain feature or features in common. Thus an object A possessing features a b c d may be said to resemble another object B possessing a b e f, because, they possess the elements a and b in common. But Hume found that this raised difficulties about simple, or unanalysable, ideas or qualities. It would follow on this theory that non-composites or simples cannot resemble each other and, consequently, we cannot genealise in their case. And yet simples do resemble each other and we do generalise in their case. Locke also saw the problem, but the solution proposed by him is different from Hume's. Locke searched for a common characteristic extrinsic to simples, for instance, 'white' and 'red' are both 'visibles', they 'get into the mind' in the same way, and so may be said to resemble each other in this respect and 'comprehended under the genus or name colour.'[42] But does it not imply that the entities with which Locke now deals are in fact composites and not simples, consisting of two characteristics; (a) being white or red and (b) being visible ? If so, the problem remains unsolved.

Hume's own solution of the problem is indicated in the following passage.[43]

---

occurrences. That is, they must recognise what logicians have called 'type-token' distinction. Any occurrence of the word 'table' is particular (a token), and two occurrences of what would be called the same word (Table as a type) are occurrences of the same word only in that they resemble each other in the relevant ways. Thus the general word 'Table' is nothing but the class of the resembling particular words 'table', 'table' and so on.

42. See *Essay*, III, iv, 16. In the same way, Locke holds, colours, sounds, smells, tastes, etc. which 'come into the mind only by one sense' and so resemble one another in this respect, may be comprehended under the genus or the term 'quality', as distinguished from 'extension, number, motion, pleasure and pain, which make impressions on the mind and introduce their ideas by more senses than one'.

43. Op. cit., footnote, p. 313.

"It is evident, that even different simple ideas may have a similarity or resemblance to each other; nor is it necessary, that the point or circumstance of resemblance should be distinct or separable from that in which they differ. 'Blue' and 'green' are different simple ideas, but are more resembling than 'blue' and 'scarlet'; though their perfect simplicity excludes all possibility of separation or distinction. It is the same case with particular sounds, and tastes, and smells. These admit of infinite resemblances upon the general appearance and comparison, without having any common circumstance the same."

Here is a very definite suggestion of the modern Resemblance Theory. We may generalise not by discovering a common element or elements, but by noting resemblances where there are no identical common qualities, or at least no known identical common qualities. This is sufficient basis for generalisation, even if we know no such identities as are assumed in the traditional theory of resemblance. Hume has thus put forward quite a new account of resemblance and generalising, and the modern Resemblance Theory is merely a development of this suggestion. It has developed it by applying Hume's suggestion not merely to simples but also to composites. Even in the case of composites, is it so necessary, as we supposed, to find identities before we generalise? Must we first make quite certain that the quality a^1 in A is identical with quality a^2 in B, before we can group A and B for purposes of generalisation? Would it not be enough to say that these qualities resemble one another? This is a matter to which we shall have to return later. It is enough now to note that the solution proposed by the adherents of the Resemblance Theory is already suggested by Hume, though he did not develop his own suggestion.

It must however be pointed out that Hume's account of resemblance was not free from ambiguity, for he slips back into speaking of even simples as resembling one another in respect of an identity. He says that we group all simple ideas together under the abstract term 'simple idea', because, all 'these resemble each other in their simplicity.'[44] Now, in accordance with the theory of resemblance suggested by Hume, this should mean that the simplicity of one simple idea is similar to, but not identical with, the simplicity

44. Loc. cit.

of another simple idea. Yet this hardly seems to be Hume's meaning. He surely seems to mean that the simplicity in both the cases is identical.

5. *The Rationalist Protest*

The empiricists, speaking generally, advocated the theory that the universal is identical with the concept. It is the workmanship of the mind, and is fabricated out of materials given in experience. The rationalists agreed with the empiricist's view that the source of universals was the mind itself, that is, they accepted the conceptualism of the empiricist theory. But they protested against its empiricism. They could not agree that all universals were fabricated out of empirically derived material. Some universals were no doubt fabricated in this manner, but not all; there are universals of outstanding importance which, being fundamental to human knowledge, are not derived from experience. So the empiricist theory, according to the rationalists, was superficial and only partially true. A deeper analysis of concepts was necessary.

All this is clearly brought out by Descartes' reply to Gassandi and Leibniz's criticism of Locke's conceptualism. In his fifth *Meditation* Descartes held that the geometrical triangle was 'an immutable and eternal nature' known independently of sense experience.[45] Gassandi agreed with Descartes that the geometrical triangle was a universal, but he doubted whether it was known independently of experience. He thought that it was also known in the same way as other universals, i. e., by abstracting common features of particular triangles which are observed to resemble one another. There is no justification for supposing that we possess the knowledge of an ideal triangle prior to all experience of triangles.[46]

Descartes would agree, as we have pointed out in the beginning of this Chapter, that the existence of empirical universals was brought about in the manner described by Gassandi, but he would not agree that all universals are of this kind. Certain universals, for example, mathematical objects, are known in a non-empirical manner, and these are 'immutable natures'. The main argument of Descartes in support of his view is that it is impossible to derive

45. *Works of Descartes*, Haldane and Ross, I, p. 180.
46. *Objection* V, op. cit., II, p. 182.

universal concepts of mathematics, e. g., of triangle and straight line, from observed triangles and straight lines, since in fact we never observe a genuine triangle or a genuine straight line.[47] The argument is clearly Platonic with the difference that it does not purport to prove the existence of transcendent universals, but only of *a priori* concepts. Thus mathematical concepts, according to Descartes, are not empirical universals framed by abstracting the common features of the observed instances, as Gassandi holds. They are innate concepts known by intellectual intuition.[48] In the same way the notions of God, Substance, Mind, Body and all such essences are known by intellectual intuition, or are innate.[49]

Descartes' account of universals obviously requires clarification which he does not give. But one thing comes out very clearly, namely, his opposition to empiricism. He does not, of course, deny the need for observation through the senses in the field of science; nevertheless, he is convinced that empiricism fails to give a satisfactory account of those universals which, in his view, can be drawn from the thought itself, and not from sense-experience.

Leibniz's criticism of Locke's conceptualism brings out the rationalistic position more clearly. He too denies, like Descartes, that all universals are derived from sense-experience. Locke's denial of innate knowledge, according to him, makes a satisfactory theory of knowledge impossible. He holds with Plato that 'the soul originally contains the principles of several notions and doctrines, which are merely roused on certain occasions by external objects.'[50] The senses, he agrees, 'are necessary for all our actual acquiring of knowledge', but they are, he holds, 'by no means sufficient to give us the whole of our knowledge, since senses never give anything but instances, that is to say, particular or individual truths.' Sense-experience cannot give us universal and necessary truths, since however numerous the instances of a general truth may be, 'it does not follow that what has happened will happen in the same way.'[51] Again, 'the senses furnish

47. Ibid., II, p. 227.
48. Ibid.
49. See *Notes against Programme*, op. cit., I, p. 442.
50. See Leibniz's '*Introduction to New Essays on Human Understanding*' in '*The Monadology and other Philosophical Writings*', tr. by Robert Latta, Oxford University Press, 1951, p. 360.
51. Op. cit., p. 362.

us with matter for reasoning, and we never have thoughts so abstract that something of sense is not mingled with them; but reasoning requires in addition something other than that which is of sense.'[52] It is noteworthy how completely Leibniz foreshadows Kant's position: Human knowledge begins with sense-experience, but it cannot be explained entirely in terms of sense-experience.

Thus, according to Leibniz, we possess the knowledge of necessary truths in the realms of pure mathematics (especially in arithmetic and geometry), logic, metaphysics, ethics, whose 'demonstration can come only from the inner principles which are called innate.'[53] That is to say, some of our knowledge, the knowledge of necessary truths, is innate and *a priori*. Now, what does Leibniz mean by innate knowledge? Does he mean by it a knowledge which we are always conscious of since our birth? He certainly does not mean so, for he clearly says that 'we must not imagine that we can read these eternal laws of reason in the soul as in an open book,.....but it is enough that we can discover these laws in ourselves by means of attention, for which opportunities are furnished by the senses;.....'[54] What Leibniz seems to mean is that the human mind comes to experience prepared and disposed to think in certain ways. Locke, in his doctrine, ignored the essential fact that the mind prior to experience has a nature of its own, and what it comes to know later must be explained partly in terms of this nature. If we neglect the mind itself, we neglect half the explanation of knowledge.

Leibniz further points out that Locke in the opening sections of the second book of his *Essay* admits that the ideas which do not originate in sensation come from reflection, but his account of reflection was superficial. Reflection, according to Leibniz, 'is nothing but an attention to that which is in us, and the senses do not give us what we already bring with us.'[55] Locke would have found answers to many of his difficulties if he had looked into his own mind. He never understood, for instance, how we gain the notion of substance. Leibniz thinks we know it in so far as we are aware of ourselves. In ourselves 'there are being, unity, substance, duration, change, activity, perception, pleasure and thousand other objects of our intellectual

52. Op. cit., footnote 22, p. 362.
53. Op. cit., pp. 363-64.
54. Ibid., p. 364.
55. Op. cit., p. 366.

ideas.'[56] These 'intellectual ideas' are not gained empirically, but by the mind's reflection upon itself. They are inherent in the constitution of our active mind which, having a nature of its own, orders the given of experience in its own way. Our mind, according to Leibniz, is disposed from the outset to think in certain ways and this disposition lies at the root of all subsequent knowledge. We are determined to think thus by our very nature as intellectual beings. The said disposition of the mind is not a custom-bred habit, as Hume would say; it is innate, and *a priori* disposition of the mind itself.

Thus, for Leibniz, there are two kinds of universal concepts: *a priori* and empirical. The former (those of being, unity, substance, etc.) underlie human knowledge as synthesising principles. They, thus, play a most important function in human knowledge. Locke who denied the existence of such innately known principles and tried to derive them from experience, failed to see that they by their very nature cannot be so derived. A question, however, arises: how does Leibniz justify the assumption that *a priori* principles apply to natural world discovered in experience? His answer would be that there is a 'pre-established harmony' between the principles of the mind and the constitution of the natural world. All the rationalists maintain their central position, namely, that the mind of itself can think the truth about the real, only by assuming that, as Spinoza puts, it, 'the order and connection of ideas is the same as the order and connection of things.'[57] But how is this latter assumption itself justified? Any justification they attempt of this assumption rests on a dogmatic metaphysics and Kant is right in maintaining that the assumption is in fact never justified by them.[58] Locke by insisting upon experience for obtaining universal concepts is saved at least from this dogmatic assumption.

56. Loc. cit.
57. *Ethics*, II, prof. 7, Everyman's Library, 1928.

Spinoza also shares in the rationalist protest against the empiricist theory of universals. The universals with which empiricists are concerned are gained by the mind at the level of *Imaginatio*. But there is another level of knowledge namely, *Ratio*, which also has its universals. The former are confused and contingent, while the latter are distinct and necessary. Any account of universals which neglects the latter is incomplete, and empiricism is defective in so far as it attempts to conceive the universals in terms of *Imaginatio* alone. (See *Ethics*, II, prof. 40 note I and II). For a detailed account of Spinoza's position, see Aaron: *The Theory of Universals*, pp. 87 ff.

58. See *Critique of Pure Reason*, tr. N. K. Smith, Macmillan, London, 1963, B9 and B10. Also see Preface to the second edition, B xvi, and B xvii.

Kant, who is a critic of both rationalists and empiricists, it is important to note, reasserts in essentials the Leibnizian protest against the empiricists. All concepts, he holds, are not empirically derived, for 'pure concepts of understanding', which play an important part in our knowledge, are not empirically derived.[59] Kant however, does not give us a detailed account of empirical concepts. In the *Critique* he is wholly concerned with 'pure concepts', such as substance, relation, being, causality, and so on, and what he says of empirical concepts, such as 'dog' 'table', etc., is somewhat incidental. Empirical concepts, he thought, do not require any justification (or 'deduction'), 'since experience is always available for the proof of their objective reality.'[60] But this is not so in the case of pure concepts; in their case a justification of their use in our knowledge is necessary, since they are not derived from experience. It is for this reason that Kant concentrates on the 'Transcendental Deduction' of pure concepts, and as for empirical concepts, he accepts Locke's account of them as products of the act of thought on the material supplied by sense-experience. Kant praises Locke for 'opening a new line of enquiry' into the way we 'advance from particular perceptions to universal concepts.'[61] But he adds that deduction of pure concepts can never be obtained in the manner suggested by Locke, 'for in view of their subsequent employment, which has to be entirely independent of experience, they must be in a position to show a certificate of birth quite other than that of descent from experience.'[62]

It is important to note that, in Kant's view, pure concepts are not only obtained independently of experience, they are also presupposed in the coming into being of empirical concepts. "Experience", he holds, "contains two very dissimilar elements, namely, the 'matter' of knowledge (obtained) from the senses, and a certain 'form' for the ordering of this matter, (obtained) from the inner source of pure intuition and thought which, on occasion of the sense-impressions, are first brought into action and yield concepts."[63] Thus concepts are brought into being only when the 'matter' of the senses is ordered by the 'form' of the understanding, an ordering of the manifold which is essentially what

59. *Critique*, B 127.
60. A 84.
61. A 86, B 119.
62. B 119.
63. A 86.

Kant means by an act of understanding and a judging. Such an act is essential if concepts are to be brought into being, and such an act necessarily involves pure concepts. If the mind did not already know how to order the given in terms of pure concepts, no empirical concept would ever come into being.

Thus Kant's objection against the empiricists is that they ignore pure or *a priori* concepts which are presupposed by all knowledge. He calls these concepts 'categories'[64] and, perhaps more appropriately, as 'keys to possible experience.'[65] In the preface to the second edition of the *Critique*, he says : 'Experience is a species of knowledge which involves understanding, and understanding has rules which I must presuppose as being in me prior to objects being given to me, and therefore as being *a priori*.'[66] A very significant assertion is made here, namely, that pure concepts are rules which are essential for human knowledge. It explains how they are used in understanding and judging. Not only pure concepts, but also empirical concepts, according to Kant, function as rules; 'A concept is always as regards its form, something universal which serves as a rule.'[67] This comes out very clearly in his three-fold analysis of the judgment.[68] A judgment, he says, involves first a synthesis of apprehension in intuition, secondly a synthesis of reproduction in imagination and, thirdly, a synthesis of recognition in a concept. Thus concepts have an important part to play in judging; one should not be able to say, for instance, 'this is a triangle', if he did not already possess the concept of triangle. The concept is a rule by which synthesis of recognition, an essential element of all judgment, becomes possible. This is true, not only of *a priori* concepts, but of empirical concepts also.

The main criticism directed against Kant is that his account of pure concepts is far from clear. He criticises the empiricists for neglecting pure concepts which are fundamental principles of human knowledge, yet he himself does not explain how we come to possess these all-important concepts nor does he make their nature clear. All that he tells us of their origin is that they are not given in sense-experience but are *a priori*. As to their nature, we should not expect to know

64. A 111.
65. A 513, B 370.
66. B xvii.
67. A 106.
68. A 99-106.

much, if anything at all, since they transcend experience. Thus Kant can tell us little about pure concepts and consequently his criticism of the empiricists loses much of its force.[69]

It is true that we do not experience substance, cause, and the rest of the categories directly; yet we possess these notions as guiding principles in ordering our experience. How do we come to possess them? Hume regarded them as custom-bred dispositions which are empirically derived, but are yet part of our being. Leibniz, on the other hand, held that the categories are 'subjective dispositions of thought, implanted in us from the first moment of our existence, and so ordered by our Creator that their employment is in complete harmony with the laws of nature in accordance with which experience proceeds.'[70] Kant rejected both these theories on the ground that they could not possibly explain the necessity and universality of science. Against the Leibnizian theory he observes that "the necessity of the categories, which belongs to their very conception, would then have to be sacrificed. The concept of cause, for instance, which expresses the necessity of an event under a presupposed condition would be false if it rested only on an arbitrary subjective necessity, implanted in us, of connecting certain empirical ideas according to the rules of causal relation. I would not then be able to say that the effect is connected with the cause in the object, that is to say, necessarily, but only that I am so constituted that I cannot think this idea otherwise than thus connected. This is exactly what the sceptic most desires."[71] The categories, according to Kant, are objective and necessary; they have nothing to do with anyone's dispositions, for then they would be subjective. The same criticism would apply to the empiricist theory also. One may be disposed to think in a certain way as the result of his past experience. This gives subjective necessity. But what he needs is objective necessity and this it does not give. Kant thus rejects both the Humean and the Leibnizian theories of disposition.

Yet it is disputed whether Kant has succeeded in showing us the nature of this objectively necessary knowledge which he argues must be there. As Aaron puts it, 'we are left in doubt whether such knowledge does in fact exist, whether, that is to say, the necessity of mathematics is known by *a priori* in sight independently of experi-

69. Cf. Aaron, op. cit., p. 115.
70. B 167.
71. B 168.

ence and whether the other sciences do reveal objective necessity in Kant's sense'.[72] It is further alleged that Kant's analysis of concepts has not been thorough enough. The notion of concepts which occupies a place of supreme importance in his philosophy remains vague, both in regard to empirical as well as pure concepts. Nevertheless, it is true that Kant shared in the rationalist protest against the empiricist theory of universals, inasmuch as he held that there are universals, pure concepts, which are not derived from sense-experience. He accepted the conceptualism of the empiricists (particularly of Locke), but rejected their empiricism so far as pure concepts were concerned.

Kant's view of universals may be compared with that of the Buddhist nominalist. Universals, for both, originate in the understanding. They agree that sense-experience and understanding are two separate sources of knowledge; the one being the source of the knowledge of particulars, and the other being the source of the knowledge of universals. Understanding is acknowledged by both as the faculty which synthesises and reconstructs the 'given' of the sense-experience under its own 'forms' and this synthesis, it is agreed, constitutes our empirical knowledge. Nevertheless, there are important differences between the two. For Kant, universals are of two kinds : *a priori* and empirical. While the former have their source purely in the understanding, the latter, though originating in the understanding, are yet grounded on the resemblances apprehended in sense-experience. For the Buddhist, on the other hand, the distinction of the *a priori* and the empirical does not exist. All universals for him are *a priori* constructions having no objective basis whatsoever. The difference between Kant and the Buddhist in this regard originates from the difference of their views concerning the various faculties of cognition. For Kant, the senses and the understanding are the sources of true knowledge, while Pure Reason is the source of Transcendental Illusion. The Buddhist, though emphasising the difference of the senses and the understanding, does not recognise the difference of the latter from Pure Reason. Consequently, for him, senses alone are the source of true knowledge, and understanding is the source of Transcendental Illusion.

The above difference between the views of Kant and the Buddhist has its roots in their different conceptions of the 'given'. For Kant empirical objects are 'given' in sense-experience, though they are

72. Op cit., p. 117.

once more reconstructed by the understanding in the concept. Such reconstruction does not yield false knowledge, since the 'given' of the sense conforms to the concept of the understanding. For the Buddhist, on the other hand, only the unique particular point-instant is 'given', and all the rest, including the empirical object of Kant, are universals constructed by thought. Further, all thought-constructions (universals and empirical particulars), are negative in nature; they are 'negations of their negations.' The only positive entity is the point-instant. For Kant, the universal concepts of the understanding as well as empirical objects are positive, and the two conform to each other. There is no opposition between sense-experience and understanding. The Buddhist, on the contrary, makes a radical difference between sense-experience and understanding. The former is the knowledge of the real, whereas the latter is the knowledge of imaginary universals. There can be no real conformity between the two. The universal form is imputed to the 'given' of the senses by the understanding; it does not belong to it. The Buddhist contends that if universals originate in thought and not in the sense-experience of the real, then all knowledge involving universals must be illusory. Kant would not agree with this. For him universal concepts, though originating in thought, are yet legitimately applicable in the sphere of sense-experience; an application of them beyond sense-experience, to the things-in-themselves, is, however, illegitimate. The Buddhist, on the contrary, holds that things-in-themselves, the point-instants, being what are 'given' in sense-experience, the application of universal concepts even within the sphere of sense-experience is illegitimate, and such an application yields nothing but illusions. The Buddhist thus makes all empirical knowledge subjective, while Kant tries to safeguard its objectivity.

With the discussion of Kant we conclude our historical investigation on the problem of universals in Western Philosophy. The problem, however, continued to be discussed after Kant, and sometimes at considerable length, but most of the answers given are not essentially different from those we have already examined. Hence, it is not necessary for us to consider in detail the view of each individual philosopher on this problem. It should suffice if we discuss the main issue in this regard in Contemporary Philosophy, namely, the issue between the Philosophy of Universals and the Philosophy of Resemblances. Our historical survey has also revealed that the various theories of universals discussed fall under two broad categories: one holding universals (in some sense) and the other holding resemblances among particulars as the ontological basis of concepts and the usage of words. Some of the Indian Systems, namely, the Jaina and the Viśiṣṭādvaita, have also sought to replace universals by resemblances. Hence, it is important to consider the rival claims of these contending philosophies and make a proper assessment of them.

CHAPTER XIV

UNIVERSALS VERSUS RESEMBLANCES IN CONTEMPORARY PHILOSOPHY

We may begin our discussion by first noting some of the important arguments on the side of universals. For this purpose we propose to consider briefly the views of three contemporary philosophers, namely, Russell, Stout and Moore. It is not that others have nothing significant to say on the side of universals, but that we consider these philosophers as fairly representing the case of universals against the protagonists of resemblances. It will, however, be noted that although these philosophers advocate the reality of universals they do not hold exactly the same view concerning the nature of universals and their relation to particulars.

1. *Russell's Defence of Universals*

Bertrand Russell, to start with, advocates a modified form of Platonism. He holds that except proper names which stand for particulars, all words, substantives, adjectives, prepositions and verbs stand for universals.'[1] Again, he says, 'all truths involve universals, and all knowledge of truths involves acquaintance with universals.'[2] The universals that we know by acquaintance, according to him, are 'sensible qualities, relations of space and time, similarity, and certain abstract logical universals.'[3] Of these the first, he says, cannot be strictly proved if someone denies the existence of such entities as common qualities, but the existence of the universals of relation can be strictly demonstrated.[4]

One might deny, for example, universals 'whiteness' and 'triangularity' (as Berkeley and Hume did) and maintain that anything is white or is a triangle if it has the right sort of resemblance to some

1. *The Problems of Philosophy*, Hume University Library, 1962, p. 93.
2. Loc. cit.
3. Op. cit., p. 109.
4. Op. cit., p. 95.

particular white patch or some particular triangle. 'But then', Russell points out, 'the resemblance required will have to be a universal.' There cannot be different resemblances for each pair of 'white' or 'triangle', 'for then we shall have to say that these resemblances resemble each other, and thus at last we shall be forced to admit resemblance as a universal. The relation of resemblance, therefore, must be a true universal.'[5] And having been forced to admit this universal, Russell argues, there is no point in denying such universals as whiteness and triangularity.[6]

Is it possible to explain away the universal 'similarity' itself ? Russell thinks that it is not possible without being involved in an endless regress. He takes for example two discs of 'red' (not necessarily of exactly the same shade), and two utterances of the word 'red' following the perception of the two discs successively. The two discs of 'red' are similar and so are the two utterances of the word 'red'. Now, are we saying the same thing about the discs and about the utterances when we say the discs are similar and when we say the utterances are similar? Or are we only saying similar things? 'In the former case', Russell says, 'similarity is a true universal; in the latter case, not.' The difficulty in the latter case is the endless regress. We shall say, if we adopt the latter alternative, that the two wholes—the one of the two similar discs of red and the other of the two similar utterances of the word 'red'—are of the same kind, i.e., the two are similar wholes. In this way, we shall try to avoid defining the kind by reference to a universal. But, Russell says, 'I do not see how we are to avoid an endless regress of the vicious kind if we attempt to explain similarity in this way.'[7]

Thus the reality of universals, according to Russell, is undeniable.[8] He emphasises that the being of universals must not be regarded as mental. 'Whatever being belongs to them is independent of being

---

5. Op. cit., p. 96.
6. Op. cit., p. 97. Cf. Russell's *An Inquiry into Meaning and Truth*, Pelican, 1962, p. 325.
7. *Inquiry*, p. 327.
8. In the later phase of his thought Russell was not so sure of the reality of universals as he was in the earlier phase. The following passage from the *Inquiry* is significant: "I conclude, therefore, though with hesitation, that there are universals, and not merely general words. Similarity at least will have to be admitted; and in that case it seems hardly worthwhile to adopt elaborate devices for the exclusion of other universals." Loc. cit.

thought of or in any way apprehended by minds.'[9] He gives the example of the relation 'north of' between Edinburgh and London asserted by the proposition 'Edinburgh is north of London.' This relation is as independent of our knowledge as the two places it relates. We do not cause the truth of the above proposition by coming to know it; on the contrary, we merely apprehend a fact which was there before we knew it. 'The part of earth's surface where Edinburgh stands would be north of the part where London stands, even if there were no human beings to know about north and south, and even if there were no minds at all in the universe.'[10]

Russell, however, admits that the relation 'north of' does not 'exist' in the same sense in which Edinburgh and London exist. "There is no place or time where we can find the relation 'north of'." Hence the relation is radically different from everything that can be apprehended by senses or by introspection. 'It is neither in space nor in time, neither material nor mental; yet it is something'.[11] Russell emphasises that it must not be thought of as an 'idea' or an 'act of thought', for then we shall rob it of its essential character of universality. All acts of thought are necessarily particulars; they differ not only with different individuals, but also with different moments of the mental life of the same individual. Hence 'universals are not thoughts, though, when known, they are the objects of thoughts.'[12] Yet we cannot speak of them as 'existing', since they are not 'in time'. Thoughts and feelings, minds and physical objects exist, but universals do not exist in this sense. They may be said to 'subsist' or have 'being', where 'being' is opposed to 'existence' as 'being timeless.'[13] Thus, for Russell, there are two worlds: the world of being (universals) and the world of existence (particulars). According to one's temperament one may prefer the contemplation of the one or of the other, and consider the one that is not preferred as hardly worthy of being regarded in any sense real. But the truth, according to Russell, is that 'both have the same claim on our impartial attention, both are real, and both are important to the metaphysician.'[14]

9. *Problems*, p. 97.
10. Ibid., pp. 97-98. Cf. *Inquiry*, p. 325.
11. Ibid., p. 98.
12. Ibid., p. 99.
13. Ibid., p. 100, Russell's distinction of 'Existence' and 'being' is similar to the Nyāya distinction of *sattā* and *bhāvatva*. For the Nyāya also universals do not have *sattā* (existence), but they have *bhāvatva* (being).
14. Op. cit., p. 100.

The crucial question, however, is: how are the two worlds, the world of universals and the world of particulars, related? Russell anticipates the question, but does not answer it. If he holds the same view as that of Plato, then all the objections urged against the latter can be urged against his view also.

2. *The Theory of Stout*

G. F. Stout advocates a theory of universals quite different from that of Russell. He denies that there are any common attributes characterising numerically different particulars. 'A character characterising a concrete thing or an individual is as particular as the thing or the individual which it characterises.'[15] All the attributes of a substance are particular, because they are spatially separated from the attributes of other substances. 'The roundness of one ball is locally separate from the roundness, smoothness and whiteness of the other.'[16] Thus, attributes, according to Stout, can occupy space and endure through time. He criticises Russell for calling them spaceless and timeless. He charges that Russell disjoins particulars and universals as two intrinsically independent realms of experience. He finds it possible to do this because for him qualities and relations are, as such universals. In as much as they are universals they cannot in any way form part of the being of the particular things which they qualify or relate.'[17]

Now, if the 'redness' of one flower, for example, is different from the 'redness' of another flower, for they occupy different places, then how do we call both the flowers 'red'? Does not Stout's theory logically involve him in the position of nominalism according to which the universal is merely the name and all that exists is the particular? Stout denies that his theory necessarily lands him in nominalism. He says that although 'agreeing with the nominalist that characters are particulars as the things or substances which they characterise, the inference I draw from the thesis is not that there are really no universals, but that the universal is a distributive unity.'[18] So, for Stout, universals are not mere names; they exist as 'distributive unities'.

15. *Studies in Philosophy and Psychology*, Macmillan, 1930, p. 386.
16. Op. cit., pp. 389-90.
17. Op. cit., pp. 402-3.
18. Op. cit., p. 388.

Now, what does Stout precisely mean by a 'distributive unity'? He certainly does not mean by it an identical character, since, for him, there is no identical character common to different members of the same class. Nor does he mean by it a unity based on resemblance, since resemblance, according to him, cannot be the basis of identity; on the contrary, it presupposes identity. That is to say, resemblance, being a relation, presupposes a complex unity within which the terms 'resembling one another' have any significance.[19] The nominalist, Stout argues, tries to explain a class on the basis of resemblance, but he cannot explain resemblance without presupposing the notion of a class. The class of 'triangles', for example, is said to be based on the resemblance between different figures in certain respect and the respect in which they are said to resemble is nothing but their being 'triangles, i.e. members of the class triangular figures'. "This" Stout argues, "is plainly a vicious circle, when what requires to be explained is precisely the meaning of the words 'class' or 'kind'."[20] Thus, for Stout, the universal, that is, 'distributive unity', is neither an identical character common to numerically different particulars, nor a unity derived from resemblance between them. It is the unity of the class of which particulars are instances. It is a fundamental category presupposed by all classification.

It must, however, be remarked that Stout's notion of the universal as distributive unity is not quite intelligible. It is said to be a unity which is neither an identical quality nor one derived from resemblance. Yet it is a unity binding different particulars into a class. But what precisely is the nature of this unity? Stout can tell us nothing more than that "the distributive unity of a class or kind is an 'ultimate' and unanalysable type of unity."[21] But calling it 'ultimate' does not solve the problem. If the said unity is objective, then it must, it seems, be either an identical character, or a unity based on resemblance. And if it is subjective, then it is not clear how Stout's position can be different from nominalism. It is, however, clear that Stout seeks to avoid nominalism and at the same time safeguard particularity of characters. But in this attempt he makes his theory obscure.

19. "A relation of above and below as subsisting between a and b presupposes a spatial complex including both a and b and the spatial relation between them. In like manner resemblance presupposes a complex unity of the particular type which I call the distributive unity of a class." Op. cit., p. 388.
20. Loc. cit.
21. Op. cit. p. 388.

Further, Stout's contention that all the features characterising a concrete thing are particulars also does not seem to be true. If it were true, then we could not assert of two things A and B that both are 'red', or both are 'round'. Stout holds that a character belonging to a concrete thing is absolutely particular. But how can he prove it without being dogmatic about it, that is, without asserting *a priori* that it must be so. Certainly no empirical procedure can be suggested for ascertaining that a character belonging to a concrete thing is absolutely particular, i.e., it belongs to no other thing in the universe. It is, however, logically possible that it is absolutely particular, but the possibility to the contrary cannot logically be denied. Hence, even if a character belonging to a concrete thing is, as a matter of fact, absolutely particular, yet Stout cannot logically assert that it is so. And if he asserts that it must be so, he is certainly in the wrong. Moreover, we do observe identical colours and identical shapes recurring over and over again. This evidence of experience is too strong to be rejected.

The main argument of Stout in favour of his contention is that, since two concrete things, say A and B, are 'locally separate', the specific characters belonging to the one must also be 'locally separate' from those belonging to the other. From this he infers that the specific characters belonging to A cannot be identical with the specific characters belonging to B. This inference, as G.E. Moore points out, is not logically justifiable.[22] Even if it be true that the characters belonging to two locally separate things are locally separate, it does not follow that they are not identical. Stout obviously assumes that there is no distinction between the sense in which two concrete things are 'locally separate' and that in which two characters can be said to be so, and this assumption seems to be wrong.[23] So far as concrete things are concerned, Stout's contention may be admitted. It is impossible for a self-identical thing to be locally separate from itself, i. e., to be in two different places at the same time. But when we speak of two qualities as 'locally separate', we seem to be using the phrase in an entirely different sense. All that we mean, or can mean,

22. *Philosophical Papers*, George Allen and Unwin, 1969, p. 25.
23. "I deny", says Moore, "that any two characters can ever be 'locally separate' in the sense in which two concrete things can be, or 'temporally separate' in the sense in which two events can be." Op. cit., p. 26.

by it is that the one belongs to a concrete thing which is locally separate (in the first sense) from a concrete thing to which the other belongs. And in this sense of 'locally separate', two qualities which are locally separate, may be identical. As Moore says "with this sense of 'locally separate', it seems to me perfectly obvious that a quality can be 'locally separate' from itself; one and the same quality can be in two different places at the same time."[24] Thus there being absolutely no reason to suppose (as Stout does) that two characters are locally separate in the same sense in which two concrete things are, Stout's contention that all characters are particulars is not logically justifiable.

3. *Moore's Analysis*

Now, what is Moore's own conception of universals?[25] We may begin by noting that Moore distinguishes between three main types of universals: (1) relations, (2) relational properties and (3) non-relational properties.[26] The first is exemplified by such relations as 'being a member of', 'being at a distance from', etc. These relations are universals because they hold identically in innumerable cases. The examples of the second type of universals are such properties as 'being a member of a certain group', 'being at a distance from some one or the other thing', etc.[27] To these Moore adds such properties as 'being white', 'being of a shade of white', etc.[28] All these relational properties are universals because they belong identically to several things at the same time. The third type of universals are exemplified by such properties as 'being two', 'being three', etc. which belong to groups of things in a non-relational way. To these may be added such properties as 'being a shade of white', 'being pure white', etc. which also belong to white shades in a non-relational manner.[29] All these three types of universals, according to Moore, are real, because they

24. Op. cit., p. 25.
25. Moore elaborates his view of universals in his work, '*Some Main Problems of Philosophy*', Chapters XVII to XX. But later on he realised that some of the things he said there were mistaken and, therefore, he wrote an Appendix in which he corrected those mistakes. We shall discuss Moore's view in the light of these corrections.
26. '*Some Main Problems of Philosophy*', George Allen and Unwin, 1953. p. 369.
27. See op. cit., pp. 312, 320 and 323.
28. See Appendix, p. 378.
29. See op. cit., pp. 368-69, and Appendix, pp. 374, 378.

are discovered by us in the external world. Of these the universals which are properties, either relational or non-relational, belong to things, but this is not so in the case of the universals of relation. 'The relation', Moore says, 'does not belong to anything whatever in the sense in which this property does; it merely relates two things to one another.' The relation, as a matter of fact, holds 'between' the things it relates.[30]

Moore has made above certain important distinctions which are noteworthy. In the first place, relations are distinguished from relational properties because they are presupposed by the latter. The relational property of 'being at a distance from A', for example, presupposes the relation 'at a distance from' which cannot be identical with it.[31] The second distinction made by Moore is between the various determinate shades of a colour and the colour itself; for example, between the various shades of white—pure white, creamy white, bluish white — and the colour white. The various shades of white are, as a matter of fact, different colours, and are not colours in the same sense in which, e.g., 'white', 'blue', 'red', etc. are colours.[32] The difference consists in this : Things having a particular shade of white, say creamy white, exactly resemble one another in respect of that shade, whereas things included in the class of 'white' do not so resemble, for they belong to different shade-groups of white. That is to say, the colours 'pure white', 'creamy white', etc. are identical qualities, while the colour 'white' obviously is not an identical quality. The same holds true in the case of all qualities whatsoever.

The above consideration leads Moore to the third distinction, namely, the distinction between 'being white' and 'being of a shade of white.' The former means being related to one or the other shade of white, whereas the latter means being related to an identical shade of white. Nevertheless, both are relational properties, since, according to Moore, "the colours only belong to sense-data in the sense of having a certain relation to them; but, of course, the relational properties of having those colours or being of those colours 'belong' in quite a different sense."[33] That is to say, a colour belongs to a sense-

30. Op. cit. p. 325.
31. Op. cit., p. 312.
32. Op. cit., p. 376.
33. Op. cit., Appendix, p. 378.

data in a relational sense, while the property of 'being of that colour' belongs to it in a non-relational sense. The reason why Moore holds this is quite obvious. If the relational property of 'being white', for example, belonged to white things in a relational sense, then the relational property of having that relational property will also belong to it in a relational sense, and so on *ad infinitum*. Hence, all relational properties must be held to belong to things in a non-relational sense.

The fourth important distinction made by Moore is between the property of 'being white', or 'being of a shade of white' and that of 'being a white', or 'being a shade of white.' The former belongs only to things, or sense-data, and not to the colour white, while the latter belongs only to colours (determinate shades of white) and not to things, or sense-data. The former is a relational property, while the latter is a non-relational property. The latter is an instance of the universal of the third type.[34] It is clear from this that, for Moore, having an identical quality is a relational property, for a quality can only be related to a thing, but being that identical quality is not a relational property, for it does not consist in having a relation to anything else.

With reference to those philosophers who hold that there are no universals but only resemblances of different degrees, Moore says that the notion of resemblance requires a careful examination. In the first place, it must be asked: what is the property peculiar and common to all patches, e.g., of white, by virtue of which they are all called 'white'? The answer from the side of the resemblance theory would be that certain patches of colour are called 'white' because they closely resemble a patch of, say, pure white. So the property peculiar and common to all white patches is the property of closely resembling a patch of pure white. But this, Moore says, does not really give us the property common to all white patches, for it excludes the particular pure white patch which is chosen as a standard. The property of closely resembling a pure white patch is indeed peculiar and common to all white patches except the pure white patch taken as a standard, for 'that particular white patch does not resemble itself; it is itself'.[35] The same difficulty arises if we consider the patches of an

34. Loc. cit.
35. Op. cit., p. 333.
"Resemblance is a relation which a thing cannot certainly have to itself; it is a relation which can hold between two different things—things which are, at least, numerically different—are two." Op. cit., p. 334.

identical shade of white, say pure white. If we try to define their peculiar and common property in terms of resemblance, we would say that all those patches which exactly resemble a particular patch of pure white, say A, are pure white. But the property of 'exactly resembling' A, though common to all the other patches of pure white, does not belong to A, for A is not exactly similar to itself; it is itself.[36] Hence, the resemblance theory, according to Moore, fails to give us the required common property in both the cases we have considered.

Another objection which is frequently raised against the resemblance theory is that resemblance always involves a common property. When we say that two things resemble one another, what we mean by this is always merely that they have some property in common. And if resemblance thus consists in the possession of a common property, then it is quite plain that the common property in question cannot consist in resemblance. We are thus forced to recognise a universal. Moore thinks that this objection cannot be pushed too far. There may be a kind of resemblance which does not consist in the possession of a common property. This comes out very clearly if we consider the class of patches of all colours. What is the property peculiar and common to all patches of colours, which distinguishes them from everything else in the universe? It seems clearly impossible to distinguish such a property, apart from a relational property based on resemblance. Hence, we must admit a kind of resemblance which is 'immediate' and 'internal', that is, one which does not consist in the possession of a common property. "We might say that every patch of colour has to every other a relation, called likeness, which nothing else in the universe has to them, and that this is a relation which does not consist in the possession of any common property."[37]

But the real difficulty in the resemblance theory, according to Moore, arises when we try to define the property peculiar and common to all patches of colours, or patches of a particular colour, in terms of the resemblance between them. As has already been shown, the resemblance theory fails to define the property peculiar and common to all patches of white or all patches of a particular shade of white. In the same way, it fails also to define the property

36. Op. cit., p. 350.
37. Op. cit., p. 365.

peculiar and common to all patches of colours. If we say that the property peculiar and common to all patches of colours is that of having some sort of resemblance to a particular patch of colour, then it obviously leaves out the particular patch of colour which we have chosen as a standard. It is not, therefore, a property common to all patches of colours. Moore suggests that this difficulty may be got over if we accept that the property peculiar and common to all patches of colours, or all patches of a particular colour, is a 'disjunctive property'.[38] That is to say, the property peculiar and common to all patches of colours is that of either being in some degree similar to an arbitrarily chosen patch of colour, or being that patch of colour. Similarly, the property peculiar and common to all patches of white is that of either being similar to an arbitrarily chosen patch of white, or being that patch of white.

One might, however, object that the disjunctive property cannot be regarded as a common property at all. It only means that one of the members of a class fulfils one condition and the rest fulfil the other condition. It is as if we should say that the only property which belongs to every member of human race and to nothing else is the disjunctive property of being either man or woman. Moreover, there is always an arbitrary element in choosing the particular patch which all others are said to resemble. Two persons might choose different patches of white as standards and, consequently, what they mean by 'white' would not be the same. Moore admits that these are serious objections to the theory of disjunctive property. Nevertheless, he says, 'I am inclined to think that this may be the true solution.'[39] But the acceptance of disjunctive property, according to Moore, does not constitute the acceptance of a new kind of universal. It being a relational property, is a universal of the second type.[40]

Moore thus holds that the resemblance theory logically leads to the acceptance of a relational universal, namely, the disjunctive common property. Universals are, therefore, inescapable. He severely criticises those philosophers who hold that universals are 'the work of the mind.' "I only want to say that I cannot see any shadow of reason for it."[41] This mistaken view about universals, according to

38. Op. cit., p. 363.
39. Op. cit., p. 365.
40. Op. cit., p. 339.
41. Op. cit., p. 370.

Moore, arises due to the confusion between two different things, viz., the act of thought and the object of thought. The act of thought is, of course, something dependent on the mind, but the object thought of, e.g. number two or the relation of resemblance, is not so dependent. As soon as this distinction is realised, there remains no reason to suppose that these objects of thought are 'the work of the mind'. "It becomes plainly quite possible that there should have been two things in the universe, and two things which resembled one another, before there was any mind at all."[42]

Moore admits that all universals are, in a sense, 'abstractions', or they are 'abstract things'. But it is wrong to suppose, as some philosophers have done, that universals, for this reason, are 'the work of the mind'. Indeed, 'abstraction' is a psychological process by which we become aware of universals. So, 'it is our awareness of them which is the product of the process; not the universals themselves.'[43] Moore points out further that it is not possible to define abstraction itself without reference to universals. "What we mean by abstraction is just the process by which we first learn to distinguish universals, and there is no other way of defining it."[44] Hence, to suppose that universals, being abstractions, are unreal, that they are hardly better than pure fictions like 'griffins' and 'chimaeras', is, according to Moore, a grossly mistaken notion about them. Some philosophers (e.g. Russell) make a distinction between 'existence' and 'being', and hold that particulars alone have 'existence', while universals have only 'being'. Even if this distinction be valid, Moore says, it is not so important as the distinction between the things which do have being and those which do not have it, are purely imaginary and do not belong to the universe at all. It is this distinction which underlines the distinction between truth and falsehood. And it is this fundamental distinction which is overlooked by those who hold that universals, being abstractions, are pure fictions. If we fix in our mind clearly the sense in which there are no such things as 'griffins' or 'chimaeras', then it would seem quite plain that universals are not in any way to be classed with them. It would seem, on the contrary, that "there is the most fundamental difference in the universe between the two, a difference

42. Op. cit., p. 371.
43. Loc. cit.
44. Loc. cit.

ever so much more important than that which separates universals from particulars."[45]

4. *The Protagonists of Resemblance*

We have considered above some important arguments for the Philosophy of Universals. Let us now consider the arguments for the Philosophy of Resemblances. We have already considered the theories of Locke and Hume who sought to replace universals by resemblances. The modern Philosophy of Resemblances is only a development of their views. According to modern empiricists, the problem of universals like every other metaphysical problem arises entirely from erroneous view about language. The superstitious belief from which arises the notion of universals is: all words are names; so general or abstract words must be the names of general or abstract entities. The Philosophy of Universals, it is alleged, abolishes the distinction between general words and proper names. This the Philosophy of Resemblances repudiates.[46] According to the Resemblance. Theory a general word is the name of anyone of a group of objects, not the name of a specific entity or property common to all those objects. There is no ground whatever, it is argued, for treating a general word as if it were a proper name. The word 'red' for example, is not the name of any entity common to all red objects; it is the name of anyone of the red objects. As Quine puts it, "One may admit that there are red houses, roses and sunsets, but deny, except as a popular and misleading manner of speaking, that they have anything in common....There is not, in addition, any entity whatever, individual or otherwise which is named by the word 'redness', nor, for that matter, by the word 'household', 'rosehood', 'sunsethood'. That the houses and roses and sunsets are all of them red may be taken as ultimate and irreducible."[47]

It might be urged by the realist that the predicates such as 'red', etc. must be regarded as names each of a single universal entity in order that they may be meaningful at all. This, Quine holds, is a baseless assumption. Russell's theory of 'Descriptions', he points out,

45. Op. cit., p. 373.
46. See Woozley, A. D. : '*Theory of Knowledge*', Hutchison's University Library, London, 1949, pp. 92-93. Also see Morris Lazerowitz : '*The Structure of Metaphysics*', Routledge and Kegan Paul, London, 1955. p. 191.
47. W. V. O. Quine : '*From a Logical Point of View*', Harward University Press, 1953, p. 10.

has shown that we might use words and phrases meaningfully without supposing the existence of entities allegedly named by them.[48] "We need no longer labour under the delusion that meaningfulness of a statement containing a singular term presupposes an entity named by the term. A singular term need not name to be significant."[49] The realist might again urge that even if it be granted that there is distinction between meaning and naming, and that general words are not names of attributes, still it must be admitted that they have meanings. And these meanings, whether they are named or not, are still universals, and some of them might even be attributes. Quine counters this argument by refusing to accept 'meanings'. He holds that there are no 'meanings', but words and sentences which are 'meaningful.'[50] Meaningfulness does not consist in having some abstract entity as meaning. "The fact that a given linguistic utterance is meaningful (or significant, as I prefer to say so as not to invite hypothesis of meanings as entities) is an ultimate and irreducible fact."[51] Thus, according to Quine, we can use singular terms or predicates in our sentences without assuming the singular and abstract entities which they purport to name. Also we need not assume a realm of entities called 'meanings' in order to understand the significance or meaningfulness of an utterance.[52]

According to Wittgenstein also, we are trapped by the noun form of the "meaning of a word" and are thus led to assume that meanings are entities. We "think of meaning as a thing of the same kind as the word, though also different from the word. Here the word, there the meaning." If a philosopher asks 'what is meaning?', we feel we ought to be able to point to something. "We are up against one of the great sources of philosophical bewilderment; we try to find a substance for the substantive."[53] Now, it is true that many substantives do have a naming function, e.g. proper names, like 'John' and general names, like 'chair', (though amongst these there are important differences).

---

48. For a detailed discussion on this point see Quine, op. cit., pp. 5-9. For Russell's theory of Descriptions see '*The Problems of Philosophy*', Ch. V. Also see Stebbing, L. S.: '*A Modern Introduction to Logic*', Methuen, London, 1950, pp. 145 ff.
49. Op. cit., pp. 8-9.
50. Op. cit., p. 11.
51. Loc. cit.
52. For a detailed discussion on this point see Quine, op. cit., pp. 12 ff and 72 ff.
53. See Alice Ambrose: *Wittgenstein on Universals* in *Metaphysics*, ed. by W. E. Kennick and Morris Lazerowitz, Prentice-Hall Inc., New Jercy, p. 87.

But not all words stand for things that can be pointed to, that is to say, "it is part of their grammar that they cannot be explained by pointing to something. 'Meaning' is such a word. Yet there is a great propensity upon hearing the substantive 'meaning' to think of it as naming an ethereal entity." To break up this spell Wittgenstein urges speaking, not of the meaning of words, but of the use of words. The advantage of this replacement is that 'use' carries with it no suggestion of an object corresponding to a word.[54]

Now, if there are no common features corresponding to words, how do we make successful use of them? Wittgenstein answers that we make use of general words and decide whether an object is of a certain sort, not by discovering an identical feature (or complex of identical features), but by discovering something vague, something which he calls 'family resemblances'. By this phrase he means the vague and overlapping likenesses which one sees between the different members of a family. He gives the example of what we call 'games', meaning by it 'board-games', 'card-games', 'ball-games'. 'Olympic games', and so on. "What", he asks, "is common to them all?—Don't say: 'there must be something common, or they would not be called games'—but look and see whether there is anything common to all. For if you look at them you will not see something that is common to all, but similarities, relationships and a whole series of them at that."[55] It is hard to discover a universal which is exactly the same in each of its instances, so that they are different only numerically and not qualitatively. We classify particulars according as they resemble each other, and it is very seldom that the particulars we classify together exactly resemble each other. It is also very seldom that the particulars we classify together are totally different from other particulars which we do not classify with them. Very often we have to decide by decree of convention about border-line cases. This shows that the world is not a neat and tidy place, sharply divided into compartments as the philosophy of universals assumes. We classify

---

54. See Alice Ambrose, op. cit., pp. 87, 88.
55. *Philosophical Investigations*, Tr. G. E. M. Anscombe, Basil Blackwell, Oxford, 1953, Part I, 66.
Cf. "The fact with regard to abstract words is that they are applicable to each of a number of things because the things resemble each other more or less, without there being anything common to all of them to set exact application of words." Lazerowitz, op. cit., p. 96.

objects into groups and give them a common designation (a) according to their degree of likeness and unlikeness, and (b) according to our decision where and how to limit membership of the group.[56] Thus, the Philosophy of Resemblances, it is claimed, is clearer and closer to facts.

The philosophy of Universals will agree that the objects characterised by a universal do resemble each other, but it would maintain that resemblance is always derivative; it is a consequence of the fact that the same universal characterises all the objects. The Philosophy of Resemblances would deny this. It would maintain that resemblance can be underivative. It would point out that the above view of resemblance involves a serious flaw: it leaves no room for inexact resemblances. Resemblances have degrees of intensity and cannot be treated as if degreeless—either present in its maximum degree or else not present at all. Two coins may be exactly alike in their shape, if so, one may say that the very same shape, say round, is present in both of them and resemblance is based on this. But what about an apple and an orange? They certainly resemble each other in shape, but not exactly. So, there is no identical shape present in them both upon which the resemblance could be based. Resemblance here seems to be ultimate and underivative. The philosophy of universals, it is argued, fails to provide any room for the important and familiar notion of the degree of instantiation.[57]

The protagonists of universals, as we have noted, have advanced two main objections against the resemblance theory: (1) Resemblance is always resemblance 'in respect of', so it invariably involves reference to a universal, and (2) resemblance itself is a relational universal, a universal of a special kind. How does the resemblance theory meet these objections? To the first objection Woozley replies that although it is true that if two objects are similar to each other there must be some respect in which they are similar, it is not true that this respect is an additional something common to both, i.e., a universal. Red

56. Cf. Woozley, op. cit., pp. 82 and 93.
Referring to the Platonist's attempt to state the boundaries of a concept by an exact definition, Wittgenstein says "Can you give a boundary? No. You can draw one; for none has so far been drawn....... The boundary will never entirely coincide with the actual usage, as this usage has no sharp boundary." Quoted by Alice Ambrose, op. cit., p. 89.
57. Cf. Price, H. H., '*Thinking and Experience*', Hutchison, London, 1953, pp. 17-18.

objects, for example, are to be called 'red' because they resemble each other in respect of being red, that is, there is a similarity between the red of the one and the red of the other, and the similarity might be anything from being virtually exact to being only approximate and generic. This similarity, it is held, is 'a fundamental and not further analysable relation.'[58] One might argue that if similarity between two reds can be exact, then it amounts to the admission of identity, a universal. Woozley replies that there is no harm in it 'as long as we are clear that what we mean is that one is exactly like the other.' There is harm in it if we think that the identity of two reds is analogous to the identity of an individual. It is, therefore, preferable to say not that the red of the one is identical with the red of the other, but that it is exactly like it.[59]

The Philosophy of Resemblances may answer the above objection in another way. It may maintain that resemblance is always 'resemblance towards' and not resemblance 'in respect of.' It is resemblance towards certain standard objects or exemplars. Both the philosophies agree that there is a class of, e.g., red objects, but they differ in their conceptions of this class. According to the Philosophy of Universals all members of the class are instances of the same universal 'redness'. But according to Philosophy of Resemblances the structure of class is more complicated. Every class has an inner ring of key members consisting of a small number of standard objects, or exemplars. The exemplar of a class of red objects might be a certain tomato A, a certain brick B and certain post-box C. Then a red object is any object which resembles A, B and C as closely as A, B and C resemble one another. Similarly, the exemplars of the class of coloured objects might be a summer sky, a lemon, a post-box and a lawn. These resemble one another though not very closely. Accordingly, the class of coloured objects consists of everything which resembles these four exemplars as closely as they resemble each other. In the same way all classes can be explained without assuming universals.[60]

In reply to the second objection, namely, that resemblance itself is a universal, the advocates of the resemblance theory point out that the objection really begs the question. It assumes, what it ought to

58. See Woozley, op. cit., pp. 97-98.
59. Op. cit., p. 98.
60. See Price, op. cit., pp. 20-21.

prove, that resemblance being admittedly a general word it must stand for a universal, whereas this is the very question at issue. "The criticism", Woozley says, "seems to assume the principle that if A is similar to B and B is similar to C, then both similarities must be the same, and consequently that both are instances of a universal similarity. But this is to take advantage of an ambiguity in 'same'."[61] We must distinguish, he says, between two usages of the word 'same' If, for instance, A, B and C are blue objects of different shades, then, according to usage (i) which does not provide for the difference of shades, we say that they are all of the same colour, and following this usage we say that similarity between A and B is the 'same' as the similarity between B and C. But, according to usage (ii) which provides for the difference of shades, we do not say that they are all of the same colour, and , consequently, we do not say that the similarity between A and B is the same as the similarity between B and C. Again, in usage (i) when we say that the similarity between A and B is the same as the similarity between B and C, all that we mean, according to Woozley, is that 'A and B and C are like each other in being blue; and therefore that the similarities are the same does not entail that they are instances of a universal similarity'. And in usage (ii) 'the similarities are not the same, and that they are not the same also does not entail they are instances of a universal similarity'.[62]

It is further pointed out that the objection that similarity must be a universal overlooks the fact that similarities are of different orders. Two cats A and B are similar to each other and two sounds C and D also are similar to each other. These are 'first-order' similarities. But it is also true that the two cat-similarity 'is similar to' the two sound-similarity and 'is similar to' many other similarities too. This is the 'second-order' similarity. In virtue of this second-order similarity, a similarity between similarities, we may apply the same general word to both of them, and the word we happen to use for this purpose is the word 'similarity,' or 'resemblance,' in the second-order sense.[63]

There is nothing wrong or unintelligible, according to the resemblance theory, in the notion of second-order resemblance. And if the advocates of universals say that there is, then the same may be held against their theory also. It can be argued that 'universality' must

61. Op. cit., p. 100.
62. Op. cit., pp. 100-101.
63. See Price, op. cit., pp. 24-25.

itself be a universal; since the word 'universal' is a general word like the word 'man', so, according to the Philosophy of Universals, there must be a universal called 'universality' corresponding to it. And if it is a universal, then the infinite regress argument directed against the resemblance theory would apply to the theory of universals also. Again, there will be another anomaly; if 'universality' is a universal, then it must logically be an instance of itself. But this will be a contradiction, for according to the theory of universals, anything that is an instance of a universal is *ipso facto* a particular and not a universal. To get out of these difficulties the Philosophy of Universals too must introduce the notion of 'different orders'. The word 'universal', it has to say, stands for a second-order universal whereas the words red, man, etc. stand for first-order ones. That is to say, 'universality' can be called a 'universal' only in a second-order sense.[64]

The Philosophy of Resemblances in this manner vindicates its stand that generalisation and use of words can be explained on the basis of discovered resemblances amongst particulars without assuming identical properties, or universals. One of the main criticisms of the theory of universals made by the advocates of resemblances was that the notion of universals arises from a linguistic confusion, a confusion between general words and proper names. This criticism seems to be quite unjustified. The Philosophy of Universals seems to be as natural a result of reflections about what things are as the Philosophy of Resemblances is. It is quite misleading to suggest that, for one who believes in universals, there is no distinction between a general word and a proper name. The issue between the two philosophies is not one of how words are to be classified, but how resemblances of characters are to be understood. The contrast between general words and proper names itself can be made only if we have settled already what they mean, and this in turn can be settled only by considering whether there are any identities among things to refer to, or only resemblances.

Another criticism of the theory of universals made by the advocates of resemblances was that it has no room for inexact resemblances, since it holds that all resemblance is derivative. The Philosophy of Universals does have an answer to this criticism, whether this answer is considered to be satisfactory or not. It meets the objection by

64. Cf. Price, op. cit., p. 25.

distinguishing between *determinable* and *determinate* universals. 'Colouredness', for example, is a determinable universal and 'redness' a determinate one. 'Redness', again, is a sub-determinable having under it the determinates, such as being 'scarlet', 'brick-red', etc.[65] Thus, in the case of an inexact resemblance, say, between A and B, we can say that both have the same determinable, if not the same determinate, universal. By this expedient the Philosophy of Universals maintains its thesis that all resemblances, including inexact ones, are derivative and not ultimate.[66]

5. *Concluding remarks*

Now, what conclusions are we to draw from the controversy between the Philosophy of Universals and the Philosophy of Resemblances? It is plain that both cover the same facts and answer the same questions, though in different ways. The problem they seek to answer is : how it is that we can (indeed, must) experience in terms of kinds and generality, that we form concepts, that we develop language for communication. The Philosophy of Universals answers that experience, thought and language become possible because there are universals in the external world. The Philosophy of Resemblances, on the other hand, answers that there are no discoverable universals; what we discover in the world are resemblances of various degrees, and it is on these resemblances that experience, thought and language depend. We have already indicated that a satisfactory solution of the problem cannot be found exclusively in any one philosophy. The truth seems to lie in both and we may briefly state what we consider to be the true solution of the problem.

It must be said in the first place that we undoubtedly discover recurrences in the world. The same quality, the same relation, the same number are repeated over and over again in our experience. This specific white of the writing paper, for example, is a universal, for it is identically repeated in so many instances. Similarly, the relations, e.g. of 'being side by side', 'inside of', etc., are universals, for they obtain identically in innumerable cases. In the same way, numbers two, three, etc., are universals recurring in innumerable groups of twos, threes and so on. The Philosophy of Resemblances

65. This corresponds to the Nyāya distinction of '*para*' and '*apara*' *sāmānya*.
66. Cf. Price, op. cit., pp. 27-28.

tries to replace these discovered identities by resemblances. It maintains that when we say that two shades are identical what is really the case that they are exactly similar to each other. But what does exact similarity mean? It seems we must distinguish between two cases of exact similarity. Two coins may be exactly alike in all respects, yet they are not identical. Exact similarity in such cases does not mean identity; it is compatible with numerical diversity. But in the case of qualities, relations and numbers, exact similarity means identity, and diversity means dissimilarity. If two hues, or two relations, are exactly alike, i.e., if they are not discernible, they are not two, but one.[67] That is to say, a self-identical thing cannot be in two places at the same time; but this is not true of qualities and relations, for these can be, or are really found to be, in two places at the same time.

The protagonists of resemblance theory might argue that the so called identical qualities and relations are not really identical but only apparently so. The evidence in their favour being wholly empirical, it is not infallible. It is conceivable that the qualities which we perceive to be identical may in reality be different, and the difference may be so minute that we human beings cannot perceive them. But this takes the resemblance theory into a most controversial field. It is now assuming the difference between what appears and what is real. Although a direct disproof of this assumption is impossible, yet this makes the position of the resemblance theory fundamentally weak. For, in the first place, just as it is conceivable that there are no identical qualities and relations in reality, so it is conceivable that there are. In the second place, the empirical evidence points to the existence of identical qualities and relations. To deny their existence would be closing one's eyes to the facts for the sake of the theory. Logically the resemblance theory would lead to the view that nature never repeats itself either in quality or in relation, and this is a position contrary to experience.

But all that our argument proves, or purports to prove, is that there are identical qualities and relations in the world we experience. It does not prove, nor seeks to prove, that there are absolute identities in the non-experienced, or the transcendental, world. The question whether there are such identities is irrelevant for our purpose. What

67. Cf. Wisdom, John, *Problems of Mind and Matter*, Cambridge University Press, 1934, p. 208. Also see Brand Blanshard, *Reason and Analysis*, George Allen and Unwin, 1962, p. 395.

we seek to know is whether there are identical qualities and relations in the experienced world, which provide a foundation for our generalisations and use of general words. And it seems there is sufficient evidence to affirm that there are.

So the Philosophy of Universals seems to score over the Philosophy of Resemblances so far as the existence of identical qualities and relations is concerned. But the resemblance theory also has its strong points. The strength of this theory lies in the assertion that in many cases our generalisations are based on the observation of resembling qualities and in the denial that we can generalise only when we have observed an identical quality. We have argued in more than one place that many of our generalisations are not based on the discovery of identical quality or qualities possessed by all the members of a class. For example, in the case of the class of blue objects, or the class of human beings or chairs, one cannot discover an identical quality common to the whole class. These classes and the corresponding usage of words seem to be based on observed resemblances which do not involve any identical quality. Indeed, we should distinguish between two kinds of resemblances; the one that involves an identical quality, and the one that does not. A class may be constituted on the basis of resemblance which involves an identical quality, e.g., the class of scarlet red objects. But a class may also be constituted on the basis of resemblance which does not involve any identical quality, e.g., the class of colours, or human beings, or animals. In other words, a concept or a word does not necessarily require an identity in the objects which it applies to; it is sufficient that there is some degree of resemblance between all the objects which satisfy a given concept. That is to say, resemblance, at least in some cases, may be ultimate and unanalysable.[68]

Russell has argued against the resemblance theory that even if it rejects all abstract universals, it must admit at least one universal, namely, the universal 'resemblance', in order to avoid infinite regress. And if it admits the existence of one such universal, then, there can

68. Cf. "Classes need not be based on identity, and are not destroyed by its removal. A class based upon similarity to a given character is as good a class as any other, and as truly existent in nature....... The classes of living beings, constituted as they are by numberless resemblances, and standing into each other on all sides, answer in fact to the resemblance theory more nearly than to its rival."
Brand Blanshard, op. cit., p. 417.

be no objection in principle to the existence of others. We have noted the answer given by the resemblance theory to this objection. It seems that two kinds of resemblances must be distinguished; (i) Resemblances between particulars constituting a class, say, 'blue', or 'man', or 'chair'; and (ii) resemblance between resemblances constituting different classes. In the first case it seems resemblance, like identical qualities and relations, is a recurrent feature and, in this sense, a universal. Instead of saying that resemblances between different shades of blue, or different individual human beings, are similar, it seems more correct to say that these resemblances are recurrent features on the basis of which we classify things and qualities, and designate them with a common name. Similar qualities, similar shapes, similar situations constantly recur in our experience. The recurrence of these similarities is as useful a basis for classification as is the recurrence of identical qualities and relations. Here too are universals. It is, of course, not easy to identify them as in the case of identical qualities and relations. They are recurring likenesses empirically observed and consciously used for classification and ordering of our experience.

It may be objected that we should have to distinguish between different kinds of resemblances corresponding to different general terms. For every general term we should have to admit a specific kind of resemblance. So, would it not be better to admit an objective universal corresponding to each term rather than admit all these resemblances?[69] We have already suggested an answer to this objection. It is not a question of what we should admit, rather it is the question of what we discover. Certainly, what we admit should not conflict with what we discover. The terminology of universals is undoubtedly elegant and free from the clumsiness which the terminology of resemblances involves. By distinguishing between determinable and determinate universals the Philosophy of Universals offers a very neat account of classification and generalisation. But do we discover in the external world what are called determinable and sub-determinable universals? The answer seems to be negative. So, the distinction of determinable and determinate universals, though elegant from the point of view of terminology, does not solve the ontological question as to what there is in the external world

69. See Ewing, A. C., *The Fundamental Questions of Philosophy*, Routledge and Kegan Paul Ltd., London, 1953, p. 213.

corresponding to the general terms which we use. From the point of view of what we discover in the external world the Philosophy of Resemblances seems to give a more cogent account of what the Philosophy of Universals calls 'determinable' universals. We may, however, use the terminology of universals for the sake of convenience, and there is no harm so long as we keep in mind that the universals corresponding to such terms as 'red', 'man', 'tree', 'colour', etc. are recurring similarities and not recurring identities.

With regard to the second kind of resemblance, namely, the resemblance between resemblances constituting various classes, the Philosophy of Resemblances has explained that it is not a universal as alleged, but resemblance of a second-order. By this explanation it answers the charge of infinite regress levelled against it by Russell. Resemblance between resemblances is not of the same order of which resemblance between particulars is. In our terminology, it is not a recurrent similarity, but resemblance between recurrent similarities. By virtue of this second-order resemblance we use one and the same word 'resemblance' for different resemblances. Also, we use the same word 'resemblance' for this second-order resemblance not in the sense in which we use it for resemblances among particulars, but in a second-order sense. This explanation is certainly complicated, but there is nothing unintelligible about it. Even in the Philosophy of Universals the notion of 'second-order' has to be used. All general terms, in this philosophy, correspond to universals in things. So, the term 'universal' must correspond to a universal in universals, say, to 'universality' Now, this latter has to be a second-order universal in order to avoid infinite regress. Also, if 'universality' is regarded as one amongst universals there will be self-contradiction, for then we will have to say that it is its own instance, i.e., both universal and particular. The term 'universal' can be used for 'universality', only in the second-order sense. It is for this reason that the Nyāya does not call 'universality' (*jātitva*) a universal (*jāti*) at all. It calls it *upādhi* in order to avoid confusion between it and the universals residing in things. So we can call resemblance between recurring resemblances as 'resemblance' in the second-order sense, or, if we choose the Nyāya terminology, we may call it an *upādhi* corresponding to the word 'resemblance', as universality (*jātitva*) is an *upādhi* corresponding to the word 'universal'

Finally it must be pointed out that the Philosophy of Resemblances, like the Philosophy of Universals, is an ontological doctrine. It has been used, as we have seen, as the starting-point of the epistemological doctrines of conceptualism and nominalism, just as the Philosophy of Universals has been used as the starting-point of the realist epistemology. The Philosophy of Resemblances would aver that resemblances observed in nature are not subjective; they are there, have been there and will be there even if no one is there to think and speak of them. Thought and language depend upon the apprehension of resemblances, and not vice versa. So, there is nothing subjectivistic about the Philosophy of Resemblances. It denies that there are real universals, but it affirms that there are real resemblances. Things and qualities, according to it, resemble one another whether anybody knows it or not, just as for the Philosophy of Universals, objects are instances of universals whether they are known to be so or not. Thus, the Philosophy of Resemblances, in this respect, is as realistic as the Philosophy of Universals.

CHAPTER XV

CONCLUSION

We may now summarise the results of our inquiry. We would only state the general conclusion without repeating the arguments. The question with which we started was whether the generality of our experience, thought and language had any basis in outside reality, or, in other words, whether our classifications and the usage of general words had any objective foundation, or not. We examined in this connection several theories advanced by different systems of thought, but found none of them to be entirely satisfactory.

Extreme realism, both of the Nyāya-Vaiśesika and the Mīmāṁsā type and the Platonic type, was found to be untenable. There is neither any evidence for the existence of universal essences apart from the particulars, nor any logical necessity of postulating them in order to explain our classifications of things. It is quite naive and uncritical to assume that our general conceptions of things as 'cow', 'man', 'animal', 'coloured', etc. necessarily imply identical class-essences having a being of their own apart from the particular things. Besides, extreme realism, as the Buddhist, the Advaitist and others have shown, involves innumerable difficulties which it fails to surmount. The greatest difficulty is that of explaining the relation of universals to particulars. Plato did realise the difficulties which his theory involved, but never tried to answer them. The Nyāya-Vaiśeṣika and the Mīmāṁsaka tried to answer them, but succeeded only in making certain dogmatic assertions without providing a satisfactory explanation of the difficulties. We, therefore, rejected extreme realism as an unsatisfactory theory of universals.

Like extreme realism we found extreme nominalism also to be quite unsatisfactory. There is only one example of a well developed and self-consistent form of extreme nominalism in the history of thought, namely, the *apohavāda* of the Buddhist. This theory recognises no objective basis for general conceptions and designations. All class-concepts, on this theory, are thought-constructions having their source in the innate conceptualising tendency of the mind. This theory is rooted in a particular ontology, the ontology of unique momentary particulars (*svalakṣaṇas*). It denies all identity and similarity in the real world. If we accept this ontology of the Buddhist, there is no escape from the extreme nominalism advocated by him. If all that exists is absolute point-instant, then all notions of identity and similarity must be mere fictions of thought, or mere words. But why must we accept this ontology? Vācaspati Miśra and Udayana have shown that the Buddhist doctrine of momentariness is an unfounded assumption. Our experience, on the contrary, attests the stability of the objects and their mutual relationships. The objects display identical qualities and relations and similarities of various degrees. There is no reason whatsoever to suppose that these are illusions of the mind, unless of course we are biased in favour of the particular ontology advocated by the Buddhist. Moreover, the nominalism of the Buddhist involves certain disastrous consequences for his epistemology. On this theory, all class-notions and usage of words, would be completely arbitrary. There could neither be any common notion, nor any common understanding and agreement, nor any communication of ideas. All knowledge would be completely subjective. To avoid these consequences, the Buddhist postulates a metaphysical principle, namely, the universal constructive disposition innate to the minds of all human beings. This is said to account for the belief in common understanding and mutual communication of thought. But why make these assumptions at all? Why assume, first, that the real is absolute particular, and then, in order to account for common empirical knowledge, assume that all human beings innately possess a common constructive disposition? Is it not more reasonable to accept the identities and similarities given in uncontradicted experience as real, and explain class concepts and usage of general words on their basis?

Moderate realism, conceptualism and moderate nominalism avoid most of the difficulties of the two extremist theories stated above. In Indian Philosophy the Jaina, and in Western Philosophy Aristotle and his followers advocated a moderate form of realism. This theory asserts that 'humanity' and 'redness', for example, are not entities different from particular human beings and particular red objects, but essences immanent in them. It is by virtue of these essences that they are what they are. We might abstract these essences and form concepts of 'man' and 'red', but they do not exist in this abstracted state. This theory no doubt avoids many of the difficulties of extreme realism, but there are two main objections which it has to face. Firstly, there is no evidence for the existence of such essences as the immanent characters of particular things. They are neither observable nor even conceptually separable from the general features possessed by the particulars. And secondly, if such essences were really there and discoverable by us in some manner, then we should have no difficulty, as Locke pointed out, with regard to border-line cases wherein we find it very hard to assign a particular thing or a quality to a determinate class. It is for these reasons that the modern exponents of moderate realism do not talk of metaphysical essences, but of observable characteristics or features recurring in numerous instances. These features, recurring singly as well as in groups, form the foundation of our numerous classifications of objects. But even in this modified form moderate realism is only partially true. It explains concepts pertaining to identical qualities and relations; but it does not explain concepts, such as 'man' 'animal', 'colour', etc., which do not rest on any observable common feature or features. These concepts can be explained only by going beyond moderate realism, that is to say, by recognising resemblances also, besides identity, as the basis of classifications.

A different form of moderate realism was advocated in Indian Philosophy by the Advaitist. Universals, according to him, are not real essences but names and forms (*nāmarūpa*) of Being (*Brahman*) which alone is ultimately real. They are said to be categories of Being generated by the primordial nescience. They are thus empirically real, though ultimately illusory. This view can be characterised also as a kind of conceptualism, since universals are said to be the products of transcendental activity; they are conceptual divisions of one uniform universal Being. But they are not conceptual in the sense of being subjective. They are, on the contrary, objective, i.e., empirically real, though ultimately non-different from Being. This view of universals is a necessary consequence of an absolutistic stand-point. It is inescapable if one accepts the Advaitic view of the ultimate identity of all existence. But to accept this view is to go beyond empirical evidence, and it does not seem to be necessary to do so in order to give a satisfactory account of our general conceptions.

Moderate realism, as we stated above, does not provide a complete theory of universals. So also conceptualism and moderate nominalism provide only a partial explanation of our class-notions. In Indian philosophy, conceptualism was advocated by the later Jaina thinkers and the Viśistādvaita. Both of them accepted only resemblances and not identities as the bases of class-concepts. In Western Philosophy, Ockham, Locke and his followers advocated conceptualism, while Hobbes advocated moderate nominalism. We have already shown that both conceptualism and moderate nominalism rest on the same ontology, the ontology of particulars having different degrees of resemblance to one another. These resemblances are accepted by both as the ontological bases of classifications. There is thus no fundamental difference between these two epistemological theories. It is for this reason that modern empiricists have abandoned the terminology of conceptualism and nominalism and talk in terms of resemblances into which both these theories ultimately resolve.

It is generally contended by the modern empiricists that resemblances are ultimate, and these resemblances alone, not identities, form the bases of classifications and usage of words. On the other hand, realists, like Russell and Moore, insist that identities, or universals, can alone be regarded as the bases of our general conceptions. We have found both these views to be only partially justified. The resemblance view does not do justice to the observed identities, viz., identical qualities and relations, which have equal claim for recognition. Many of our classifications are based on these observed identities. Similarly, the realist's view fails to do justice to the observed resemblances which do not involve any discoverable identities. Such resemblances are ultimate and they form the bases of many of our classifications. The realist's contention that all resemblance is derivative, i.e., based on some identity, was found to be untenable. Resemblance, as we have shown, may be of two kinds; the one that involves an observable identical quality, and the other that does not. In the former case it is derivative, but in the latter case it is ultimate. The modern empiricists take an extreme position when they deny all identities and make ultimate resemblances the sole ground of all classifications. Similarly, the realists take an extreme stand when they declare all resemblances to be derivative and insist that some kind of identity alone can be regarded as the ground of classifications. We have held that both these extreme views are erroneous. Neither resemblances alone nor identities alone can explain all our classifications. We must combine both of them in a single comprehensive view in order to give a satisfactory answer to the problem of universals.

Thus we have maintained that there are identical qualities and relations which recur over and over again in our experience. In the same way, there are also resemblances—resembling qualities, resembling objects, resembling situations—which repeat themselves in innumerable instances. All these recurrences involve universals. The term universal, in our view, is applicable not only to identical qualities and relations, but also to similarities, because the essential meaning of the term, as we understand it, is recurrence. These recurrent identities and similarities are the principles of grouping; they form the foundations of our thought and speech. There is nothing subjective about them, as the Buddhist maintains. The apprehension of recurrence no doubt involves operation of the mind, but all mental activities are not creative. Mind is the instrument of discovery also. If the observed recurrences were creations of the mind, i.e., if there were no universals in the world, there could be no conceptual knowledge of the world at all, since concepts, in that case, would be pure fabrications of the mind having nothing to do with the external reality. All conceptual knowledge would, in that case, be completely erroneous. Only immediate intuitions or sensations, which are free from the operation of the mind, would be true. Thought and speech would be completely divorced from reality. There could neither be any common knowledge, nor any communication of thought. All belief in common understanding and agreement would be completely erroneous. These consequences are strong enough reasons to make us reject the premises from which they follow. They evidently fail to do justice to our valid empirical knowledge.

The view of universals which we have held cannot evidently be identified with any of the traditional theories. We go beyond realism when we recognise similarities too as the principles of classification. Similarly, we reject conceptualism and nominalism when we recognise identical qualities and relations along with similarities as the principles of grouping. In one sense, however, our view may be called realistic; it is on the side of realism inasmuch as it insists on some kind of objective basis for our empirical concepts.

Finally, it must be observed that when we say that the identities and similarities, on which our empirical concepts and usage of general words rest, are constituents of the external world, we do not mean that they are some kind of entities over and above the particulars manifesting them. They are real only as features of individual objects or as relations holding between them. Some philosophers have found in this the reason for regarding universals as fabrications of thought. But this, we have maintained, is a grossly mistaken view. The apprehension of universals—identities and resemblances—no doubt involves abstraction, but that does not mean that they are mind-dependent. Abstraction is a psychological process by which we become aware of universals. So it is our awareness of them which is the product of the process, not the universals themselves. Some other philosophers make a distinction between 'existence' and 'subsistence' and hold that particulars alone have existence, while universals have only subsistence. Even if this distinction be valid, though it is not very clear, it is not so important as the distinction of universals from pure fictions. It is this distinction which, as Moore has pointed out, underlies the distinction of truth and falsehood. If we clearly understand the sense in which pure fictions like 'horned hares' and 'sky-lotuses' do not exist, it would seem quite plain that universals, namely, identical qualities, identical relations and similarities, are not to be classed with them. It would seem, on the contrary, that there is a fundamental difference between the two, a difference much more important than the difference between universals and particulars.

A SHORT BIBLIOGRAPHY

(Excluding texts listed under ABBREVIATIONS)

Aaron, R. I. — *The Theory of Universals,* Oxford, 1952.
Two senses of the Word Universal, Mind, 1939.

Allan, D. J. — *The Philosophy of Aristotle,* Oxford University Press, 1952.

Ambrose, Alice — *Wittgenstein on Universals,* in *Metaphysics* Ed. by W. E. Kennick and Moris Lazerowitz, Prentice-Hall Inc., New Jercy.

Aristotle — *Metaphysics,* tr. by Richard Hope, Columbia University Press, New York, 1952.
Categories, tr by A. E. Wardman and J. C. Cread, in *The Philosophy of Aristotle,* Mentor Classics, 1963.

Athalye and Bodas — *Tarka-saṁgraha* of Annambhaṭṭa, BORI, Poona, 1974.

Ayer, A. J. — *Language Truth and Logic,* Gollancz, 1936.
On Particulars and Universals, Proceedings of the Aristotelian Society, 1933-34.

Bambrough, Renford — *Universals and Family Resemblances,* PAS, Vol. 61 (1960-61)

Berkeley, George — *Treatise Concerning The Principles of Human Knowledge,* in *British Empirical Philosophers,* Ed. by A. J. Ayer and Raymond Winch, Routledge and Kegan Paul, London, 1952.

Bhaduri, Sadananda — *Studies in the Nyāya-Vaiśeṣika Metaphysics,* Bhandarkar Oriental Research Institute, Poona, 1947.

Blanshard, B. — *Reason and Analysis,* George Allen and Unwin, 1962.

Carre, M. H. — *Realists and Nominalists,* Oxford University Press, 1946.

Copleston, F. S. J. — *A History of Philosophy,* London, Burns, Oates and Washbourne Ltd., 1950.

Crombie, I. M. — *An Examination of Plato's Doctrine,* Routledge and Kegan Paul, London, 1963.

Dasgupta, S. N. — *History of Indian Philosophy,* Cambridge, 1932.

Descartes, Rene — *The Principles of Philosophy, Meditations, Notes Against a Programme and objections,* in *The Philosophical Works of Descartes,* tr. by Haldane, E. S. and Ross, G. R. T., Dover, 1931. Vols. I and II.

Ewing, A. C. — *The Fundamental Problems of Philosophy,* Routledge and Kegan Paul Ltd., London, 1953.

Field, G. C. — *The Philosophy of Plato,* Oxford, 1951.

Hiriyanna, M. — *Outlines of Indian philosophy,* George Allen and Unwin Ltd., London, 1932.

Hobbes — *Leviathan,* Ed. by Michael Oakshott, 1947.

Hume, David — *A Treatise Concerning Human Nature,* Book I, in *British Empirical Philosophers,* Ed. by A. J. Ayer and Raymond Winch, Routledge and Kegan Paul, London, 1952.

Jha, Ganganath — *Pūrva Mīmāṁsā,* Banaras Hindu University, 1942.

Kant, Immanuel — *Critique of Pure Reason,* Tr. by N. K. Smith, Macmillan, London, 1963.

Keith, A. B. — *Indian Logic and Atomism,* Oxford, Clarendon Press, 1921.

Lawande, G. N. — *The Problem of Universals,* New Book Company, Bombay, 1943.

Lazerowitz, Moris — *The Structure of Metaphysics,* Routledge and Kegan Paul, London, 1956.

Leibniz, G. W. — *Introduction to New Essays on Human Understanding,* in *The Monadology and Philosophical Writings,* Tr. by Robert Latta, Oxford University Press, 1951.

Locke, John — *An Essay Concerning Human Understanding,* Ed. by Raymond Wilburn, Everyman's Library, 1947.

Moore, G. E. — *Some Main Problems of Philosophy,* George Allen and Unwin, 1953.

Philosophical Papers, George Allen and Unwin, 1959.

Mukherjee, Satkari — *The Buddhist Philosophy of Universal Flux,* Calcutta University, 1935.

Introduction to Bhāṣāpariccheda with Siddhānta-muktāvalī, Tr. by Swami Madhavananda, Advaita Ashram, Almora.

Pears, D. F. — *Universals,* in Philosophical Quarterly, 1950-51.

Plato — Dialogues, Tr. by B. Jowett, Oxford, Third ed. 5 Vols.

Price, H. H. — *Thinking and Experience,* Hutchison, London, 1953.

Quine, W. V. O. — *From a Logical Point of View,* Harward University Press, 1953.

Radhakrishnan, S. — *Indian Philosophy,* George Allen and Unwin, London, 1940, 2 Vols.

Raju, P. T. — *Thought and Reality,* George Allen and Unwin Ltd., London, 1937.

Russell, B. — *The Problems of Philosophy,* Home University Library, 1962.

An Inquiry into Meaning and Truth, Pelican, 1962.

Ross, W. D. — *Plato's Theory of Ideas,* Oxford, 1951.

Aristotle, Methuen, London, 1949.

Sastri, G. N. — *Philosophy of Word and Meaning,* Calcutta Sanskrit College Research Series No. 5, 1959.

Shastri, D. N. — *Critique of Indian Realism,* Agra University, 1964.

Spinoza, Benedict — *Ethics,* Everyman's Library, 1928.

Stebbing, L. S. — *A Modern Introduction to Logic,* Methuen, London, 1950.

Stout, G. F. — *Studies in Philosophy and Psychology,* Macmillan, 1930.

Taylor, A. E. — *Plato, The Man and his Work,* Methuen, 1952.

Windelband, W. *A History of Philosophy,* Macmillan, New York, 1950.

Wisdom, John *Problems of Mind and Matter,* Cambridge University Press, 1934.

Wittgenstein, L. *Philosophical Investigations,* Tr. by G. E. M. Anscombe, Basil Blackwell, Oxford, 1953.

Woozley, A. D. *Universals* in Encyclopedia of Philosophy, Macmillan, New York, 1967, Vol. 8.

Theory of Knowledge, Hutchison's University Library, London, 1949.

Wulf, M. D. *History of Medieval Philosophy,* Thomas Nelson and Sons Ltd., 1935.

INDEX